REMEDIAL READING
Classroom and Clinic

SECOND EDITION

REMEDIAL READING
Classroom and Clinic

edited by

Leo M. Schell, *Associate Professor of Education*
Kansas State University
Paul C. Burns, *Professor of Education*
University of Tennessee

Allyn and Bacon, Inc., Boston

Contents

4 CREATING A LEARNING ENVIRONMENT 257

5 PUTTING IT ALL TOGETHER 369

6 THE EXTRAS THAT COUNT 511

Preface

There are several justifications for this collection of source materials. A single, summarizing book is unable to deal in depth with all the kaleidoscopic aspects of reading difficulties. There is simply too much literature available for one author to survey the field comprehensively, digest it, and encapsulate it within the covers of a book in enough detail for readers to implement the ideas in educational practice. Readers must go to the original sources for the details necessary for this type of understanding. Also, a book that summarizes whole concepts in a single paragraph may prevent the reader from learning to read and to think on his own — things he must do once he leaves the confines of the college classroom.

Every author has a distinct point of view and definite opinions about his special field that need not be shared unanimously by other specialists in the field. Students of reading must be exposed to several ways of looking at a topic. They must be aware that controversy and alternatives exist, that many problems have not yet been — and may never be — resolved, and that the future may hold more answers than the past and present combined.

The following principles guided us in the selection of articles for this anthology:

Reading difficulties are a highly individual problem, the roots of which can be varied and multiple.

Prevention is more desirable than remediation and must, in the long run, be the responsibility of the classroom teacher.

Accurate diagnosis and interpretation of results is the core of a corrective program in classroom or clinic.

Procedures and materials must reflect the individualized nature of reading difficulties.

The teacher is the single most important element in both prevention and correction of reading difficulties.

A successful program of prevention and correction demands both school- and community-wide cooperation and is a joint venture of many people.

The number of meritorious ideas conceived by specialists in reading is staggering, and the competition to have them printed in professional journals is fierce. Many of these ideas never appear in professional journals and are not disseminated beyond a small group of people fortunate enough to hear them at a convention. Even professional libraries subscribing to Educational Resources Information Center (ERIC) cannot provide students total access to the vast range of professional literature that exists in the field of reading. Therefore, many articles included in this anthology were originally presented at professional conventions or were written especially for this book. Thus, in one small sense, this book is a "convention in print."

The editors acknowledge their deep indebtedness to all the people who have made this book possible: authors and organizations who gave permissions, specialists who wrote original articles, and reviewers who helped clarify and organize the book. Our names may appear on the cover and title page but this is not "our" book; it belongs to all those who made it possible. Our goal was not to produce a book but to help children with reading problems. We pray we have achieved that goal.

LEO M. SCHELL
PAUL C. BURNS

REMEDIAL READING
Classroom and Clinic

1

What, Why, and Who

Unanswered questions remain the hallmark of the field of reading difficulties. In order to provide a foundation for the remaining sections of this book, this first part will focus upon some pervasive questions.

First, what is our reading target for the seventies? Until we have identified and accepted some goal, we cannot intelligently set in motion the efforts that will be required to achieve it. And the commitments will have to be dedicated, considering the magnitude of reading deficiencies.

Another question that must be early dealt with is, What is involved in learning to read? Studying a person's attempt to read is a formidable task, but it will help us to obtain a better grasp of that extremely complex, high-level cognitive act. Until we sense the "fit" of the numerous reading pieces into an overall pattern, we are not likely to offer the necessary type of reading program, nor are we apt to be successful with any prevention / correction reading program.

How has reading disability been treated in the past? Knowledge of the past may not be essential to understanding the present or to prophesying the future, but it is helpful in gaining a perspective on, and an overall view of, a situation. Current goals, materials, and procedures are often an outgrowth of roots that go far back. Thus, to understand current programs better and to evaluate newer trends, one must know something of the past. A study of the past decades of remedial reading should help us to formulate better guidelines for our reading programs and to avoid some pitfalls in developing our reading services.

Who should teach children with reading problems? What academic background, experience, and personality traits are most desirable? The quality of education is highly related to, and influenced by, the teacher preparation; therefore, in the absence of definitive research, professionals must agree on the general characteristics desired in teachers of reading. Teacher-training institutions, state departments of education, school administrators, and classroom teachers are all vitally interested in the answers to these questions.

The editors of this anthology do not pretend that the following four articles answer these questions definitively; but we do believe they offer some new ways of thinking about them.

JAMES E. ALLEN, JR.

The Right to Read—Target for the '70's

The following statement presents a challenge to our democratic society in general and to schools and educators in particular. Calling for a total commitment, the article not only serves as a cogent introduction to this part, but also provides a justification for the whole anthology.

Do you think the suggested goal is feasible? Why or why not? What plans or programs have been made to consider how the goal of universal readers can be achieved in your state? in your city? school? classroom? How many children in your classroom and in your school system have significant reading deficiencies? How can public support for this goal be secured?

Imagine, if you can, what your life would be like if you could not read, or if your reading skill were so meager as to limit you to the simplest of writings, and if for you the door to the whole world of knowledge and inspiration available through the printed word had never opened.

For more than a quarter of our population this is true. For them education, in a very important way, has been a failure, and they stand as a reproach to all of us who hold in our hands the shaping of the opportunity for education.

These individuals have been denied a right — a right as fundamental as the right to life, liberty, and the pursuit of happiness — the right to read.

The suppression of the individual which for so long characterized the governance of nations rested on the ignorance of the many and the learning of the few. With the

From an address given to the 1969 Annual Convention of the National Association of State Boards of Education while the author was United States Commissioner of Education. Reprinted with permission of James E. Allen, Jr.

invention of movable type there was created a source of widespread learning that held hope for the eventual abolishment of ignorance and for removal of the barrier to the participation of the common man in the determination of his destiny.

The education for all, necessary as a foundation of a democratic society, became a possibility, making feasible the quest for the realization of this concept which honors the dignity and worth of the individual.

Thus, from the beginning of our Nation, the importance of education has been recognized. Education has come to mean many things and to encompass a wide range of information and experiences, but certainly it must still include, as it did in the beginning, the ability to read.

Those who do not gain this ability in the course of their early education lack a skill necessary to all other areas of learning and are being denied a fundamental educational right — the right to read.

It is true, of course, that the inability to read effectively is only one of the many vexing problems facing American education, just as heart disease and cancer represent only limited dimensions of our national health problems. Yet, we have seen the value of concentrating attention on such medical concerns.

The inability to read effectively, contaminating as it does every other dimension of education, is clearly one challenge deserving of our concentrated efforts. As we learn how to attack this deficiency cooperatively, we will not only be getting at this foundation of learning, but will be gaining the strength and the skills to meet together many other educational problems.

From a variety of statistical information accumulated by the Office of Education regarding reading deficiencies throughout the country these shocking facts stand out:

One out of every four students nationwide has significant reading deficiencies.

In large city school systems up to half of the students read below expectation.

There are more than three million illiterates in our adult population.

About half of the unemployed youth in New York City, ages 16-21, are functionally illiterate.

Three-quarters of the juvenile offenders in New York City are two or more years retarded in reading.

In a recent U.S. Armed Forces program called Project 100,000, 68.2 percent of the young men fell below grade seven in reading and academic ability.

The tragedy of these statistics is that they represent a barrier to success that for many young adults produces the misery of a life marked by poverty, unemployment, alienation, and, in many cases, crime.

It must be recognized also, however, that for the majority who do acquire the basic reading skills, there can also be a barrier which limits the fulfillment of their right to read. This barrier exists when the skill of reading is not accompanied by the desire to read. We fail, therefore, just as much in assuring the right to read when the desire is absent as when the skills are missing.

It is inexcusable that in this day when man has achieved such giant steps in the development of his potential, when many of his accomplishments approach the miraculous, there still should be those who cannot read.

While still in New York State, I had begun to develop plans for launching a statewide, concentrated attack on reading deficiencies. Now I have national responsibilities and my view of the educational scene from this level convinces me that there is no higher nationwide priority in the field of education than the provision of the right to read for all, and that the Office of Education and the Department of Health, Education, and Welfare can do no greater service for the cause of education than to spearhead a nationwide attack to eliminate this failure of our education efforts.

Therefore, as U.S. Commissioner of Education, I am herewith proclaiming my belief that *we should immediately set for ourselves the goal of assuring that by the end of the 1970's the right to read shall be a reality for all — that no one shall be leaving our schools without the skill and the desire necessary to read to the full limits of his capability.*

This is education's "moon" — the target for the decade ahead. With the same zeal, dedication, perseverance, and concentration that made possible man's giant step of last July 20, this moon too can be reached.

While it is obviously impossible to expect that our target could encompass the complete elimination of the reading deficiencies of the out-of-school population also, this decade devoted to the improvement of reading should include a new and intensive attack in this area of need, bringing to bear the kind of widespread concentration of effort and resources that will be given to inschool youth.

I have chosen to set forth this target at the meeting of the National Association of State Boards of Education because you bear the responsibility for shaping basic educational policies for the primary and secondary schools of our Nation. The responsibility for the provision of educational opportunity, traditionally and legally, rests with the States. The public education system of our Nation has developed on the premise that education belongs to the people and its control shall be in the hands of lay boards. It is you, therefore, who have the original responsibility and authority within the framework established by your respective legislatures, for the setting and enforcement of standards, and for the evaluation of per-formance. It is you also who must be accountable for your stewardship. You are at the center of any effort to raise the level of achievement in our educational system.

State boards are, of course, not alone in this responsibility, for it falls also upon all those who participate in the ad-ministration and operation of the educational enterprise. Therefore, in presenting the challenge of this target to you I am also presenting it to groups such as the Education Commission of the States, the Council of Chief State School Officers, State education departments, local school boards and their staffs, the American Association of School Administrators, the National Education Association and the American Federation of Teachers and their State and local affiliates, the National Congress of Parents and Teachers, students and their organizations — indeed, to all individuals and organizations comprising the total educational endeavor of our Nation. Essential also, of course, will be the intensive participation of the colleges and universities and their schools of teacher education.

But to hit the target by the end of the 70's, to achieve a goal of such enormous dimensions, involvement will have to reach far beyond the forces of education.

Necessary will be committed participation and support of the Congress; State and local political leaders and legislative bodies; business, industry, and labor; civic and community groups; publishers; advertising organizations; television, radio, and the press; research and scientific organizations; foundations; the entertainment industry; the sports world; and, perhaps most essential of all, the understanding and support of an enlightened and enthusiastic public. In other words, *I am calling for a total national commitment to and involvement in the achievement of the "right to read" goal.*

This is a proper goal for our society because it will not only correct the injustice done to individuals by the denial of their right to read, but it will also, because of its widespread social and cultural effect, benefit and strengthen the entire fabric of our society.

I hope that by this point in these remarks I have succeeded in arousing your enthusiasm, but I suspect that certain doubts as to the practicability of the timing and scope of the goal have also crept into your thinking. Indeed I can already hear the excuses, the expressions of fear and reservation, the "yes, buts" with which many will greet this challenge. To accept these is to continue the rationalization, the justifications for failure that for too long have persisted, demoralizing our will and generating a defeatist attitude.

Of course, this goal cannot be easily attained. It will be far more difficult than the landing on the moon. But the time is right, I believe, to try, for so much is at stake and there are so many favorable auguries for success.

This is a time when we have accumulated an enormous amount of research and expertise in the field of reading. Few other areas of learning have been so thoroughly and widely studied. May I add here parenthetically, however, that we must avoid the danger of allowing education's reading "moonshot" to become bogged down in debate over *methods* of the teaching of reading. It is the *goal* with which we must be concerned.

This is a time when science and technology have given us a whole new array of resources to apply to the solution of the reading problem.

This is a time when school boards and school administrators are less preoccupied than at any time since World War II with the pressing problems which have been created by ever-increasing student enrollment.

This is a time of growing understanding of the effects of environment
and other factors on the ability to learn.

This is a time when preschool educational opportunities are being
more generally incorporated into the public education system.

This is a time when new Federal legislation has provided increased
funds for attacking problems such as that of the improvement of
reading.

This is a time when there is a great readiness to support a program
that holds promise for the improvement of reading. The concern of
parents, public officials, and the general citizenry about the effectiveness of the schools seems to find a focus in the problem of
reading failures. The failure to teach everyone to read is a strong
factor in the loss of full confidence in our schools that is finding
expression in large numbers of defeated budgets and bond issues, in
student and community unrest, and in the growing tendency to seek
new instrumentalities for educational reform outside of the
traditional system. This is in a sense a negative situation that needs
only a believable expectation of success in solving the problem to
transform it into a tremendous positive force. The relatively simple,
universally understood objective, implicit in the "right to read" goal,
standing out clearly amidst the confusions of the complexity of the
educational endeavor of these days, can be the rallying point for the
renewed confidence in our schools that will gather to them a new
surge of enthusiastic public support.

The cumulative effect of the conjunction of so many
positive factors at this particular time can but serve to reduce
doubts and to support that reasonable degree of assurance of
success that mandates the attempt.

While the main task of carrying out the activities necessary
to achieve the goal of the right to read for all by the end of the
70's will fall upon the States and localities, the Federal
Government has a vital supportive role to play. It is not the role
of the Federal Government to make specific plans, nor to
prescribe the programs and methods to be used. The diverse
needs and conditions of the various States and their communities require the flexibility of approach that our decen-
tralized system makes possible. The main contribution that can
be made at the Federal level will be the coordination of the
effort, the marshaling of forces and resources on a nationwide
basis, and the provision of the technical, administrative and
financial assistance required, all done in a spirit of total and
fervent commitment.

Once more then, I proclaim my belief that it is possible for the 70's to be the decade in which the right to read becomes a reality for all, with no one leaving our schools lacking the skill and the desire necessary to read to the full limits of his capability — and that it is our duty to set for ourselves this target.

The months immediately ahead should be a time of preparation in the hope that next summer will see the beginning of the countdown, with the launch scheduled for the opening of the 1970-71 school year.

I therefore call upon you to take upon yourselves the obligation of assuring that every child in your State will learn to read, and I request that you begin immediately in your own State to consider how this goal can be achieved, to assemble resources, to plan, and to report back to me what actions you have taken under State leadership so that the school year 1969-70 can be recorded as the year when together we set in motion the nationwide effort that will erase this intolerable deficit in American education.

The Office of Education has already begun this kind of activity, and we shall be consulting with you and all other educational forces, as well as with representatives of the total national community, as to procedures.

The decade of the 70's will see the 200th anniversary of our Nation. A most appropriate celebration of that event — a celebration that would honor the true spirit of the democratic concept, and recognize the fundamental importance ascribed to education from the beginning of our Nation, would be to secure for all of our citizens that right to read which so long ago made possible the feasibility of a democratic society and continues to undergird its strength.

Continuing toleration of the failure to give everyone the ability to read breaks faith with the commitment to equality of opportunity which is the foundation of our public education system. Having arrived at a time which holds forth the possibility of eliminating this failure we must, in all justice, seize the opportunity with the utmost vigor and determination.

Remarkable success has been achieved by our educational system, but so long as there is one boy or girl who leaves school unable to read to the full extent of his capability, we cannot escape the charge of failure in carrying out the responsibility entrusted to us.

LEO M. SCHELL

Reading Difficulties:
Heuristic and Explanatory Models

Models are valuable for helping the student to recognize and to understand abstract ideas. Through the models presented in this article, the reader will see the complexity and interrelationships of reading difficulties and, perhaps, will sense some potential implications for instructional practices.

What additional components of the reading process might be listed? What growth periods or reading development stages might be identified? What additional correlates and determinates would you consider important enough to add to the writer's categories? How do Models I and II compare? How do they contrast? What defects are inherent in the two models? How does the idea of the models compare with the taxonomy proposed by Cohen in Part Five? The reader is encouraged to consider seriously the two questions posed at the conclusion of the article.

For many years scientists have successfully used tangible models to illustrate unseeable natural phenomena. No one has ever seen an atom, yet models of them composed of styrofoam balls and wire circles are an essential part of most chemistry, biology, and physics courses and clutter the offices of Nobel-prize winners.

They are considered so understandable that diagrams of them are used repeatedly in elementary school science textbooks, and constructing them is a common learning activity for pupils and teachers studying certain topics. Their "understandability" is a direct function of their oversimplification and lack of realism. In these models, protons and electrons are unmagnetized, and relative sizes and weights of various

An original paper written for this book by Leo M. Schell.

10

components are inaccurate. Furthermore, they are jerked out of context in relation to adjacent nuclear particles, and they are not in motion. However, because they make it easy to learn and remember the parts and their functions, they are considered indispensable for students; and because they promote speculation about possible behaviors and relationships, they are considered valuable for scholars. Thus, their defects are more virtues than serious handicaps.

Similar models have been produced by serious social scientists to help explain concepts as abstract and complex as intelligence.[1]

MODEL I: COMPLEXITY OF READING PROBLEMS

Learning to read printed symbols must obviously be an extremely complex, high-level cognitive act. And the forces influencing the success or failure of this learning are numerous, varied, and not totally known. Furthermore, there is a complex interrelationship between (1) the various facets of the reading process, (2) the stages of reading development, and (3) the correlates and determinates of learning or not learning. Until the potential complexities are recognized, prevention, intervention, and correction are likely to be oversimplified and possibly ineffective.

Components of the Reading Process

Reading is not thought to be a global, unitary, undifferentiated act. Rather, it is thought to be composed of relatively distinct components. For purposes of illustration and discussion, the reading process will be arbitrarily divided into six major components, as follows:

1. Word recognition	4. Reading-Study skills
2. Word meaning	5. Oral reading
3. Comprehension	6. Interest in reading

Schematically they could be arranged on a continuum like this, each in a separate segment:

---

[1] J. P. Guilford, "The Structure of the Intellect," *Psychological Bulletin*, 52 (1956), 267-293.

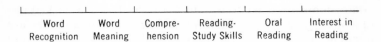

Word	Word	Compre-	Reading-	Oral	Interest in
Recognition	Meaning	hension	Study Skills	Reading	Reading

Figure 1. Components of the Reading Process

Stages of Reading Development

It should be clear, however, that each of the foregoing components is a growth area. That is, each component grows gradually over a period of time, becoming more and more complex and well developed, and hopefully culminating in reading maturity. Thus, there is a sequence of development for each component of the reading process (and for the reading process as a whole). This sequence can be divided into growth periods or stages during which certain skills, attitudes, or interests are stressed and developed. The segmented, one dimensional model above is inadequate to illustrate this expanded concept. Another dimension, stages of reading development, must be added. (Again, the number of stages decided upon is purely arbitrary and for illustration only.)

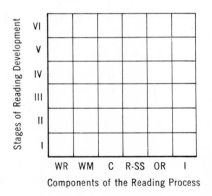

Figure 2. Two-dimensional
Model of Reading Components
and Stages

By itself, this model is quite valuable, because it graphically illustrates the point that any one reader may be at varying stages of development within each of the components of reading. And with readers with problems, that is almost always the case! However, the reading process — and the problem of reading difficulties — is still more complex; a more sophisticated model is therefore required.

Correlates and Determinates of Learning to Read

Reading is not learned in a vacuum; numerous forces influence the rate of learning and the relative success or lack of it that any individual experiences. For purposes of illustration and discussion, these correlates and determinates will be arbitrarily divided into six major categories as follows:

1. Educational factors
2. Environmental factors
3. Physiological factors
4. Language factors
5. Cognitive factors
6. Adjustment factors

When related to the components of reading and their developmental stages, the completed three-dimensional model looks like Figure 3.

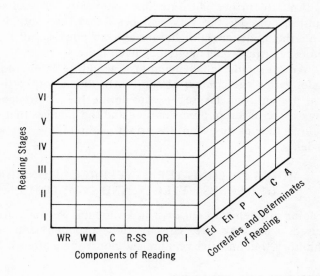

Figure 3. Model I, Complexity of Reading Problems

Each cell in this model represents an aspect of possible reading difficulty that can be described in terms of (1) components of the reading process, (2) stages of reading development, and (3) correlates and determinates of learning to read. Thus, each cell is a unique combination of these three variables. Theoretically it is possible to describe the reading difficulties each individual has in terms of this model. We could say that child A was performing at stage five in all components of reading except Word Meaning and Interest in Reading, where his functioning was at stages three and two respectively, and that these deficiencies were the result of a combination of educational and environmental factors. Such a precise description would permit a closer integration of diagnosis and remediation as urged by Spache [2] and a greater individualization of instruction, since each cell implies certain emphasis in order to achieve improvement.

Even though this and other models may have some potential implications for instructional practices, that is not their primary intent. The intent is merely to verify the complexity and interrelationships of reading difficulties. All else is extra.

And to further illustrate the complexity of reading difficulties, consider the very real possibility that not all lines within the model are straight, nor all cells equal-sized! Perhaps a more realistic model might look like Figure 4.

An even more challenging task would be to envision this model within the context of the fourth dimension of time — past, present, and future — considering the differences that may exist at different points in time and the changes that surely occur as time passes. And this brings us directly to our second model.

MODEL II: . LONG-TERM INTERRELATIONSHIP OF CAUSES, EFFECTS, AND SYMPTOMS

Reading problems do not exist in a vacuum. Not only are they caused, but they are causal; they produce detrimental, inhibitory, and negative reading and nonreading effects. This is

---

[2] George D. Spache, "Integrating Diagnosis with Remediation in Reading," *Elementary School Journal*, 56 (Sept., 1955), 18-26.

the "vicious circle" phenomena that has been recognized for so long. One typical example, a two-dimensional model, is presented in Figure 5.

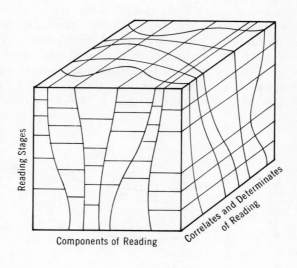

Figure 4. Model I with Unequal Cells

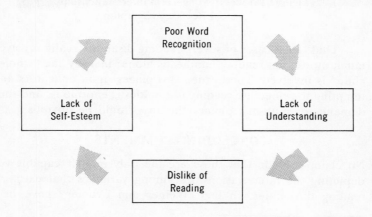

Figure 5. "Vicious Circle" Model of Reading Difficulties

As valuable as this model is, it is far from a realistic description of the actual interrelationships among the variables involved. Its primary weakness is that it fails to consider that reading difficulties typically produce more and more negative and detrimental effects the longer they exist. As reading disability becomes increasingly severe, academic learning suffers, self-esteem decreases, social relationships change (frequently for the worse), initiative turns into apathy and energy into lethargy, measured intelligence diminishes, oral and aural language may be impaired, etc., ad infinitum. A "vicious spiral" may be a truer picture than a "vicious circle." (See Figure 6.)

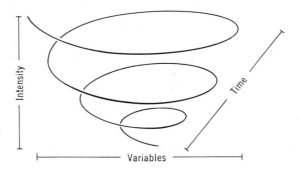

Figure 6. Model II, Long-Term Interrelationships
of Causes, Effects, and Symptoms

Thus, most cases of severe reading disability really involve much more than reading handicaps alone; literally the "whole child" is involved. The burden this places upon educators attempting to remediate reading difficulties is enormous, and the demand for multidisciplinary therapy should be obvious.

CONCLUDING COMMENTS

No claim is made that these are the only models capable of depicting the interrelationships among variables that exist in reading difficulties. In fact, Weiner and Cromer [3] have de-

---

3 Morton Weiner and Ward Cromer, "Reading and Reading Difficulty: A Conceptual Analysis," *Harvard Educational Review*, 37 (Fall, 1967), 620-643.

scribed various models but have not translated them into visual depictions. Neither are these two necessarily accurate or comprehensive. They contain all the defects inherent in any such models and, hopefully, all the virtues. They are proposed for explanatory and heuristic purposes rather than as ends in themselves. Readers are urged to ponder the inferences these models hold, to try modifying or adapting them, and even to try creating others. What kind of a model, for example, would best illustrate the desirable interplay between child, teacher, and learning environment? Or, can you conceptualize the reading process as an arrow with the forces necessary to put it in flight as facilitating factors, influences preventing it from hitting the bull's-eye as impeding variables, and the bull's-eye as reading maturity?

ALBERT J. HARRIS

Five Decades of Remedial Reading

Reviews of historical trends provide important information concerning the effects of certain practices that may suggest programs for future action. They also offer explanations of the how and why of many of the theories and practices that now prevail in the schools. They help educational workers to identify and evaluate fads and bandwagon schemes. Finally, they help us understand the significance of education and the interrelationship between the school and the society from which the school derives its functions. In this article, Dr. Harris presents an overview of the significant events in the field of remedial reading from 1916 to 1965. Few persons are more competent to evaluate the events of the past fifty years in the field of reading.

What were the most important happenings in each decade? What themes seem to occur in each decade? Why? After taking time to look at where we have been, do you have some sense of where we seem to be headed?

The Year 1965 marked the close of the first fifty years of American interest in remedial reading. When I was invited to choose a topic, it occurred to me that an historical overview of the 50-year period might be appropriate. As I read again some of the contributions that were written over 30 years ago, I rediscovered many an idea that had been new and exciting when I had first encountered it. I developed a new respect for the pioneers and a conviction that much of our present thinking has roots that go far back. It began to appear that each of the five decades had its own distinctive characteristics.

Reprinted from *Forging Ahead in Reading*, J. Allen Figurel, ed., (Newark, Delaware: International Reading Association, 1968), pp. 25-34. Reprinted with permission of the International Reading Association and Albert J. Harris.

Since this paper is an attempt to provide an historical overview and perspective, the five decades will be discussed in sequence. For each ten-year period, major trends will be noted and the particular developments that seem to me most noteworthy will be briefly described. Obviously, the selection of what to include from a vast and nearly overwhelming literature is a matter of personal opinion; and while I have tried to be objective, my own beliefs and interests necessarily have influenced my choices and what I shall say about them.

THE FIRST DECADE: 1916 to 1925

The idea that some children have special difficulty in learning to read and can be diagnosed and given special teaching seems to have sprung into prominence in American education almost full grown. The first journal article on the subject appeared in 1916; by 1922 there already were two books and a body of periodical literature on the subject.

Concern with reading disability did not originate on this continent. A case study written in 1896 by a British physician, W. Pringle Morgan, is generally thought to be the first writing on the subject *(41)*. Morgan used the term "congenital word-blindness" to describe a fourteen-year-old boy who had not learned to read although he seemed intelligent in other respects. But for the next twenty years interest was confined almost entirely to a few European medical practitioners and did not cross the Atlantic.

The first American paper on remedial reading was probably one written by Willis Uhl and published in the *Elementary School Journal* in 1916 *(59)*. Uhl gave silent and oral reading tests to all pupils in grades three to eight of an elementary school, listed ten kinds of faults, and suggested remedial procedures. Within the next four years diagnostic procedures, case studies, and school survey results were published by such people as Augusta Bronner *(5)*, Charles Judd *(31)*, W. S. Gray *(25)*, Clarence T. Gray *(34)*, and Laura Zirbes *(62)*. By 1921 William S. Gray authored a book of case studies *(26)*, and in 1922 Clarence T. Gray attempted to cover the field in a book entitled *Deficiencies in Reading Ability: Their Diagnosis and Remedies (24)*.

The first American paper in the European mode was by

Clara Schmitt and appeared in 1918 *(50)*. She used the terms "developmental alexia" and "congenital word-blindness" and advocated a systematic phonic method of remedial instruction. She introduced one new sound at a time in a continued story in which bells rang *(l)*, dogs barked *(r)*, cows mooed *(m)*, etc.

At the same time Grace Fernald, who had worked under Dr. Shepherd Ivory Franz in the retraining of soldiers with head wounds, was developing the kinesthetic method for teaching nonreaders. Her first paper, published in 1921, was widely read and influential *(18)*.

The first decade drew to a close with the publication of the Report of the National Committee on Reading in 1925 — the famous 24th Yearbook of the National Society for the Study of Education *(46)*. In this highly influential volume there was a chapter entitled "Diagnosis and Remedial Work." That chapter consisted mainly of a table with three parallel columns: *evidences of deficiency, diagnosis and remedial suggestions*. The table occupied ten pages and contained suggestions that are still worth reading.

There is an interesting contrast in the basic approach of the early medical and educational writers on reading problems; one which I believe continues to this day. The physicians were concerned primarily with differential diagnosis and only secondarily with remedial help. The educators were concerned mainly with developing tests to measure reading skills and with practical teaching techniques. They were interested in diagnosis — especially the kind of diagnosis that tries to establish causation — to a far lesser degree. This difference is still quite evident in the 1960's.

THE SECOND DECADE: 1926-1935

The later 1920's saw the development of many new ideas. Most important, probably, was the development of batteries of tests for use in diagnosing reading difficulties. First to appear were the *Gates Reading Diagnosis Tests* in 1927 *(21)*. Monroe's *Diagnostic Reading Examination* was published in 1928 *(39)*, and the *Durrell Analysis of Reading Difficulty* was first copyrighted in 1933. These three batteries are still used widely in reading clinics, two of them in revised editions.

Among the research studies of the decade, perhaps the

most valuable was Monroe's *Children Who Cannot Read (38)*. This book summarized previous research, reported on a detailed study of hundreds of severe reading disability cases, and described in detail a teaching method emphasizing phonics with a good deal of kinesthetic reinforcement. It ranks, in my opinion, among the best researches on reading disability. Other important research contributions were made by Gates and his doctoral students, one of whom was Guy L. Bond. These studies systematically studied visual, auditory, readiness, and lateral dominance factors in relation to reading problems.

Samuel T. Orton, a neurologist, published his first paper on reading problems in 1925 *(43)*. The development of his ideas has recently been summarized usefully by Mrs. Orton *(42)*, who was instrumental in founding the Orton Society in his memory. Orton's theoretical formulation is based on rivalry between two cerebral hemispheres, neither of which has established a clear dominance over the other; as dominance shifts, the child shows a fluctuating reversal tendency. Orton's followers have generally favored a synthetic phonic or sounding-blending method of teaching.

At about the same time, Walter F. Dearborn of Harvard was reporting a high incidence of mixed dominance and left-handedness in cases of reading disability *(11)*. He explained their reversals in terms of conflicting motor tendencies, a theory that was for many years the main alternative to Orton's ideas. Dearborn also studied aniseikonia, a condition in which the two eyes form images of unequal size, and found that children with this condition were handicapped in reading *(12)*. My own first introduction to reading problems came about through Dearborn's assistant who in 1929 let me take all of the tests they were using and explained their research methodology to me.

By the early 1930's there was enough published on reading problems to make summaries very useful. Integrative summaries of research on remedial reading were published by Miles A. Tinker in the 1930's *(56, 57)*.

Still another feature of the second decade was the founding of the first reading clinics. Among the earliest were those founded at Boston University by Durrell and at Shaker Heights, Ohio, by Betts.

Aside from Monroe's monograph, referred to earlier, the

most influential book on remedial reading of the second decade was Gates', *The Improvement of Reading*, first published in 1927 and revised in 1935 *(22)*. Although Gates concentrated mainly on his own tests and teaching materials, his was the best text-book on remedial reading for many years.

THE THIRD DECADE: 1936-1945

The period from 1935 to the beginning of World War II was marked by a continued output of new books. First to appear were Betts', *Prevention and Correction of Reading Difficulties (2)* and the first book on remedial reading in secondary schools, by McCallister *(35)*, both of which were published in 1936. The next year came *Remedial Reading* by Monroe and Backus *(40)*, and *Prediction and Prevention of Reading Difficulties* by Stanger and Donohue, two followers of Orton *(54)*. In 1938 Luella Cole's *The Improvement of Reading* called for multilevel boxed materials for individualized practice and predicted the coming of reading laboratories which arrived commercially about 20 years later *(9)*. Russell, Karp, and Kelly issued a compendium of useful reading exercises and games in the same year *(49)*. In 1940 two textbooks appeared, *How to Increase Reading Ability* by Harris *(28)* and Durrell's *Improvement of Basic Reading Abilities (16)*. During the early 1940's, the years of World War II, the only other important new book was Fernald's definitive description of her kinesthetic method *(17)*.

The mid- and late-1930's also saw the development of the first large-scale remedial program in a public school system. The presence of many hundreds of unemployed college graduates led to some bold ventures in finding useful things for them to do while receiving federal aid. Under the supervision of some of Gates' assistants, the Federal Writer's Project prepared a series of 80 practice booklets for use in remedial reading. Several hundred people with no previous teaching experience were put through a short training program and then were assigned to teach small groups of retarded readers in the public schools of New York City. Most of my earliest students in remedial reading courses were involved as teachers or supervisors in that remedial program, which lasted for several years until our entry into World War II caused the program to be discontinued.

The accelerating pace of research and writing on all aspects of reading instruction during the 1930's produced an appreciative welcome for Traxler's *Ten Years of Research in Reading,* which appeared in 1941 *(58).* This summary and annotated bibliography listed and briefly summarized more than 100 articles on remedial reading and 18 articles on diagnosis and included in addition references on many other topics. Traxler was encouraged to prepare three later volumes of the same kind, each covering a period of several years *(58).* These have been extremely valuable to scholars and research workers in reading.

During this decade the mental hygiene movement discovered reading disability; and case studies, theoretical discussions, and research reports began to appear in such journals as *Mental Hygiene, American Journal of Orthopsychiatry,* and the *International Journal of Psychoanalysis.* Blanchard's case studies of children with reading problems of apparently emotional origin attracted wide attention *(3).* In 1941, Gates estimated that among children with marked reading disabilities about 75 percent show personality maladjustment and that in only about 25 percent is the emotional difficulty a contributing cause of the reading failure. He was widely quoted in educational circles *(23).* Child guidance specialists, however, regarded his figures as marked underestimates. While in educational situations remedial teaching was the preferred treatment, child guidance clinics often gave priority to psychotherapy for child and parent.

This decade also saw the development of what may be called the machine approach to remedial reading. For diagnosis, the major development was the production of a commercially manufactured eye-movement camera called the *Opthalm-O-Graph,* designed by Earl A. Taylor; previously such cameras had to be individually designed and custom built. Taylor's 1937 book provided new information on the use of eye-movement photography in diagnosis *(55).*

On the remedial side, there were three main machine developments. One was the first reading pacer, designed by Guy T. Buswell *(6).* It contained a motor-driven shutter that would come down over a page of print at a rate that could be controlled. A second was the first set of motion picture films for reading practice at controlled speeds, developed at Harvard for use with college students. A third was Earl Taylor's *Metron-O-Scope (55)*. This was a large and cumbersome device which had three shutters and could expose a line of print one third at a time at a controlled rate. All of these appeared between 1935 and 1940. Improved devices to accomplish the same purposes are currently in wide use, particularly in college and adult reading programs.

In 1940 I summarized the results of the research then available on the effectiveness of improving reading by attempting to train eye movements or by controlling the exposure of reading material, as follows: "Experimental evidence indicates that motivated practice produces as much improvement in rate of reading as programs of eye-movement training do, while it has a somewhat more favorable effect on comprehension. Another point of practical importance is the fact that motivated practice requires no special material while eye-movement drills require the use of specially prepared material or expensive apparatus. There is no reason for the teacher who relies on motivated practice to feel that his method is inferior to the formal methods of training eye movements or the use of complex machines to pace the reader" *(28)*. Now, 27 years later, I have found no reason to change that opinion.

America's entry into World War II caused a depletion of the graduate schools; and during the war and for a couple of years after it, little that was new about remedial reading appeared in print.

THE FOURTH DECADE: 1946-1955

Of the research studied that appeared during the ten years that followed World War II, the one that had the greatest influence in America was Helen Robinson's *Why Pupils Fail in Reading*, published in 1947 *(47)*. The first part of the book contained a scholarly review of the literature on the causation of reading disability. The rest of it was a detailed report of the intensive study of 22 cases, by a staff representing ten different professional specialties. Robinson stressed the absence of any one causal factor present in all cases. In these children many anomalies were present that were not considered to have causal importance for the reading problem, as well as many that were. For example, while 73 percent of the cases had visual problems, the visual problem was considered *causally* significant in only 50 percent. Social, visual, and emotional problems appeared most frequently. Inappropriate teaching methods, neurological difficulties, and speech or functional auditory difficulties seemed less frequently to be causal. Endocrine disturbances, general physical difficulties, and insufficient auditory acuity appeared to be least important. Robinson's book provided strong support for a pluralistic view of the causation of reading disabilities.

The major European research study of the decade was Hallgren's monograph on the inheritance of specific dyslexia, which was published in 1950 *(27)*. Hallgren's study of 79 clinic cases and 43 other "word blind" cases included family histories. He reported some evidence of reading disability among the parents or siblings in all but 13 cases and concluded that a primary reading disability is inherited as a unitary Mendelian dominant characteristic. He also accepted the idea that there are other reading disabilities caused by such factors as emotional disorders or environmental conditions.

Hallgren's monograph is widely cited by recent writers on dyslexia, such as Hermann in Denmark *(30)*, and Critchley in England *(10)*, as providing evidence of a special kind of "pure" reading disability. I am inclined to agree with M. D. Vernon, who commented, "What seems much more plausible is that there is a congenital disposition in certain cases towards the occurrence of certain related defects: reading disability, speech defects or infantile speech; motor incoordination; left-handedness or ambidextrality" *(61)*.

In the textbook field, 1947 saw the publication of Kottmeyer's *Handbook of Remedial Reading (33)*, as well as revised editions by Gates and Harris.

This decade saw the birth of the two organizations which later merged to become the International Reading Association. The National Association for Remedial Teaching, known as NART was started in New England by a group among whom Elva E. Knight was prominent and shortly attracted to its board of directors many of the leading authorities on reading problems. The International Council for the Improvement of Reading Instruction (I.C.I.R.I.) was started around 1947 by graduate students at Temple University. Following the naming of its publication as *The Reading Teacher* in 1951 and its issuance as a printed magazine in 1952, I.C.I.R.I. grew steadily. By 1954 the majority of the people on the board of one of these organizations were also on the board of the other, and the desirability of a merger was evident. The last day of their independent existence was December 31, 1955, a fitting close to the decade.

The Orton Society was also founded during this decade and issued its first bulletin in 1950.

The preference of many psychiatrists and clinical psychologists for emphasis on emotional causation and treatment of reading problems by psychotherapy continued strongly through these ten years. One of the most influential papers was by Gerald Pearson, a highly regarded psychoanalyst, and described several kinds of personality deviations that could produce reading disability as a sympton *(44)*. I can recall being a member of a symposium on ego problems in reading difficulties at the annual convention of the American Orthopsychiatric Association in 1953; I described remedial reading as a form of non-interpretive, ego-strengthening psychotherapy. Numerous theses were done about that time in which personality tests were given to a reading disability group and a group of normal readers. Nearly all of those studies found a wide range of scores in both groups and no significant differences in group averages. By the end of the decade the suspicion was growing that the psychology of personality was not providing the key to the understanding of reading disability.

This decade from 1946 to 1955 was also marked by a general expansion of interest in remedial reading, an expansion which was shown in many ways. Scores of colleges and universities organized reading clinics, and many started graduate training programs for reading specialists. The number of remedial teachers in public school systems continued to grow. Remedial reading programs began to spread upward from elementary schools to the secondary schools. Commercial organizations offering everything from tutoring the nonreader to speed reading for executives sprang up in the larger cities.

With a growing market, materials written specifically for use in remedial reading began to appear, and several writers compiled lists of books that combined a mature interest level with low difficulty.

As this decade ended, in 1955, a new theory burst upon the

public: children were failing to learn to read just because they weren't being taught phonics. Rudolf Flesch's *Why Johnny Can't Read (19)* became a best seller, and public and parental criticism of the schools quickly intensified. Looking back, it is easy to see both that the argument was a gross over-simplification, put across with blatant use of propaganda techniques, and that it had a partial basis in fact. The merger resulting in the birth of IRA came just when public interest in reading was reaching a peak of intensity. So closed a most interesting decade.

THE FIFTH DECADE: 1956-1965

The year 1956 opened the fifth decade on a level of high emotional tension. Reading specialists were busy showing that disabilities existed in countries where the graphemephoneme relationship was regular and phonic instruction was the rule and informing the public about all the factors that may help to produce a reading difficulty other than method of teaching. Flesch had, however, done remedial reading a great service: he had convinced hundreds of thousands of parents than when Johnny had trouble with reading, he was not necessarily stupid; and this viewpoint led to public pressure both for improved developmental reading programs and for more diagnostic and remedial facilities.

On January 1, 1956, IRA officially came into existence; and its phenomenal growth since then has been a source of con-tinuing amazement to me as well as of satisfaction. Before and shortly after the merger some remedial specialists expressed fears that their interests would be neglected in the new organization. By now, I hope, such fears are things of the past.

New books continued to appear. New textbooks included one by Bond and Tinker in 1957 *(4)* and one by Roswell and Natchez in 1964 *(48)*. Revised editions were brought out by Harris in 1956 and 1961 and Kottmeyer in 1959. The 1962 University of Chicago Reading Conference was devoted to underachievement in reading *(60)*. Scholarly contributions included Vernon's review of the literature on backwardness in reading *(61)*, Malmquist's study of reading disability in the first grade *(36)*, the books by Hermann and Critchley mentioned previously, and a useful collection of papers edited by Money

(37). Although papers on diagnostic and remedial reading continued to appear in scores of educational, psychological, and medical journals, the various IRA publications became increasingly helpful. Annual reviews of reading research by Helen M. Robinson for IRA* and Theodore Harris for the *Journal of Education Research* continued the pioneer efforts of Gray and helped to keep reading specialists in touch with new developments.

The major shift in theory was away from psychodynamics and toward renewed emphasis on physiological, neurological, and constitutional factors. In 1956 Rabinovitch first published his distinction between primary reading disabilities, which he considered to be the result of constitutional deviations in neurological functioning, and secondary reading disabilities which may be induced by a variety of environmental factors *(45).* The next year Lauretta Bender attributed severe reading disability to a maturational lag, a delayed development of certain brain centers *(1).* Rabinovitch and Bender were both psychiatrists with excellent reputations and their papers were influential. Both avoided the trap of attributing deficiencies in perceptual or motor skills necessarily to brain damage, a diagnosis made all too often on flimsy evidence.

In 1959 a brave effort was made to explain all reading disabilities with a single theory. Smith and Carrigan, after an intensive study of about 40 cases, concluded that all of the varied symptoms could be explained by a lack of balance between two chemicals controlling the transmission of nerve impulses in the brain *(52).* The theory was impressive; the evidence, unfortunately, was less than convincing.

Another unconventional approach was that of Delacato, whose background was in work with brain-damaged children. Delacato attributed reading disability to an arrest of neurological development *(14).* Some children were thought to be arrested at a level of one of the lower brain centers; their treatment might start with practice in creeping, crawling, and sleeping in a preferred position. For other children the problem was thought to be failure to establish unilateral dominance, and unconventional measures to enforce unilateral dominance were used, including such practices as forbidding the child to listen to

---

*In *The Reading Teacher* through 1964 and in the *Reading Research Quarterly* from 1965 on.

music. Delacato's theories have been widely discussed, but most specialists on reading disability remain skeptical.

At IRA pre-conference institutes efforts were made by Harris in 1961 *(29)* and deHirsch in 1962 *(13)* to clarify the nature of the perceptual difficulties in reading cases. Both stressed the Gestalt aspects of perception, particularly with regard to part-whole relationships and failures in integration of one experience with another.

Experimentation with drugs as an adjunct to remedial treatment was started but did not get very far. Smith and Carrigan were encouraged by their results with a few cases; Staiger, on the other hand, obtained negative results *(53)*. Considering the variety of drugs now used in psychiatric settings, this area of reading research has barely been started.

New trends in diagnostic testing included growing skepticism about intelligence tests, a new and warmly greeted test based on psycholinguistic principles, and considerable attention to testing of perceptual abilities. While reading clinics continued to rely on the Stanford-Binet and Wechsler intelligence scales which are individually administered, there was growing recognition that group tests of mental ability are not very satisfactory with retarded readers. The Illinois Test of Psycholinguistic Abilities measured nine aspects of visual, auditory, and motor functioning relevant to language development and was welcomed in many reading clinics *(32)*. The Frostig Developmental Test of Visual Perception attempted to provide measures of the five aspects of visual perception: eye-hand coordination, figure-ground, form constancy, position in space, and spatial relations *(20)*. Auditory perception tests were found useful, and favorable validity data were reported for the Wepman Auditory Discrimination Test *(8)*, and an auditory blending test devised by Roswell and Chall *(7)*.

The outpouring of new ideas about how the teaching of beginning reading can be improved that has taken place since 1960 has had its counterpart in remedial teaching. Advocates of perceptual training — i.t.a., words in color, materials based on linguistic principles, programed materials, programed tutoring, talking typewriters, and specific phonic systems — have all been clamoring for attention. Most of these approaches are still too new to be properly evaluated, and we will have to wait a few years for the dust to settle.

The 1960's have also seen an outburst of interest in the

massive reading retardation among disadvantaged children, particularly those belonging to minority groups. So far, most of this attention has been focused on improving the developmental reading program, providing preschool enrichment, and working with the school dropout and adult illiterate. We need to take a careful look at the child who is both disadvantaged and a case of special disability.

Remedial reading began during this decade to be accepted as a field of special education, requiring specially trained teachers and deserving financial support. The first state certification of remedial teachers was begun, although most states still do not certify remedial teachers as such.

The climax of the decade, however, came with the passing of the new education acts of 1965. The Elementary and Secondary Education Act provided hundreds of millions of dollars for new programs to meet the needs of the disadvantaged. Much of this money under Title I and Title III has gone into an almost infinite variety of remedial reading projects and programs. One of the immediate results was that the previously inadequate supply of trained reading specialists was totally insufficient to meet the demand, and hundreds of untrained or insufficiently trained people have had to fill a great many of the new positions. How seriously this condition may have affected the quality of the new programs is still a matter of guesswork.

In 1965, also, federal recognition of the critical need for reading personnel was shown by the addition of reading to the fields of study in which special training institutes could be supported under the National Defense Education Act. The December 1965 issue of *The Reading Teacher* listed 67 NDEA institutes in reading to be held in 1966. This institute program, which is continuing, holds promise of lessening somewhat the critical shortage of trained reading specialists.

Thus, the fifth decade closed with recognition by the public and by the government that remedial reading is a necessary special service and that it should be staffed with properly trained teachers.

We have taken a birds-eye-view of five decades. The year 1916 marked the first publication on reading difficulties in America; 1965 ended with federal support for a vast program of new diagnostic and remedial services and with support also for the training of needed personnel in this field. We have come far in these 50 years.

As the 50 years came to a close, however, much remained open and unsolved, and still is. We still do not have definitions of reading disability and remedial reading which everyone is willing to accept. Controversy continues over the causation of reading failure. Many varieties of remedial treatment are in use, some long established, others very new. While reading clinics and remedial programs have proliferated, there is no set of standards as to how they should be organized, how they should operate, or how they should be staffed. Research is lagging far behind innovation, making it possible for the program with the best press agent to get the most attention. The many professions interested in reading problems are just beginning to pay attention to one another's findings and opinions.

There is, then, a great deal still to be accomplished. The work of predicting, preventing, diagnosing, and correcting reading failure has been well started. But final answers are a hope for the future rather than a present reality. Much remains to be done.

REFERENCES

1. Bender, Lauretta. "Specific Reading Disability as a Maturational Lag." *Bulletin of the Orton Society,* 7 (1957), 9-18.

2. Betts, Emmett A. *Prevention and Correction of Reading Difficulties.* Evanston: Row, Peterson & Co., 1936.

3. Blanchard, Phyllis. "Psychogenic Factors in Some Cases of Reading Disability,"*American Journal of Orthopsychiatry,* 5 (1935), 361-374.

4. Bond, Guy L., and Miles A. Tinker, *Reading Difficulties: Their Diagnosis and Correction.* New York: Appleton-Century-Crofts, Inc., 1957.

5. Bronner, Augusta F. *The Psychology of Special Abilities and Disabilities.* Boston: Little, Brown & Co., 1917.

6. Buswell, Guy T. *Remedial Reading at the College and Adult Levels: an Experimental Study.* Supplementary Educational Monographs, No. 50. Chicago: Department of Education, University of Chicago, 1939.

7. Chall, Jeanne; Florence G. Roswell; and Susan H. Blumenthal.

"Auditory Blending Ability: A Factor in Success in Beginning Reading," *The Reading Teacher,* 17 (1963), 113-118.

8. Christine, Charles, and Dorothy Christine. "The Relation of Auditory Discrimination to Articulatory Defects and Reading Retardation," *Elementary School Journal,* 65 (1964), 97-100.

9. Cole, Luella. *The Improvement of Reading.* New York: Farrar and Rinehart, 1938.

10. Critchley, Macdonald. *Developmental Dyslexia.* London: William Heinemann Medical Books Ltd., 1964.

11. Dearborn, Walter F. "Structural Factors Which Condition Special Disability in Reading." *Proceedings of the American Association for Mental Deficiency,* 1933, 38, 266-283.

12. Dearborn, Walter F., and Irving H. Anderson. "Aniseikonia as Related to Disability in Reading." *Journal of Experimental Psychology,* 1938, 23, 559-577.

13. deHirsch, Katrina. "Psychological Correlates in the Reading Process." In *Challenge and Experiment in Reading,* J. Allen Figurel, (Ed.). *International Reading Association Conference Proceedings,* 7 (1962), 218-226.

14. Delacato, Carl H. *The Treatment and Prevention of Reading Problems.* Springfield, Illinois: Charles C. Thomas, 1959. *The Diagnosis and Treatment of Speech and Reading Problems.* Charles C. Thomas, 1963.

15. Durrell, Donald D. *Durrell Analysis of Reading Difficulty.* Tarrytown, New York: World Book Co. (Harcourt, Brace & World), 1937.

16. Durrell, Donald D. *Improvement of Basic Reading Abilities.* Yonkers-on-Hudson: World Book Co., 1940.

17. Fernald, Grace M. *Remedial Techniques in Basic School Subjects.* New York: McGraw-Hill Book Co., 1943.

18. Fernald, Grace M., and Helen B. Keller. "Effects of Kinesthetic Factor in Development of Word Recognition," *Journal of Educational Research,* 4 (1921), 355-377.

19. Flesch, Rudolph. *Why Johnny Can't Read.* New York: Harper & Bros., 1955.

20. Frostig, Marianne; Welty Lefever; and J.R.B. Whittlesey. *Administration and Scoring Manual for the Marianne Frostig Developmental Test of Visual Perception.*

21. Gates, Arthur I. *Gates Reading Diagnosis Tests.* New York: Bureau of Publications, Columbia University, 1927.

22. Gates, Arthur I. *The Improvement of Reading.* New York: The Macmillan Co., 1927; 2nd Ed., 1935.

23. Gates, Arthur I. "The Role of Personality Maladjustment in Reading Disability," *Journal of Genetic Psychology*, 59 (1941), 77-83.

24. Gray, Clarence T. *Deficiencies in Reading Ability: Their Diagnosis and Remedies*. Boston: D. C. Heath and Co., 1922.

25. Gray, William S. "Diagnostic and Remedial Steps in Reading," *Journal of Educational Research*, 4 (1921), 1-15.

26. Gray, William S. *Remedial Cases in Reading: Their Diagnosis and Treatment*. Supplementary Educational Monograph, No. 22. Chicago: Univ. of Chicago Press, 1922.

27. Hallgren, Bertil. "Specific Dyslexia," *Acta Psychiatrica et Neurologica*, Supplement 65 (1950).

28. Harris, Albert J. *How to Increase Reading Ability*. New York: Longmans, Green and Co., 1940.

29. Harris, Albert J. "Perceptual Difficulties in Reading Disability." In *Changing Concepts of Reading Instruction*, J. Allen Figurel, (Ed.). *International Reading Association Conference Proceedings*, 6 (1961), 282-290.

30. Hermann, Knud. *Reading Disability:A Medical Study of Word-Blindness and Related Handicaps*. Springfield, Illinois: Charles C. Thomas, 1959.

31. Judd, Charles H. *Reading: Its Nature and Development*. Supplementary Educational Monographs, No. 2. Chicago: Univ. of Chicago Press, 1918.

32. Kirk, Samuel A., and J. J. McCarthy. "The Illinois Test of Psycholinguistic Abilities — An Approach to Differential Diagnosis," *American Journal of Mental Deficiency*, 66 (1961), 399-412.

33. Kottmeyer, William. *Handbook for Remedial Reading*. St. Louis: Webster Publg. Co., 1947.

34. Lloyd, S.M., and C.T. Gray. *Reading in a Texas City: Diagnosis and Remedy*. University of Texas Bulletin No. 1853. Austin: Univ. of Texas, 1920.

35. McCallister, James M. *Remedial and Corrective Instruction in Reading*. New York: D. Appleton-Century Co., 1936.

36. Malmquist, Eve. *Factors Related to Reading Disabilities in the First Grade of the Elementary School*. Stockholm: Almqvist & Wiksell, 1958.

37. Money, John (Ed.). *Reading Disability: Progress and Research Needs in Dyslexia*. Baltimore: Johns Hopkins Press, 1962.

38. Monroe, Marion. *Children Who Cannot Read*. Chicago: Univ. of Chicago Press, 1932.

39. Monroe, Marion. *Monroe Diagnostic Reading Examination.* Chicago: C. S. Stoelting, 1928.

40. Monroe, Marion, and Bertie Backus. *Remedial Reading.* Boston: Houghton, Mifflin Co., 1937.

41. Morgan, W. Pringle. "A Case of Congenital Word-Blindness," *British Medical Journal,* 2 (1896), 1378.

42. Orton, June L. "The Orton-Gillingham Approach." Chapter 8 in *The Disabled Reader,* John Money, (Ed.) Baltimore: The Johns Hopkins Press, 1966.

43. Orton, Samuel T. "'Word-blindness' in Children," *Archives of Neurology and Psychiatry,* 14 (1925), 581-615.

44. Pearson, Gerald H. J. "A Survey of Learning Difficulties in Children," *Psychoanalytic Study of the Child,* 7 (1952), 372-386.

45. Rabinovitch, Ralph, *et al.* "A Research Approach to Reading Retardation," *Neurology and Psychiatry in Childhood.* Proceedings of the Association for Research in Nervous and Mental Disease, 34, 363-396. Baltimore: Williams and Wilkins, 1956.

46. *Report of the National Committee on Reading.* Twenty-fourth Yearbook, Part I, of the National Society for the Study of Education, Guy M. Whipple, (Ed.). Bloomington, Illinois: Pub. Sch. Publg. Co., 1925.

47. Robinson, Helen M. *Why Pupils Fail in Reading.* Chicago: Univ. of Chicago Press, 1947.

48. Roswell, Florence, and Gladys Natchez. *Reading Disability: Diagnosis and Treatment.* New York: Basic Books, Inc., 1964.

49. Russell, David H.; Etta E. Karp; and Edward I. Kelly. *Reading Aids through the Grades.* New York: Bureau of Publications, Teachers College Columbia University, 1938.

50. Schmitt, Clara. "Developmental Alexia: Congenital Word-Blindness or Inability to Learn to Read," *Elementary School Journal,* 18 (1918), 680-700, 757-769.

51. Sievers, Dorothy J., *et al. Selected Studies on the Illinois Test of Psycholinguistic Abilities.* Madison: Photo Press, Inc., 1963.

52. Smith, Donald E. P., and Patricia M. Carrigan. *The Nature of Reading Disability.* New York: Harcourt, Brace & Co., 1959.

53. Staiger, Ralph C. "Medicine for Reading Improvement," *Journal of Developmental Reading,* 5 (1961), 48-51.

54. Stanger, Margaret, and Ellen K. Donohue. *Prediction and Prevention of Reading Difficulties.* New York: Oxford Univ. Press, 1937.

55. Taylor, Earl A. *Controlled Reading.* Chicago: Univ. of Chicago Press, 1937.

56. Tinker, Miles A. "Diagnostic and Remedial Reading, I and II," *Elementary School Journal*, 33 (1932-33), 293-306, 346-357.

57. Tinker, Miles A. "Trends in Diagnostic and Remedial Reading as Shown by Recent Publications in This Field," *Journal of Educational Research*, 32 (1938), 293-303.

58. Traxler, Arthur E. *Ten Years of Research in Reading: Summary and Bibliography.* Educational Records Bureau Belletin, No. 32. New York: Educ. Rec. Bur., 1941. *Another Five Years of Research in Reading,* Educational Records Bureau Bulletin, No. 46 (1945). *Eight More Years of Research in Reading,* Educational Records Bureau Bulletin, No. 64 (1955). *Research in Reading During Another Four Years,* Educational Records Bulletin No. 75 (1960).

59. Uhl, Willis W. "The Use of the Results of Reading Tests as a Basis for Planning Remedial Work," *Elementary School Journal*, 17 (1916), 266-75.

60. *The Underachiever in Reading.* Compiled by H. Alan Robinson, (Ed.). Supplementary Educational Monographs, No. 92, Chicago: Univ. of Chicago Press, 1962.

61. Vernon, M. D. *Backwardness in Reading: A Study of Its Nature and Origin.* Cambridge: Cambridge Univ. Press, 1957.

62. Zirbes, Laura. "Diagnostic Measurement as a Basis for Procedure," *Elementary School Journal*, 18 (1918), 505-552.

THE PROFESSIONAL STANDARDS
AND ETHICS COMMITTEE
OF THE
INTERNATIONAL READING ASSOCIATION

Roles, Responsibilities, and Qualifications of Reading Specialists

Acts by the federal government in the sixties have helped cause a "reading teacher explosion." Many special reading teachers are inadequately prepared for their positions. The following guide indicates the qualifications that a group of specialists in the area believe desirable for those persons who spend the majority of their time in developmental or remedial reading activities. Notice that the clinical worker, consultant, and supervisor or director of reading need training and experience beyond the minimum standards set forth for the special teacher of reading.

With which recommendations do you agree most strongly? With which do you disagree? Are there any responsibilities or qualifications you would add? How do you rank on the desired qualifications? What are your state's requirements?

THE PURPOSE OF THIS STATEMENT

This statement of the roles, responsibilities and qualifications of reading specialists has been formulated by the Professional Standards and Ethics Committee and approved by the Board of Directors of the International Reading Association. It is intended that these minimum standards will serve as guides to:

1. Teachers and administrators in identifying the reading specialist.
2. State and provincial departments of education in certifying specialists in reading.
3. Colleges and universities offering professional programs in reading.
4. Individuals planning to train as reading specialists.

These standards are under constant study and are periodically revised by the committee. This 1968 guide is a revision and extension of the brochure, "Minimum Standards for Professional Training of Reading Specialists," published in 1965.

THE NEED FOR ESTABLISHING STANDARDS

Reading is a complex process that develops within an individual throughout years of formal schooling and adult life. As a result of expanded knowledge, the demand for trained personnel in reading at all levels has increased tremendously. With the demand high and the supply relatively short, the danger of unqualified persons attempting those tasks which only a trained reading specialist should undertake has become a very real one. One means of preventing such occurrences is by establishing minimum standards for the professional training of reading specialists.

The reading specialist may be designated as that person (1) who works directly or indirectly with those pupils who have either failed to benefit from regular classroom instruction in reading or those pupils who could benefit from advanced training in reading skills and/or (2) who works with teachers, administrators, and other professionals to improve and coordinate the total reading program of the school.

Definition of Roles

Reading personnel can be divided into two categories: those who work directly with children either as reading teachers or reading clinicians; and those who work directly with teachers as consultants or supervisors with prime responsibility for staff and program.

A. Special Teacher of Reading

A Special Teacher of Reading has major responsibility for remedial and corrective and/or developmental reading instruction.

B. Reading Clinician

A Reading Clinician provides diagnosis, remediation, or the planning of remediation for the more complex and severe reading disability cases.

C. Reading Consultant

A Reading Consultant works directly with teachers, administrators, and other professionals within a school to develop and implement the reading program under the direction of a supervisor with special training in reading.

D. Reading Supervisor (Coordinator or Director)

A Reading Supervisor provides leadership in all phases of the reading program in a school system.

Responsibilities of Each Reading Specialist

A. Special Teacher of Reading

*Should identify students needing diagnosis and/or remediation.

*Should plan a program of remediation from data gathered through diagnosis.

*Should implement such a program of remediation.

*Should evaluate student progress in remediation.

*Should interpret student needs and progress in remediation to the classroom teacher and the parents.

*Should plan and implement a developmental or advanced program as necessary.

B. Reading Clinician

*Should demonstrate all the skills expected of the Special Teacher of Reading and, by virtue of additional training and experience, diagnose and treat the more complex and severe reading disability cases.

*Should demonstrate proficiency in providing internship training for prospective clinicians and/or Special Teacher of Reading.

C. Reading Consultant

*Should survey and evaluate the ongoing program and make suggestions for needed changes.

*Should translate the district philosophy of reading with the help of the principal of each school into a working program consistent with the needs of the students, the teachers, and the community.

*Should work with classroom teachers and others in improving the developmental and corrective aspects of the reading program.

D. Reading Supervisor

*Should develop a system-wide reading philosophy and curriculum, and interpret this to the school administration, staff, and public.

*Should exercise leadership with all personnel in carrying out good reading practices.

*Should evaluate reading personnel and personnel needs in all phases of a school-wide reading program.

*Should make recommendations to the administration regarding the reading budget.

Qualifications

A. General (Applicable to all Reading Specialists)

*Demonstrate proficiency in evaluating and implementing research.

*Demonstrate a willingness to make a meaningful contribution to professional organizations related to reading.

*Demonstrate a willingness to assume leadership in improving the reading program.

B. Special Teacher of Reading

*Complete a minimum of three years of successful classroom teaching in which the teaching of reading is an important responsibility of the position.

*Complete a planned program for the Master's Degree from an accredited institution, to include:

1. A minimum of 12 semester hours in graduate level reading courses with at least one course in each of the following:

   (a) *Foundations or survey of reading*
   A basic course whose content is related exclusively to reading instruction or the psychology of reading. Such a course ordinarily would be first in a sequence of reading courses.

(b) *Diagnosis and correction of reading disabilities*
The content of this course or courses includes the following: causes of reading disabilities; observation and interview procedures; diagnostic instruments; standard and informal tests; report writing; materials and methods of instruction.

(c) *Clinical or laboratory practicum in reading*
A clinical or laboratory experience which might be an integral part of a course or courses in the diagnosis and correction of reading disabilities. Students diagnose and treat reading disability cases under supervision.

2. Complete, at undergraduate or graduate level, study in each of the following areas:

   (a) Measurement and/or evaluation.
   (b) Child and/or adolescent psychology.
   (c) Psychology, including such aspects as personality, cognition, and learning behaviors.
   (d) Literature for children and/or adolescents.

3. Fulfill remaining portions of the program from related areas of study.

C. Reading Clinician

   *Meet the qualifications as stipulated for the Special Teacher of Reading.

   *Complete, in addition to the above, a sixth year of graduate work including:

   1. An advanced course or courses in the diagnosis and remediation of reading and learning problems.
   2. A course or courses in individual testing.
   3. An advanced clinical or laboratory practicum in the diagnosis and remediation of reading difficulties.
   4. Field experiences under the direction of a qualified Reading Clinician.

D. Reading Consultant

   *Meet the qualifications as stipulated for the Special Teacher of Reading.

*Complete, in addition to the above, a sixth year of graduate work including:

1. An advanced course in the remediation and diagnosis of reading and learning problems.
2. An advanced course in the developmental aspects of a reading program.
3. A course or courses in curriculum development *and* supervision.
4. A course and/or experience in public relations.
5. Field experiences under a qualified Reading Consultant or Supervisor in a school setting.

E. Reading Supervisor

*Meet the qualifications as stipulated for the Special Teacher of Reading.

*Complete, in addition to the above, a sixth year of graduate work including:

1. Courses listed as 1, 2, 3, and 4 under Reading Consultant.
2. A course or courses in administrative procedures.
3. Field experiences under a qualified Reading Supervisor.

CODE OF ETHICS

The members of the International Reading Association who are concerned with the teaching of reading form a group of professional persons, obligated to society and devoted to the service and welfare of individuals through teaching, clinical services, research, and publication. The members of this group are committed to values which are the foundation of a democratic society — freedom to teach, write, and study in an atmosphere conducive to the best interests of the profession. The welfare of the public, the profession, and the individuals concerned should be of primary consideration in recommending candidates for degrees, positions, advancements, the recognition of professional activity, and for certification in those areas where certification exists.

Ethical Standards in Professional Relationships

1. It is the obligation of all members of the International Reading Association to observe the Code of Ethics of the organization and to act accordingly so as to advance the status and prestige of the Association and of the profession as a whole. Members should assist in establishing the highest professional standards for reading programs and services, and should enlist support for these through dissemination of pertinent information to the public.

2. It is the obligation of all members to maintain relationships with other professional persons, striving for harmony, avoiding personal controversy, encouraging cooperative effort, and making known the obligations and services rendered by the reading specialist.

3. It is the obligation of members to report results of research and other developments in reading.

4. Members should not claim nor advertise affiliation with the International Reading Association as evidence of their competence in reading.

Ethical Standards in Reading Services

1. Reading specialists must possess suitable qualifications for engaging in consulting, clinical, or remedial work. Unqualified persons should not engage in such activities except under the direct supervision of one who is properly qualified. Professional intent and the welfare of the person seeking the services of the reading specialist should govern all consulting or clinical activities such as counseling, administering diagnostic tests, or providing remediation. It is the duty of the reading specialist to keep relationships with clients and interested persons on a professional level.

2. Information derived from consulting and/or clinical services should be regarded as confidential. Expressed consent of persons involved should be secured before releasing information to outside agencies.

3. Reading specialists should recognize the boundaries of their competence and should not offer services which fail to meet professional standards established by other disciplines. They should be free, however, to give assistance in other areas in which they are qualified.

4. Referral should be made to specialists in allied fields as needed. When such referral is made, pertinent information should be made available to consulting specialists.

5. Reading clinics and/or reading specialists offering professional services should refrain from guaranteeing easy solutions or favorable outcomes as a result of their work, and their advertising should be consistent with that of allied professions. They should not accept for remediation any persons who are unlikely to benefit from their instruction, and they should work to accomplish the greatest possible improvement in the shortest time. Fees, if charged, should be agreed on in advance and should be charged in accordance with an established set of rates commensurate with that of other professions.

2

How the Child
Got That Way

Nowhere is the cliche, "the whole child learns" more true than in learning — or failing to learn — to read. A constellation of forces almost defying enumeration have been catalogued as enhancers or inhibitors of reading growth. These forces occur in every growth area of child development: physical, social, emotional, psychological, and educational. A few seem universal, some are frequent, and others are strangely infrequent. Some are definitely causal; others occur in conjunction with reading disability but for inexplicable reasons. Occasionally one factor can be specified as the causal agent; other times several factors intertwine while remaining identifiable as primary causes. But too often even intensive diagnosis cannot specify why the disability occurred. And to complicate the matter, any factor may emerge at any time during the reader's life.

Three major areas for study are evident when dealing with the causes of reading disability: multiple causation, relative frequency, and instructional implications. The first has been discussed so frequently that it may have lost much of its initial impact (as have "the whole child" and "individual differences"). But its truth remains. The fact that each article in this section deals with a single factor rather than several interrelated ones does not indicate that either the authors of the articles or the editors of this book believe in a theory of single causation; variables must be isolated for careful study and to emphasize their existence.

The problem of relative frequency is both dismaying and puzzling. Literally innumerable factors have been related to reading disability, yet the consensus of educators intimately involved with such children is that at least 75 percent of them are the victims of improper and inadequate instruction in the basic skills. It is imperative that we never permit ourselves, the profession, and the public to forget this fact! We must never be swept off our feet by persuasive voices peddling the latest fad in either causation or instruction. Critical reading is a skill to be practiced — as well as taught — by reading teachers.

Instructional implications are not easily dealt with. Because research in education is in its infancy, it is easier to identify causal or associated factors than it is to specify the kind of treatment uniquely appropriate for each one. But by studying the various factors, reading specialists will eventually learn to choose remediation consonant with discovered and suspected causation and to institute measures to prevent or diminish future cases of reading disability. Unless we apply what we know about how the child got that way, we may just as well forget about it. The only justification for investigating causal and associated factors is that knowledge of them will be used in the correction and prevention of reading disability.

The editors of this anthology do not pretend that the following articles systematically investigate the multiplicity of causal and associated factors. Several ideas in these articles have not made significant contributions at the present time, although they may represent definite potential breakthroughs in how we think about the etiology of reading disability. It is equally possible that further investigation may prove them untenable. Part of what the editors hope to convey in this section is that we know surprisingly little for certain about how the child got that way. Research will continue to unearth new possibilities, which in turn, may be either trivia or triumph. One thing is certain, however. The profession will not be satisfied with yesterday's knowledge. And neither must the teacher of reading.

THEODORE A. CHANDLER

Reading Disability
and Socio-Economic Status

Socio-economic status is a potent influence on reading achievement, yet its impact is little understood and oft-ignored. This review takes a penetrating and sobering look at research findings and challenges us to discover the implications of its conclusions in our own teaching and community.

Is socio-economic status a causal or relational factor in reading disability? In what ways could it be implicated in learning word identification skills? in learning comprehension? How is this article related to Baratz's and to Coleman's in this section, to Stanchfield's in Part Four, and to Robinson's and Wynn's in Part Six? What do these findings mean to the teachers of children from lower socio-economic classes?

Twenty years ago when she wrote that "there seems to be little relationship between reading failure and education or ability of parents, socio-economic status, foreign language in the home, or recordable attitudes," Robinson *(26)* did not have the benefit of subsequent studies. This is not to say that she would refute this statement of hers: "It thus appears that studies to date have not given objective evidence of the relationship of socio-economic status to reading disability or reading progress." Obviously, in her plea for "objective evidence" she means well-designed, controlled experimentation yielding substantial correlations. Although some of the studies cited here may not meet her criteria, the gross result should indicate serious circumstances demanding serious consideration.

In a monumental work, Warner observed:

Reprinted from *Journal of Reading,* 10 (October 1966), pp. 5-21, by permission of Theodore A. Chandler and the International Reading Association.

> Social class research demonstrates that our educational system
> performs the dual task of aiding social mobility and, at the same
> time, working effectively to hinder it.... It has been estimated
> that, whereas 80% of the upper- and upper-middle class children
> actually go to college, only 20% of the lower-middle and 5% of
> the lower-class children get there.... If the teachers and school
> administrators in grade and high schools know the class positions
> of the children who enter their schools they can predict who will
> and who will not get to college....

Let us see how Warner's study operates in Berkeley, California,
but with the focus changed to the effect of residential
segregation upon educational achievement (specifically
reading) and educational-vocational aspirations. In 1960
Wilson *(33)* analyzed this problem in Berkeley. Unique in
topography, Berkeley illustrates a kind of mobility which very
interestingly parallels Warner's concept of social mobility.
Looking at a map and table compiled by the Berkeley Urban
Renewal Office, *(23)* one sees that property value (cost of
housing) follows a generally consistent pattern. The "flats"
represent the lowest in topography and in cost of housing; next
are the "foothills"; finally the top of the socio-economic ladder
is reached in the "hills." The census tracts (geographic areas of
the city based upon the latest census figures) having the least
expensive housing tend to have higher concentrations of
nonwhites than the city-wide average percentage of nonwhites.
All seven of the census tracts composing the lowest quartile of
tracts by median value of owner-occupied homes (i.e., $13,500
or less) had 27.9 percent or more nonwhites. Six of the seven
tracts composing the lowest quartile of tracts by average
monthly contract rent (i.e., $70 or less) had 43.7 percent or
more nonwhites.

Is it not surprising then that racial social distance is directly
proportional to geographic height! Yet the so-called liberals in
the "hills" would certainly deny that they are practicing
segregation — new style. They merely want their children to
attend the "best" schools in Berkeley and associate with peers
whose parents have the same values as they do. Wilson *(33)*
suggests how this pattern of geographic racial segregation
manifests itself in terms of school achievement patterns.

Using the California Reading Achievement Test at the high
sixth-grade level, Wilson found that 90 percent of the upper

strata were reading at grade level, while only one-third of the children of semi-skilled or unskilled manual laborers were. The mean test score was 106 in the Hills, 92 in the Foothills, 73 in the Flats. And analyzing the variability within each school stratum, he found that the higher occupational strata reflect higher achievement. But another variable apparently has an even more profound influence than occupation of the parents. The children of professionals in the Hills attained a higher average than their compeers in the Foothills; and the children of manual workers in the Foothills, though almost equalling the white-collar group in the same schools, proved quite superior to their compeers in the Flats. Only five children were not reading at grade level in the Hills, but only within a year of grade level. (Although there were three children of manual workers living in the Hills, interestingly none of these were among the five not reading at grade level.) Whereas almost all the children of professionals and white-collar workers were reading at grade level in the Hills, a third of them in the Foothills, and a quarter of them in the Flats were retarded in reading. Also, as can be surmised by this, the variability (standard deviation) was greater in the Flats and Foothills than in the Hills.

Keeping in mind that occupational status follows the topography in Berkeley, Table 1, reproduced from Wilson's thesis, *(33)* also tells us that other factors (such as teachers' evaluations of students, IQ, arithmetic achievement scores, and educational aspirations) follow a strikingly similar pattern to the reading achievement scores. There are, however, some exceptions that should be noted. In evaluating the professional and white-collar groups in the Hills and Foothills, the teachers gave the same proportions of A's and B's to the outstanding readers in both the Hills and Foothills. One wonders if this really reflects superiority or if it reflects the "halo effect" in ratings. Perceptual bias, as it relates to a criteria of excellence, seems to be influenced not so much by an unwavering criterion measure but by the norms of the strata. As Wilson *(33)* says, "The normalization of a lower standard of performance in the less-favored stratum provides the same circular reinforcement for the group that the normalization of past performances does for the individual."

Another exception relates to the Negroes' occupational aspirations. In the Flats, where they form a majority, there is a

Table 1

Teacher and Test Indications of Academic Achievement
by Father's Occupations: High-Sixth-Grade Boys,
Berkeley, California, 1959*

Father's Occupation	Achievement Variables[a]					
	1	2	3	4	5	6
Executive	73%	65%	92%	106	81	125
	(26)	(26)	(26)	(25)	(25)	(23)
Professional	67	56	91	105	82	126
	(93)	(93)	(93)	(92)	(88)	(74)
Merchant: self-employed	63	67	90	105	83	125
	(30)	(30)	(30)	(29)	(29)	(26)
Upper white collar	54	46	84	101	79	122
	(37)	(37)	(37)	(37)	(34)	(32)
Lower white collar	32	29	65	84	63	107
	(31)	(31)	(31)	(29)	(29)	(27)
Artisan: self-employed	39	61	39	88	66	114
	(18)	(18)	(18)	(17)	(18)	(16)
Skilled manual	27	31	42	84	59	103
	(48)	(48)	(45)	(43)	(42)	(35)
Semi- and unskilled manual	11	20	33	75	55	101
	(75)	(75)	(72)	(70)	(66)	(55)
All Occupations	42%	42%	65%	92	69	114
	(405)	(405)	(396)	(387)	(377)	(327)

[a] The indexes of achievement are as follows:
1. Percentages to whom teachers would assign A or B grades in reading.
2. Percentages to whom teachers would assign A or B grades in arithmetic.
3. Percentages reading at grade level (in a high-sixth-grade reader) in April.
4. Mean California Reading Achievement Test scores.
5. Mean California Arithmetic Achievement Test scores.
6. Mean California Mental Maturity Test (IQ) scores.
* Blanket permission on file in Main Library, University of California,
Berkeley.

higher level of occupational aspiration than in the Foothills,
where they are obviously a minority. And apparently this same
reversal holds true for educational aspiration, since nearly
three-fourths of the Negroes in the Flats want to go to college as
Wilson *(33)* explains: "A segregated social minority can
generate and maintain higher hopes than when integrated. It
can develop its indigenous leadership, and is not demoralized
by continuous tokens of their imposed inferiority." Although
this may be true, there may be other possible explanations. For
example, he used a forced-choice type of measuring instrument

for educational aspiration with only one open-ended question regarding occupational interest. He had a measure of internal consistency for education but not for occupation. Furthermore, what may we deduce from a child's expressed occupational interest at Grade Six? The fact that 75 percent of the Negro children residing in the Flats express a desire to go to college in no way seems like an unusual phenomenon. One wonders what happens to this stated desire during junior and senior high school.

Only 10 percent of the Negroes — but 52 percent of the whites — were marked as outstanding readers by their teachers in the Foothills. In the Flats the percentage was 17 for the Negroes and 24 for the whites. Fourteen of the 81 Negro students were mentioned as outstanding readers in the Flats as opposed to 2 out of 20 Negro students in the Foothills. But of course ratings generally do not have particularly high or even moderate correlation coefficients.

In an earlier study of eight high schools in the San Francisco-Oakland area, Wilson *(32)* found large discrepancies in the modal educational and occupational aspirations of their student bodies, even though the schools were by no means homogeneous. Nevertheless, he was apparently able to distinguish predominantly middle-class schools from predominately working-class schools. While fewer than two-thirds of the sons of professionals at the working-class schools wanted to go to college, nearly 93 percent of the same stratum at the highest status schools wanted to. And similarly, a third of the sons of manual workers at the working-class schools wanted to go to college as opposed to more than half who attended the predominantly middle-class schools. Again, we see that the socio-economic milieu of the school does exert its influence.

In an attempt to show the relationship between socio-economic status and performance of junior high school students, Coleman *(6)* selected three groups on the basis of the Sims Socio-Economic score card: Group I was the high status group; Group II, normative; Group III, low status. His sampling, which included 43 states and various types of schools and communities, indicated that as a group the poor readers were children of low socio-economic status. He found the differences to be reliable in each grade. Consistent with this finding is the additional fact that pupils from Group I had the largest number of hobbies, with even some qualitative differentiation in terms of choice of hobby. For example, they might as a rule choose reading, playing musical instruments, or collecting. And in terms of extracurricular activities, there was greater participation by pupils from the high socio-economic group. It is possible that the extracurricular programs in the schools are geared to meeting the needs of the higher socio-economic status student. In any case, Coleman was not quite ready to conclude that superior achievement is a result of socio-economic status. Nor was he ready to admit that it is a result of superior intelligence, even though he found differences in median IQ's which favored the higher status groups. And since intelligence, as operationally defined by intelligence tests, is really an indication of achievement rather than ability (IQ tests are essentially achievement tests), Coleman's reluctance is understandable.

If we presume that the number of books in the home and the educational level of the parents reflect socio-economic status, then it might be possible to make a quantitative analysis as Sheldon and Carrillo *(29)* did. Beginning with an original 868 youngsters in eight schools in central New York State, they selected five percent of the good readers and five percent of the poor readers on the basis of achievement test scores, ratings by teachers, and IQ test scores. With a final sample of 290 good readers and 95 poor readers, they compiled the following:

Table 2

Percentage of Good and Poor Readers
by Number of Books in the Home

No. of books in home	Good Readers	Poor Readers
0	33%	67%
1–25	35%	21%
25–100	37%	24%
over 100	75%	11%
over 500	78%	9%

The relationship appears abundantly clear: As the number of books in the home increases, the percentage of good readers increases while the percentage of poor readers decreases. Also significant is that 217 of 290 parents (93 percent) of the good readers responded, as opposed to 63 of 95 parents (66 percent) of the poor readers. The accuracy of this kind of reporting remains dubious because of the parents' desire to look good. Table 2 might show that the number of books in the home is proportional to the quality of reader in the home. In other words, good readers might ask for books and receive them while poor readers would not necessarily ask for them.

In terms of highest grade reached by the parents, we find 35 percent of the good-reader parents completed college as contrasted to only 7% of the poor-reader parents. Again, poorer cooperation from the parents of the poor readers was noticed. But this time only approximately two-thirds of the parents of the best readers responded. This apparently is a much more emotionally-charged issue, and hence more prone to defensiveness. Other limitations of the study were noted by the author. For example, the selected sample had a geographic bias and the educational levels of the parents were contaminating the teachers' ratings. Nevertheless, the study did indicate that children who were good readers tended to come from homes where there was some reading matter and some value placed upon education as indicated by achieved parental goals. In addition, the author found that children who were good readers had fathers in professional and managerial occupations 55% of the time, while children who were poor readers had fathers in this classification only 27% of the time.

In Denver, Colorado, Granzow *(13)* confirmed some of Sheldon and Carillo's findings In comparing underachievers with normal achievers at the sixth- and seventh-grade levels with a representation covering 51 of the 69 schools, the following was learned: (a) the underachievers in reading came from homes of lower socio-economic status; (b) the percentage of parents who were indifferent to reading was higher for the underachievers in reading; (c) the parents of the underachievers in reading had fewer educational advantages. A sampling of 40 each is rather small, but related studies reveal similar patterns.

Extending this concept of socio-economic status geographically, we find Vernon, *(30)* an Englishwoman, declaring: "It would probably be accepted immediately that in this country (England) at least the reading achievement of children of lower socio-economic status is generally inferior to that of children of higher socio-economic status." But she goes on to say: "Thus so

far as low socio-economic status is connected with backwardness, it may be that the cultural factors are of relatively
greater importance than is sheer poverty."

Dawson measured the IQ's of and obtained reading and
arithmetic quotients for 289 children whose parents moved
from a slum area in Glasgow to a slum clearance estate. Tests
were given at the time of the move, and then 12-18 months later.
The reading scores improved more than the arithmetic scores
and IQ's; all the differences except one were significant. A
control group of children who remained in the slum showed
increases in some scores and decreases in others, but no overall
improvement.

Engle *(10)* asked: "Do pupils from financially dependent
homes do less satisfactory work in school than pupils from more
fortunate homes?" He found a higher percentage of pupils from
the privileged homes pursuing academic subjects than those
from under-privileged homes. And by the same token, the
percentage of pupils from the under-privileged homes who were
studying vocational subjects was much larger than the percentage of pupils from the privileged homes. Analyzing the
academic marks, he found a similar pattern. Those from the
under-privileged homes had a distribution of marks distinctly
skewed toward the lower marks, while the opposite was true of
the marks of the pupils from the privileged group. What is
particularly significant is that even in vocational subjects the
pupils from the privileged homes made better marks than those
from the under-privileged homes.

Although Mills *(20)* fails to name the study, he says, "The
most careful study available reveals that in many cases the
father's income rather than the boy's brains determines who
shall be college trained." In fact, Sexton *(28)* devotes an entire
book to the relationship between income and several facets of
education. Making a careful sociological analysis of the schools
of Big City (reportedly Detroit), she saw certain relationships
between median income schools (that is, median income of the
parents of the pupils attending a particular school) and reading
achievement.

As is indicated in Table 3, the reading disabilities of the
lower income groups tend to perpetuate a self-fulfilling vicious
circle, which was cited earlier. Unable to read adequately, the
lower income groups fail to qualify for the skilled and higher

paying jobs and thus are obliged to follow in their parents' footsteps, remaining in the same types of occupations. Apparently income does follow socio-economic status, at least at the unskilled and semiskilled levels. However, seemingly there would be many exceptions even at these lower strata, as witnessed by the many instances of laborers earning more than some professionals.

Table 3

Fourth-Grade Iowa Achievement Scores

Major income group	Reading*
$3000	− .14
$5000	− .06
$7000	+ .07
$9000	+ .20

(* relative to total composite score: above or below)

The indictment that Sexton makes in her book is characterized by what she calls the inverted pyramid concept. Those youngsters who need help the least (children from parents who have an income of $7000-$9000) receive more service (such as reading improvement programs, gifted classes, best facilities, best teachers, etc.) than those who need the services the most — those in the lowest-income schools. For example, 3.9 percent of all schools in the lower-income half have an all-day reading teacher, whereas 4.9 percent of the schools in the upper half do. Sexton is quite critical of how this inequity occurs. "The ground rules work like this: A child is given a reading test (an IQ test). If he does poorly on this reading test he cannot get remedial reading aid. A strange logic, but one which is all too often applied in our schools." Unable then to "qualify" for remedial instruction, the children with reading disabilities may be forced into non-academic curricula, which just by coincidence (or by design) also reflect the vocational standing of the parents. Even in the university there is a general differentiation in choice of curricula as reflected by family income. According to Mills, [20] "Students of law, medicine, or liberal arts generally come from families having twice the yearly income of students in nursing, teaching or commercial work."

The curriculum of the elementary school, especially, reflects middle-class values. And no doubt the material that lower-income children are required to read is based largely on the vocabulary, experiences, and interests of middle- and upper-income groups. Rarely do any of these texts speak the language of lower-income students or communicate to them in any meaningful way. For example, in Big City Sexton noted that the zoo was located in the middle-class section of town, and virtually no Negroes visited it. Yet in the Reading Readiness test used in Big City, there were animals which city children would normally see only in a zoo. If one looks into the first-grade pre-primers, primers, and readers used in most school systems, one wonders if the experiences depicted are really typical. Usually there's a family of four (brother and sister) living in the suburbs. The children are neat and clean and their faces always lack "color." There are always a father and a mother, who also are neat and clean all the time even when father is working on the car. Never is there an interpersonal problem in the home. Usually the lives of the characters in these stories are exceedingly sterile. How difficult it must be then for the Negro children to painfully see that the reading experts do not consider them worthy of consideration in most basal readers. Can we totally ignore the content? Does not *meaningful* reading material improve reading skills?

Sexton cites an experiment conducted by the University of Kentucky using this very premise. It was assumed that simple, readable, meaningful reading materials would improve the general standard of living of low-income children. Without changing the curriculum, specially-prepared reading materials dealing with problems of health and diet were introduced in two Kentucky schools, with the teachers being instructed by guides how best to use these materials. After ten years, the experimental group showed a pronounced improvement in fundamental learning skills (especially reading) in comparison with students in schools not taking part in the projects. Also, these reading materials had a positive effect on the attitudes of people in these communities and improved their standard of living. However, Sexton neither cites statistical evidence for this nor indicates the rating procedures.

Just as class values influence school curriculum, so class values influence behavior, as can be examined along the dimensions of peer-group relationships like social acceptance. Neugarten *(22)*, for example, found that the children of the upper and upper-middle classes were rated high by all other children for such traits as good looks, liking for school, leadership, friendship, and other personal traits. The reverse was true for lower-class children. They were said to be bad looking, dirty, and "people you would not want for friends." Here, already in the fifth and sixth grades, children's personalities and even life careers are being shaped and influenced.

Brown and Bond *(4)* examined the school records of children identified with the lowest social status groups and found that they received fewer school rewards such as marks, elective offices, and other symbols of recognition than children of higher social status. Furthermore, more punishments were received by children of low social status. Again, this was in the sixth grade. But note that this study was made in an impoverished Southern community, using only Negro children! Not surprising was the fact that 70 percent of the youngsters were in the lower-lower and upper-lower classes and the other 30 percent in the middle class, based on the Warner Index to Social Status.

Milner *(21)* pushed the problem down to the first grade, hypothesizing that "high reading ability in grade one children is related to 'higher' family social status; and conversely, low reading ability in grade one children is related to 'lower' family social status." She did find support for this in a Pearson correlation of .86 between family's Index of Social Characteristics (per Warner) and the "language IQ," as represented by the California Test of Mental Maturity. Through an interview schedule, she also discovered that the high-scoring children were surrounded by a much richer verbal family environment and had more opportunity for emotionally positive interaction with parents than the low-scoring children. One might then question, as this author undoubtedly did, Davis' *(7)* contention that less weight on verbal-skills training should be emphasized with the children from low socio-economic status. Yet if we presume that communication skills are essential to all children, then apparently more weight should be placed in this area, especially for the children of lower socio-economic status. Milner advocates publicly-supported nursery schools and kindergartens among the lower-class population as an immediate consideration. But she also suggests a revised curricular program in which these children in small groups can be provided with needed positive interpersonal relationships between pupils and the teacher.

"Any extension of experience, improvement of goals and motivation can be achieved only by methods which do not ignore or insult the learner's origins and present value system, thus preserving his security while challenging to growth and improvement. The values and beliefs of any one social class cannot be imposed upon the society. Certain usually ignored values and processes of the lower class may well possess social value," Burton *(5)* says in a provocative article. According to his figures, children are drawn from the social classes in this proportion: 3 percent upper, 38 percent middle, 58 percent lower. In this case, then 41 percent determines what the remaining children will experience in their early, formal training in learning to read. And since the majority of the teachers come from the middle-class, one might conservatively say that the bulk of the youngsters — those in the lower classes — are out-classed and consequently at a decided disadvantage. And when its time to rate the youngsters, the middle-class teachers naturally are committed to their own values. The middle and upper classes particularly stigmatize in the lower classes what they prefer to call laziness, shiftlessness, irresponsibility, ignorance, and immorality. Hence, teachers in general will rate lower-class children lower than the children in their own classes, frequently because they neither understand nor accept alien values. The lower classes probably find many of our middle-class values also repugnant and alien. Even some "rebel" middle-classers are questioning some of these values. But for the vast majority of students in the pre-collegiate curriculum at the high school level, middle-class, traditional values still prevail — Puritan morality, individualism, work-success ethic, future-time orientation.

In devising a Differential Values Inventory containing 64 forced-choice items, Prince *(25)* attempted to pair Traditional value orientation with an Emergent value system (relativistic moral attitudes, conformity, sociability, present-time orientation). An interesting finding emerged: value patterns of seniors and freshmen within each type of school (public, religious, private) showed no significant difference, and both were similar to the teachers' value patterns in that particular school. The religious schools showed more traditional value orientations, the private schools more emergent, and the public schools somewhere in between. The acquisition of values is indeed a most complex phenomenon. As Getzels *(12)* maintains:

> When the school is caught in an area of sharp cleavage along regional, occupational, or social-class lines...the various significant figures in the school setting and in the community provide inconsistent and contradictory models for the child. In such situations, identification, if it occurs at all, results in conflict and anxiety, for to incorporate one model means to reject another. To incorporate the parents' values as a model may mean to reject the teachers' values.

Holmes *(16)* reaffirms a similar notion: "When self-fulfilling behavior is reinforced, the child is able to mobilize more and more of energies for the purposive-pursuit of his task, but when such behavior is in conflict with authoritative and parental notions of what the child ought to be doing, then the converse would tend to be true." Obviously, if the child's milieu is pleasant, rewarding, and tends to increase his self-esteem, he will likely stick around and possibly do well; however, if it is punishing and tends to diminish his self-respect, he is likely to do poorly and want to quit.

It then seems to follow that possibly the object of hostility will be different for children of lower socio-economic status than for middle-class children when there's a reading problem. Frequently in middle-class children the hostility is directed primarily against the parents. But in the case of the lower-class child, where there is a reading disability the acting-out behavior will be directed primarily against the teacher and the school. (Thus there should be much less discrepancy between parental attitudes about their children and children's self-attitudes in the case of lower-class reading disability than in higher-class reading disability cases, but this needs to be tested empirically.)

Changing the focus slightly, this question may be raised: What is the relationship, if any, between delinquency and reading disability? Roman, Margolin and Harari *(27)* made an intensive survey of the New York City Children's Court. They found that 76 percent of the children screened for educational problems were retarded at least two years in reading. More than 50 percent of the group was retarded five years or more. Although this does not necessarily mean that failure in reading results in delinquency, it does suggest that reading disability is frequently a first sign of delinquency, as confirmed by Margolin, Roman and Harari. *(19)* After all, with the low socio-economic child the imposition of learning to read really represents an act of aggression by an unfriendly, outside authority. It's "outside" because this child is rarely punished by his parents for academic failure. In fact, he is frequently praised. His peer group actually rewards him for acts of bravado which challenge authority. Invariably the father maintains an authoritarian, rigid, punitive hold on the family. He seems only to communicate to his children physically and usually impulsively. There is little verbal communication by the parents, and they apparently do not tolerate (let alone encourage) verbal exchange by the children. Is it any wonder then that these children, exposed to one set of values half their waking hours, come into conflict during the other half when forced to adhere to a set of values they don't comprehend?

Dimitz, Kay and Reckless *(9)* found that pupils who lived in the more desirable census tracts scored significantly lower on delinquency indices but significantly higher on IQ and school achievement measures. These conclusions support other studies cited. Their sample consisted of 717 sixth-grade pupils in 24 different rooms in 11 selected elementary schools of Columbus, Ohio. They were concerned with IQ, reading, and arithmetic achievement scores as a function of race, sex, teacher nomination, and type of neighborhood. Considering reading achievement scores as a function of race and neighborhood, for example, they found that the whites scored at the 6.22 grade level, whereas the Negroes scored at the 4.56 grade level (critical ratio: 13.78 P: .01). By the same token, the children from the "good" neighborhood scored at the 6.64 grade level, whereas the children from the "bad" neighborhood scored at the 4.80 grade level (critical ratio: 13.21 P: .01). The authors paint an interesting caricature: "The white female who was nominated as good and who resides in a good neighborhood occupies the most favorable position on the average ranking for all six measures in this study, while the Negro male who was nominated as bad and resides in a bad neighborhood makes the poorest average showing on all six measures." This really supports Wilson's *(33)* finding that only 6 percent of the boys in the Flats and Foothills of Berkeley indicated reading or homework as a favored activity, whereas 18 percent so indicated in the Hills. And two-thirds of the boys in the Hills say they do read, while only half of the boys in the lower strata say they read. But by now this difference should surprise no one.

If intelligence is held constant, the differences between the lower and higher social strata largely result from this differential in experience, though there are undoubtedly, as indicated, other possible facets to the problem. If this is so, then success in beginning reading should be positively related to the number of the child's responses to opportunities for reading prior to first grade. Almy *(1)* tested this hypothesis and found a significant positive correlation between success in reading and such experiences as looking at books and magazines, having someone to read to them, and interest in words, letters, and numbers.

Concerned with this lack of experience which influences reading readiness success, Herr *(14)* gave Spanish-speaking children a year of pre-first grade training. They entered in school a year before normal admission. As a result of her findings, she concludes: "Spanish-American children with pre-first grade training have a decided advantage over the children who do not have the experience of pre-first grade training, and it raises the presumption that a large percentage of failures could be eliminated in the lower grades if all Spanish-American children were given a year of preparatory training."

In studying 226 children, Pratt *(24)* found a significant superiority of kindergarten pupils over non-kindergarten pupils when both were tested on reading readiness and on achievement tests at the end of the first grade. In fact, the kindergarten group obtained an average score on the Gates Primary Reading Tests of 15.15 points higher than the other group (and with a critical ratio of 6.75, this makes the difference significant).

Gates and Russell *(11)* matched two groups of children who were underprivileged and of dull-normal intelligence (Binet IQ: 75-95). One group was given a full term of experiences without formal instruction in reading, while the other matched group was given a definite program in reading during this first term.

Their data suggests that these children profit from pre-reading activities and should be given a full year of such enrichment activities.

Anderson and Dearborn *(2)* also suggest that reading-readiness training seems to be particularly successful for children handicapped by a foreign language background or by their socio-economic class. Although they wrote nine years before Sexton *(28)*, they seem to be aware of her "inverted pyramid" concept: "Surprisingly, or not, the literature does not show that kindergarten experience has any great effect in facilitating the process of learning to read, possibly because the right children have not been involved." So again the children who seem to need kindergarten generally do not get this experience, while the youngsters who may not need it because of their rich backgrounds are usually exposed to this pre-school training.

Children can learn only what their environment provides, and what is most often seen or heard is most likely to be learned thoroughly. Using her own information tests with 47 first-grade pupils, Hildreth *(15)* indicates that children make the best scores on the topics with which they are most familiar, which demonstrates the impact of experience. Incidentally, her information tests correlated .70 with the Kuhlmann-Anderson Intelligence Test. Although modest, it does lend support to the importance of considering range of information as a factor in intelligence.

Betts *(3)* maintains that "eight out of ten retarded readers have normal or superior intelligence." But then later he seems to be falling into a typical "middle-class trap" when he says, "To be retarded in reading, his mental par must be higher than his reading par." Is this the kind of "strange logic" to which Sexton *(28)* was alluding?

In reviewing 97 studies, Loevinger *(18)* found an average correlation of .40 between test intelligence of children and the occupational level of their fathers. She also found that the highest (the professional group) was one standard deviation above the mean of the population (or an average of 116 IQ), while the lowest (the day-laboring classes) was about half a standard deviation or less below the mean of the population (or an average of 92 IQ). Hence, one would naturally expect to find a high correlation between reading achievement and social class status.

If the difference between intellectual stimulation in the upper-class home and dearth of such stimulation in the lower-class home can produce such differences in test intelligence and reading achievement, one wonders if possibly this could be induced also by changes in geographic environment. Klineberg *(17)* compared the intelligence test scores (using the National Intelligence Test) obtained by different groups of New York City Negro children, all born in the South but differing in the number of years they had lived in New York City. His investigation covered some nine different studies involving some 3,081 subjects, consisting of 10- and 12-year-old Negro boys and girls in the Harlem schools. He found that there was a definite tendency for the National Intelligence Test scores to improve as length of residence in New York City increased. It was also learned that the rural, southern Negro children begin far behind the urban, southern Negro, though after a number of years of residence in New York City the difference disappears.

After I examined carefully these studies and others not cited, several plaguing questions arose: Isn't the IQ test basically an achievement test? Could not socially disadvantaged children have the ability to learn and yet show up poorly on standardized tests? And what sort of learning tasks can we devise — paired-associates, serial learning; low and high interference measures; retroactive and proactive inhibition measure? Are there perceptual motor-visual differences between socially disadvantaged children and average children?

These and other significant questions will have to be answered before some of the socially-oriented correlates of reading disability can be resolved.

REFERENCES

1. Almy, M.C. *Children's Experiences Prior to First Grade and Success in Beginning Reading,* Contributions to Education, #954 (New York: Bureau of Publications, Teachers College, Columbia University, 1949).
2. Anderson, I.H. and W.F. Dearborn. *The Psychology of Teaching Reading* (New York: The Ronald Press Co., 1952).
3. Betts, E.A. "Are Retarded Readers 'Dumb'?" *Education,* 76 (May, 1956), 9, 568-575.
4. Brown, W.H. and L.B. Bond. "Social Stratification in a Sixth Grade Class," *Journal of Educational Research,* 48 (1955), 539-543.

5. Burton, W.H. "Education and Social Class in the U.S." *Harvard Educational Review,* 23 (1953), 243-256.

6. Coleman, H.S. "The Relationship of Socio-Economic Status to the Performance of Junior High School Students," *Journal of Experimental Education,* 9 (1940), 61-63.

7. Davis, A. *Social-Class Influences Upon Learning* (Cambridge: Harvard University Press, 1955).

8. Dawson, S. "Environmental Influence on Mentality," *British Journal of Psychology,* 27 (1936), 129.

9. Dimitz, S., B. Kay, and W.C. Reckless. "Group Gradients in Delinquency Potential and Achievement Scores of Sixth Graders," *American Journal of Orthopsychiatry,* 28 (1958), 598-605.

10. Engle, T.L. "Home Environments and School Records," *School Review,* 42 (1934), 590-598.

11. Gates, A. and D.H. Russell. "The Effects of Delaying Beginning Reading a Half Year in the Case of Under-Privileged Pupils with IQ's 75-95," *Journal of Educational Research,* 32 (1939), 321-328.

12. Getzels, J.W. "Changing Values Challenge the Schools," *School Review,* 65 (1957), 92-102.

13. Granzow, K.R. "A Comparative Study of Underachievers, Normal Achievers and Overachievers in Reading," *Dissertation Abstracts,* 14 (1954), 631-632.

14. Herr, S.E. "The Effects of Pre-First Grade Training Upon Reading Readiness and Reading Achievement Among Spanish-American Children," *Journal of Educational Psychology,* 37 (1946), 87-102.

15. Hildreth, G. "Information Tests of First Grade Children," *Childhood Education,* 55 (1933), 416-420.

16. Holmes, J.A. "Personality Characteristics of the Disabled Reader," *Journal of Developmental Reading,* 4 (1961), 111-122.

17. Klineberg, O. "The Influence of the Northern Environment on the Intelligence Test Scores of Negroes," in *The Language of Social Research* by Lazarsfeld and Rosenberg (Glencoe, Ill.: The Free Press, 1955), pp. 175-183.

18. Loevinger, J. "Intelligence as Related to Socio-Economic Factors," in *Intelligence: Its Nature and Nurture,* Thirty-Ninth Yearbook, National Society for the Study of Education, Part I (Chicago: University of Chicago Press, 1940), 159-210.

19. Margolin, J.B., M. Roman, and C. Harari. "Reading Disability in the Delinquent Child: A Microcosm of Psycho-Social Pathology," *American Journal of Orthopsychiatry,* 25 (1955), 25-35.

20. Mills, C.W. *White Collar* (New York: Oxford University Press, 1953).

21. Milner, E. "A Study of the Relationship Between Reading Readiness in Grade One School Children and Patterns of Parent-Child Interaction," *Child Development,* 22 (1951), 93-112.

22. Neugarten, B.L. "Social Class and Friendship Among School Children," *American Journal of Sociology,* 51 (1946), 305-313.

23. Office of Urban Renewal, City of Berkeley, California, April 26, 1961 (Revised October 31, 1961).

24. Pratt, W.E. "A Study of the Differences in the Prediction of Reading Success of Kindergarten and Non-Kindergarten Children," *Journal of Educational Research,* 42 (1949), 525-533.

25. Prince, R. "Values, Grades, Achievement and Careers Choice of High School Students," *Elementary School Journal,* 60 (1960), 376-384.

26. Robinson, H.M. *Why Pupils Fail in Reading* (Chicago: University of Chicago Press, 1946).

27. Roman, M., J.B. Margolin, and C. Harari. "Reading Retardation and Delinquency," *National Probation and Parole Association Journal,* 1 (1955), 1-7.

28. Sexton, P.C. *Education and Income* (New York: The Viking Press, 1961).

29. Sheldon, W.D. and L. Carrillo. "Relation of Parents, Home and Certain Developmental Characteristics to Children's Reading Ability," *Elementary School Journal,* 52 (1952), 262-270.

30. Vernon, M.D. *Backwardness in Reading* (Cambridge: University Press, 1957).

31. Warner, W.L. *Social Class in America* (Chicago: Science Research Associates, Inc., 1944).

32. Wilson, A.B. "Residential Segregation of Social Classes and Aspirations of High School Boys," *American Sociology Review,* 24 (1959), 836-845.

33. ———. "The Effect of Residential Segregation upon Educational Achievement and Aspirations" (Unpublished doctoral dissertation, University of California, Berkeley, 1960).

JOAN C. BARATZ

Linguistic and Cultural Factors in Teaching Reading to Ghetto Children

Terms such as socioeconomic status and race are global descriptions of phenomena and as such cannot be used to explain why certain children traditionally and typically fail to learn to read. More specific and causal factors must be specified and studied. This article focuses on one such factor. It is amazing and puzzling that the milieu of many children has so frequently been ignored or slighted and that the children's oral language has received so little attention until recently.

What reactions do you have when you hear, "I don't got none" or "Her went to town"? Do you agree that "ghettoese" is a language difference rather than a language deficiency? In what ways is the inner-city black child like a foreign-born immigrant? Until the suggested transitional readers are available, what seems to you to be a practical technique for helping these children learn to read? Why not change the child's oral language patterns so they conform to printed syntactical patterns rather than vice versa? What other articles in this book are related to Baratz's theme?

The low income, urban Negro child is failing in our schools. His inability to read is a major challenge to contemporary educators because of its relationship to the child's self-esteem and his ultimate social effectiveness.

Failure to acquire functionally adequate reading skills not only contributes to alienation from the school as a social institution (and therefore encourages dropping out), but it goes on to insure failure in mainstream job success. There is certainly a relationship between reading success or failure on the

Reprinted from *Elementary English*, 46 (February 1969), pp. 199-203. Copyright 1967 by the National Council of Teachers of English. Reprinted by permission of the publisher and Joan C. Baratz.

one hand, and receptivity to or alienation from the society in which those reading skills are highly valued (Labov and Robins, 1967). It is almost impossible to underestimate the chain of reactions which can be touched off by early and continued educational failure which so many disadvantaged Negro children experience in even the most well-intentioned school systems. Because the educational system has been ineffective in coping with teaching inner city children to read, the system treats the reading failure (in terms of grading, ranking, etc.) as if the failure were due to intellectual deficits of the child rather than to methodological inadequacies in the teaching procedures. Thus the system is unable to teach the child to read, but very quickly teaches him to regard himself as intellectually inadequate, and therefore, of low self worth and low social value.

Despite the enormous expenditure of energy in remedial reading programs, children in the ghetto are still not learning to read. (National Advisory Council on Education of the Disadvantaged, 1966.) Although the difficulties of teaching reading to a portion of the population is a unique problem for the United States, the problem itself is not unique. The parallels are quite clear between the difficulty we are experiencing in teaching reading to the disadvantaged Negro child with those of emergent countries which are attempting to make a multi-cultured population literate in a single national tongue.

In his recent report on the Washington, D.C. School System, Passow (1967) indicated that the central question that must be answered is: "What are the educationally relevant differences which the District's pupils bring into the classroom and what kinds of varied educational experiences must be provided by the schools to accomodate these differences?" One major educationally relevant difference for Washington, D.C., as for ghettos across the nation, is that of language. The Negro ghetto child is speaking a significantly different language from that of his middle class teachers. Most of his middle class teachers have wrongly viewed his language as pathological, disordered, "lazy speech." This failure to recognize the interference from the child's different linguistic system, and consequent negative teacher attitudes towards the child and his language leads directly to reading difficulties and subsequent school failure.

The differences between Negro non-standard and standard English have been described in some detail by Stewart (1965, 1967, 1968), Labov (1967), Bailey (1965) and others (Dillard, 1967, Baratz and Povich, 1967). Some of these differences were concerned primarily with distributions and patterning and others focused in greater detail upon syntactic differences between the Negro non-standard system and standard English. It is possible to compile a list of some of the differences between the two systems such as the following:

VARIABLE	STANDARD ENGLISH	NEGRO NON-STANDARD
Linking verb	He is going.	He _ goin'.
Possessive marker	John's cousin.	John _ cousin.
Plural marker	I have five cents.	I got five cent _.
Subject expression	John lives in New York.	John he live in New York.
Verb form	I drank the milk.	I drunk the milk.
Past marker	Yesterday he walked home.	Yesterday he walk_home.
Verb agreement	He runs home.	He run_home.
	She has a bicycle.	She have a bicycle.
Future form	I will go home.	I'ma go home.
"If" construction	I asked if he did it.	I aks did he do it.
Negation	I don't have any.	I don't got none.
	He didn't go.	He ain't go.
Indefinite article	I want an apple.	I want a apple.
Pronoun forms	We have to do it.	Us got to do it.
	His book.	He book.
Preposition	He is over at his friend's house.	He over to his friend house.
	He teaches at Francis Pool.	He teach_Francis Pool.
Be	Statement: He is here all the time.	Statement: He be here.
Do	Contradiction: No he isn't.	Contradiction: No he don't.

But what of these differences? All the linguists studying Negro non-standard English agree that these differences are systematized structured rules within the vernacular; they agree that these differences can interfere with the learning of standard English but they do not always agree as to the precise nature of these different rules. This leads to varied disagreements as to why a particular feature exists (i.e. phoneme deletion versus creolization) but it does not dispute the fact that the linguistic feature is present. No one would disagree that standard English has a grammatical structure and uniqueness and many descriptions of that structure have been written. Yet it is probably true that no two linguists would agree in all details on how to write that grammar. This equally explains the current controversy of the linguists as to how one writes the grammar of the vernacular. Controversy as to the exact nature of the vernacular does not negate the fact that the vernacular is there.

This language *difference*, not deficiency, must be considered in the educational process of the Negro ghetto child. In 1953, the UNESCO report regarding the role of language in education stated that: "It is axiomatic that the best medium for teaching a child is his mother tongue. Psychologically, it is the system of meaningful signs that in his mind works automatically for expression and understanding. Sociologically, it is a means of identification among the members of the community to which he belongs. Educationally he learns more quickly through it than through an unfamiliar medium."

Since 1953 studies employing the recommendations of the UNESCO report have clearly illustrated the importance of considering the vernacular in teaching reading in the national language (Modiano, 1965). It is clear that structural knowledge of non-standard vernacular and the ways it can interfere with learning to speak and read standard English is indispensable to teaching ghetto Negro children. Goodman (1965) and Bailey along with Stewart have all indicated the existence of interference from the dialect on ability to read. Labov (1967) has also stressed that the "ignorance of standard English rules on the part of the speakers of standard English" and the "ignorance of non-standard English rules on the part of teachers and text writers" may well be the cause for the reading failures that occur in the schools. In addition, Wiener and Cromer (1967) in their article on reading and reading difficulty discussed the need to determine the relationship between language differences and reading problems because a failure to be explicit about the relationship between reading and previously acquired auditory language often leads to ambiguities as to whether a particular difficulty is a reading problem, language problem, or both.

If the disadvantaged Negro child, like the Indian having to learn Spanish in Mexico, or the African having to learn French

in Guinea, has to contend with the interference from his vernacular in learning to read how does his task of learning to read
differ from that of the middle class "mainstream American"
child? When the middle class child starts the process of learning
to read, his is primarily a problem of decoding the graphic
representation of a language which he already speaks. The
disadvantaged Negro must not only decode the written words,
he must also translate them into his own language. This presents
an almost insurmountable obstacle, since the words often do
not go together in any pattern that is familiar or meaningful to
him. He is baffled by this confrontation with (1) a new language
with its new syntax; (2) a necessity to learn the meaning of
graphic symbols, and, (3) a vague, or not so vague, depending
upon the cultural and linguistic sophistication of the teacher,
sense that there is something terribly wrong with his language.

Although both the middle class child and the disadvantaged Negro child are first faced with the task of relating
their speech to a graphic representation that is arbitrary and
without a direct one to one correspondence to their speech (i.e.
the "silent e" in *love*, the "silent k" in *knife*, the "k" as
represented in *cut* and *kite*, and the "s" as represented in *Sue*
and in *cement*, etc.) the cards are stacked against the inner city
Negro child because his particular phoneme patterning is not
considered in the curriculum at this early phase so that when he
reads *hep* for "help", *men'* for "mend", *boil* for "ball", the
teacher presumes that he cannot read the word. Hep and help,
men and mend and boil and ball are homonyms in the inner city
child's vernacular. Similarly during the initial stages of learning
to read, the disadvantaged child is confused and presumed
ignorant and unable to comprehend concepts if when he is
taught the rhyming concept in reading he responds that *han'*
(hand) rhymes with *man*. When told he is wrong he becomes
confused for he is right: *han'* and *man* do in fact rhyme in his
speech. In instructing these children it is necessary for the
teacher to separate the concepts to be learned from the details
of standard English. Until we do this, Negro children will
continue to be confused and will continue to have great difficulty in learning to read standard English.

Despite the obvious mismatching of the "teachers and text
writers" phoneme system and that of the inner city child, the
difficulties of the disadvantaged Negro child cannot be sim-

plified solely to the pronunciation and phoneme differences that exist in the two systems. There is an even more serious problem facing the inner city child which concerns his unfamiliarity with the syntax of the classroom texts. Although the middle income child also must read texts that are at times stilted in terms of his own usage, there is no question that the language of the texts is potentially comparable to his system. That is to say, although he does not speak in the style of his reading text, he has the rules within his grammar to account for the occurrence of the textbook sentences. However, the textbook style is more deviant to the ghetto child than it is to his middle class standard speaking agemate because much of the reading text is not a part of his potential syntactic system.

Because of the mismatch between the child's system and that of the standard English textbook, because of the psychological consequences of denying the existence and legitimacy of the child's linguistic system, and because of the success of vernacular teaching around the world, it appears imperative that we teach the inner city Negro child to read using his language as the basis for initial readers. In other words, first teach the child to read, and then teach him to read in standard English. Such a reading program would not only require accurate vernacular texts for the dialect speaker, but also necessitate the creation of a series of "transition readers" that would move the child, once he had mastered reading in the vernacular, from vernacular texts to standard English texts. Of course, success of such a reading program would be dependent upon the child's ultimate ability to read standard English.

The advantages of such a program are threefold. First, success in teaching the ghetto child to read. Second, the powerful ego-supports of giving credence to the child's language system and therefore to himself, and giving him the opportunity to experience success in school. And third, with the use of transitional readers, the child has the opportunity of being taught standard English (which cannot occur by "linguistic swamping" since his schoolmates are all vernacular speakers) so that he can learn where his language system and that of standard English are similar and where they are different. Such an opportunity may well lead to generalized learning and the ability to use standard English more proficiently in other school work.

The continued failure of programs of reading to ghetto children that offer more of the same, i.e. more phonics, more word drills, etc. has indicated the need for a new orientation towards teaching inner city children to read. Any such program must take into account what is unique about the ghetto child that is impairing his ability to learn within the present system. This paper has suggested that one of the essential differences to be dealt with in teaching inner city Negro children is that of language. The overwhelming evidence of the role that language interference can play in reading failure indicates that perhaps one of the most effective ways to deal with the literacy problems of Negro ghetto youth is to teach them using vernacular texts that systematically move from the syntactic structures of the ghetto community to those of the standard English speaking community.

BIBLIOGRAPHY

Bailey, B., Linguistics in non-standard language patterns, unpublished paper, NCTE meetings, 1965.

Baratz, J. and Povich, E., Grammatical constructions in the language of the Negro preschool child, unpublished paper, ASHA, 1967.

Dillard, J., The English teacher and the language of the newly integrated student, *The Record-Teachers College,* 69, 2, 1967, 115-120.

Goodman, K., Barriers to reading comprehension, *Elem. English,* 1965, 853-860.

Labov, W., Some sources of reading problems for Negro speakers of non standard English, in *New Directions in Elementary English,* National Council of Teachers of English, Champaign, Ill., 1967.

Labov, W. and Robins, C., A note on the relation of reading failure to peer-group status in urban ghettos, unpublished paper, 1967.

Modiano, N., A comparative study of two approaches to the teaching of reading in the national language, U.S.O.E., Final Report, 1965.

Passow, A. H., *Toward creating a model urban school system: a study of the District of Columbia public schools,* Teachers College, Columbia University, 1967.

Stewart, W. A., Foreign language teaching methods in quasi-foreign language situations, *Non-standard speech and the teaching of English,* Washington, D.C., Center for Applied Linguistics, 1965.

———— Urban Negro speech: sociolinguistic factors affecting English teaching, in R. Shuy (ed.) *Social Dialects and Language Learning,*

National Council of Teachers of English, Champaign, Ill., 1964.

————— Sociolinguistic factors in the history of American Negro dialects, *The Florida Foreign Language Reporter,* 5, 1967, 4-5.

————— Continuity and change in American Negro dialects, *The Florida Foreign Language Reporter,* 6, 1968, 3-14.

Wiener, and Cromer, Reading and reading difficulty: a conceptual analysis, *Harvard Educational Review,* 37, 1967, 620-643.

JAMES C. COLEMAN
FRIEDA L. BORNSTON
JACK FOX

Parental Attitudes as Related to Reading Disabilities in Children

We have frequently focused on gross forces affecting reading achievement, possibly because they are so obvious and easy to measure. But subtle and covert forces — familial relationships, for example — may actually be more pervasive and more persuasive. Yet we know little about them and seldom take them into account in making a diagnosis, planning instruction, or implementing preventive action. Studies such as this one help us understand disabled readers better and sensitize us to the complexity of problems these children often face.

Hypothesize how maternal dominance could negatively affect reading achievement. What implication does this study have for the prevention of reading disabilities? What implications does it have for the selection and use of materials and procedures by remedial teachers? To what degree do you think there could be a relationship between this study and the findings of Chandler earlier in this section? In what way might Wynn's suggestions in Part Six need to be broadened to include the findings of this study?

Reading disability in children of normal or superior intelligence has been linked to a variety of possible etiological factors. Among those that have been stressed are parent-child relationships. Since there is a dearth of experimental evidence in this area, the present study was undertaken to delineate more clearly some of the specific parental attitudes which may be of etiological significance in reading disability.

Reprinted from *Psychological Reports,* 4 (March 1958), pp. 47-51, by permission of James C. Coleman and the publisher.

METHOD

Subjects. — The experimental group of parents (E Group) consisted of 20 pairs of parents of male children who were enrolled in the Clinical School, a center for the diagnosis, study, and treatment of reading disability cases, located on the campus of the University of California at Los Angeles. The control group (C Group) consisted of 20 sets of parents of children attending the University Elementary School, a regular elementary school in the Los Angeles City School District which is also located on the U.C.L.A. campus. The children of all members of the C Group were making normal school progress.

With respect to variables other than school progress, the children of both sets of parents were matched for IQ, age, sex, and freedom from serious physical or emotional defects.

On the basis of a supplementary data sheet filled out by all parents, it was found that the two parental groups were also relatively well-matched except for certain age and educational differences discussed in the Results section of this paper. The number of parents used in the study resulted from some attenuation of the data gathered from an originally larger group. Originally there were 25 sets of parents in the C Group and 29 sets of parents in the E Group. However, some data sheets were not filled out, some of the surveys were not completed and, in two instances, there was only one parent in the family so that data could not be obtained from the father. Also, some parents qualified their answers with side comments that made it impossible to score their surveys objectively. All such forms were discarded, leaving the resultant groups, each consisting of 20 sets of parents. The data gathered from these Ss served as the basis for all computations reported in this paper.

Procedure. — The University of Southern California Parent Attitude Survey (PAS) was administered to both the E and C Groups of parents. Both sets of parents also filled out a Supplementary Data Sheet covering information with respect to number, ages, and sex of the children in the family, educational level, religious preferences, and occupation of the parents.

The PAS was then scored according to Shoben's *(1)* weighted method and scores were obtained for each parent on

the four scoring categories yielded by this instrument:
domineering, possessive, ignoring, and unclassified. (The last is
a scale of 10 items tapping attitudes toward sexual, religious,
moral, and monetary behaviors.) A fifth score was also obtained. This was the total score and consisted of a simple sum of
the scores of the four main categories.

The data were then treated statistically to determine
whether any significant differences in parental attitudes existed:
(a) between the E and C Groups of mothers; (b) between the E
and C Groups of fathers; and (c) between discrepancy scores of
E mothers and fathers and C mothers and fathers.

In addition to using Shoben's weighted scores as a basis for
computations, another scoring device was also used. The PAS is
so constructed that it requires S to reply to a statement of attitude in one of four ways, either, Strongly Agree, Mildly Agree,
Mildly Disagree, or Strongly Disagree. It was reasoned that it
was not, perhaps, the actual attitudes held that might be of
greatest psychological significance, but rather the certainty or
strength of emotional reaction measured by this instrument
which might be most revealing of relevant differences among
the groups under study. Consequently a simple tally was made
of the number of extreme responses (Strongly Agree and
Strongly Disagree) made by each S. Comparisons were then
made between E and C mothers, between E and C fathers,
between E mothers and fathers, and between C mothers and
fathers to see whether they differed significantly in the number
of extreme judgments they made.

RESULTS

From supplementary data sheets. — The two parental
groups were relatively well-matched, but the one significant
difference that existed between them (and an important difference, as Shoben points out) was the difference in the
educational levels attained by the members of the different
groups. Differences significant beyond the .01 level of confidence were obtained when comparing the mean educational
levels of E and C fathers and E and C mothers. Both the C
mothers and fathers showed superior educational attainment
over the E Groups. Further, within the C Group itself, the
fathers were significantly superior in their educational at-

tainments to the mothers. No statistically significant difference existed between the educational levels of E mothers and fathers, although the mean level was higher for these fathers than the mean obtained for the mothers. It is interesting to note, however, that in 50% of the cases, E mothers equaled or exceeded the educational levels of their husbands whereas this was true for only 10% of the C mothers.

Despite differences in educational background, the groups were very similarly constituted with respect to occupation. In the E Group of mothers, 18 were housewives, 1 was a nurse, and the other was a teacher. The C mothers contained 16 housewives and 4 teachers. The E fathers had 11 men in occupations classified as professional and managerial, 6 in clerical and semi-intellectual occupations, and 2 skilled workmen. The C fathers had 16 men in professional and managerial positions and 4 in clerical and semi-intellectual occupations.

E fathers were older than C fathers, the mean difference being significant at the .05 level of confidence. No significant differences existed between the mean ages of the two groups of mothers, although E mothers tended to be older. Some of the age difference in the two groups may be accounted for by the fact that the ages of the children of E parents went up to 15, whereas children of C parents only went up to the age of 12. In any case, the number of children in the family was almost exactly equal for the two groups.

Insofar as religious preferences for the two groups were concerned, the groups were also very similar. The E group contained 14 Protestants, 4 Catholics, 12 Jews, and 10 persons who stated no preference. The C Group contained 20 Protestants, no Catholics, 11 Jews, and 9 persons who stated no preference.

From the Parent Attitude Survey. — Table 1 shows the mean scores obtained by all groups on the PAS when scored by Shoben's weighted method. In comparisons made between the means of the weighted scores, the following results were obtained. (a) The E mothers showed higher scores on the Domineering scale than the C mothers. This difference was significant beyond the .05 level but at less than the .01 level of confidence. (b) Although no significant differences were obtained on any of the other scales when considered separately, E mothers showed Total Scores higher than those obtained by C

mothers. The difference between their mean scores on this
scale was significant beyond the .01 level of confidence. (c) No
significant differences were obtained between the E and C
fathers on any scale.

Table 1

Shoben's Weighted Scores on the Parent Attitude Survey

Scale	Experimental Fathers			Experimental Mothers		
	Mean	Range	δ	Mean	Range	δ
Total	299.95	272–332	16.96	314.75	284–379	21.44
Domineering	138.60	114–150	25.33	144.45	130–176	11.67
Possessive	73.40	63– 80	4.04	76.95	69– 94	6.04
Ignoring	52.15	47– 60	3.83	53.95	47– 62	4.72
Unclassified	35.80	30– 38	3.78	39.40	33– 48	4.53

Scale	Control Fathers			Control Mothers		
	Mean	Range	δ	Mean	Range	δ
Total	299.70	262–319	23.30	295.70	269–320	19.53
Domineering	136.75	117–163	17.04	134.40	113–154	11.37
Possessive	73.70	63– 97	7.27	71.95	60– 81	5.23
Ignoring	51.70	46– 62	4.50	52.40	45– 60	3.95
Unclassified	37.10	29– 44	4.70	36.50	26– 47	4.16

N = 20 for each of the 4 groups.

When comparisons were made between the number of
extreme judgments made by the several groups, the following
results were obtained. (a) E mothers made more extreme
judgments than were made by E fathers. The difference between their mean scores was significant beyond the .05 level but
at less than the .01 level of confidence. (b) No significant differences were found between the number of extreme judgments
made by C mothers and fathers, nor did any significant differences appear between E and C fathers or between E and C
mothers in this measure.

DISCUSSION

The inferences which may be drawn from the results of this
study shed some light on the background of male children who
suffer from reading disabilities. Although clearly experimental

verification is needed, these results would seem to indicate a general family patterning in which the mother's domineering tendency seems to be a pivotal factor.[1] It is not the actual amount of dominance, however, that is crucial. More important than the actual extent of the domineering trait is the discrepancy in dominance exhibited by our E mothers when compared with E fathers. No such discrepancy was evident in the C group, but the statistically significant differences in extreme judgments made by mothers and fathers in the E group, coupled with the E mother's greater tendency toward dominance, probably creates an atmosphere of feminine superiority in the household. By comparison with the mother, the father in the family appears to be a "weak" and indecisive figure.

This "weakness" in the male adult figure in the household is further enhanced by the fact that, in 50% of our E cases, the mother is superior in her educational attainments. Even where she is not, however, she seems to lay great stress on educational achievement and to see it as a symbol of "strength." The father's position in these families seems to be further "belittled" by the fact that these mothers apparently desire their male offspring to become "stronger" figures than their fathers.

The pressure of the domineering mother on her male child to develop "strength," often equating this strength with educational achievement, coupled with a male parental model in the household who appears weak, possibly presents the male child with difficulties in making a masculine identification. This problem is reflected in his approach to and feeling of adequacy in the performance of educational tasks.

SUMMARY

A study was conducted in which the U.S.C. Parent Attitude Survey was administered to two groups of parents to determine whether significant differences would be obtained between the mean scores obtained by parents whose male children make

---

[1] E mothers in the present experiment scored significantly lower on the Domineering Scale than Shoben's group of mothers of well-adjusted children. But Shoben reports that the higher the educational level, the lower the Domineering score tends to be. Our E mothers score significantly higher on this scale than other mothers of comparable educational background.

normal school progress and those whose male children have been unable to master basic skills, despite their adequate intellectual endowment.

These parent groups were similar with respect to age, occupation, number, and sex of children in the family, and religious preferences. They differed in educational attainment, the control group having achieved a significantly higher educational level than the experimental group, although both groups were higher in this regard than what would be expected from a representative sample of the general population.

The PAS was scored according to Shoben's weighted method and comparisons were made between the mean scores obtained by the groups on the four scoring categories. Differences significant at beyond the 5% but at less than the 1% level of confidence were obtained on the Domineering Scale between the E and C mothers, with the E mothers being higher on this train. Although none of the other scales yielded significant differences, when their scores were combined to compute the Total Scale, the differences between E and C mothers increase and reach a degree of significance beyond the 1% level of confidence.

In addition to the weighted scores, the PAS was treated so as to obtain a score of "extreme judgments." When comparisons are made among the several groups on the mean number of extreme judgments, differences beyond the 5% but below the 1% level of confidence are obtained between the E mothers and the E fathers, with the mothers making the greater number of such extreme judgments. No comparable difference was found to exist between the fathers and mothers of the C Group.

The results of the present investigation point to a family background of the boy with reading disability that includes a domineering mother who exerts pressure on her male child to develop "strength," often equating this strength with educational achievement. In addition, the father in the household appears as an inadequate model for the child's behavioral development leading to difficulties in making a masculine identification. The combination of these parental factors is apparently reflected in the child's ineffective approach to and feeling of inadequacy in the performance of educational tasks.

REFERENCE

1. Shoben, E.J., Jr. The assessment of parental attitudes in relation to child adjustment. *Genet. Psychol. Monogr.,* 1949, 39, 103-147.

RICHARD S. ALM

Causes of Reluctance

Disinterest in the reading act is possibly the most persistent and serious problem presented by children with reading difficulties. In this essay, aimed at both prevention and correction of reading difficulties, Alm suggests that inability to read may be too simple an explanation of this problem.

What implications do the causes discussed have for the total reading program? What does a careful analysis of these causes tell us about the society we live in? What does it tell us about the type of educational system children are compelled to attend? What kind of a remedial program must we offer if we are to overcome these factors?

The reluctant reader presents the most serious kind of reading problem in our schools today. A non-reader at age fourteen — lacking basic reading skills but with the *will* to learn — is, relatively, an easier problem for a teacher than a child who denies that reading is, for him, a part of the natural order of life.

Who is this child? The reluctant reader is "a student who is capable of reading at his grade and age level or above, but doesn't make use of or enjoy reading." What are his characteristics? He may have one or more of these identities: one who shuns reading, who ignores reading tasks, who seeks activities of all other kinds in preference to reading, who tries to compensate for his not reading by developing other skills such as listening, who substitutes — or tries to substitute — talking for reading, who intensely dislikes reading. He is a serious problem

Reprinted from *The Underachiever in Reading,* Supplementary Educational Monographs, No. 92, H. Alan Robinson, ed. (December 1962), pp. 101-109, by permission of The University of Chicago Press and Richard S. Alm. ©1962 by The University of Chicago Press.

because the causes of reluctance are many and complex. They are usually subtle; they are often deep-seated.

LACK OF READING SKILL

The most obvious cause of reluctance is that an individual does not know *how* to read well. It is a challenge to establish a relationship between every child and *some* book, to awaken, to stimulate, to build an interest in reading. But the task is a difficult one, and we understand the reluctant reader's conflict: none of us *likes* to do what is difficult.

A child's inability to read well is usually the result of a combination of factors. The *why's* — the causes of a child's failure to read, to learn to read well — involve these general areas: perceptual difficulties, other physical deficiencies, environmental factors, limitations of intelligence, poor or inadequate instruction and/or learning, emotional difficulties.

These areas are discussed in other papers in this section. Let us examine one area, however, to note its relationship to reluctance: instructional factors. The child may not have been properly taught or he may have learned improperly. He may be left to bridge the gap between a reading lesson learned in isolation and a later demonstration of that learning. He may be assigned reading activities with which he cannot adequately deal.

John had been taught to read by a narrow spelling method. As a twelfth-grader, he was a slow, painstaking reader who spelled out every word he did not immediately grasp or about which he had some doubts. His progress was so tortuous that he avoided any and all reading situations. Even a story which his classmates found thrilling was drudgery for him.

Note Robin's plight: In sixth grade he was assigned a review lesson in a reading workbook. The lesson required the reader to draw comparisons among the stories read in the unit, to determine some generalizations, to note relationships. Robin knew the stories well. He could summarize them accurately and in some detail. He seemed very much interested in the stories themselves. But he delayed doing the workbook lesson in class, and it became a homework assignment. Even then, he postponed it, and why? He did not know how to cope with the reading tasks required. The teacher had assigned the lesson, assuming that Robin and his classmates all knew what to do. Robin failed the assignment, chiefly because the teacher had failed to grasp that the reading skills involved had not been learned and had to be *taught*. Robin was reluctant to face that reading situation because there he saw only defeat.

LACK OF READING GUIDANCE

But good teaching and satisfactory learning of reading skills are not sufficient. A second major reason for reluctance is not knowing *what* to read. The older the child, the greater is this problem. Countless children who can read do not. They do not know how to select books themselves. They receive little or no appropriate guidance either at school or at home.

Children all over the country are regularly scheduled for what is called a "library period." This may be a treasured experience. Or it may mean merely being deposited in the library for thirty minutes or an hour to browse. The child, meager in reading experience, his reading interests dulled or undeveloped, turns to shelves of books, with only these self-determined criteria: The book must be thin or small; it must have large print and few pages; it must be "easy." It is ironic that for the young child — at the age of greatest interest in reading — books are colorful, varied, and plentiful. Many youngsters have been beguiled by the illustrations of Dr. Seuss, Virginia Lee Burton, Taro Yashima, Don Freeman, and Maurice Sendak into dealing with the printed page. As children grow older, the number of reluctant readers increases. For them, books become larger, plainer, heavier, and more forbidding.

Readers are sometimes faced with such assignments as "Read a biography" or "You must read one book every six weeks and report on it." What does the reluctant reader do? He selects a book at random based on the criteria *he* has devised. He seeks a simple version of a standard work. He finds a synopsis from a dust jacket or a book review. Or he seeks an even more unorthodox solution.

The child's plight in not knowing *what* to read may be the result of the teacher's lack of knowledge and ability. The teacher may know few books and may not know which books will motivate which youngsters. Such a teacher cannot then individualize his guidance of a child's reading program.

The teacher may be ignorant of the reading interests of students. Also, he may be insensitive to the level of his students' reading tastes. By scorning their choices, he will alienate them from reading anything and prevent them from expressing their ideas about what they appreciate and what they find dull. Young readers must be encouraged to be honest in their reactions toward everything they read.

Further, the teacher may have a very distorted point of view about the variation in the reading pattern of most readers. Children and adults who read widely read both the good and the bad, the beautiful and the trite. To attempt to maintain a reading pattern of only the best in literature will lead to youngsters' finding their teacher stuffy, out of touch.

Another characteristic which teachers must accept is that readers often have extended periods of devotion to certain types of books. The junior high school girl who has a passion for horse stories — and is reluctant to read anything else — must be allowed to let that passion run its course. To force her to shift allegiances might well lead to rebellion, would at the least result in her setting a double standard: one kind of book for the teacher but a quite different kind of reading for her own personal enjoyment.

LACK OF OPPORTUNITY TO READ

A third cause of reluctance is that the child has little or no opportunity to read. Here availability of books is a crucial factor. Investigations of reading — quantitative — have shown that *the* crucial factor is nearness of the reader to books.

But books are not readily available today to all would-be readers, young or old:

> More than 40,700 schools in the United States have no school libraries, and 10,600,000 children attend these schools.
> Twenty-five million Americans have *no* public library service, and fifty million have only sub-standard service.
> Public schools with libraries have, on the average, only five books per pupil.
> Fewer than half of all college libraries have 50,000 volumes.
> There is only one professionally trained librarian for every 4,200 children in elementary schools.

The ratio for all schools is one librarian for 1,740 pupils.[1]

A child who has meager library resources or none — and these children are still in the majority in this world of abundance in 1962 — has little opportunity to develop reading interests either in breadth or intensity. His reluctance may be actually an absence of desire, because desire has never been stimulated.

Availability is only one factor. In some instances where there are books, there are barriers which prevent effective use of them — for example, the librarian who sets herself up as a guard rather than a guardian. Teachers in her school dread the library period each month. The librarian does not want more than one child in any section of the library; her fear is that two will talk! Her formula for library periods can be summarized thus: "Get your books as quickly as possible. Then go to your seats and read." Here silence is the password. Here no "librarian" works but is rather a "Keeper of the Tomes."

Even when books are available, sometimes there is not *time* for the child to read. A teacher may not provide time, because she fears that a classroom of students reading library books looks as if she is not working. Thus, the reading of library books is reserved for a kind of homework. This homework may or may not be accomplished, because the distractions at home are too many, and the day is not long enough to encompass them all.

READING LACKS PRESTIGE

A fourth cause of reluctance to read is that we live in a culture in which the activity of reading has very little prestige. Lip service is given to the importance of reading, but our actions belie our words.

Gordon Dupee, president of the Great Books Foundation, reminds us of Plato's observation that what is honored in a country will flourish there. Dupee declares:

> Ours is a society which does not honor reading. We turn our own depreciation of reading to indignation and blame the school. . . . We think of school as the only place of schooling. All this has a certain convenience, of course, for it absolves us from doing battle against a wider field, against the aspects of society

---

[1] These figures appear in "Some Notes on Libraries," *Elementary English,* XXXIX (May, 1962), 477.

which shape and motivate our children, including ourselves. Bluntly put, if Johnny's parents don't read, why should he submit to the rigors of acquiring that discipline?[2]

Roper[3] compares the reading of adults in the United States — 17 percent currently reading a book at any given time — with the reading of adults in other countries: Canada, 31 percent; West Germany, 34 percent; England, 55 percent. These figures are especially significant when one considers that America has what we call universal education. Roper contends that if we are to have an intellectual renaissance in America, it must begin in the homes of our country. In elaborate detail, he points out the esteemed place held by baseball in our culture. In contrast, he notes, there are "no 'little leagues' of the mind. . . . There is no widespread folk tradition that seeks out and trains and takes pride in exceptional intellectual talent."

Dupee[4] reports that 42 percent of houses in the United States are without bookcases or bookshelves of any kind. A survey conducted by one of the leading encyclopedia companies showed that 84 percent of the families purchasing the encyclopedia had not opened it within one year after purchase. "It was bought as cultural furniture."[5]

Many children grow up in an environment in which no one who is important to them does any reading. The parents may be eager to have their children read; they may coax, threaten, or bribe their youngsters. But if these children are surrounded by people who only talk about reading and do none of it themselves, they are not likely to view reading as important. These children become our reluctant readers.

LIMITED CONCEPTS OF READING

Another cause of reluctance is the limited concepts held by many people about the process of reading. Reading is regarded too often as a simple skill, to be learned early in life, once and forever. For example, sounding out words is for some teachers

---

[2] Gordon Dupee, "Can Johnny's Parents Read?" *Saturday Review,* XXXIX (June 2, 1956), 5.

[3] Elmo P. Roper, "The Intellectual Renaissance," *Vital Speeches,* XXVI (June 15, 1960), 524-28.

[4] Dupee, *op. cit.,* p.5.

[5] *Ibid.*

and parents the act of reading. Many children, as the first stage in reading, are required to mouth meaningless sounds. They may not have any understanding of — nor are they told — what relationship these lessons have to the complete act of reading. "Reading" for them becomes a series of exercises divorced from meaning. Mastery of these elements may mean to teacher or parent that the child has learned to read. Nothing here — even the skills which may be gained — will lead automatically to the delights in the world of books. In a day of unparalleled wonders in the realm of children's books, no child should miss, from his first day in kindergarten onward, the wonders and the joy in such writers as Robert Lawson, Lynd Ward, Marcia Brown and Leslie Brooke.

The individual who is reluctant to read fails to understand, usually, what reading can do that other media cannot do: *(a)* provide an unending source of pleasure, whether you are a science fiction fan, a devotee of the arts, a student of the writings of great thinkers, an amateur cook, a scholar in languages, a would-be novelist . . . ; *(b)* enable one to return again and again to the laughter of Robert McCloskey's *Homer Price* (Viking, 1943) or to the poignancy of Doris Gates' *Blue Willow* (Viking, 1940); *(c)* give one the opportunity to mull over such complex statements as one finds in biblical or philosophical literature; *(d)* permit one to savor, by reading and returning to, such a line as "One could do worse than be a swinger of birches," or "The land was ours before we were the land's."6

In the upper grades of the elementary school and thereafter, the child faces increasingly a flood of information that threatens to inundate him. Here, the factual book may be his only experience unless a teacher, sensitive both to the needs of children and the variety of books, focuses attention on the pleasures of reading. To develop in a child this fascination with books, teachers must be steeped in works commonly labeled "children's literature." Those who teach in junior and senior high school must know literature for adolescents, the transitional books which help the young reader move from the world of children's literature to the rich fields of adult books.

Another limited concept about reading is that instruction

---

6 The two lines are from *The Poems of Robert Frost* (New York: Modern Library, 1946), pp. 129, 399.

should focus, at any level, on skills alone. Skills — whether they deal with word-recognition techniques, with consulting the dictionary, with using library reference tools — are important, but individuals must develop, in addition, varied reading interests, cultivated reading tastes, positive attitudes about reading, and a broad understanding of the roles of reading in peoples' lives.

READING IS A BORE

Another cause of reluctance to read is boredom. How does a child become bored? No one is concerned about his interest in reading. He may have, as his lot, no books, dull books, difficult books, or inappropriate books. Thus, the problem involves two aspects: the reading material and what is done with it.

People react to books in different ways; yet we often teach as though a basal reader in the elementary school or a literary work in the high school were sacred. Note the literary classics with which the high school curriculum has become saddled in the last six decades: *Silas Marner, The Idylls of the King, Julius Caesar, Macbeth, Ivanhoe.* There is little differentiation in reading assignments; these classics are taught in some schools to all students, even if teachers must resort to simplified versions or classic comics!

Duff records the rebellion of her teen-age daughter and her classmates when a young, inexperienced teacher began a detailed study of "The Rime of the Ancient Mariner":

> Simply read through as the wonderful adventure of a ghostly ship and its crew, it would probably have been well liked. But discussion of its mystical and metaphysical aspects went against the grain because it was neither understandable nor interesting to eighth graders, and they refused to take it seriously. Inexperience betrayed the teacher into the further blunder of mistaking his students' perfectly legitimate — if ineptly expressed — protest for rebellion against his authority, and perhaps too for a flouting of a poem he particularly admired. As a corrective measure he required every one of them to memorize all twenty stanzas of Part I! Nothing could have quenched more thoroughly any latent spark of response, and it was hard to know whom to feel sorrier for, the young man who had spoiled his honest intention of teaching the meaning of a magnificent poem,

or the youngsters who unwillingly learned the words alone as a penalty for showing their own honest feeling.[7]

Here both the timing and the teaching of this literary selection were wrong. These factors are surely important reasons why junior and senior high school students are not only reluctant readers but reluctant English students as well.

For every high school student who has thrilled to the magnificence of Shakespeare, there are many whose interest in any literature has been killed. Is Shakespeare at fault? Of course not — rather it is the age at which youngsters are given a particular play to read, or the way it is taught — a line-by-line analysis or one-scene-a-night reading assignments. If the dramatic intensity of *Macbeth* is dissipated over a many-weeks' period of snail-paced reading, the impact of the play for any reader is lost.

Most elementary school youngsters are restricted — through lack of funds or overcrowded classrooms — to a set of basal readers only. Their reading experiences are thus highly circumscribed. They may have difficulty in reading because the material is foreign to their experience. The schoolteacher in Ashton-Warner's *The Spinster* discovered that only by writing in the idiom of, with the experiences of, and at the level of the young Maoris in her classroom could she teach many of them reading. She wondered, "What terrible power there must be in words for little children if only we could tap it and harness it!"[8]

She developed what she called *Key Vocabularies* in which with a caption she described an experience which a child had had and which — in his own private vocabulary — he could then read. The problem for the Maori children was that the imported books were so far removed from their experience that they could not — or could only with great difficulty — bridge the gap.

Sometimes books are not difficult enough. Youngsters are often bored, because we do not let them forge ahead. We read the grade labels on books or note their level of difficulty and accept these not as guides but as strait jackets. Once all youngsters in a fifth grade were given a fifth-grade reader. Now

[7] Annis Duff, *Longer Flight,* pp. 113-14. New York: Viking Press, 1955.
[8] Sylvia Ashton-Warner, *The Spinster,* p. 162. New York: Simon & Schuster, 1958.

teachers have recognized the range of differences in a classroom, and it is commonplace to find in a fifth-grade classroom books with second-, third-, and fourth-grade labels. But, books labeled six, seven, or eight — not yet do we find these in any but the rarest fifth-grade classroom. This too, will come to pass.

What does *interest* mean? At an earlier University of Chicago Conference on Reading, an interest was defined as "a characteristic disposition, organized through experience, which impels an individual to seek out particular objects, activities, understandings, skills, or goals for attention or acquisition."[9] Factors which create boredom in reading either block the development of interests or kill any interest which may exist.

SUBJECTED TO PRESSURES

Another cause of reluctance to read is *pressure*. Pressure may come from many sources — parents, teachers, or the readers themselves.

Parents frequently create in their minds a mold into which they try to push, pull, squeeze, cajole their child. This mental image may not match the child's abilities, personality, background, or educational opportunities. Reactions by young readers to pressure may be rebellion, apathy, withdrawal, or antagonism. For any of these, the logical consequence is a reluctance to read.

Another kind of pressure is the kind of reading demand made on the individual. Often the school presents reading tasks that a child cannot achieve. Often the child's family sets up similar hurdles. One sin of countless parents is their insistence that youngsters read aloud to them. Too often the youngster is a poor reader or one who does not enjoy reading. Parents do not teach anything about reading with this activity; it is their way of checking on a child's progress. I have had a seemingly endless series of conferences with parents in which they admit to scolding, nagging, even several instances of beating children who did not read aloud well enough. Typically, the child is

---

9 Jacob W. Getzels, "The Nature of Reading Interests: Psychological Aspects," in *Developing Permanent Interest in Reading*, p. 7. Compiled and edited by Helen M. Robinson, Supplementary Educational Monographs, No. 84. Chicago: University of Chicago Press, 1956.

asked to read material he has not read before, material with which he may have difficulty in the classroom — a place which is, incidentally, probably far less weighted with emotional overtones than his own home. It is always a surprise to these parents that their children do not like to read, that they try to hurry through an oral reading session to escape to the elsewhere.

Another kind of problem is self-pressure. A child, for one reason or another, sets goals toward which he *tries* to move. He may try to emulate the academic performance of an older brother or sister or of a classmate. He may feel — perhaps subconsciously — that he is not doing as well as his parents want him to. He may feel the need — in elementary school or in college — to excel. The pressure, instead of leading to increased reading, often results instead in an individual's turning away from books.

DEMANDS ON READER'S TIME

Another cause of reluctance to read is that today there are many competitors for everyone's time. The reluctant reader may have so many activities which give him satisfaction that he does not try to find time for reading. The physically active child may find that his skill in playing football or his speed in running the 100-yard dash more than compensates for his inability to read all that his teacher or his parents want him to read.

Stuart, for example, was absorbed primarily in playing football, building models, flying kites. His teacher, however, felt that he should read better and more. His parents were concerned and sent him to a tutor. Stuart was perfectly willing to do everything asked of him in the tutoring session, but reading was really of little consequence in his life. His parents finally had to accept the fact that his was a problem of maturity. And, finally, Stuart did find that to accomplish all that he wanted to in Boy Scouts and in high school classes he had to read. This motivation led him to change his point of view about reading in all areas, in and out of school.

Another competitor for a reader's attention probably is the comic book, a medium that children absorb more by osmosis than by reading. Today, millions of copies are ground out each week on every conceivable subject. All children are exposed to comic books whether home or school approves of them or not. And for many children, the comic book is the only "book" they ever "read."

Television — that "vast wasteland" — is the center of interest for children several hours a day. The latest of Witty's annual reports[10] on children and TV indicates that children in elementary school watch television an average of twenty hours per week; high school students, thirteen hours.

Television may motivate a youngster to read a particular book, or to read more about a particular subject, *but* if children watch *on the average* twenty hours a week, these hours must substitute for other activities. For too many of them television is a substitute for reading. SoRelle and Walker[11] have made a study about the influences of television in the lives of 2,000 junior and senior high school students in Texas. They discovered that the junior high school student in the study watched television, on the average, for more hours during a year than he spent in school. The high school student watched fewer hours but still spent 87 percent of the number of hours he spent in a year in front of the television set.

For many young people work is a factor which permits them to do little or no reading: chores, after-school jobs, long homework assignments. The latter may involve reading, but this is not a matter of choice. Each of these activities may be so demanding in time and physical effort that the individual is left with no interest in and no energy for reading. Teachers, too, understand this problem: a busy schedule forbids certain activities. The teacher — with the students — wails, "Where is the time?" This poses a problem of priorities, putting first things first.

EMOTIONAL IMPLICATIONS

As a backdrop to some of these causes, as a concomitant to others, as an aftermath to still others are emotional difficulties. The reactions, the feelings, the frustrations of a reader may lead to emotional overtones in every one of his reading encounters.

---

[10] Paul A. Witty and Paul J. Kinsella, "A Report on Televiewing in 1961," *Elementary English,* XXXIX (January, 1962), 24-32.

[11] Zell SoRelle and Jack Walker, "What Is Television Doing to Our Children?" *Journal of Educational Research,* LV (February, 1962), 236-37.

An embarrassing experience, or a series of them, being held up to ridicule, for example, or being compared unfavorably to brother or sister may affect an individual's perspective about his own abilities or about the learning activities which confront him. The child who is in the poorest group year after year must certainly develop negative feelings toward reading.

Continued failure to read well may so dominate an individual's background that he faces each reading lesson with dread. Sometimes these reactions form a defense: "Why should I read? I'll do a miserable job!" To overcome this self-concept of defeat is one of the most difficult — and subtle — of the problems facing the teacher of reading.

SUMMARY

The causes of reluctance to read cluster around three centers: the learner, the teacher, the environment in which the learner lives. Eight possible causes of reluctance have been discussed here:

1. The individual does not know *how* to read.
2. The individual does not know *what* to read.
3. The individual has little or no opportunity to read.
4. The individual discovers early that in his world reading has little or no prestige.
5. The individual is often never given any glimpse of the wider horizons of reading.
6. The individual is bored with reading.
7. The individual is faced with pressures of many kinds.
8. The individual has innumerable demands on his time, many more fascinating or satisfying for him than reading.

Each of these is inextricably bound to the emotional status of the readers involved. In dealing with these causes, one must pay careful attention to the emotional factors.

These causes are complex and far-reaching. They influence an individual's school achievement, his emotional development, his future career, his leisuretime pursuits. There are implications here for teachers, parents, librarians, administrators, publishers, and, of course, for the readers themselves. The burden of dealing with these causes is not for any one person or group alone. All of us who are concerned with the reading welfare of others — in elementary school, high school, or college — must be aware of these problems and work toward their solutions.

LILLIAN BELMONT
HERBERT G. BIRCH

The Intellectual Profile of Retarded Readers With Normal IQs

Since reading is a cognitive act and because reading disability is defined in terms of discrepancy between achievement and potential, it is imperative that we know as much as possible about the intellectual functioning of children with reading difficulties. What abilities do the children possess? What ones are they deficient in? Which intellectual traits seem most related to reading achievement and disability? We desperately need more research of the quality and revelation of this investigation

To best understand this study and its significance, familiarize yourself with a Wechsler Intelligence Scale for Children (WISC). The authors do not speculate about whether the differences between normal and retarded readers on the Verbal and Performance scales are genetic or acquired. Have you an opinion? Does Verbal, Performance, or Full Scale IQ seem most suitable for accurately specifying retarded readers? What implications might these findings have for prevention, diagnosis, prognosis, and instruction of disabled readers?

The present report is an analysis of the patterning of intellectual functions on the Wechsler Intelligence Scale for Children (WISC) in an age-homogeneous, representative sample of children who are significantly retarded in reading but whose IQs are within the normal range. Knowledge of such patterning can contribute to a better understanding of specific intellectual deficits, which may underlie reading disability and so be of

---

Reprinted with permission of author and publisher: Belmont, L., & Birch, H. G. The intellectual profile of retarded readers. *Perceptual and Motor Skills,* 1966, 22, 787-816, M6-V22. Available as a separate from journal.

This is a modified and abridged account, written especially for this book by the authors of the study.

potential worth for more effective management as well as for an analysis of the effects which poor reading may have on the course of intellectual development. Previous studies which have used the WISC to analyze the intellectual strengths and weaknesses of retarded readers have contained serious methodologic flaws. The present study has in large part overcome methodologic shortcomings in terms of representativeness of sample, sample size, and age range studied.

METHOD

The analysis of intellectual pattern in retarded readers is based upon an epidemiologic study of reading ability of all children born between the years 1951 and 1955 inclusive who were attending public, private, independent and parochial schools in the city of Aberdeen, Scotland. The entire population of school children of this city, within the birth years specified, was tested in December, 1962. Absentees were tested as soon after their return to school as was feasible. This procedure resulted in the standardized reading testing of 99.87% of all children in five birth years who were attending any school in the city. For the present study, 9- and 10-year-old children born in 1953 were selected for intensive analysis.

The tests used for assessing reading skills were a British sentence reading test and three parts of the American Metropolitan Achievement test: word knowledge, word discrimination, and reading. All tests were given in the classroom by standard procedures.

WISC evaluation was restricted to a sampling of children who had achieved an IQ score of 80 or more on a group test of intelligence administered routinely by the schools to all 7 year olds. Intelligence testing was done 6 months after the reading survey. Only boys were used for the purposes of our study because of the greater frequency of reading disability among them *(4)* and for sex homogeneity in analysis of findings.

The patterning of intellectual abilities was compared in two groups, one of boys who were retarded readers and the other of boys who were reading at normal levels. The groups were as follows: Retarded readers were 150 boys who were randomly selected from the 173 boys in the 1953 birth year whose raw scores on at least 3 of the 4 reading tests fell at or below the tenth percentile of the population tested. Normal comparisons consisted of boys in the same birth year whose performance was above the criteria for identifying retarded readers. One hundred and seventy-three boys were matched with the poor readers on the basis of birth date and school class. From this sample, 50 boys were randomly chosen to serve as normal comparisons.

The mean ages of the retarded and normal readers were respectively 9 years 10 months (SD = 3.6 mo.) and 9 years 9 months (SD=3.3 mo.). The difference in age between the two groups was not statistically significant.

The differences between the two groups on the 4 reading tests were all statistically significant (p < .001). On the average, the retarded readers were one and one-half years behind the normal readers on the tests, and fully one-third of them lagged by more than 2 years behind the average performance of the normal comparison group. Such differences represent significant degrees of retardation especially when such retardation is related to the number of school years and the age of the Ss.

The subjects were classified for social class based on the father's occupation at the time of reading testing. As would be expected, since the children of the comparison group were drawn from the same school class as the retarded readers, the social class distributions of the two groups were basically similar. The retarded readers were somewhat underrepresented in (upper) Social Classes I and II (6% vs. 12% for normal readers) but the differences in the distributions by social class position were not statistically significant (chi^2 = 1.44).

Intellectual assessment in both groups was carried out by means of all 12 subtests of the Wechsler Intelligence Scale for Children (13) using the test item alterations recommended for British children by the Committee of Professional Psychologists of the British Psychological Society. Testing was done by 3 qualified examiners who had had previous experience in testing Scottish children. All testing was done "blind," the examiners having no knowledge of the reading group to which the child belonged.

RESULTS

This condensation presents data on those subjects with WISC Full Scale IQs of 90 or better. All except one of the normal readers and 90 of the retarded readers were included in this classification. Several analyses were done: (1) All retarded readers of IQ 90 and over were compared with all normal readers. (2) The WISC subtest patternings of only those retarded and normal readers in the average range (IQ 90-109) of intellectual functioning were examined. (3) The final analysis was a comparison of the poorest readers within the average intellectual range with normal readers individually matched to them for Full Scale IQ.

Total Group Findings for Ss with IQs of 90 or Better

The mean IQ values for both the retarded readers and the normal comparison group are presented in Table 1. Although

Table 1

Mean Wisc IQs for 90 Retarded Readers and
49 Normal Readers with Full Scale IQs of
90 and above

WISC IQ	Retarded Readers	Normal Readers	t*	p
Full Scale	97.2±5.5	105.5±9.3	5.92	<.001
Verbal Scale	96.2±7.1	107.0±9.5	7.20	<.001
Performance Scale	98.9±7.9	102.8±10.7	2.29	<.05
M v-p Diff	-2.7	+4.2		
t	2.37	2.66		
p	<.02	< .02		

* Since there were significant differences in the variances, the Cochran correction of the *t* test was applied.

the mean IQs of both groups fall within the normal range, the retarded readers were significantly lower on all three IQ measures. A comparison of the mean Verbal and Performance IQs for each of the groups resulted in small but significant differences favoring (1) Verbal IQ among normal readers and (2) Performance IQ among the retarded readers. A more sensitive measure of differences in Verbal and Performance IQ patterning in the 2 groups may be obtained by determining the number of Ss in each group who had either higher Verbal or Performance IQs. The results of this analysis indicate that there was a difference between the 2 groups in the number of individuals who had higher Verbal than Performance IQs. Whereas 60% of the retarded readers had higher Performance than Verbal IQs, 60% of the normal comparison group had higher Verbal than Performance IQs. This difference is significant (chi^2 = 8.05, df = 1, p <.01). The relationship is even stronger when one determines the numbers of individuals who had a difference of 10 or more points between Verbal and Performance IQ; among retarded readers 12 subjects had higher Verbal IQs and 28 had higher Performance IQs. Among normal readers, frequencies were 15 and 4 (chi^2 = 10.54, df = 1, p <.01). The retarded readers of normal IQ, then, appear to have relatively greater difficulty with the demands of the Verbal, rather than of the Performance portion of the intelligence test.

Since there were significant differences between the 2 groups both in mean IQ levels and in verbal and performance patterning, it would be expected that the mean Scaled Scores

Table 2

Mean Wisc Subtest Scores for 90 Retarded and
49 Normal Readers with Full Scale IQs of
90 and Above

WISC Subtests	Retarded Readers	Normal Readers	t	p
Information	9.0±1.7	10.6±2.5	4.00	<.001
Comprehension	8.6±2.3	9.4±2.5	2.00	<.05
Arithmetic	10.2±2.2	12.6±2.2	6.00	<.001
Similarities	10.0±2.3	11.5±2.6	3.75	<.001
Vocabulary	8.9±2.2	11.0±2.4	5.25	<.001
Digit Span	9.6±2.1	11.5±2.3	4.75	<.001
Picture Completion	10.8±2.4	11.4±2.8	1.50	N.S.
Picture Arrangement	10.4±2.4	11.1±2.6	1.75	N.S.
Block Design	9.5±2.1	10.8±2.8	2.83	<.01
Object Assembly	9.6±2.8	9.9±2.9	.60	N.S.
Coding	9.4±2.0	9.6±2.4	.50	N.S.
Mazes	9.3±1.8	9.5±1.9	.67	N.S.

and subtest profiles would reflect these trends. Table 2 contains the mean subtest scores for the two groups. Significant differences in mean subtest scores were restricted to Verbal Scale subtests, with the single exception of Block Design on the Performance Scale. Thus, the Full Scale IQ differences between the normal readers and the normally intelligent retarded readers reported in Table 1 appear, in the main, to reflect abilities tested by the Verbal Scale of the Intelligence test.

The relative similarity or dissimilarity in subtest profile between the two groups was explored in two ways. The first method employed was to determine the degree of relationship between the ranked mean subtest scores of the two groups. The rank-order correlation coefficient (rho = .71) indicated that the subtest profiles were similar in the two groups. The second method was graphic. A zero abscissa was established by using the deviations of each subtest score of the normal readers from the mean of their subtest scores as a base. Thus, if both the retarded readers and the controls had deviations of –1.0 from their own mean of subtest score, the plotted difference would be zero and would fall on the abscissa. If, however, the control deviated by +1.0 from the mean of their subtest scores on a given subtest and the retarded readers by –1.0 on the same subtest, the retarded readers would be plotted as having a –2.0 deviation. This shifting zero permits a direct depiction of relative distance in subtest performance profile between the two groups. Thus, even when both the retarded readers and the normal readers have a subtest performance which deviates in the same direction from each group's own mean of subtest scores, greater positive deviation or a lesser negative deviation on the part of the retarded readers will both be reflected in positions above the abscissa. Conversely, greater negative deviations or lesser positive deviations in subtest score of the retarded readers will be reflected in positions below the abscissa. Figure 1 indicates that a relative weakness in Verbal subtest scores and relative strength in Performance scores were present in the retarded readers of normal intellectual level.

Comparison of Retarded and Normal Readers of Average IQ

Since the comparison of subtest patterns can be affected by differences in the intellectual levels of the groups compared, a further analysis was carried out in which IQ range was

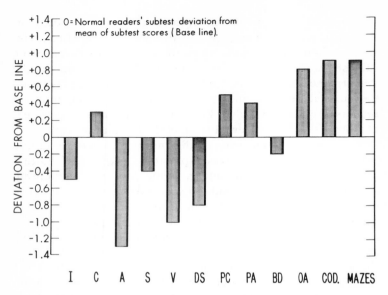

Figure 1. WISC Subtest Divergences of Retarded Readers
of Normal IQ (N = 90) from Normal Readers (N = 49)

restricted to Full Scale IQs between 90 and 109. This
necessitated the elimination of 2 retarded readers and 15
normal readers whose IQs were above 109.

Even when IQ range was restricted, Full Scale IQ differences (100.6 ± 5.5 vs. 96.9 ± 5.2) continued to favor the
normal readers. This difference in IQ derives entirely from the
normal reading group's superiority in Verbal Scale IQ (102.8 ±
7.0 vs. 95.9 ± 6.8; Performance IQ : 98.3 ± 6.7 vs. 98.6 ± 7.8).
It is of further interest in this connection that whereas Verbal
Scale IQ is significantly higher than Performance Scale IQ in
normal readers, the reverse obtains for the retarded readers. In
mean subtest scores, all significant differences obtained were
on Verbal Scale subtests (Information, Comprehension,
Vocabulary, Digit Span). The restricted group analysis confirmed the earlier findings.

Comparison of the Most Severely Retarded Readers with Normal Readers Individually Matched for IQ

Factors of heterogeneity in intellectual level and in degree of
reading retardation may continue to influence comparisons of

pattern even when IQ range is restricted. Stringent control can only be obtained when the individuals compared are matched for IQ and when degree of reading retardation is homogenized.

To control for both factors a subgroup of retarded readers of normal intelligence with reading below the tenth percentile on *all four* reading tests was defined. This group of 28 boys all had severe reading disability; 22 of them were matched for Full Scale IQ with normal readers (exactly in 15 cases, within 1 or 2 points in the remaining 7). This procedure eliminated Full Scale IQ differences and ensured that only significantly retarded readers were included. The overall difference in reading between the matched groups of retarded and normal readers was 1.8 school yr. (Word Knowledge, 1.9 yr.; Word Discrimination, 2.0 yr.; Reading, 1.4 yr.).

Table 3

Mean Wisc IQs for 22 Poorest Readers and
22 Normal Readers Matched For
Full Scale IQ

WISC IQ	Poorest Readers	Normal Readers	t	p
Full Scale	97.9±4.8	98.0±4.7	.71	N.S.
Verbal Scale	94.8±7.4	100.5±6.9	2.89	<.02
Performance Scale	102.0±9.2	95.6±6.2	2.67	<.02
Mv-p Diff.	−7.2	4.9		
t	2.37	2.28		
p	<.05	, <.05		

The WISC IQ data for the matched IQ groups presented in Table 3 indicate that, though equal in Full Scale IQ, the two groups differed significantly from one another in both Verbal and Performance IQ. The retarded readers achieved a significantly higher Performance IQ and a significantly lower Verbal IQ than did the normal readers. Within each group, the differences between Verbal and Performance IQs were significantly different but opposite in direction. The Performance IQ was higher than the Verbal IQ in the retarded readers and the Verbal IQ greater than the Performance IQ in the normal readers.

Table 4

Mean Wisc Subtest Scores for 22 Poorest Readers and
22 Normal Readers Matched For
Full Scale IQ

WISC Subtests	Poorest Readers	Normal Readers	t	p
Information	8.4 ± 1.7	9.5 ± 1.6	2.20	<.05
Comprehension	8.8 ± 1.7	8.6 ± 1.6	.40	N.S.
Arithmetic	10.3 ± 2.2	11.7 ± 1.9	2.33	<.05
Similarities	9.1 ± 2.8	10.0 ± 1.8	1.28*	N.S.
Vocabulary	8.2 ± 2.0	9.9 ± 2.0	2.83	<.01
Digit Span	10.1 ± 2.0	10.6 ± 2.3	.76	N.S.
Picture Completion	10.5 ± 2.7	10.1 ± 2.0	.57	N.S.
Picture Arrangement	10.8 ± 2.9	10.4 ± 2.7	.47	N.S.
Block Design	9.8 ± 2.4	9.3 ± 2.0	.76	N.S.
Object Assembly	11.0 ± 3.5	8.4 ± 2.6	2.77	<.01
Coding	9.9 ± 2.2	8.8 ± 1.8	1.83	<.10
Mazes	9.6 ± 2.2	9.2 ± 1.9	.67	N.S.

*Since there was a significant difference in the variances, the Cochran correction of the t test was applied.

The analysis of subtest scores for the two matched IQ groups (Table 4), indicates that the normal readers achieved a higher mean subtest score on all but one (Comprehension) of the Verbal Scale subtests. Conversely, the poorest readers achieved a higher mean subtest score on all the subtests of the Performance Scale. This difference in pattern was significant (p = .01; Fisher's exact probability test).

When the various subtest differences were individually considered, the differences between the two matched IQ groups were statistically significant for the Vocabulary, Arithmetic and Information subtests. When individual subtests on the Performance Scale were considered, only one mean subtest score difference, Object Assembly, was significant. In light of frequent reports that Coding is especially poor in retarded readers, the finding that the retarded readers had a higher mean subtest score on the Coding subtest than did the normal readers is of particular interest.

When the mean subtest scores were ranked, the rank-order correlation coefficient between the relative position of subtests in the two groups was .20, a value which indicates that the patterning of subtest scores in the matched IQ groups of normal and retarded readers was different.

A graphic analysis (Figure 2) illustrates relative and absolute strengths and weaknesses. These findings in the matched IQ groups reaffirm and strengthen the previously noted tendencies.

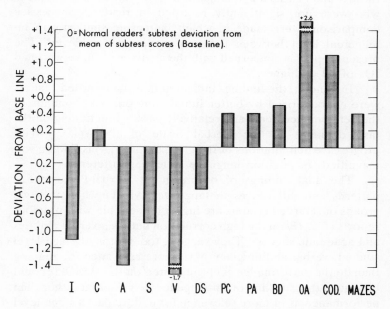

Figure 2. WISC Subtest Divergences of Poorest Readers
(N = 22) from IQ-matched Normal Readers (N = 22)

Vocabulary Subtest Analysis

In order to understand the nature of the deficiency suggested by the generally poorer performance of retarded readers on the Verbal Scale, vocabulary was more intensively analyzed. The analyses were related to two aspects of the vocabulary response: (a) number of words defined and (b) types of definition offered. Retarded readers both "knew" fewer words and demonstrated differences in features of language style in that they defined more words descriptively and fewer words categorically than did the normal readers.

DISCUSSION

The present study reports the patterning of intellectual functioning in a group of retarded readers who were limited to a
narrow age range and representative of retarded readers in a
total population of school boys. The patterns of intellectual
functioning in these 9- to 10-year-old boys were compared with
those found in a socially comparable group of similar aged boys
who were not significantly retarded in reading. Successive
comparisons were made in which increasing similarity in intellectual level between the two groups was achieved. The
present report is concerned with the analyses of those who had
IQs of 90 or higher.

In general, the findings indicated that the retarded readers
were characterized by better functioning on task demands of
the Performance Scale and relatively poorer functioning on the
task demands of the Verbal Scale of the WISC. With
progressive delimitations of the groups studied, this finding was
magnified. In addition language style was different.

The dual findings of difference in Verbal-Performance
patterns and differences in language style between the two
groups of retarded readers are highly compatible with previous
reports *(7, 8, 12)* on the high correlation between verbal abilities
and academic success. They suggest, too, that at the age level
studied, verbal abilities may have more relevance for reading
than do the performance skills measured on the WISC. It could
be argued that the kind of "intelligence," e.g., verbal rather than
performance, is of more relevance for children at this age level
matched for Full Scale IQ than intellectual level, as such. The
differences in language style may be seen as a reliance on more
direct inputs on the part of the retarded readers than on a more
indirect, symbolic use of language. Our findings do not answer
the question of whether retarded readers have a verbal deficit
because of their poor reading or because language is a primary
deficit of etiologic significance for reading dysfunction.

Negative findings are perhaps as important as the positive
ones. Other workers (whose work is summarized in [*1*]) have
repeatedly reported weakness in functioning in retarded
readers on the Coding subtest. In none of our comparisons was
this subtest performance found to be notably weak. Further, at
all levels of analysis in the age group of retarded readers

studied, Performance Scale demands as a whole tended to be well responded to and weaknesses were generally to the demands made by subtests of the Verbal Scale. The difference in Coding score found in the studies of other workers may be a function of undetected sampling biases, inappropriate comparison groups, wide age ranges or of the method of analysis of the data. The work of Neville *(9)*, who used a valid comparison group and who found low Coding scores for *both* normal and retarded readers, suggests that the nature of the comparison groups used may be the reason for the finding.

Our findings of weakness on the Verbal Scale and strengths on the Performance Scale are not idiosyncratic. Rather, detailed analyses of the subtest patternings reported in other investigations are in accord with this general conclusion. However, little or no effort has been made in other studies to analyze this most general difference. It is probable that this failure derives in part from an excessive focus on perceptual and other performance factors rather than on language inadequacy in the intellectual organization of retarded readers. In general, the findings of the present study indicated that for 9- to 10-year-old retarded readers, intellectual weakness, when subnormal intellectual functioning is excluded, is sharply restricted to verbal demands. The intellectual problem appears to be one of language and its usage rather than of perceptual or manipulative skills as measured by the subtests of the WISC.

These findings do not comprise the complete picture of cognitive lacks in retarded readers. In other studies we have found evidence of dysfunction in integrating auditory and visual information *(5)* and in lateral awareness *(2)*. Further, very young children with reading disability may well be ones in whom perceptual and performance skills are generally more markedly affected and older groups of children retarded in reading, ones with different patternings of defect *(3)*. Findings, therefore, are generalizable only to children of the same age range as those studied.

One possible additional area of concern in the interpretation of our findings may derive from the manner in which the representative group of 9- to 10-year-old retarded readers was defined. These were not clinic cases but rather Ss drawn from the total body of male readers who were functioning at a level inferior to 90% of their age and classmates and

a total normal school population. They therefore were selected
epidemiologically for reading retardation, as such, and did not
come to notice for a variety of other behavioral and conduct
disorders that so frequently bring schoolchildren retarded in
reading to clinical notice *(6)*. They therefore were relatively
free from the clinically associated neuro-behavioral concomitants that have been described in clinically obtained
groups of retarded readers *(10, 11)*. Our sample, then, is
representative of the population of retarded readers in a
community and not of any clinical group. In this sense our
findings cannot be directly compared with those of other
workers who have studied WISC intellectual patterning in
retarded readers because of the undefined reference
populations to which the earlier studies pertain.

A final difference stems from the fact that our retarded
readers, as well as the normal comparison group, were Scottish
children. It is possible that the noted differences in findings may
derive from differences in educational practices and cultural
milieu. Such a question, though fruitful for speculation, is
presently not answerable. An answer must await the findings of
a comparable epidemiologic survey currently being conducted
in the United States (D. Bryant, personal communication).

REFERENCES

1. Belmont, L., & Birch, H.G. The intellectual profile of retarded
readers. *Perc. motor Skills,* 1966, 22, 787-816.
2. Belmont, L., & Birch, H.G. Lateral dominance, lateral awareness
and reading disability. *Child Developm.,* 1965, 36, 57-71.
3. Benton, A.L. Dyslexia in relation to form perception and directional sense. In J. Money (Ed.), *Reading disability; progress and
research needs in dyslexia.* Baltimore: Johns Hopkins Press, 1962.
Pp. 81-102.
4. Bentzen, F. Sex ratios in learning and behavior disorders. *Amer. J.
Orthopsychiat.,* 1963, 33, 92-98.
5. Birch, H.G., & Belmont, L. Auditory-visual integration in normal
and retarded readers. *Amer. J. Orthopsychiat.,* 1964, 34, 852-861.
6. Gilbert, G.M. A survey of "referral problems" in metropolitan
child guidance centers. *J. clin. Psychol.,* 1957, 13, 37-42.
7. Gunderson, R. O., & Feldt, L.S. The relationship of differences
between verbal and nonverbal intelligence scores to achievement.
J. educ. Psychol., 1960, 51, 115-121.

8. Huge, D.S., & Stroud, J.B. Reading proficiency and intelligence scores, verbal and nonverbal. *J. educ. Res.,* 1959, 52, 258-262.

9. Neville, D. A comparison of the WISC patterns of male retarded and non-retarded readers. *J. educ. Res.,* 1961, 54, 195-197.

10. Rabinovitch, R.D. Dyslexia: psychiatric considerations. In J. Money (Ed.), *Reading disability; progress and research needs in dyslexia.* Baltimore: Johns Hopkins Press, 1962. Pp. 73-79.

11. Silver, A.A., & Hagin, R.A. Specific reading disability: follow-up studies. *Amer. J. Orthopsychiat.,* 1964, 34, 95-102.

12. Vernon, P.E. Ability factors and environment. *Amer. Psychologist,* 1965, 20, 723-733.

13. Wechsler, D. *Wechsler Intelligence Scale for Children, manual.* New York: Psychological Corp., 1949.

PHYLLIS A. KATZ
MARTIN DEUTSCH

The Relation of Auditory-visual
Shifting to Reading Achievement

Many non-educators — neurophysiologists, psychiatrists, and physiological psychologists — have speculated that some cases of reading disability may be due to subtle impairments of perceptual functioning. The following study is representative of some of the new directions and thinking that research is taking into some of the basic yet unexplored aspects of learning disabilities. Yet even when results are valid and unequivocal, two questions must be asked: Are these deficiencies causes or effects of reading problems? Are they causal or merely related factors?

What are the theoretical bases of this study? What is the researchers' explanation of this phenomenon in terms of learning principles? Katz and Deutsch fail to make clear how auditory-visual shifting could detrimentally affect reading achievement. What components of the reading process involve auditory-visual associations? If this ability is truly basic to reading performance, could it be used as a predictor of success even before children are taught to read?

Educators have long suggested that defective perceptual functioning may play a role in producing reading retardation. The relationships between specific auditory and visual skills and reading disability have therefore been widely investigated (e.g., Witty & Kopel, 1936; Betts & Austin, 1940; Poling, 1953; Goins, 1958). These investigations have focused primarily on children with gross anatomical defects in vision or audition. Although it is apparent that such gross defects place severe limitations on the child's learning capacity, it has been noted that such cases

Reprinted with permission of author and publisher:
Katz, Phyllis A. and Deutsch, Martin, Relation of auditory-visual shifting to reading achievement. *Percep. Mot. Skills,* 1963, 17, 327-332.

constitute a very small proportion of the retarded reading population (Johnson, 1957). The possibility exists that other cases of early reading difficulties might be due to more subtle impairments of perceptual functioning.

Since reading instruction typically involves the presentation of both auditory and visual information, any inability to process such stimulus information would be expected to reflect itself in learning problems. Such attentional difficulties might occur either with respect to the individual communication channels (auditory or visual), or to the sequential processing of visual and auditory stimuli in combination. In the latter instance, the child might be quite capable of attending to either auditory or visual information when presented alone, but would experience difficulty in shifting attention from one mode of stimulation to the other. The hypothesis advanced in the present investigation was that retarded readers would exhibit poorer performance than normal readers on a task requiring rapid attentional shifts between modalities.

In an earlier study employing adults, Mowrer (1941) found that reaction times increase when stimuli from a different modality are introduced into a series of stimuli in a single modality. The amount of this increase in latency associated with shifts in stimulus modality has been shown to be differentially related to certain kinds of population variables. Sutton, *et al.* (1961), for example, demonstrated that the behavior of schizophrenic patients on shifting tasks differs from normals. Benton, *et al.* (1962) have obtained similar results with neurological patients. In the only study investigating this phenomenon in children, Raab, Deutsch, and Freedman (1960) found a relation between modality shifting efficiency and reading achievement. The Raab study, however, was restricted to a sample of sixth-grade children. Thus, the issue of the temporal relationship between modality shifting efficiency and reading problems is difficult to evaluate on the basis of this earlier work. The present investigation represents an attempt to obtain evidence on the developmental aspects of this relationship. Toward this end, three age groups were studied. If perceptual difficulties of this type do indeed impede reading progress, they should be present not only at the upper elementary school grades, but should also be observable in young children, prior to reading instruction.

METHOD

Subjects. — The sample was composed of 48 Negro males drawn from the first, third, and fifth grade classes of two New York City elementary schools at the beginning of the school year. This particular racial and sex group was chosen both because of the high incidence of reading disability associated with it, and in order to keep the sample as homogeneous as possible.

Each age group was further subdivided according to reading ability. The Gates Advanced Primary Reading Test was administered to all third and fifth grade Negro males and the final sample of "high" and "low" readers was selected from the upper and lower 30% of the obtained frequency distribution for each grade. The mean reading scores of the third and fifth grade samples are presented in Table 1.

On the first grade level, the Reading Prognosis Test of the Institute for Developmental Studies was employed to differentiate the potentially good and poor readers. These two groups were also selected from the upper and lower 30% of the distribution. This Reading Prognosis test has been found to correlate .81 with reading achievement scores at the end of the first grade in a similar group of Ss (Weiner & Feldman, 1963). At all age levels, children with known auditory or visual defects were eliminated from the sample.

Table 1

Means of the Gates APR Test

Grade	Condition	
	Low	*High*
Third	2.2	3.9
Fifth	2.9	4.8

In addition to reading tests, Lorge-Thorndike Intelligence Tests were first administered to all Ss. The high and low reading groups differed significantly with respect to IQ scores ($F = 17.62$, $df = 1/46$, $p < .001$). The mean IQs for the high and low groups were 97.9 and 82.1, respectively.

Apparatus. — A bimodal reaction time apparatus was

employed. This equipment has previously been described by Sutton, *et al.* (1961). It is capable of automatically presenting four separate stimuli: a red light, a green light, a high tone of 1200 cps, and a low tone of 400 cps. S's task was to lift his finger from a button every time a stimulus was perceived. Reaction times to each stimulus were automatically recorded. The stimulus program was designed so as to appear random to Ss. Each stimulus was preceded by every other one an equal number of times. The time-between stimuli was varied randomly at either 1.5, 2.0, or 3.0 sec. There was a 1-min. delay at the end of each block of 33 trials.

Procedure. — All Ss were tested individually in the school. Upon entering the experimental room, S was seated in front of the apparatus and instructed as follows:

> We are going to play a game with lights and sounds. See this window? Well, every now and then you will see some lights here, a red light or a green light. Other times you will hear some sounds, a high sound or a low sound. Now I would like you to put your finger down on this button. Every time you see a light or hear a sound, pick your finger up as fast as you can. Then put your finger down again and wait for another light or sound. When another one comes, pick up your finger again as fast as you can, and put it right down again and wait for another.

The presentation of the stimuli automatically terminated if S did not repress the button. Each S received 198 trials.

RESULTS

Two measures of reaction were employed in the analysis: (a) mean reaction time to stimuli which were preceded by a stimulation in a different modality and (b) mean reaction time to stimuli preceded by same-modality stimuli. These measures will subsequently be referred to as cross-modal and ipsi-modal reaction times, respectively. Both of these conditions occurred equally often in the sequence. The mean reaction times of each group are presented in Table 2.

A mixed Type III analysis of variance (Lindquist, 1953) was conducted on the scores. This analysis indicated that, as expected, all Ss took longer to respond to stimuli which were preceded by a stimulus in a different modality ($F = 50.93$, $df = 1/42$, $p < .001$). The main effect of age was statistically significant ($F = 14.44$, $df = 1/42$, $p < .001$), indicating that older children have faster over-all reaction times. The mean total reaction times for the first, third, and fifth grade groups were 726, 541, and 438 msec., respectively. Although the poor readers responded more slowly, the main effect of reading level was not significant ($F = 3.87$, $df = 1/42$, $p < .10$).

The result of major interest to the hypothesis initially advanced is the interaction between type of reaction time (i.e., ipsi- and cross-modal) and reading level. This interaction was significant at the .01 level ($F = 7.37$, $df = 1/42$), indicating that retarded readers exhibited greater difficulty than normal readers in shifting from one modality to another. The mean increase from the ipsi- to the cross-modal condition for the retarded readers was twice that for the high reader groups. Thus, this interaction supports the hypothesis that poor readers cannot shift attention between modalities as rapidly as normal readers.

Table 2

Mean Reaction Times in Milliseconds

Group	Type of Reaction Time	
	Ipsi-modal	Cross-modal
First grade — low	772	862
First grade — high	612	644
Third grade — low	501	586
Third grade — high	507	559
Fifth grade — low	449	491
Fifth grade — high	397	418

Although the difference between good and poor readers was somewhat greater at the earlier age levels, the interaction of age by reading level did not reach the generally accepted level of significance. None of the other interaction effects was statistically significant either.

Since the two reading groups differed with respect to IQ scores, the question can be raised as to whether intellectual factors played a role in the differences in modality shifting behavior. In order to obtain information on this question, difference scores between cross- and ipsi-modal reaction times were computed for each S, and these were correlated with Lorge-Thorndike IQ scores. The resulting Pearson product-moment correlation coefficient was $-.21$ which was not significantly different from zero ($Z = 1.46$). In addition, the correlation obtained between IQ and total reaction time was not significant ($r = .22$). Thus, it may be concluded that performance on this bimodal reaction time task is not significantly related to intelligence.

DISCUSSION

The findings of the present study indicate that normal and retarded readers differ in the ease with which attention is shifted from one modality to another. Although all children took longer to respond in the cross-modal condition, the poorer readers had the greatest difficulty in shifting sequentially from one channel of communication to another. This result corroborates Raab's earlier study (Raab, *et al.,* 1960).

There are several alternative points of view which may be offered to explain this finding. First, the differences in performance of the two groups may be reflecting some more basic neurophysiological differences. Hernandez-Peon, *et al.* (1956) observed that evoked potentials in the auditory pathways of cats disappear when a prominent visual stimulus is attended to. Although the above cited study was not completely analogous to the present one in that auditory and visual stimuli were presented simultaneously rather than sequentially, it may be that stable and large individual differences could be found in the rate at which such neurological potentials decrease in humans.

Another possible explanation may be offered in terms of learning principles. In the experimental task employed in this study, the child was instructed to make the same response to different stimuli. It is conceivable that retarded readers took longer to respond to cross-modal shifts because they are generally poorer at response generalization, i.e., it may take them longer to transfer an identical response (including the speed of the response) to a different cue. A prediction which would follow from this reasoning is that the smallest differences between poor and good readers should occur during the latter part of the test. In order to obtain evidence on this point, the data were further analyzed according to performance on the first and second half of the test. This analysis revealed that differences in shifting efficiency between the reading groups were at a maximum during the first half and they diminished markedly on the second half of the task ($F = 3.88$, $df = 1/26$, $p <$ .06). This finding then supports the learning explanation. The poorer readers shifted more rapidly on the second half of the test. Further work on response generalization and its relationship to reading achievement is indicated.

The results reveal that modality shifting capacity is not directly related to intellectual ability. Although IQ is clearly related to reading ability, which in turn is related to modality shifting, the perceptual behavior is not related to intelligence. This suggests that non-intellective factors, which are not ordinarily included in assessments of children's ability, may be playing a very important role in reading performance. The possibility suggests itself that such factors might be used profitably as predictors of achievement in reading.

The question can be raised whether the relationship between the capacity to shift attention and achievement in reading is a causal one. It should be noted that on the basis of Raab's study, which used only older children, an alternative explanation can be posited, namely, that attentional deficiency is a partial result of not learning to read well. The results of the present investigation cast doubt on this position, however, since a relationship was found to exist on the first-grade level, prior to the time the children were actually taught to read. The finding that modality shifting differences can be related to potential as well as actual reading achievement tends to support the notion that this particular perceptual skill is basic to reading performance.

REFERENCES

Benton, A.L., Sutton, S., Kennedy, J.A., & Brokaw, J.R. The cross-modal retardation in reaction time of patients with cerebral disease. *J. nerv. ment. Dis.,* 1962, 135, 413-418.

Betts, E.A. & Austin, A.S. *Visual problems of school children. Chicago: Professional Press, 1940-1941.*

Goins, J.T. Visual perceptual abilities and early reading progress. *Suppl. Educ. Monogr.,* 1958, 87, 1-108.

Hernandez-Peon, R., Scherrer, H., & Jouvet, M. Modification of electric activity in cochlear nucleus during attention in unanaesthetized cats. *Science,* 1956, 123, 331-332.

Johnson, M.S. Factors related to disability in reading. *J. exp. Educ.,* 1957, 26.

Lindquist, E.F. *Design and analysis of experiments in psychology and education.* Boston: Houghton Mifflin, 1953.

Mowrer, O.H. Preparatory set (expectancy) — further evidence of its "central" locus. *J. exp. Psychol.,* 1941, 28, 116-133.

Poling, D.L. Auditory deficiencies of poor readers. *Suppl. Educ. Monogr.,* 1953, 77, 107-111.

Raab, S., Deutsch, M., & Freedman, A. Perceptual shifting and set in normal school children of different reading achievement levels. *Percept. mot. Skills,* 1960, 10, 187-192.

Sutton, S., Hakerem, G., Zubin, J., & Portnoy, M. The effect of shift of sensory modality on serial reaction time: a comparison of schizophrenics and normals. *Amer. J. Psychol.,* 1961, 74, 224-232.

Weiner, M., & Feldmann, S. Measurement of reading skills of lower socioeconomic status children. Paper presented at American Psychological Association, August, 1963.

Witty, P.A., & Kopel, D. Factors associated with the etiology of reading disability. *J. educ. Psychol.,* 1936, 27, 119-134.

JOHN B. ISOM

Some Neuropsychological Findings in Children With Reading Problems

The proper functioning of the central nervous system is vital to normal development and progress in any task, and it seems crucial in ones as complex as learning to read. Yet we cannot directly examine the CNS of humans with reading problems; all we can do is make inferences on the basis of performances on certain tasks. The paucity of reliable information in this area is overwhelming. We know almost nothing with certainty! And even when we think we have formed sound conclusions, we are still uncertain what implications they have for instructional procedures and material selection. Yet some people have been so eager, feeling that the need for better reading instruction is urgent, they have not been willing to wait for the tedious, time-consuming process of research to produce definitive answers, but rather they have forged ahead imputing questionable causation, using unproven materials and techniques, and evangelizing with fervor. Such people may not be pleased with Isom's relatively inconclusive findings and his relative lack of specific conclusions and instructional suggestions.

Although Isom draws from his findings no definite conclusions about the relationship between laterality and reading, what do you think they would be if he had? In what ways does Schilder's arm-extension test and right-left concept development seem related to laterality and dominance? Does Isom generally support or refute Katz and Deutsch's findings on auditory-visual shifting reported in the previous article? Isom suggests that poor readers may be deficient in the "rote processing of non-meaningful material." What components of the reading process demand this type of processing? What do you think the future holds for research into this area? Will it be bleak or promising?

Reprinted from *Self and Society,* thirty-second yearbook of the Claremont Reading Conference, Malcolm P. Douglass, ed., pp. 188-198. By permission of Claremont College and John B. Isom.

The data in this presentation and the conclusions drawn therefrom are based upon observations of several hundred children during the last four years. The majority of these children were in attendance in school systems in the greater Portland area at the time they were seen at the University of Oregon Medical School. The immediate source of the referral was the child's teacher or parent, in the majority of cases, and various third parties originated the referral in the remaining cases.

REASON FOR MEDICAL EVALUATION

The children were referred directly to the essayist for neurological evaluation or they were referred because of locally known interest in reading disabilities in children. This is a selected population and the findings are not to be construed as necessarily characteristic of poor readers detected in a randomly selected group of school children.

SELECTIVE FEATURES
OF CHILDREN INFLUENCING REFERRAL

That the children referred to a medical facility for evaluation of reading disability represent a selected group is further attested to by examining the ratio of the boys to the girls in several school settings. The ratio of boys to girls in the present series is approximately 6 to 1. Ratios equal to or higher than this have been noted in other diagnostic referral clinics, whether the clinic is in a medical or pedagogic setting. Ratios of boys to girls from 2.0 - 2.4 to 1 have been noted in remedial reading classes in public schools in Portland, Oregon; Boston, Mass. *(1)*, and Stoke-on-Trent, England *(2)*, extending over a 35 year period. The ratio of boys to girls in regular classrooms in the larger public school system is approximately 1 to 1. The degree of reading retardation, whether or not "corrected" for I.Q. is not the only factor that determines whether a child will be referred from his regular classroom to a remedial reading class or from the latter to a diagnostic or evaluation clinic in a medical or educational setting. Doubtless there are many factors which, in general, reflect subjective evaluation of the child by the child's teacher, either in the regular classroom or in the remedial reading class. These factors have not been precisely defined but to the author it appears that they may be grouped under the heading of *pupil-teacher interaction*. In effect, this is a measure of the teacher's acceptance or rejection of the child's reading and non-reading behavior. It is not implied that this is the only factor operating, nor necessarily, the most important one, in all instances. However, it is almost certainly important in a significant number of cases and is probably responsible for the ratio of boys to girls in the referral populations.

The children ranged from 7 to 16 years of age; all but a few were between 9 and 14 years of age. The I.Q., as measured by the WISC or Stanford-Binet, was between 80 and 90 in a small percentage of cases and between 90 and 120 in the bulk of the remainder, a very small number of children had I.Q. scores in the range from 120 to 130 and only one or two above 130. They had no obvious neurological deficit, their vision and hearing were intact. The children showed varying degrees of skill and ease of accomplishment in performing such tasks as tandem walking, standing on one foot, standing with feet together and eyes closed, and execution of rapid, repetitive or sequential movements. These operations are commonly employed to assess the degree of "awkwardness" or "incoordination" that a child demonstrates. These concepts are difficult to define and almost impossible to quantitate. Suffice it to say that the majority of children performed these tasks well and were considered by their parents to be reasonably well, and in some cases, exceptionally well coordinated. Some of the children had been considered ill-coordinated in early childhood and this had persisted but did not prevent the children's dressing themselves completely, including tying shoe laces, or engaging in such activities as riding a bicycle, skating, etc.

We can distinguish two general groups of children by the history given by the parents. In the first group, much the larger, the age of onset of intelligible speech and subsequent oral language development was within expected limits and was not different from that of the child's siblings who do not have reading problems. In the other group, the onset of speech and/or the age of intelligible speech was delayed. In almost all instances, the speech subsequently became normal, with or without speech therapy. A few individuals have a persistent lisp or other speech impediment that does not interfere with speech production.

LATERALITY IN POOR AND AVERAGE READERS

We determined the eye which the children preferentially used for monocular sighting and the hand which they preferentially used for unilateral tasks. "Eyedness" is defined by the eye which the child uses to look through a kaleidoscope when it is presented to him in the mid-line and he grasps it with both hands before putting it to his eye. "Handedness" is determined by the hand the child uses when writing, holding a fork, and throwing a ball. If the individual uses the same hand for all three of these tasks, he is considered "handed" for that side. If the hand used for these three tasks is on the same side as the eye used for monocular sighting, he is said to have consistent laterality. If "handedness" and "eyedness" are on opposite sides of the body, then he is said to have crossed laterality. If he does not use the same hand for all three tasks, he has mixed "handedness" and mixed laterality. Obviously, by this operational definition, an individual can be only left- or right-eyed. The frequency of left handedness is approximately 10% in the poor readers and in the average readers. Left-eyedness occurs twice as often in the poor readers as in the average. Consistent hand-eye laterality is noted in 50% of the poor readers as compared to 75% of normals; crossed hand-eye laterality in 47% of the poor readers and 15% of the normals; mixed hand-eye laterality in 3% of the poor readers and 10% of normals. These figures suggest that mixed or consistent hand-eye laterality, but not crossed, right-eyedness, or right handedness, are associated with better reading ability. The group of poor readers and normals were equated for intelligence.

LATERALITY IN SUPERIOR READERS

To further test these conclusions, it was decided to examine a group of superior readers of the same age. We were unable to equate the groups for I.Q. since the superior readers were all in the I.Q. range of 125 to 170, considerably above average-normal or high-average levels. However, the findings are of interest and cast considerable doubt on the suggestion that right-eyedness or consistent hand-eye laterality are causally related to reading ability. Of the 50 advanced readers examined, 6% were left-handed and 33% were left-eyed. The superior group demonstrated consistent hand-eye laterality in a larger percentage of cases than the dyslexic, but in a smaller percentage than the average readers. Superior readers demonstrated crossed hand-eye laterality in a larger percentage than the average readers but in a lesser percentage than the poor readers. They showed mixed hand-eye laterality in a percentage equal to that found in average readers.

In summary, comparisons of these three groups indicated that left-handedness occurred with approximately equal frequency in all three; left eyedness was seen with approximately equal frequency in the advanced and normal groups and yet the difference in reading ability between these two groups was enormous. The advanced readers were five to six years ahead of their grade placement level in reading ability. Consistent hand-eye laterality was found in the advanced readers in a higher percentage than the poor readers, but in a lesser percentage than in the normals. Crossed hand-eye laterality was noted less often in the advanced than in the poor readers but more often in the advanced than in the average readers. Mixed hand-eye laterality was seen more often in the advanced and in the normal groups than in the poor readers.

A recent report by the English Ministry of Education *(3)* compares the hand-eye correspondence in 11 year olds as it relates to their reading ability which is qualitatively judged to be poor, fair, or good. The ratio of the number of children with crossed hand-eye laterality and consistent hand-eye laterality at each of the three reading levels is approximately unity. This indicates that no advantage in reading is conferred upon the individual with consistent hand-eye laterality at 11 years of age.

LATERALITY IN FIRST GRADERS

We examined the reading achievement as it relates to hand-eye correspondence in several hundred children who were in the eighth month of the first grade. The children were divided into three groups, those reading at or below a grade level of 1.7, those reading at a level from grade 1.7 to 1.9, and those reading above grade 1.9. The ratio of the percentage of children with consistent laterality to those with crossed laterality was approximately unity in each of the three reading levels. This indicated no advantage in reading achievement, measured late in the first grade, conferred by consistent vs. crossed laterality.

CHANGING LATERALITY IN CHILDHOOD

We have had opportunity to perform serial examinations over several years on the same children, currently numbering several hundred. One of the findings of this systematic observation on a single population is that handedness and eyedness are not constant in all children in the late pre-school and early school grades. Approximately two hundred and fifty children were seen at age four, again prior to entering kindergarten, and then prior to entering the first grade. It is of interest that approximately 20% of the children changed "eyedness" and a little less than 10% changed "handedness" during the period of observation. The definitions of eyedness and handedness that have been previously applied are the ones operable here. These findings clearly indicate that one cannot speak of "handedness" and "eyedness" in children unless operational definitions are presented and the age of the children examined is clearly stated.

EXTENSION TEST

Silver and Hagin *(4)* have employed the so-called extension test of Paul Schilder as a presumed manifestation of cerebral dominance. The test is a relatively simple one in that the subject is asked to fully extend his arms parallel to the floor, with his eyes closed. After the passage of several seconds, sometimes a minute or a minute and a half may be required to gain an endpoint, one may see one arm elevated with respect to the other or both arms may remain at the same level. The normal response consists of relative elevation of the hand and arm which are used for writing. If neither arm is elevated, with respect to the other, or if the arm other than the one used for writing is elevated, the response is abnormal. The test is based upon the presumption that the relatively higher arm will reflect greater muscle tone because the "dominant" cerebral hemisphere will deliver more impulses to the peripheral musculature than will the "non-dominant" hemisphere. Silver and Hagin *(4)* have found this a useful tool in a relatively limited number of individuals, in that more than 90% of individuals with reading disability will have an abnormal extension test or more than 90% of individuals with the abnormal extension test will be found to have reading difficulty. We have not found such a high incidence of abnormal responses in the children with reading disability and it is of interest that 27 out of 50 superior readers had an abnormal response to Schilder's extension test.

The significance of preferential use of an eye and/or a hand on one side of the body for certain tasks and the significance of so-called "crossed" or "consistent" laterality or dominance is obscure. It is evident from this study, as well as several others published in recent years, that observations on various aspects of laterality or so-called cerebral dominance do not serve to distinguish the individual poor reader from the good reader nor do they shed any light on the etiology of reading disability or indicate a consistently successful remedial program.

RIGHT-LEFT CONCEPT DEVELOPMENT

In contrast to the preferential use of eye or hand, an individual's awareness of the concept of right and left on his own body, on that of a second person and of the right and left relationships of objects in extracorporeal space does seem to be significantly related to reading achievement.

Our findings in this area parallel those of Belmont and Birch (5), as well as others, although the precise meaning of the association is unclear at this time. We have found that practically all children, whether average or poor readers, are able to identify right and left upon their own person by eight or nine years of age.

The ability to identify right and left on another person lags behind that of identifying right and left on one's own person. There is a distinction between the poor and average readers in the age at which right-left identification on another person can be made. The majority of normal readers are able to identify right and left on another person by age 7 and in another year or two they can do this on a second person. Poor readers lag markedly in this skill. Less than half are able to identify right and left on a second person at age 9 and it is not until 13-14 years of age that virtually all poor readers can perform this task.

The recognition of the right and left relationships of two or three objects in extra-corporeal space is the most difficult of these identification-tasks and the test with two objects is easier than the test with three objects. Normal children are able to identify the relationship of two objects two or three years before then can that of three. Almost all children can order correctly two objects by the end of the first decade of life. It is not until 11-12 years of age that the majority of children can orient correctly three objects. In contrast, the poor readers are markedly delayed in the acquisition of this facility. By age 14 years, only 84% of our sample could order correctly two objects and only 66% could order correctly three objects. These findings indicate that in the normal and the poor reader, the acquisition of this facility reflects the maturation of an underlying process(es) which reaches functional completion by the end of the first decade, or early in the second decade, of life in the normal but is not complete in poor readers several years later. However, there is a cumulative increase in the percentage of poor readers who can perform these tasks as they grow older.

In general, strongly right-handed individuals tend to develop facility in right-left identification at an earlier age than do those who are left-handed. Strongly right- or left-handed individuals are more advanced than those who do not have well-defined handedness. However, this association is not absolute.

A BASIC PROCESS IN POOR READERS

Our observations on poor readers suggest a basic difficulty in poor readers. These observations focus on the child's ability to process sequentially presented information, particularly via the auditory channel. The assessment of this function obviously requires a minimal level of auditory-perceptual and visual-perceptual functioning. In none of our children were we able to detect aberrant auditory or visual perception. The tasks set to the children are, in part, a measure of short term or mnemonic memory and the ability to learn and remember common information, whether formally taught or not. Poor readers have particular difficulty acquiring this kind of information.

The tasks are oral and written. The child is asked to state his complete birthdate, the days of the weeks, the months of the year, in order, and to write his name, address, phone number and the letters of the alphabet in order. These tasks apparently reflect maturation of an underlying process(es) of the central nervous system.

Children who are poor readers show a cumulative increase in the percentage who can perform these tasks at successive age levels. They are decidedly retarded in development of this function compared to normals and strikingly retarded when compared to superior readers. The three groups are of comparable chronological age. Excluding recitation of the months of the year and production of the written alphabet, almost all poor readers can perform these tasks by age 16. Only 50% of the group can state the months of the year in order and only 50% can write the alphabet. The distribution of poor readers is such that only 25% of all poor readers who are 16 years of age or more* are able to accomplish both of these tasks.

Comparison of the advanced, the average and the poor readers in the 10-12 year age range indicates that all of the superior readers could perform all of the tasks with the exception of stating the months of the year. Eleven percent of the superior readers were unable to recite the months of the year. Almost all of the average readers could perform all of the tasks except recitation of the months of the year. Approximately 50% of the average normal were unable to state the months of the year in correct order. None of the tasks were accomplished by 100% of the poor readers and, in general, they were decidedly retarded in the rate of development of their ability to perform these tasks. Only 15% of the poor readers knew the months of the year and only 37% could write the alphabet.

These tasks reflect an auditory or auditory-visual skill and in an attempt to distinguish the more important channel, the auditory digit span retention of each of these three groups of individuals was determined. The results were rather similar, in pattern, for all three groups. Each of the three groups showed progressive increase, with age, in the number of digits they could repeat. The advanced readers were superior to the average and they, in turn, were strikingly advanced with respect to the poor readers.

Observations made by Rosenberger *(6)* would suggest that "sequencing" is also at fault in poor readers as contrasted to good readers. In their study, a three by three matrix was visually presented and the child was required to match letters in the central cell with combinations of the same letters in the surrounding cells. The word "the" was in the central cell in two matrices. In one matrix, the surrounding cells were blank or contained various combinations of the three letters in "the." In

---

* We have examined 18 poor readers who range from 18-44 years of age.

the other matrix, cells were blank or contained combinations of the three letters in the word "the" or substitution of an "l" for a "t" in "the" or the "o" for an "e" in "the." Another matrix contained the letters "laj," meaningless in English, in the central cell and blanks or various combinations of these three letters in the surrounding cells. The fourth matrix presented a circle, a square, and a triangle in that order in the central cell and blanks or various combinations of these geometric figures in the surrounding cells. It is of interest that there was no differentiation of the poor readers versus the good readers on the task employing geometric figures. However, there was a striking difference between the poor readers and the good readers when the center cell contained "laj," or "the," and the comparison was with combinations of "t," "h," "e." There was a lesser degree of distinction between poor and good readers when the central cell contained "the" and some of the possible comparisons include substitution of "l" and "o."

Lecours *(7)* and Lecours and Twitchell *(8)* have indicated that poor readers make sequential errors in written language. We have noted similar errors and have also found that poor readers make sequential errors in spoken language when the material is unfamiliar or difficult. The children are asked to repeat motorically complex speech units such as "persistence," "essential," and "success" and the sentence, "Persistence is essential to success" *(9)*. Poor readers perform much less well than the average readers.

In summary, it appears that the poor readers differ significantly from average or superior readers in the facility with which they may process sequentially presented information. Depending upon the complexity and the familiarity of the material to be processed, they appear to have more difficulty with the auditory than the visual aspects of this process. Conversely, those who perform well on tests designed to assess the ability to process auditorily and visually presented, sequential information, in general, are good or superior readers.

The poor readers we examined have average-normal intelligence and are able to use spoken language adequately. They may have less facility with language than the more accomplished readers, particularly those with superior ability. The poor reader does not have language disability in the sense of an individual with *aphasia*.

Our observations suggest that poor readers may be distinguished from good readers by deficiency of short-term memory, or in the rote processing of nonsense or non-meaningful material — so called automatic or mnemonic memory. This is in contrast to the extraction of meaning from printed words.

To the beginning reader, all printed words are nonsense and he appears to process them in rote fashion. Initially, he processes them word-by-word, later by groupings of words or phrases or sentences. Once the reader is able to speak or name the printed word, he learns the meaning of that word. Learning the meaning of the word is made easier if the reader can associate the spoken word with some object, person or situation in his own experience. When these serial processes have been accomplished, the word may be considered part of the reader's active, oral vocabulary. The individual cannot read skillfully or create meaning from what he reads until he has reached this stage of development in the art of learning to read.

We need not dwell upon those factors influencing the creation of meaning for printed material except to emphasize that it *must* follow the process of associating spoken word with written word.

Most children accomplish these two tasks, association of auditory and visual symbol and learning the meaning of either or both easily and simultaneously *(10)*. Individuals who have difficulty with reading also have difficulty with the first stage of learning to read. This is reflected in their difficulty with other kinds of mnemonic or rote tasks which we ask them to perform. This study is, in a sense, a retrospective one and we cannot conclude that individuals who have difficulty with these tasks at the time they enter school will necessarily show subsequent difficulty with reading although it is our impression and tentative opinion that such would be the case.

Theoretically, if reading is composed of two discrete processes, and one must precede the other, then we should find, in clinical practice, two different kinds of reading disability. All of us are only too familiar with individuals who have difficulty with the rote processing of written material and also have difficulty creating meaning from printed material. Only rarely do we encounter individuals who are very skillful in the rote processing of printed material and have great difficulty or are unable to appreciate the meaning of the material. Such individuals do exist but they are only rarely encountered. Why one kind of disability should be so frequently encountered and the other so rarely encountered is obscure.

REFERENCES

1. Durrell, Donald D., *Improvement of Basic Reading Disabilities*. Yonkers-on-Hudson, New York: World Book Co., 1940.
2. *The Health of the School Child*. Report of the Chief Medical Officer of the Ministry of Education for the year 1960 and 1961. London: Her Majesty's Stationary Office, 1962 (Reprinted 1963), pp. 22.
3. *Ibid.,* p. 23.
4. Silver, Archie and Hagin, Rosa, "Specific Reading Disability: Delineation of the Syndrome and Relationship to Cerebral Dominance," *Comprehensive Psychiatry,* Vol. I (April, 1960), 126-133.
5. Belmont, Lillian and Birch, Herbert G., "Lateral Dominance and Right-Left Awareness in Normal Children," *Child Development,* XXXIV (1963), 257-270.
6. Rosenberger, Peter, "Visual Recognition and Other Neurologic Findings in Good and Poor Readers," *Neurology,* XVII (1967), pp. 332 (abstract).
7. Lecours, Andre-Roch, "Serial Order in Writing — A Study of Misspelled Words in 'Developmental Dysgraphia,'" *Neurophsychologia,* IV (1966), 221-241.
8. Lecours, Andre-Roch and Twitchell, Thomas E., "Sequential Errors in Written Language: Their Form, Occurrence and Nature," *Neurology,* XVI (1966), pp. 313 (abstract).
9. Blakely, Robert, "Oral Sequencing Ability: Norms for Ages 5-12 Years," ASHA, Vol. 7 (September, 1965), Pg. 321, Paper presented at the 41st Annual Convention of the American Speech and Hearing Association, October 30, 1965.
10. Bateman, Barbara, "Reading: A Controversial View, Research and Rationale," Curriculum Bulletin No. 278, XXIII, Eugene, Oregon: School of Education, University of Oregon, 1967, p. 14 (Mimeographed).

VERNON L. SIMULA

Anxiety — and the
Learning-to-Read Process

We speak rather glibly about "emotional problems and
"personal-social maladjustment" as causes or concomitants of
reading problems. Yet personality factors of lesser severity may
be more widespread and just as debilitating—but far less
recognized. Anxiety is one such factor.
      Does the phrase "test anxiety" refer only to formal pencil-
and-paper tests? Make a list of some evaluative situations
children face daily in school, particularly in reading instruction;
then list some ways to assure that they are non-anxiety
producing situations. Explain in your own words how anxiety
inhibits learning to read. Relate this discussion to the articles by
Root and by Otto and McMenemy in Part Four.

Learning how to read is perhaps the principal task which a child
undertakes during the first years of school. For many children,
the learning-to-read process is a manageable, and often an
enjoyable, task. For others, the acquisition of reading skills
presents a formidable experience.

      Numerous reasons have been advanced to explain why
some children encounter difficulty in the learning-to-read
process. Factors which are frequently cited include visual and
auditory problems, intellectual deficiencies, personality
problems, neurological anomalies, and physiological anomalies.
Educational factors, the methods and materials used, are also
cited. The discussion here will focus upon "personality
problems."

      The literature on the relationship of personality problems
and reading difficulty is characterized by several factors. First,

      Reprinted from *Academic Therapy,* 1 (No. 4), 209-214, by permission of
Vernon L. Simula and Academic Therapy Publications.

it appears that what is meant by a personality problem may not always be clear to the classroom teacher. The term "personality problem" has been used loosely to include such characteristics as "emotional maladjustment," "selfconsciousness," "aggressiveness," "conscious refusal to learn," etc. The classroom teacher who perceives a child's behavior in such terms is likely to gain only a superficial understanding of the learning problem.

Moreover, many reports of research and clinical observations relating to reading difficulties have dealt typically with the obvious or the more serious types of personality problems. The outward symptoms of such problems are obvious to the classroom teacher. The relationship of serious personality problems to reading difficulties is similarly apparent.

There remains, however, the possibility that personality factors of lesser severity may be operating to contribute to a child's learning problem. That is, a child need not possess what is commonly labeled a "behavior disorder" before his learning ability is affected. Rather, there may be children within the typical classroom who exhibit "acceptable" or "normal" behavior but whose learning ability is still affected because of personality factors. One such factor is that of anxiety.

THE NATURE OF ANXIETY

Anxiety is generally recognized as a basic element within the construct of the personality. It is described as a condition of the individual which is characterized by conscious feelings of unpleasantness, tension, or apprehension. Such feelings of anxiety are said to be evoked by inter-personal situations which the "self" perceives as psychologically threatening.

According to the psychoanalytical position, anxiety originates in the individual at the moment of birth when the immature nervous system is flooded with sensory, motor, and physiological stimuli. The reaction to this state of helplessness is termed by Freud as the prototype of later anxiety reactions (8:30-2).

As the infant develops, he is able to effect a progressively greater differentiation of his environment. Gradually, he learns to associate the appearance and disappearance of feelings of "unpleasantness" with the appearance and disappearance of "objects," which at this early stage is predominantly the mother. Thus, anxiety generalizes from the feelings of helplessness or "unpleasantness" to the danger of "losing the objects" which, the child has learned, determine his well-being (8:33).

The role of anxiety in personality formation becomes more specific during the early stages of socialization experiences, e.g., toilet training and the internalization of parental values. During these years, the child is repeatedly reinforced for "acceptable" behavior and scolded for behavior which is not condoned by his parents, or other adults. It is from these early "evaluative" experiences that a child learns that he is at times "good" and at times "bad," that he is sometimes "nice," and sometimes "naughty." The result of such day-to-day experiences is that the child forms some notion of the adequacy of his "self" in the eyes of his "significant others" (8:35).

As a consequence, any situation in which the child feels that his adequacy is being evaluated may constitute a psychological threat to the child and thus give rise to anxiety. Such anxiety Sarason has termed "test anxiety" (8:7 - 10).

While test anxiety has both conscious and unconscious elements, there are available to the classroom teacher certain observable characteristics which may suggest that test anxiety is operating. A child who is afflicted with "high test-anxiety" may be one:

1. who fidgets, squirms, or bites his nails, especially during a test or when he is asked to recite,
2. whose voice trembles or who even stammers slightly when he is asked to recite — but whose voice is normal during ordinary conversation,
3. who frequently complains of headaches or sickness, especially near test time or when he knows that he is to recite in front of the class,
4. who appears nervous when he has to read orally or when he has to write on the chalkboard,
5. who gets upset because he received a poor grade on his paper or who worries about failing even though he is in no danger of actually failing (8:313-4, 9).

ANXIETY AND SCHOOL EXPERIENCES

The primary classroom and particularly the learning to-read setting, appears replete with evaluative situations. The classroom teacher, for instance, tells the child which of his pronunciations are correct and which are incorrect. She gives shiny gold stars for perfect papers; she slashes errors with ugly red checks. Children label some of their peers as "sharpies," others as "dummies." The teacher typically designates some children as belonging to the "high" reading group and others as belonging to the "low" reading group. Evaluation and test-like situations are seemingly unavoidable in beginning reading instruction.

The teaching of reading, it must be noted, requires a very intimate relationship between the teacher and the child. According to Sarason, the chief element in a school "test-like situation" is the teacher. For the text-anxious child, the anxieties already associated with the parents often generalize to the classroom teacher who now serves as a parent-surrogate in a similar authoritarian role.

THE EFFECTS OF ANXIETY ON LEARNING-TO-READ

The effects of high levels of anxiety on learning are generally debilitating, especially where the learning task involves material that is relatively difficult and highly symbolic.

The function of anxiety as a suppressor of performance during learning is essentially one of interference. Sarason explained that the child is more concerned with the internal, anxiety-produced stimuli aroused by the threat emanating from the evaluative nature of the learning situation than he is with the cues or the instructions relevant to the learning task (8:20).

Early recognition of the effects of anxiety upon reading and other areas of school achievement were typical reports of clinical observations. Blanchard *(1),* in describing 73 cases of reading disability admitted to the Philadelphia Child Guidance Clinic during the years 1925 to 1933, contended that the disabilities were, in many cases, preceded by emotional maladjustments. She described such maladjustments as being the result of the child's efforts to solve ambivalent guilt conflicts. From a Freudian theoretical position, the reading disability provided the child a means to relieve his anxieties and guilt feelings through the self-punishment he received in the form of disapproval and criticism. Blanchard also contended that the sex differences observed in reading achievement could

plausibly be due to differences in the psychosexual development of boys and girls.

Sylvester and Kuntz cited the importance of the child's
early stages of personality development in relation to the later
acquisition of reading skill. They referred particularly to the
curiosity and body exploration activities which characterize the
behavior of a young child during the Freudian oral and anal
stages of personality development. If such activities are
traumatically inhibited, the curiosity drive becomes associated
with anxiety which, in turn, may become conditioned to the
persons who exercise the external control over the child — but
upon whom the child is also dependent. Sylvester and Kuntz
then reasoned that any learning task which requires curiosity
and self-assertion, such as the task of learning how to read, will
elicit anxiety reactions on the part of the child. According to
these writers, the reading disability then becomes a defense
against such anxiety.

The use of anxiety as a research variable in experimental
investigations was first conducted within the construct of the
drive theory formulated by Hull. Several instruments have been
designed to measure anxiety defined in this manner. Castaneda,
McCandless, and Palermo *(2)* have adapted the Taylor Manifest
Anxiety Scale for use with elementary children. This form has
been designated as the Children's Manifest Anxiety Scale.

Experimental studies utilizing this scale revealed that high
and very low levels of anxiety generally tend to depress learning. High levels of anxiety have been observed to facilitate
performance on simple tasks whereas it becomes debilitating as
the difficulty of the task was increased. Within the school
setting, the effects of manifest anxiety in children have been
demonstrated by McCandless and Castaneda *(6)* who found that
high levels of anxiety tended to have a greater debilitating effect
upon complex skills such as reading and arithmetic as compared to skills such as spelling.

Feldhusen and Klausmeier *(3)* investigated the effects of
anxiety, defined as a generalized and diffuse fear response,
upon various areas of school achievement. These investigators
used the Children's Manifest Anxiety Scale to study a
population of 120 fifth-grade children divided into three groups
of low, average, and high intelligence levels. Correlations of -.48
and -.38 between CMAS scores and reading scores were

reported for boys and girls, respectively.

Grimes *(5)* studied the reading achievement of two groups of third-grade children, utilizing the variables of (1) toilet training stress, (2) compulsivity, (3) manifest anxiety, and (4) intelligence. One group of children was located in a school whose curriculum provided a highly structured type of beginning reading instruction. This approach was predominantly a phonics type of program which, according to Grimes, was low in perceptual ambiguity of cues. The second group attended a different school where they received beginning instruction that was relatively unstructured and high in perceptual ambiguity of cues. The second approach to reading instruction was termed by Grimes as the "whole word method."

The principal finding reported by Grimes pertained to the differential performances between the high anxious subjects that were subjected to the two different methods of reading instruction. He found that the high anxious subjects enrolled in highly structured curriculum obtained significantly higher scores on a test of reading achievement than did the high anxious subjects who had received highly unstructured reading instruction.

The concept of test anxiety proffered by Sarason as a research variable is formulated as a psychoanalytical construct. Sarason described test anxiety as a conscious "danger signal" which alerts the individual to external, situational threats, whereas Spence and Hull defined anxiety in terms of drive or motivation. Such danger signals, according to Sarason, are associated not only with the immediate situational stimuli but also with unconscious elements of previously unresolved conflicts. Sarason designated the early, pre-school, parent-child relationships as being the principal source of such conflicts.

Situations within the school setting which may evoke responses for a child are those where the teacher is perceived as an authoritarian figure whose principal role is to evaluate the adequacy of the child's performance. Class discussions, oral reading at the reading circle, and spelling tests are examples of common classroom activities which may constitute anxiety-provoking threats to some children. Such reactions toward evaluation, in addition to being disproportionately strong, are, according to Sarason, an extension of the evaluative situations which the child has previously experienced within the home (8:12).

Sarason has reported low, negative correlations between TASC scores and reading scores for children in grades two through five. When control for "excessive lie scores" was exercised, Sarason obtained correlations between TASC scores and reading achievement scores ranging from –.232 in Grade Two to –.412 in Grade Four. The increase in the size of the negative correlations was predicted by Sarason who reasoned that children at the higher levels would encounter a greater number of tests and testlike situations (8:128).

Clifford *(4)* used the Test Anxiety Scale for Children in studying the effects of test anxiety upon reading rate, comprehension, and the flexibility of reading rate among fourth-grade boys. She found that high levels of test anxiety were significantly related with low reading rate and low comprehension scores.

This writer *(9)* has used the Test Anxiety Scale for Children to study the acquisition of word recognition skills among second-grade children. Significant differences in word recognition test scores were observed between the group of children who were described as being high in test anxiety on the basis of their TASC scores and the group of children who were described as being "not-high" in test anxiety.

IMPLICATIONS FOR CLASSROOM PRACTICES

Perhaps the principal implication of the anxiety literature is that it demonstrates for the classroom teacher that it is not only the child with the "obvious" emotional problem who may have difficulty in learning to read due to personality reasons. The research suggests that anxiety may play a critical role in the learning processes of the test anxious child. Such a child is not typically the "seriously disturbed" child nor is he necessarily even the unruly "discipline case." More often, the anxious child is one who is withdrawn, who sometimes feels helpless, and who at times is very dependent upon the teacher.

Another implication is that the construct of test anxiety enables the classroom teacher to understand better her specific relationship to the child and his learning problem. In dealing with the test anxious child, whether in the classroom or in the remedial reading clinic, the teacher must first devote considerable effort in developing a relationship in which the child will feel that his "adequacy" is not threatened.

Similarly, the notion of anxiety is pertinent to the problem of reading readiness. Traditionally, there have been two general approaches for developing readiness for reading. One is to allow more time for maturation to occur while the other approach provides for specific types of training. Where anxiety contributes to the lack of readiness, it seems unlikely that either of the two traditional approaches is appropriate. Instead, the solution would lie principally in the development of the teacher-child relationship. The highly anxious child will be ready to learn how to read only when he feels that his adequacy is not threatened by the interpersonal nature of the learning situation.

BIBLIOGRAPHY

1. Blanchard, Phyliss, "Psychogenic Factors in Some Cases of Reading Disability," *American Journal of Orthopsychiatry,* 5:361-74, 1935.
2. Castaneda, Alfred, Boyd R. McCandless and David S. Palermo, "The Children's Form of the Manifest Anxiety Scale," *Child Development,* 27:317-26, 1956.
3. Feldhusen, John F. and Herbert J. Klausmeier, "Anxiety, Intelligence, and Achievement in Children of Low, Average and High Intelligence," *Child Development,* 33:403-409, 1962.
4. Clifford, Edith M., "Test Anxiety, Reading Rate, and Task Experience," an unpublished study, mimeographed, 1964 (?).
5. Grimes, Jesse W., *The Interaction of Certain Pupil Personality Characteristics With Methods of Teaching Reading in Determining Primary Grade Achievement,* unpublished dissertation, Harvard University, 1958.
6. McCandless, Boyd R. and Albert Castaneda, "Anxiety in Children, School Achievement, and Intelligence," *Child Development,* 27:379-391, 1956.
7. Lighthall, Frederick F., *Anxiety As Related to Thinking and Forgetting,* What Research Says to the Teacher, Number 30. Washington, D. C. National Education Association, 1964.
8. Sarason, Seymour B. and others, *Anxiety in Elementary School Children,* New York: John Wiley and Sons, Inc., 1960.
9. Simula, Vernon L., *An Investigation of the Effects of Test Anxiety and Perceptual Rigidity Upon Word Recognition Skill of Second Grade Children,* unpublished dissertation, Indiana University, 1964.

JANET W. LERNER

A Thorn by Any Other Name:
Dyslexia or Reading Disability

Are there any readers of this book who haven't repeatedly used, heard, or read the term dyslexia in the past several years? Yet how many of us really know much or have thought deeply about it? "A little learning is a dangerous thing!" This article should be read in conjunction with the following one by Natchez.

In what ways is this article related to the preceding one by Isom? Do you know what some of the commonly accepted symptoms of dyslexia are? What do you make of the fact that dyslexia is defined in so many ways and attributed to so many different causes? Does it surprise you that the field of medicine would attempt to ascribe a single etiological factor as causal while educators seek a combination of causes? What differences in points of view and training could account for this fact? Do you know of any diagnostic instruments, instructional techniques, or materials supposedly for specific use with dyslexics?

The label, *dyslexia*, is appearing with increasing frequency in professional circles and before the general public.

The professional organization that concerns itself mainly with the field of reading, the International Reading Association, has become aware of dyslexia. While this word was not used in the title of any of the annual conference meetings from 1960 to 1967, dyslexia was part of the title of five different sessions of the 1968 conference. The multi-disciplinary journal, *The Journal of Learning Disabilities,* devoted an entire recent issue to dyslexia. The editor noted that dyslexia has become so

From *Elementary English*, 48 (January 1971), pp. 75-80. Copyright © 1971 by the National Council of Teachers of English. Reprinted by permission of the publisher and Janet W. Lerner.

respectable that "it now qualifies for inclusion in society's 'blue book' of medico-educational terminology" (March, 1968, p. 45).

The layman, as well as the professional, is being confronted with the term, *dyslexia*. A recent column in the *New York Times* (February 5, 1968) reported that reversals and inversions were among the symptoms "of a little understood learning disability called dyslexia," affecting as much as 15 per cent of American school children. The article continued:

> Although dyslexia — derived from the Greek for "difficulty in reading" — was first identified more than 70 years ago, it has not been considered a serious impediment to reading until very recently.

There is little doubt that professionals in the field of reading, language arts, and learning disabilities will be questioned about the phenomenon of dyslexia. Questions must be clarified. What is dyslexia? Have scholars in the field of reading been aware of dyslexia as a factor in reading failure? What theoretical frameworks led some diagnosticians to use the term *dyslexia*, and others to prefer the term, *reading disability*? The purpose of this paper is to raise and discuss these questions.

WHAT IS DYSLEXIA?

A review of the literature reveals that the word, *dyslexia*, is currently being used in a variety of ways by different authors. Its diverse definitions include a) evidence of an etiology of brain damage, b) the observation of behavioral manifestations of central nervous system dysfunctions, c) the indication of a genetic or inherited cause of the reading problem, d) the inclusion of a general language disability along with the reading problem, e) the presence of a syndrome of naturational lag, f) a synonym for reading retardation, and g) the description of a child who has been unable to learn to read through the regular classroom methods.

The quotations below illustrate these diverse definitions.

Brain damage	Brain damage can obviously produce loss of an ability to read (alexia) in an adult and prevent learning ability (dyslexia) in a child (Bryant, 1963, p.144).

Brain impairment (sometimes)	Dyslexia is a partial inability to read or to understand what one reads silently or aloud. The condition is usually, but not always, associated with brain impairment (Frierson and Barbe, 1967, p. 491).
Brain dysfunction	Our concern is with the group who cannot read because of a dysfunction in the brain. This disorder has been designated word blindness, developmental dyslexia, dyslexia. These designations concerned children with normal intelligence and no significant emotional disturbance, but who could not read (Johnson and Myklebust, 1967, p. 147).
Neurological dysfunction	Dyslexia is a genetic, neurological dysfunction, uncomplicated by other factors. The dyslexic child is unable to perceive the word of symbols through his senses and record what he sees and hears without distortion (Money, 1962, p. 48).
Genetic or hereditary factor	...there exists a "vulnerable family" syndrome. It is these families with specific generic characteristics, which are most likely to produce a child who will suffer the handicap of a learning disability....an inherited anomaly, which alone may cause some forms of learning disorders, i.e., dyslexia...(McGlannan, 1968, p. 190).
Psycho-linguistic breakdown	Dyslexia is being re-examined as a concept and reinterpreted as a breakdown in psycholinguistic functioning...(McLeod, 1966, p. 186).
Reading disability	...children who are dyslexic, that is, children who are of average intelligence or above who are finding it difficult to learn to read....The four sub species of dyslexia are primary emotional communicative dyslexia, minimal neurological dysfunctional dyslexia, genetic dyslexia, and dyslexia due to social or cultural or educational deprivation (Bannatyne, 1966, pp. 67-68).
Defective reading	Dyslexia...simply means that there is something wrong with the person's reading (Harris, 1963, p. 129).

> Dyslexia means defective reading.... Dyslexia
> is a specific condition of primary con-
> stitutional reading difficulty which may occur
> electively and which, in its pure form, differs
> distinctively from reading difficulties of other
> endogenous or exogenous origins (Eichen-
> wald, 1967, p. 31).

This large and diverse range of current uses and definitions suggests that an examination of the historical development of the term, dyslexia, would be useful. The literature reveals two almost independent strands of development of thought. One strand is found in the literature on reading which developed from the fields of medicine, psychiatry, neurology and speech. Much of this literature originated in Europe. The other discussion of dyslexia is to be found in the writings of educators and psychologists, particularly in the field of reading, and originated largely in the United States. A brief review of each of these two strands of literature follows.

STRAND 1: THE MEDICAL PERSPECTIVE

In 1896, Morgan, an English physician, described a condition he called "congenital word-blindness" in a fourteen-year-old boy with extreme reading difficulties in spite of good arithmetic abilities. The report, published in the *British Medical Journal*, attributed a neurological etiology to congenital word-blindness (Morgan, 1896).

In defining word-blindness some years later in 1917, Hinshelwood, an ophthalmologist in Scotland, concluded that it was a pathological condition due to a disorder of the visual centers of the brain which produced difficulty in interpreting printed and written language. He further stated that the condition was not due to visual or intellectual defects; yet ordinary teaching methods had failed to teach the child to read (Hinshelwood, 1917).

Schmidt, in 1918, used the terms "developmental alexia" or "dyslexia" to signify cases of congenital word-blindness (Schmidt, 1918). Schmidt's rationale for the term, *dyslexia,* had its roots in the term, *alexia,* defined as a loss of ability to read because of a known injury to the brain, such as a cerebral stroke. Alexia, also called acquired word-blindness, occurs in an adult who has already learned to read. Making a few assumptions, then, Schmidt assigned the term, *developmental dyslexia,* to cases of children who were having difficulty in learning to read. The hypothesis was formulated that in cases of dyslexia or developmental word-blindness the same areas of the brain had been damaged as in cases of adults with alexia or acquired word-blindness. Such children were described by Schmidt as unable to learn to read although they were normally endowed mentally and without defects of vision or other physical factors that would interfere with the process of learning to read.

In 1937 Orton, an American neurologist, broadened the concept of dyslexia to a specific language disability and developed a theory based on the lack of the establishment of cerebral dominance as a cause of language and reading difficulty (Orton, 1937). Orton, objecting to the term *word-blindness,* coined the word, *strephosymbolia,* meaning twisted symbols, to describe the problem of reversals and inversions.

Working in Sweden, Hallgren, 1950, made a statistical analysis of 276 cases called specific dyslexia and concluded that it is a monohybrid autosomal dominant heredity characteristic. According to Hallgren, the dyslexia pattern is inherited and the condition is genetic in nature (Hallgren, 1950).

Hermann, a Danish neurologist, in 1961 attempted to establish a medical explanation for extreme reading handicaps, which he called word-blindness or congenital dyslexia (Hermann, 1961).

Money reported on symposiums held at Johns Hopkins University Medical School in 1962 and 1966 which met for the purpose of evolving a syndrome of dyslexia (Money, 1962 and Money, 1966).

An English neurologist, Critchley, in 1964 continued the search for a concept of dyslexia by endeavoring to detect common symptoms of the group of learners with reading problems (Critchley, 1964). After critically examining such etiological theories as congenital language disorders, brain damage, and cerebral dominance, he concluded that there is no single clinical feature which can be accepted as "pathognomonic."

Working within the medical and speech schools at Northwestern University, Johnson and Myklebust concluded that dyslexia is a reading disorder which results from a dysfunction in the brain (Johnson and Myklebust, 1967). These authors view dyslexia as not only a reading disorder, but as part of a basic language and learning disability, and as a disorder of symbolic behavior. They subdivide the condition into auditory dyslexia and visual dyslexia.

In summary, the medical perspective of the phenomenon called dyslexia has been under study for about seventy years, and over 20,000 books, articles and papers have been published on the subject (Eichenwald, 1967). These studies have sought for a common behavior pattern of all dyslexic children and for clear-cut evidence of a neurological etiology. To date, conclusive evidence is still lacking from both a statistical and pathological standpoint to clearly isolate and identify the dyslexic child.

STRAND 2: THE EDUCATIONAL PERSPECTIVE

The other group of scholars concerned with the problem reader and reading problems comes from the disciplines of education, psychology, and reading. Although these writers are fully aware of the theoretical views of those scholars who seek and perceive a dyslexia syndrome, they question the operational value of this view. The workers within the educational framework are concerned with children who display symptoms which appear to be identical to those symptoms described as dyslexic by workers within the medical framework of Strand 1. However, they see insufficient evidence to place such symptoms within a diagnostic entity called dyslexia. In addition, the reading educators see the label of dyslexia as confusing and adding little or no knowledge of either diagnostic or therapeutic value.

The early reading studies of Monroe (1932) and Robinson (1946), which were careful investigations of the causes of reading failure utilizing the research available at those periods, discussed the neurological factor but concluded that early theories had not been strongly established.

The indirect methods of investigation have been used in the study of most reported cases of alexia, or word-blindness. The neurologists apparently have noted the symptoms, ruled out all other causes, and made a diagnosis of alexia or word-blindness, since no other cause could be located. Differences of opinion may exist and may not be proved correct or incorrect because the direct approach is not possible (Robinson, 1946, p. 38).

In 1958 Vernon, an English psychologist, examined the available evidence of congenital word-blindness and cerebral dominance and found "no clear evidence as to the existence of any innate organic condition which causes reading disabilities" (Vernon, 1958). Further, she asserted that the term, *dyslexia*, was unacceptable because it is not comparable to alexia, the loss of reading ability produced by cortical injury.

Harris, 1961, stated that early views of reading disabilities assumed that when the child showed no observed differences of general mental development or health, the reading difficulties were the result of brain defects which made it difficult or impossible for the child to remember and identify printed words (Harris, 1961). Harris felt this hypothesis held little value for the reading clinician.

> Imposing technical terms were proposed . . . dyslexia . . . by those medical men who looked for a fundamental defect or deficiency in the children's nervous system as the reason for his failure to learn to read. . . . it seems probable at the present time that only a small proportion of the reading disabilities to be found in the schools are of this type (Harris, 1961, p. 229).

Bond and Tinker also view the concept of dyslexia as having little diagnostic and prognostic value (Bond and Tinker, 1957).

> There is such a thing as an acquired defect in adults known as word-blindness or alexia that is attributable to a pathological condition in certain areas of the brain . . . . The child who has experienced extreme difficulty in learning to recognize printed and written language exhibits symptoms analogous to disabilities caused by known cerebral lesions in acquired word-blindness. Because of this, Hinshelwood has, in the opinion of most authorities, wrongly and unwisely, applied the term congenital word-blindness to very young nonreaders. His attempt to distinguish two varieties of word-blindness is not of value to students of reading deficiencies (p. 99).

In a later work Bond and Tinker maintain that it is practically impossible to distinguish "specific dyslexia" cases from others of severe reading disability and suggest that the "clinical worker may question the value of the term" (Bond and Tinker, 1967, p. 19).

SUMMARY

In summary, scholars from the field of education have found it difficult to accept the term, *dyslexia*, as a diagnostic entity. They reason that when no other cause for the reading problem could be found, workers within the medical perspective made an assumption, based on a leap of faith, and assigned brain injury and neurological dysfunction as the single cause of the reading failure. Although the educational perspective workers preferred not to use the dyslexia concept, the research from this field did probe such basic issues as the ways that different children learn to read and the manner in which individual children perceive the world (Goins, 1958). Because researchers from the field of reading generally conclude that a single cause of a reading problem cannot be ascertained, they examine emotional, social, psychological, cultural, and language factors along with the neurological in their attempt to diagnose the causes of reading disability. Moreover, this group concludes that the case of an adult who has lost his ability to read through cortical damage (alexia) cannot be likened to the child who is unable to learn the reading process.

IMPLICATIONS OF THE DIFFERENCES IN PERSPECTIVE

What are some of the basic implications of the differences in these two perspectives? For the purposes of discussion, the scholars working within the framework of Strand 1 will be called the *medical perspective* while those working within the framework of Strand 2 will be called the *educational perspective*.

1. While the scholars working within the medical perspective search for a single etiological factor as causal, the scholars from the educational perspective seek a combination of causes, feeling that it is not likely that a single factor can be shown to be causal.

2. The educators are likely to place greater emphasis on the developmental sequence of reading skills with more search for the child's break on the developmental reading sequence. The

medically oriented student is likely to place greater focus on the language related areas such as speech, oral language, and on other related disabilities such as arithmetic, perception, motor development, and social skills.

3. For the educator, alexia, or the loss of reading skill in the case of an adult is different from the inability to learn to read in the case of a child. Therefore, the term, *dyslexia*, is not generally used among this group. They emphasize the difficulty of differentiating "maturational lag" from central nervous system dysfunction.

4. Educators see the diagnosis of dyslexia as lacking operationality in that it does not lead to appropriate teaching strategies. After the diagnosis of dyslexia is made, one must still investigate what reading skills are lacking, how the child best learns, find appropriate materials, etc. The diagnosis of dyslexia alone provides few clues as to the appropriate treatment and remedial measures.

5. While the medically oriented clinician is likely to focus chiefly on the handicapped child, emphasizing individual treatment, the educationally oriented worker is likely to perceive a broader role and function within the school, devoting a portion of his time and energy to the developmental reading program of the entire school in seeking preventive measures.

The conclusion to be drawn is not an argument for or against the approach of either discipline. Each researcher should study the child with reading problems in terms of his own discipline and its framework and tools. Each discipline has built a substantial body of literature, but neither is benefiting from the work and foundation that has already been made by the other. As a consequence, in tracing the literature, an inescapable observation is that the literature of one field is almost completely ignored by the other. Few authorities have been able to bridge the gap between the two fields, speaking in a voice that is meaningful to both while utilizing the framework and findings of each.

Our challenge is to strengthen links between these two perspectives by encouraging channels of communication. The plea to be made is to forget labels and begin to work together.

REFERENCES

Bannatyne, Alex. "The Etiology of Dyslexia and the Color Phonics System," *International Approach to Learning Disabilities of Children and Youth.* Conference of the Association for Children with Learning Disabilities, 1966.

Bond, Guy and Miles Tinker. *Reading Difficulties: Their Diagnosis and Correction.* N. Y.: Appleton-Century-Crofts, 1957. Also 2nd ed., 1967.

Bryant, N. Dale. "Learning Disabilities in Reading," *Reading As An Intellectual Activity,* International Reading Association Annual Conference Proceedings, 1963.

Critchley, MacDonald. *Development Dyslexia.* Springfield Ill.: Chas. C. Thomas, 1964.

Eichenwald, Heinz F. "The Pathology of Reading Disorders: Psychophysiological Factors," *Corrective Reading in the Elementary Classroom,* (ed.) M. Johnson and R. Kress. Newark, Dela: International Reading Association, 1967.

Frierson, Edward C. and Walter B. Barbe, *Educating Children with Learning Disabilities.* N.Y.: Appleton-Century-Crofts, 1967.

Goins, J. *Visual Perception and Early Progress.* Supplementary Educational Monographs, No. 87. Chicago: University of Chicago Press, 1958.

Hallgren, B. "Specific Dyslexia: A Clinical and Genetic Study," *Acta Psychiat. Neurol* (Supp. 65), 1950, pp. 1-287.

Harris, Albert. *How to Increase Reading Ability.* N.Y.: David McKay, 1961.

———. "The Diagnosis of Reading Disabilities," in *Readings on Reading Instruction* (ed.) H. Harris, New York: David McKay, 1963. 129-133. 1963.

Hermann, Knud. *Reading Disability: A Medical Study of Word-Blindness and Related Handicaps,* Springfield, Ill.: Chas. C. Thomas, 1961.

Hinshelwood, James. *Congenital Word-Blindness.* London: H.K. Lewis, Ltd., 1917.

Johnson, Doris J. and Helmer Myklebust. *Learning Disabilities: Educational Principles and Practices. N.Y.: Grune & Stratton, 1967.*

Journal of Learning Disabilities, March, 1968.

New York Times, February 5, 1968.

MacGlannan, Frances K. "Familiar Characteristics of Genetic Dyslexia: Preliminary Report from a Pilot Study," *Journal of Learning Disabilities,* March, 1968.

McLeod, John. "Psychological and Psycholinguistic Aspects of Severe Reading Disability in Children: Some Experimental Studies," *International Approach to Learning Disabilities of Children and Youth.* Conference of the Association for Children with Learning Disabilities, 1964.

Money, John (ed.) *Reading Disability: Progress and Research Needs in Dyslexia.* Baltimore: Johns Hopkins Press, 1962.

————. *The Disabled Reader: Education of the Dyslexic Child.* Baltimore: Johns Hopkins Press, 1966.

Monroe, Marion. *Children Who Cannot Read.* Chicago: University of Chicago Press, 1932.

Morgan, W. P. "A Case of Congenital Word-Blindness," *British Medical Journal,* II, November, 1896, 1378.

Orton, Samuel T. *Reading, Writing and Speech Problems in Children.* N.Y.: W. W. Norton, Co., 1937.

Robinson, Helen M. *Why Pupils Fail in Reading.* Chicago: University of Chicago Press, 1946.

Schmitt, Clara. "Developmental Alexia," *Elementary School Journal,* May, 1918, pp. 680-700 and 757-69.

Vernon M. *Backwardness in Reading.* London: Cambridge University Press, 1957.

GLADYS NATCHEZ

Is There Such a Thing as Dyslexia?

Argument and debate are nothing new to education (witness the continuing 25 year debate on phonics!). Thus it should be no surprise that something as amorphous as dyslexia should have created great controversy. This paper takes the point of view that reading difficulties are more likely the result of a complex interplay between numerous variables than the result of a single specific factor.

After reading this article, how would you answer the questions asked in the title — yes, no, or maybe? How might Isom (see article earlier in this section) answer the question asked in the title? To what extent do you think children suffering to some degree from a dysfunction of the central nervous system would be afflicted with psychological problems such as those displayed by Baxter and Trevor in this paper? Are these typical or atypical children? Just assuming that Natchez's contention is valid, what implications has this for teachers? And how does this contention relate to the article in Part Six by Robinson on auxiliary services?

The term *dyslexia* is used by many as a catchall for various kinds of reading difficulty. However, most authorities use it to designate a reading disorder that results from a dysfunction of the central nervous system or an actual brain lesion *(6, 10).* Confusion occurs because there are children with reading disabilities which are caused by brain damage and others with brain damage who show no difficulty learning to read. Then too, there are conditions which are closely associated with brain injury, such as neurological disorganization, maturational lag, structural brain deviations, and the like, which may or may not

Reprinted from *Current Issues in Reading,* Nila B. Smith, ed. (Newark, Delaware: International Reading Association, 1969), pp. 384-391, by permission of Gladys Natchez and the International Reading Association.

affect language development and reading. Determining the presence of frank brain damage is comparatively easy, but it becomes increasingly delicate to distinguish minimal cerebral injury as distinct from delayed development *(13)*. This identity by no means ends the confusion. For purposes of brevity, it is advantageous to classify factors that impair learning into four major categories: those which show central nervous system disorders; those caused by impairment of the peripheral nervous system; those due to inadequate socioeducational conditions; and those resulting from psychological disturbance.*

The substance of this paper concerns the interaction of these forces. Although it is conceded that there is indeed such a thing as dyslexia, its course is influenced significantly by the interrelationships of various causative components. The interaction of these components is far greater in complexity than are any of the elements taken individually *(1, 8, 15, 16)*. Thus the important question in dealing with dyslexia is how the reading disorder is embedded in and affected by the tangential pressures surrounding it.

Despite the wealth of investigations and the recognition of multiple causation, few researchers have shown the intricate interaction of separate components. This lack is due partly to the complexity of the problem and partly because most children have suffered at least one or more years of failure before they come for thorough examination. By this time the factors are so intertwined that we do not know which ones take precedence. For instance, did the neurological difficulty cause the failure which in turn caused emotional disturbance? Or did the psychological problem intensify the developmental difficulties? Did exposure to poor teaching impede the integration of cognitive factors? Did unfavorable home and school conditions heighten the conflicts in an unusually sensitive child?

Let us examine two boys in first grade (age 6, IQ average) who had similar diagnoses and follow them to sixth and seventh grades, respectively. Both boys were referred by their separate schools for psychological evaluation. It so happens that, in turn, they were referred to the identical neurologist. Both had normal intelligence. To summarize the psychological examination

---

*Intellectual deficits are not considered here since reading difficulty is defined in terms of potential; i.e., achievement which is significantly below intellectual ability constitutes a reading disability.

briefly, both boys had a preponderance of intrapsychic conflict, poor self image, and repressed anger.

Results from the neurologist's examination showed that each suffered from a dysfunction of the central nervous system which affected visual abilities and motor coordination. One of the boys, whom we shall call Trevor, displayed difficulty with auditory discrimination as well.

When the parents of the first boy, called Baxter for convenience, were apprised of the results, they were disbelieving and angry. They blamed the school for his learning difficulty. The mother said that she had no trouble with him in his early years at home. She refused to have him undertake psychotherapy (although she did enter analysis herself) and considered it the school's responsibility to teach him.

The school did what it could; the reading specialist worked individually with Baxter; his classroom teacher devoted extra time to him each day. When he was in third grade and remained at a beginning reading level, he was placed in a special class for slow learners. His mother kept complaining, but the school staff claimed that they were doing their best. By seventh grade, Baxter was reading at third-grade level. He had been uncooperative through the years, but by December of seventh grade, he rebelled with fury. He claimed that he was not a mental case or an idiot and was simply not going to attend the special class any longer. The boy went through a period of truancy which forced the parents into further consultation. After weighing many alternatives, Baxter and his parents decided that he should go away to boarding school. When last contacted, he was in eighth grade reading at fifth-grade level. His attitudes had improved, and the teachers were optimistic regarding further progress.

Let us leave Baxter for a moment and take a look at Trevor. When his parents learned about the nature of his psychological and neurological involvement, they became apprehensive. They had high aspirations for the boy. The father was a doctor; the mother, a school teacher. Although nothing had been mentioned regarding future achievement, they worried that he would not be able to complete college. Despite several counseling sessions (they had postponed the idea of psychotherapy for Trevor or themselves), they continued to apply subtle pressure for achievement. However, they were genuinely concerned and went a long way toward understanding Trevor and lending their support. By second grade, he had accomplished little, and they decided to enroll him in a Montessori school. Here he made decided progress which strengthened him academically and emotionally. This success in turn pleased the parents who relaxed their pressure to a great degree. Trevor continued to make solid progress through the years, and now in sixth grade he is reading at approximately sixth-grade level.

In examining these two cases in a little greater depth, we may begin to see the interplay among constitutional, psychological, and environmental forces. First, we can infer that the similar organic and psychological condition in both boys restricted their learning process, although Trevor had the additional problem of auditory difficulty which Baxter did not. How much or in what way did the parents' attitudes and the school's role contribute other features?

In Baxter's case, his mother found it most difficult to accept him or even allow any expression of individuality on Baxter's part. The mother herself reported that she felt so guilty toward him that she forbade him to criticize her. Part of the guilt seemed centered around her reluctance to have another child. From the inception of her pregnancy, she wished she were rid of him. In his early years, her resentment dwindled. He proved to be little trouble as a youngster, and she was able to control him to her own satisfaction. When he became a school problem, however, her pent-up resentment returned. Despite her discussions in psychotherapy, she continued to reject and rail at him. In a way, he fulfilled her forebodings that she never should have "born him in the first place." This play on words is intriguing for one might well have wondered from the start how long Baxter could have borne her abuse.

With regard to his teachers who seemed to make appropriate provision for Baxter's difficulties, his parents continued their criticism of school policy. This act may have caused sufficient antagonism among the teachers (without their necessarily being aware of it) to cause minimally effective instruction. All these forces intensified Baxter's problem and undoubtedly interfered with optimum use of those assets which he possessed.

In Trevor's case, parental and school attitudes were more

benign. Despite subtle pressure for progress, his parents were willing to cooperate with the school and to help Trevor when he needed it. They kept a watchful eye on him and did not sabotage the teachers' efforts. These factors seemed to mitigate the learning problem, and by sixth grade he was able to achieve in school commensurate with his ability.

In comparing the two boys, one could say that the attitudes of Baxter's parents toward him and the school resulted in a serious hindrance. Even though he had somewhat less central nervous system involvement and his mother consented to undertake psychotherapy to clarify her attitudes, Baxter made very little progress through the years. In contrast, Trevor benefitted from a more favorable management of his problems.

There is no question that this summary is a simplified version of all the possible interactions. Certainly Baxter's parents wanted the best for him, too. Indeed, in reporting on his early years, they waxed enthusiastic about his lovableness and charm. But they could not tolerate his school failure. For whatever reasons, they could not demonstrate the magnanimity and understanding that Trevor's parents did when this failure occurred. Without question, there must have been many moments when Trevor's parents lost their patience and hope. But the fact remains that two boys with comparable problems showed a marked contrast in achievement, the one remaining a school failure for years and the other reaching a reasonable degree of proficiency.

Needless to say, this sparse presentation is, of necessity, suggestive rather than conclusive. Many other possibilities can accelerate or minimize a reading difficulty. One major factor in cases of neurological impairment concerns the discovery of regeneration of neurons within the central nervous system, even in adult tissue *(9)*. This factor suggests that the reading problem can diminish through the organism's growth. There is also the matter of compensation. Many investigators suggest that the organism can bypass inadequate components and develop competent ways of functioning despite handicap *(3, 7)*. Finally, the growth of the child is a complex, dynamic process subject to constant change. Not only does the organism gain in dexterity and integration, the nature of development changes. As Murphy *(11)* puts it: "Man, as a result of...discovering more and more about his nature is undergoing a change himself."

Likewise Vygotsky *(18)* states that development is "not an innate, natural form of behavior but is determined by a historical cultural process...."

The significance for any child, including one with brain injury, maturational lag, or emotional disturbance is obvious: one can begin to understand him only by being cognizant of the interaction between organic components, the child's own personal or psychological world, and the environment in which he lives *(14)*.

Although investigations of the interaction between organic factors and the individual's psychological and cultural environment are few, two recent studies address themselves to the problem. One by Craviolo, et al *(2)* investigated the relationship between nutritional growth and neurointegrative development. It was assumed that significant lags in maturation of the nervous system and in mental development may occur in children who have suffered from malnutrition in early childhood. The investigation considered that intersensory performance, as measured by visual, haptic, and kinesthetic sense modalities, would have a significant association with social impoverishment. The striking result was that although such impoverishment was kept constant, neurointegrative function was significantly better developed in those children whose mothers had the higher educational level. Apparently the greater desire of better educated mothers to nurture their children more fully and to resist those traditional customs which were detrimental to the child's growth enabled their children to develop a higher degree of intersensory functioning. This conclusion implies that their children would have least difficulty in school learning.

The other study investigated individuality in infants. Thomas, et al *(17)* examined eighty infants during their first two years of life to determine whether children are discriminably different in their behavior patterning and, if so, whether this pattern continues to characterize the child later on. Such traits as activity, adaptability, approach, intensity, distractibility, and so on were observed. They found evidence of identifiable primary patternings, but these patternings were in turn reactive to the particular environment. It should come as no surprise that it was considerably easier for the mother to care for a responsive, cheerful child than one who was moody, cranky, and aloof. Naturally, the opposite obtained also; enthusiastic, concerned mothers fostered satisfied children. Results of such interaction was particularly spectacular in sets of twins where the mother's response to the infant was to a considerable degree a function of the child's primary characteristics which at the same time influenced his parent's immediate and persistent attitude toward him. The circular result needs no elaboration.

These two studies plus the growing body of information on child development *(5, 12)* suggest that the interaction of constitutional, psychological, and environmental factors is of primary concern. To see either neurological involvement, psychological disturbance, or environmental stress as the major cause of reading disability would be to assume causality and to ignore coincidence. To be unaware of the ubiquity of neurological and psychological signs in all children with or without learning difficulties or to ignore that some children with reading difficulty manifest a minimum of obvious symptoms is gross misinterpretation of the data *(4)*.

It would seem sensible to view the reading difficulty as a symptom which may be due to a variety of factors, such as, brain dysfunction, biological variation, deviate maturation, developmental delay, emotional disturbance, or deficient socialization. In any child, some, any, or all of these factors may be acting in concert or in conflict. In most cases, it will be impossible to assign etiology with any degree of certitude, particularly if the presence of interaction among components is ignored.

REFERENCES

1. Bond, Guy, and Miles Tinker. *Reading Difficulties: Their Diagnosis and Correction.* New York: Appleton-Century-Crofts, 1967.
2. Craviolo, Joaquin, Elsa DeLicardie, and Herbert Birch. "Nutrition, Growth and Neurointegrative Development: An Experimental and Ecologic Study," *Pediatrics,* Vol. 38, No. 2, Part 2 (August 1966), 319-372.
3. Goldstein, Kurt. *Human Nature in the Light of Psychopathology.* New York: Shoken Press, 1940, 1963, Chapter 5.
4. Werry, John. "The Diagnosis, Etiology and Treatment of Hyperactivity in Children," in Jerome Hellmuth (Ed.), *Learning Disorders, 3.* Seattle: Special Child Publication (in press).

5. Hunt, J. McVicker. "Experience and the Development of Motivation: Some Reinterpretations," in Gladys Natchez (Ed.), *Children with Reading Problems:* Basic Books, 1968.

6. Johnson, Doris and Helmer Myklebust. *Learning Disabilities.* New York: Grune Stratton, 1967, 156ff.

7. Luria, A. R. *Higher Cortical Functions in Man.* New York: Basic Books, 1966, 23-30.

8. Malmquist, Eve. *Factors Related to Reading Disability in First Grades of the Elementary School.* Stockholm, Sweden: Amquist and Wiksell, 1958.

9. Masland, Richard, Seymour Sarason, and Thomas Gladwin. *Mental Subnormality.* New York: Basic Books, 1958, 137.

10. Money, John. *The Disabled Reader.* Baltimore: Johns Hopkins Press, 1966, 377.

11. Murphy, Gardner. *Personality: A Biosocial Approach to Origins and Structure.* New York: Harper, 1947.

12. Olson, Willard. *Child Development.* Boston: Heath, 1959.

13. Rabinovitch, Ralph. "Neurological and Psychiatric Considerations in Reading Retardation," Pre-conference institute lecture, International Reading Association. New York City: May 5, 1960 (mimeographed).

14. Rappaport, Sheldon. *Childhood Aphasia and Brain Damage.* Narberth, Pennsylvania: Pathway School, Livingston, 1965, 56ff, 101.

15. Robinson, Helen. *Why Pupils Fail in Reading.* Chicago: University of Chicago Press, 1946.

16. Roswell, Florence, and Gladys Natchez. *Reading Disability: Diagnosis and Treatment.* New York: Basic Books, 1964.

17. Thomas, Alexander, et al. *Behavioral Individuality in Early Childhood.* New York: New York University Press, 1963.

18. Vygotsky, Lev. *Thought and Language.* Cambridge, Massachusetts: M.I.T. Press, 1962, 51.

3

Learning More
About the Child

We must carefully identify those children who most need and can most profit from instruction, comparing them with some set standards. Then we must determine the factors that produced the disability, the specific deficient reading skills, and any enhancing strengths the child has. Finally, we must predict the kind of program likely to be most successful with each child.

Far from being a simple step-by-step sequence, this process is beset by some severe problems. One of these is defining a disabled reader. The definition will determine to a great extent the nature of our entire program, including teacher education, materials, methods, and auxiliary services. The current trend toward using discrepancy between reading potential and reading achievement as the criterion for disability is helpful but overly simplistic.

Determining how much discrepancy exists between the two variables presents another problem: Can we adequately measure these capacities? Poor readers present special problems in the accurate measurement of their general intelligence — often considered the best single indicator of reading capacity. And our best reading achievement tests are intended to test groups, not individuals, and therefore contain a considerable amount of error when used for individual diagnosis. Furthermore, some widely used tests are of questionable validity! All of this indicates that we must know all about the best techniques and instruments available to perform these tasks — including their limitations.

Assessing the cause or causes of the reading problem may require more capabilities and time than teachers have, particularly since there is a scarcity of easily administered, accurate, specialized instruments to help in the task. An interdisciplinary approach is crucial both in the long run and for a large number of students.

The primary concern of the diagnostician is discovering the reader's specific reading deficiencies. The problem is complicated: reading is not a unitary skill and most disabled readers have specific skill weaknesses rather than a general reading deficiency. In addition, reading specialists do not agree on the components of reading. A detailed knowledge of reading skills and instruments designed to measure them are crucial to a teacher's efficient and accurate performance.

Further complicating this process of identification, diagnosis, and prognosis is that it must be highly individualized. Diagnosis that treats all students alike is bound to produce a disproportionate number of failures.

A major flaw in this whole process is that it is *post hoc*; it waits until the child has severe reading difficulties before instituting remediation. Such flagrant disdain for early identification and intervention borders on being inhumane and insensitive to human suffering. We must move toward locating potential reading problems as early as possible. To do this we need techniques that are currently either nonexistent or grossly imperfect.

These are some of the topics this section intends to explore.

ARNOLD ZAESKE

The Validity of Predictive Index Tests in Predicting Reading Failure at the End of Grade One

Our educational system creates many reading problems by failing to adequately consider, understand, and provide for individual differences. Ideally, we should be able to decrease the number of children with severe reading problems by focusing on earlier diagnosis, prevention, and intervention. Even though the findings of this study indicate that we have a long way to go in designing instruments to predict probable reading failure, it seems an important contribution toward sensitizing us to the deficiencies of our current instruments and procedures and to the magnitude of the task we have facing us in making reading a right and not a privilege.

What types of procedures and instruments are you familiar with for screening children for potential reading failure? Do you think the criteria for reading failure were fair and valid? Did the author conclude that the Predictive Index Tests were the best possible means of predicting reading success or failure at the end of first grade? What conclusions can you make about the fact that there were moderate negative correlations between boys' readiness test scores and subsequent reading success? On the basis of this study, would you adopt the Predictive Index Tests for use in your school? As a result of reading this study, are you considering changing the procedures you use for screening first-grade entrants?

From *Reading Difficulties: Diagnosis, Correction, and Remediation*, William K. Durr, ed. (Newark, Delaware: International Reading Association, 1970), pp. 28-33. Reprinted by permission of Arnold Zaeske and the International Reading Association.

The book *Predicting Reading Failure (1)* by Katrina de Hirsch, Jeanette Jefferson Jansky, and William S. Langford was published in 1966. This book contained the Predictive Index Tests that were designed to predict which children of kindergarten age would be unsuccessful in reading, writing, and spelling achievement by the end of second grade. The educational value of these tests rests upon their validity to perform this function. With the aid of a faculty research grant from the University of Massachusetts and with the cooperation of the public school system of Amherst, Massachusetts, this study was undertaken to determine the validity of the Predictive Reading Tests.

The Predictive Reading Tests are comprised of a battery of ten tests: Pencil Use, Bender Visual-Motor Test, Wepman Auditory Discrimination Test, Number of Words Used in a Story Test, Categories Test, Horst Reversal Test, Gates Word-Matching Subtest, Word Recognition Tests I and II, and a Word Reproduction Test. These tests attempt to establish the maturational level of children in various motor, perceptual, and language areas. According to the authors of the tests, children who pass three or fewer of the ten tests are classified as "high-risk" children and are not likely to be developmentally ready for reading instruction. These children are predicted to have a higher probability of academic difficulties in reading, spelling, and writing several years later. The authors recommend that high risk children should be given developmental training in each area of expressed difficulty and, if possible, be enrolled in transitional type classes at the first grade level.

De Hirsch, et al found that Predictive Index Tests had a 91 percent efficiency. It correctly identified ten of eleven children who failed reading and spelling at the end of the second grade from a sampling of fifty-three. It overpredicted to the extent that four children who received a failing score on the Predictive Index Tests were subsequently successful in reading and spelling by the end of the second grade. Overprediction may be a useful practice in providing "preventive measures to a larger population in order to eliminate the possibility of overlooking potential risks."

It seems, however, that the de Hirsch study is in need of replication since the ten Predictive Index Tests were chosen from a group of 37 tests that best predicted reading failure from among 53 subjects. The problem of "shrinkage" may occur when selecting a few measures from many measures when the group is small *(2)*. Statistical data concerning the validity of the Predictive Index Tests needs to be obtained from a new sample due to the shrinkage problem.

The major purpose of the present study was to partially replicate the de Hirsch study with a new and larger sample. It modified that study by comparing the effectiveness of the Predictive Index Tests and the Metropolitan Readiness Test in predicting reading failure at the end of the first grade. The original study based its conclusions on reading failures at the end of the second grade. This study made the assumption that there is a large correlation between those pupils who are failures at the end of the first grade and those pupils who are failures at the end of the second grade. Comparisons can be made with the original study to the extent that this assumption is true.

PROCEDURE

The pupils in first grade classes in Amherst, Massachusetts, during the school year 1967-1968, constituted the sampling used in this study. The pretests were given in September of 1967 and the post-tests in May of 1968. Only ten pupils were lost for statistical purposes from the original sample of 269 tested in September. The pretests administered were the Predictive Index Tests, the Metropolitan Reading Readiness Test, and the Peabody Picture Vocabulary Test. The post-tests included a Teacher Judgment Rating, the Dolch Word List Sampling Test, and the Metropolitan Reading Test. Pupils were considered to be failures in reading if they fell below a critical level score on two of the three post-tests. The critical level scores for the various tests were as follows: pre-primer or lower on the Teacher Judgment Rating, over 35 words missed on the Dolch Word Sampling Test, and a standard score of 40 or lower on the Metropolitan Reading Test.

Five examiners were trained and employed to administer the individual tests, and the two Metropolitan Tests were administered by the classroom teachers. All test results were checked for accuracy and consistency of scoring by the researcher and his graduate assistant, Patricia Douglas. Considerable care was taken in recording test results and checking computer cards for errors.

The Pearson product-moment coefficient was used to compute correlations between pre- and post-tests. The significance of these correlations was obtained by using Hotelling's t test. The Yates chi-square technique was used to test the significance between the Predictive Index Tests and the Metropolitan Readiness Test in predicting success or failure in reading at the end of the first grade.

FINDINGS

1. The Predictive Index Tests and the Metropolitan Readiness Test predicted reading success and failure to a degree significant at the .001 level of significance. The Predictive Index Tests predicted 33 failures while the Metropolitan predicted 23 failures from the sampling of 259 pupils. The Predictive Index Tests overpredicted to the extent that 15 pupils who failed this test subsequently achieved success at the end of the first grade and it underpredicted to the extent that 18 potential achievers subsequently failed. The Metropolitan Readiness Test overpredicted to the extent that no pupils who failed this test subsequently achieved success at the end of the first grade, and it underpredicted to the extent that 28 potential achievers subsequently failed. No significant difference was found between the two tests in their ability to predict success and failure. The Predictive Index Tests were stronger in predicting the number of failures than the Metropolitan Readiness Tests, but it was weaker in predicting the number of success achievers.

		Pretest (Predictive Index Tests)				Pretest (Metropolitan Readiness)	
		Pass	Fail			Pass	Fail
Post-	Pass	193	15	Post-	Pass	208	0
tests	Fail	18	33	tests	Fail	28	23

2. The Predictive Index Tests and the Metropolitan Readiness Test were significantly related to each other at the .001 level of significance as pretests. There were 209 pupils who

had successful achievement on both pretests, 20 who failed both pretests, two who failed the Metropolitan but passed the Predictive Index, and 28 who failed the Predictive Index and passed the Metropolitan. This evidence is an indication of the more conservative nature of the Metropolitan Readiness Test.

		Metropolitan	
		Pass	Fail
Predictive	Pass	209	2
Index	Fail	28	20

3. The Metropolitan Readiness Test correlated .73 with Teacher Judgment, .67 with the Dolch Test, and .68 with the Metropolitan Reading Test. The Predictive Index Tests correlated .55 with the Teacher Judgment, .61 with the Dolch Test, and .63 with the Metropolitan Reading Test. All of these correlations for predicting success in reading achievement at the end of the first grade were significant at the .01 level of significance, with the exception of a .02 level of significance between the Predictive Reading Tests and the Dolch Test.

4. The correlations between the Metropolitan Readiness Test and the Predictive Index Tests in predicting reading success were not significantly different for the Dolch Test and the Metropolitan Reading Test at the .01 level of significance. A significant difference was demonstrated at the .01 level of significance between the correlations of the two pretests and Teacher Judgment. Although the Metropolitan Readiness Test had slightly higher correlations, the two tests are not appreciably different in predicting reading achievement at the end of grade one. The higher correlation between the Metropolitan Readiness Test and Teacher Judgment may be due to the more conservative feature of each measure.

5. The correlations between the various subtests of the Predictive Index Tests and the total Predictive Index Score were as follows: Pencil Use .39, Bender Visual-Motor Test .62, Wepman Auditory Discrimination Test .53, Number of Words Used in a Story Test .29, Categories Test .51, Horst Reversal Test .70, Gates Word-Matching Subtest .67, Word Recognition Test I .44, Word Recognition Test II .58, and Word Reproduction .69. The Bender-Visual-Motor Test, Horst

Reversal Test, and Gates Matching Test are among the tests that have the greatest correlation with the total Predictive Index Score. All three of the aforementioned subtests are in part derived from standardized readiness tests. This would indicate that the total scores of several group readiness tests could be as great or greater than the Predictive Index Tests in predicting reading success at the end of the first grade.

6. The correlations between the mental age as determined by the Peabody Picture Vocabulary Test and reading success at the end of the first grade were: .44 with Teacher Judgment, .33 with the Dolch Test, and .37 with the Metropolitan Reading.

7. There was a negative correlation between boys' readiness test scores and reading success. The correlation was -.23 with Teacher Judgment, -.33 with the Dolch Test, and -.29 with the Metropolitan Reading Test. This evidence is in agreement with most research studies that indicate that boys are not as successful as girls in reading achievement at the end of the first grade.

CONCLUSIONS

The Predictive Index Tests and the Metropolitan Readiness Test predicted reading achievement about equally well at the end of the first grade, with a slightly favorable advantage to the Metropolitan Test. The Metropolitan Readiness Test could be recommended for general predictive purposes in reading achievement since it has the advantage of being a group test.

The Predictive Index Tests, however, may be favored as a test for predicting reading failure. In fact, that was its stated purpose. The Predictive Index Tests correctly predicted 33 pupils who would fail to have adequate reading achievement, while the Metropolitan Test predicted 23 pupils. The over-prediction rate was higher for the Predictive Index Tests than the Metropolitan Readiness Test by 15 pupils, but its underprediction rate was lower by 10 pupils. From a preventative standpoint, it may be wise to overpredict with such an important developmental task as reading. To overpredict results in a more costly readiness program in the first grade. The initial expense may well be worthwhile, as it is less costly to operate preventative programs than remedial programs in terms of both monetary and human expenditure. Research studies indicate that the sooner we are able to find and overcome reading problems, the greater is the probability for adequate reading development.

REFERENCES

1. de Hirsch, Katrina, Jeannette J. Jansky, and William S. Langford. *Predicting Reading Failure*. New York: Harper and Row, 1966, 42.

2. McNemar, Quinn. *Psychological Statistics*. New York: John Wiley, 1962, 184-185.

GREGORY MORRIS

Classroom Diagnosis
of Reading Problems

Both small-scale intervention and large-scale remediation are frequently the responsibility of the classroom teacher, and desire and empathy are no substitutes for professional knowledge. This article is an attempt to fill a vast void in professional literature; it outlines a series of practical, how-to-do-it steps which, if adapted to individual situations, should help classroom teachers better diagnose and instruct children with reading problems.

What information could you gain from the permanent pupil records in your school? Have you used, or could you now use, the group reading inventory described in this article? To Morris, are reading problems broad, undifferentiated deficiencies or specific skill difficulties? How does feedback from learning activities help make diagnosis an ongoing process? In what ways is classroom diagnosis different from clinical diagnosis?

Saturday Review had a cartoon a few years back which showed a little boy and his father gazing at a flock of geese flying in a wedge formation. The little fellow asked his dad where the geese were flying and his father replied that they were flying south. The little fellow looked again at the birds and asked how they knew about flying south. Father thought for a second and said, "Oh, they follow instinct. Do you understand?" "Sure," the little fellow answered, "he's the one in front!"

The situation just described may be likened to the one in which the classroom teacher finds himself when he attempts to find out how the children in his class read. The teacher may

---

Adapted from a paper presented at the 1970 annual convention of the International Reading Association and reprinted by permission of Gregory Morris.

know about diagnosis as a word, but a deeper knowledge and understanding of the utilization of diagnosis as a means of facilitating pupil growth may be needed.

We in the teaching profession readily acknowledge that it may take new teachers several years before they develop the acumen needed to effectively provide for the wide range of abilities among the pupils in their reading classes. We must acknowledge, too, that it may take teachers some time before they really discover just how different individual pupils are. This concern is of importance to educators because the appropriate treatment of pupils' reading difficulties is a tremendously pressing need in today's schools.

The great stress we put on reading and learning is already having many concomitant effects. One serious effect is the role of reading skills. Reading was once viewed as an activity which was learned in grades 1-3 and then was used to learn in grades 4-6 and thereafter. This view is rapidly changing because of the present trend of moving much content in science, social studies, and mathematics down into the primary grades. It is not uncommon for primary children to be expected to read from social studies, science, spelling, and math textbooks in addition to basic reading texts. A youngster having difficulties in reading may be in trouble with all of his school subjects. What then of the diagnosis of reading difficulties by the classroom teacher?

Diagnosis is a broad concept, broad enough to encompass a multitude of techniques, materials, and approaches for reading instruction. As was pointed out in the national first-grade studies, children learned to read from a variety of materials, programs, and approaches. Reading authorities, after looking at the data, concluded that no matter what general method or material is used, the teacher is the crucial variable. *(3)* Diagnosis, then, can only be as effective as the teacher making that diagnosis. What leads to effective diagnosis of reading difficulties by classroom teachers?

Effective diagnosis of reading difficulties by classroom teachers is dependent upon many variables. Burnett, in an article entitled "The Classroom Teacher as a Diagnostician," identified five considerations as being pertinent *(5)*. These considerations stated in question format comprise the crux of this article.

1. Can the teacher assemble information from the pupils' record file and other sources which will provide insight as to what judgments can be made regarding these pupils' reading ability?
2. Can the teacher develop and/or utilize classroom diagnostic procedures which are valid for providing information about pupils' reading skills?
3. Can the teacher interpret the findings after he accumulates the data?
4. Can the teacher make meaningful recommendations as to how to remedy certain kinds of difficulties?
5. Can the teacher carry out an instructional program in keeping with pupils' specific difficulties?

PUPIL RECORDS

Schools maintain a permanent record file for their pupils. These files normally contain information about attendance, reading record, achievement test scores, results from individual and/or group intelligence or aptitude tests, and special tests such as hearing, vision, school readiness, and physical examinations. Pertinent comments based on teacher observations, anecdotal records, or pupil biography may also be included in these files. Reports of testing or evaluation conducted by non-school groups or agencies may be found, too, in the pupils' permanent file folder.

Since these records are usually available to the classroom teacher before his first meeting with the pupils, careful scrutiny can provide advance insights as to possible sources of difficulty. Some questions which might be raised while examining these records are:

Has reading instruction been systematic and matched to the child's achievement?

Auditory, visual, and physical defects may have been detected and noted, but were recommendations made and then implemented?

Might frequent absences or transiency have contributed to reading difficulties?

Do achievement test scores indicate a gradual or sudden decline in ability to read?

Do various individual and/or group measures confirm pupils' capacity to function at grade level?

Have previous teachers perceived any difficulties in pupils' ability to read?

These are the kinds of questions for which the classroom

teacher will want to find answers. Pupil records can help to provide some of these answers or at least a tentative hypothesis about pupils' difficulties in reading.

Records, although they can provide enough data to establish a tentative hunch as to what kinds of problems pupils may be experiencing in reading, should be used with caution and discretion. They do represent only one source of information. Once a tentative hypothesis has been established, it is imperative to expand this hypothesis by formulating and utilizing diagnostic procedures designed to provide more information as to how the pupil reads.

DIAGNOSTIC PROCEDURES
TO ASSESS READING SKILLS

Pupil records enable the classroom teacher to derive advance insights as to potential sources of reading difficulty. Another phase of diagnosis begins once pupils enter the classroom. Many school systems employ special reading teachers, reading specialists or reading consultants who assist the classroom teacher in formulating and utilizing appropriate diagnostic procedures. But for a vast number of teachers this kind of expertise is not available. The classroom teacher is therefore faced with a multitude of learning problems and often lacks the resources to utilize the more formal kinds of reading tests and diagnostic procedures.

One resource available to the classroom teacher is the informal reading inventory. Although used by Betts many years ago, the literature only recently indicates the widespread use of this instrument *(2)*. The group reading inventory, spoken of far less than the IRI, can be one of the most important diagnostic procedures utilized by the classroom teacher *(8)*. The group reading inventory is comparable to a diagnostic-teaching activity. The group reading inventory or diagnostic teaching activity is an attempt on the part of the classroom teacher to explore and discover what skills and abilities pupils are able to bring to a given instructional task in reading.

Using a selection with a known level of difficulty with a group of children, the teacher can discover whether or not pupils have the background experience to deal with specific topics and concepts; whether or not they have the ability to independently attack and analyze unfamiliar words and their meanings; whether or not they are able to establish purposes for their reading and then attempt to achieve those ends. The teacher may also determine the level of specific understanding of pupils in reacting to the key ideas, details, concepts, etc., encountered in the reading.

Pupils experiencing much difficulty in the first diagnostic teaching activity can be regrouped for another such activity with easier materials. Those pupils who exhibited confidence and facility in dealing with the material utilized in this first diagnostic teaching activity should also be regrouped for another such activity with more challenging instructional reading material. Checklists of oral and silent reading skills can be very helpful to the classroom teacher in organizing the information he is securing about his pupils' reading abilities. (See Durrell [7], Austin, Bush, and Huebner [2].)

This information when coupled with data from an attitude inventory such as the incomplete sentence blank *(10)*, diagnostic spelling tests *(8)*, word opposite and quick word tests *(4) (9)*, and on-going observation of the pupils' day-to-day reading behavior *(10)* can add immeasurably to the insights gathered from a perusal of pupil records. All of these data should enable the classroom teacher to broaden his hypothesis about his pupils' difficulties in reading.

INTERPRETATION OF DATA

Pupil records and data from many diagnostic teaching activities can provide the classroom teacher with much information. This data combined with informal observations of pupils' on-going reading behavior should enable the teacher to pinpoint many of his pupils' reading problems.

The classroom teacher must now examine all of these data and attempt to refine his hypothesis of pupils' reading difficulties. Do the data —

Indicate that the pupil has the potential for greater achievement in reading?

Indicate that the pupils' reading difficulties may be due to auditory, visual, emotional, physical difficulties or environmental differences?

Reveal that the pupil is experiencing reading difficulties because of specific skill deficiencies?

Show patterns of weakness in specific skill areas?

Perceptual Skills
> auditory
> visual
> motor

Word Recognition Skills
> sight vocabulary
> phonics skills
> structural analysis skills
> context skills
> syllabication skills

Comprehension Skills
> words
> sentences
> main ideas
> details

Rate of Reading

Oral Reading Skills

Indicate large differences in performance in specific skill areas?

In other words, what is the pupil's reading problem? This is the task then, to examine all of the data and formulate some solution for the problem. Once this is done, an instructional strategy can be formulated to deal with these difficulties. It should be pointed out that even with all of the information at his disposal, the classroom teacher, at best, can only conjecture as to what the most effective alternative will be.

DEVELOPMENT OF A TEACHING STRATEGY

Once the classroom teacher has identified the pupil's difficulties in reading, he has to pinpoint those primary instructional needs or those areas where an instructional program can be most successfully initiated.

The information gathered by the classroom teacher may suggest any number of difficulties experienced by pupils in reading. Although this number may be overwhelming, it is the task of the teacher to sort through these various difficulties and pinpoint those which are of utmost importance for developing skill in reading. John's failure to understand the main idea of paragraphs is only of secondary import when it can be shown that he has difficulty understanding words and simple phrases. Nor should we be overly concerned about Gail's inability to divide words into syllables when she fails to analyze long and short vowels and consonant blends and digraphs.

Other important aspects of a teaching strategy include selecting appropriate methods and activities, determining an appropriate instructional pace, and providing sufficient practice to assure mastery. All of these are covered in Part Five, "Putting It All Together," in this book.

IMPLEMENTATION OF RECOMMENDATIONS

How accurate can the classroom teacher be in his diagnosis of pupils' primary instructional needs in reading? Time and effort will help the teacher refine his ability to diagnose reading problems. But diagnosis does not end because an instructional program is initiated. Diagnosis is an on-going process. As the teacher begins to implement the recommendations he will want to immediately assess whether or not they are meeting the primary instructional needs previously identified.

Each lesson's objective must be assessed by teacher and pupil. Feedback to pupil and teacher should enable the teacher and pupil to do the following:

Pupil	**Teacher**
Experience success with this lesson.	Help pupil to understand the purpose of this lesson.
Perform or demonstrate some skill or activity.	Demonstrate to pupil what is expected from him at the conclusion of the learning experience.
Have the knowledge that this lesson is designed to solve a reading problem.	
See how this skill helps in other reading situations.	Take pupil through each small facet of the learning experiences.
	Provide pupil with practice and test items for teacher-pupil evaluation.
	Share examples as to how this skill can help in other reading situations.

If teacher and pupil implement the teaching strategy and utilize the feedback from the learning activities, then adjustments in terms of instructional needs and activities can be made. Diagnosis will then be an on-going continuous process.

CONCLUSION

The suggestions and ideas developed in this article place the burden of diagnosis squarely on the shoulders of the classroom teacher. Utilizing pupil records and diagnostic teaching devices, the teacher is able to develop a tentative hypothesis as to what difficulties his pupils may be experiencing in reading. After reviewing and interpreting these data, the teacher should be able to identify the pupil's most pressing or primary instructional needs. Once this has been done, an instructional strategy can be developed which should help the pupil remedy his most pressing instructional needs. Implementing the recommendations also gives teacher and pupil the opportunity to continue the diagnosis so that further modifications or refinements may be made. It's a huge undertaking, but no one is in a better position to diagnose difficulties in reading than the classroom teacher.

BIBLIOGRAPHY

1. Austin, Mary; Bush, Clifford; and Huebner, Mildred. *Reading Evaluation: Appraisal Techniques for School and Classroom.* New York: Ronald Press, 1961.

2. Betts, Emmett A. *Foundations of Reading Instruction.* New York: American Book Company, 1946, pp. 438-485.

3. Bond, Guy L. and Dykstra, Robert. "The Cooperative Research Study in First Grade Reading Instruction." *Reading Research Quarterly,* 2 (1967). pp. 9-142.

4. Botel, Morten. *Botel Reading Inventory.* Chicago: Follette Educational Corporation, 1966.

5. Burnett, Richard W. "The Classroom Teacher as a Diagnostician." *Reading Diagnosis and Evaluation.* Newark, Delaware: International Reading Association, 13 (1967), pp. 1-10.

6. Durrell, Don D. *Improving Reading Instruction.* New York: Harcourt, Brace and World, Inc., 1956, pp. 110-122.

7. Johnson, Marjorie S. and Kress, Roy A. *Informal Reading Inventories.* Newark, Delaware: International Reading Association, 1965.

8. Kottmeyer, William. *Teacher's Guide for Remedial Reading.* New York: Webster Division, McGraw-Hill Book Company, 1959, pp. 87-90.

9. Slossen, Richard R. *Slossen Oral Reading Test.* East Aurora, New York: Slossen Educational Publications, 1963.

10. Strang, Ruth. *Diagnostic Teaching of Reading.* New York: McGraw-Hill Book Company, 1964, pp. 41-59; 256-258.

ROY A. KRESS

Classroom Diagnosis
of Comprehension Abilities

Identification of reading disability is usually predicated upon a discrepancy between reading achievement and reading capacity. A perpetual perplexity has been how to measure reading capacity. Group pencil-and-paper mental-ability tests have notorious drawbacks with children with reading problems, and few classroom or remedial teachers can get individually administered test results for each child. In this article, Kress takes a rather oblique approach to the problem. Why do we want to know reading capacity? If it is to predict the level of material that the child is capable of reading and understanding, then possibly we should ask, "What is the child capable of comprehending?" rather than, "What is his IQ?"

Do you agree that it is important to understand the nature of reading comprehension before attempting to determine a child's potential level of reading ability? In what ways are Kress's suggestions more realistic than merely using results of mental ability tests? In what ways are they more complicated and demanding? Are they equally applicable in clinical situations? Based on your experiences and information, are there other factors you would want to assess in determining a child's comprehension abilities? How does this article relate to Belmont and Birch's "Intellectual Profile of Retarded Readers" in Part Two?

Among most educators today, there is a great concern about the improvement of instruction in reading in the classroom. Instructional approaches which have been used for many years in the initial teaching of reading are currently being challenged.

Reprinted from *Progress and Promise in Reading Instruction*, compiled and edited by Donald L. Cleland and Elaine Vilscek, University of Pittsburgh, 1966, pp. 33-41, by permission of the publishers and author.

New approaches are constantly being devised and extended to the classroom teacher, each as a sure-fire method of eliminating all reading difficulties among school children.

When one looks carefully at the majority of these innovations in reading instruction, it becomes evident that most appear to be based upon a very limited understanding of reading itself. Most consist of technique or material modifications designed to aid children in the mastery of the visual decoding process — word recognition. Far too often the authors make no mention of comprehension in reading, or blandly state that when a child can decode accurately, he can then read and write any words he can speak.

Although accuracy of word recognition is an important factor in reading, possession of this ability is no guarantee of understanding when one reads. The relationship between word recognition and comprehension in reading is not a unitary one in which the ability to identify a sequence of words on a printed page results in automatic understanding of what the author intended to be communicated. The ultimate purpose for reading is communication of ideas. In chess, one cannot play the game without knowing the rules for moving the chessmen about the board, but a child's learning of these rules does not mean that he understands the game.

A significant number of children in today's classrooms are not reading as well as they should be and are classed as retarded readers. However, of this retarded reader population, many more children are experiencing difficulties with the understanding of what they read than with word recognition per se. It would seem that those who feel a need to develop new techniques designed to improve reading instruction for children could make a more significant contribution by concentrating upon the problem of comprehension — the communication — rather than on different approaches to the decoding of printed language symbols.

UNDERSTANDING COMPREHENSION

Comprehension in reading is a communication activity between an author and his reader which is dependent upon the present perceptual-conceptual actions of the individual doing the reading. It requires accuracy of word perception (as distinguished from word recognition), familiarity with the things involved, the ability to recognize the relationships among them, and a certain amount of familiarity with the language employed to get the ideas across to the reader. Comprehension in reading is thinking stimulated by orthographic symbols. Except for the means of stimulation, the activity does not differ in a conceptual sense from the nature of the understanding process involved in listening and speaking situations.

Perceptual-Conceptual Bases for Comprehension

Comprehension in reading is directly dependent upon individual physiological and psychological factors operant in the reader. An individual's understanding of ideas communicated to him is related to his experience with those ideas and the objects and events from which they are derived. The richness of that experience is further dependent upon his basic sensory system for receiving external and internal stimuli and his perceptual awareness of the stimuli. The principal basis for any cognitive activity which arises in an individual while he is reading is his perceptual awareness and understanding about the environmental experiences utilized by the author in recording the ideas, objects and events involved.

1. Physiologically, the nature of an individual's perceptual activity is related to the degree to which he has an intact sensory system for the reception of stimuli. Auditory, visual, olfactory, gustatory, tactile, kinaesthetic, and proprioceptive systems all contribute basic sensory data to the integrative and associative areas of the central nervous system. Any impairment in the functioning of these systems results in a reduction of the total data available for manipulation.

2. The physiological capability for reception of sensory data provides only the potential for profiting from available experiences. Actual acquisition of experience is dependent on the degree of awareness the individual manifests in the situation. Without the psychological capability to fixate the sensory stimuli, he cannot take the first step in perceiving them and incorporating them into his present perceptual-conceptual framework. He must be able to attend to available stimuli and, through the voluntary application of that attention, concentrate in a selective way on those which are pertinent to his present needs and activities.

3. True incorporation of new sensory data, in the form of percepts, into the individual's evergrowing and changing perceptual-

conceptual reservoir demands more than inactive reception of the stimuli. To make use of current sensory experiences, he must be able to organize them so that they can both fit into and enrich or modify his present perceptual-conceptual map. Such organization is dependent on the degree to which he can abstract elements from the total experience, detect likeness and differences in various elements, and identify the similar or common essentials. Unless relationships among various elements of the experience are grasped through activity of this type, each experience exists in isolation. Generalization on the basis of relationships is impossible. Likewise, the individual has no starting point for indexing his percepts as exemplars of some class.

4. Fitting a new experience into an established framework requires the ability to make active use of previous sensory experiences and the import they have come to have. Obviously then, the individual must have retained the prior experiences and reactions to them and must be able to recall them at appropriate times. The associations which have been formed around them are the things which provide the structure and organization and, therefore, trigger the recall. The organization of the present sensory data, through the abstracting and generalizing process, establishes the base for the use of previous experiences. This organization determines what is pertinent to the present situation. Only with it can the individual integrate the current experience and his relevant past experience, do whatever reorganization is required, and thus extend and enrich his conceptual development.

5. The nature and effectiveness of perceptual activity is further influenced by the concepts which the individual has already formed. If his concepts are primarily concrete, then current sensory data will be seen as related to previous organization patterns only when there are common concrete characteristics. If, however, concepts have been formed at varying levels — concrete, functional, and abstract — far greater versatility is possible in the processing of sensory data as they become available. Because a variety of types of characteristics of the sensory data have been used in the formation of concepts, each new experience has the potential for fitting into the conceptual patterns in a variety of ways. The triggering of recall would be far more flexible and, therefore, the potential for abstracting essential elements from experience increased with subsequent increasing of the richness of the individual's conceptual background.

All of this activity, with the influences of the various physiological and psychological capabilities mentioned, is what makes possible comprehension. The concepts thus formed and perpetually enriched, deepened, broadened, and otherwise modified provide the meanings which are at the core of the communication process. It is from his reservoir that the encoder (the speaker or writer) selects the meanings he wishes to convey. It is in terms of his reservoir that the decoder (the listener or reader) interprets the message.

Language-Experience Relationships

Although certain types and degrees of communication are possible on a non-verbal level, most of human interchange of ideas is through words. Before words can function in this way, the individuals involved in the communicative process must have associated these language symbols, oral and visual, with elements of experience and the concepts formed from them. They must also have acquired certain basic understandings about language-experience relationships if verbal communication is to be effective and language is to serve as a medium for the enrichment of experience and conceptual development. A few of these essential understandings follow.

1. Language exists for purposes of communication. It involves the use of symbols to convey meanings which have been derived from experience. Each individual must, therefore, develop the attitude of expecting sense, not non-sense, to result from the use of oral and written language. However, he must continue to differentiate between the word and the thing.

2. Semantic variations occur in the use of language symbols. Meanings must be identified in terms of the total gestalt and the individuals functioning in it. Variation in meaning can occur not only from one situation to another, but also from one person to another and one culture to another. The individuals attempting to communicate must thus be aware of the fact that each will differ, somewhat, because of his particular experiences and his distinctive perceptual-conceptual background. Not only must each word be interpreted in terms of the nature of the particular situation in which it is used, but also it must be recognized as probably representing something a little different for each person.

3. Because of individual differences and variation in meaning, communication could be made virtually impossible if one were to concentrate on the variability of meaning and experience. Although the differences cannot be ignored, their recognition should lead to

the abstracting of the essential common elements in the varying meanings. It is through apprehension of these that communication occurs.

EVALUATING COMPREHENSION

Determining the adequacy of an individual student's comprehension requires that the teacher not only understand the perceptual-conceptual language foundations, but also appreciate the specific abilities which are necessary for good comprehension. Too often, the evaluation is on a rather vague and superficial level — "He doesn't understand what he reads" — instead of on the basis of specifically what is lacking in his understanding. Evaluation of the latter type is impossible unless the teacher actually knows what abilities are involved. Was his lack of understanding a lack of appreciation of pronoun reference? Was it the result of his inability to disregard unessential differences in favor of essential likenesses? Was it the result of inability to identify the topic sentence in a paragraph? Was it the lack of appreciation of a particular indefinite term? Did his lack of understanding really arise from an inability to tell what is relevant and what is irrelevant?

In essence, these questions indicate that evaluation of comprehension necessitates identification of the particular abilities involved and then investigation of the degree to which the individual has been successful in their use. It requires looking into the thinking which he is doing on the stimulus of the present situation. Because the same thinking abilities are used in the comprehension of reading materials as in the successful manipulation of concrete situations or the understanding and use of oral language, the evaluation may well go beyond the individual's reading behavior. It can and should cut across all school activities, not merely those which are planned for reading instruction. Although a certain amount of information about the child's thinking could be obtained from his performance on tests of various types, the classroom teacher will undoubtedly get the most helpful measures through alert daily observation in a variety of types of situations.

In Concrete Situations

Some of the best evaluations of a child's thinking patterns and abilities can be accomplished in the course of observation of the way he goes about the business of living in and out of the classroom. Watching him play games, settle his differences with peers, handle his work materials, or get ready to go home in the afternoon may yield important information about his problems and strengths in all thinking — including his reading comprehension. The emphasis may be on non-verbal activities and still reveal much that is relevant to evaluation of his understanding. However, if this is to be the case, the teacher must have in mind specific abilities which the child should be using in these concrete, practical, daily activities. Questions such as the following might well guide the observation.

Is the child able to judge the mood of one of his peers from his actions? Does he know when teasing him would be unwise?

Can he organize himself and his materials for a construction project he wants to do?

Does he recognize the existence of a problem? If so, can he identify the specific nature of that problem?

Does he see similarities and differences in concrete materials? Can he sort things adequately on this basis so that he can put them in their correct classroom storage places?

The list of questions might be endless. Each inquiry about the child's behavior should, however, be designed to reveal something about his specific abilities which can be helpful in the total evaluation of his comprehension and in the planning of the subsequent instructional program. Thus a negative response to the first questions above might well indicate some reasons why the child has difficulty in understanding the outcomes of the action in a particular story. The fact might be that he would have the same trouble understanding the interactions of the characters if he were actually one of them and living through the situation.

In Listening Situations

As the child listens to instructions for playing a game, a story being read to the class, a peer's description of his newest toy, or a class discussion of the various possible solutions of a math problem, further observations can be made. Again, the questions which guide the observation should be formulated to reveal his strengths and weaknesses in the handling of specific abilities.

Can he retain and follow directions which involve several

steps? How many steps can he take in, hold, and execute?

Does he react to what he hears with the kind of expression which shows he has recalled relevant experiences from his background?

Can he "picture" something which another person has described in words?

Does he respond appropriately to humorous remarks or does he miss the joke? Does he laugh at exaggeration but miss a play on words?

Each of these questions brings up the opportunity for observing a child's reactions in terms of a particular ability or cluster of related abilities. Some provide for evaluating the very specific level at which the child is currently operating and point the way quite clearly for planning of needed experience and instruction.

In Speaking Situations

As one observes the child's responses in conversation, group meetings, show tell periods, etc., the emphasis should be on what those responses reflect about his thinking abilities. His expressive abilities are important not only by themselves, but also because they reveal his thinking abilities and his resources for thinking.

Does he contribute to discussion relevant illustrations from his past experience? Do his contributions follow logically from the trend of the discussion to that point?

Can he present his ideas in a logically sequential fashion?

Does he use appropriate labels for the thing he wants to communicate about?

Can he back up his statements with real supporting evidence? Does he quote inappropriate "authorities" for support?

Does he avoid inconsistencies in his statements or even recognize them if some creep in?

What the individual says may give excellent evidence of the problems he is having in handling the total situation. His failure to ask an "intelligent" question may result from his lack of success in interpreting what he heard or what he saw in the concrete situation. His inability to state a general idea may be, actually, an inability to abstract common ideas from a number of specific factual statements.

In Reading Situations

Obviously, evaluation of reading comprehension can take place effectively when the child is actually involved in reading. Much can be done, for instance, through alert observation of an individual's reactions during silent reading (although many teachers seem to feel they can tell about a child's comprehension only by asking him to respond to specific questions). What he does as a result of his reading may be observed as a source of information about his comprehension. His discussion of the ideas he contacted and his answers to questions about them will, of course, provide further information. As in the other types of situations, careful formulation of the types of questions asked about his reading performance is necessary if maximum benefit is to be obtained from informal evaluation.

Can he skim to locate the portion of the material which will answer a specific question or does he go through from start toward finish until he stumbles on the answer?

Does he show surprise at an event which should have been unexpected by the reader?

Does he stop and puzzle over a figurative expression instead of taking it meaningfully in stride?

Does he overview material to size up its organization before he begins to read it?

Does he refer to the maps, charts, graphs, footnotes, etc., to which allusions are made?

Can he tell when the author is serious and when he is kidding the reader?

All types of pertinent observations can be made during either guided or independent reading. In like fashion, the results of both kinds of reading can be appraised after their conclusion.

In Writing Situations

Finally, informal classroom evaluation of comprehension abilities can and must be carried through into the individual's writing activities. As in speech, he reflects in his writing his strengths and weaknesses in thinking.

Does he present his ideas in a sequential, organized fashion?

Can he write a good summary, eliminating the irrelevant or inconsequential?

Can he outline effectively?

Does he paragraph and punctuate conversation sensibly?

Is the ending plausible in the story he wrote?

Is his report of the decisions reached in a meeting one which differentiates between actual decisions and points of discussion on the way to decision?

When difficulties occur in written expression, they are often evidence of problems in the thinking behind the writing. If a child uses the word *but* to introduce a clause containing no contrasting idea, it is probably because he does not understand the implications of the word. The thinking process rather than the actual writing is at fault.

CONCLUSION

Classroom diagnosis or evaluation of comprehension may have both formal and informal aspects. Particular attention has been given here to the use of informal evaluative procedures. The teacher who understands the bases of comprehension, appreciates and has carefully defined its many component abilities, and constantly tunes in on the student's thinking can come to know a great deal about his strengths and weaknesses in comprehension. With this knowledge, he can fulfill one of his major purposes as a teacher — the planning of a systematic program for the improvement of comprehension.

MARJORIE SEDDON JOHNSON
ROY A. KRESS

Individual Reading Inventories

For more than twenty years reading specialists have been using various informal instruments to help evaluate reading achievement and needs. Few articles have been detailed and comprehensive enough to be much value to the general practitioner. The following article is a notable and welcome exception.

What is implied by the statement that "only a competent examiner can accomplish the purposes" of this inventory? What is the value of determining several reading levels? Why is pupil-examiner rapport so vital? How can this best be achieved? If an accurate record of errors is crucial, how could this best be assured? Study the "Recapitulation Record." How would oral reading give insights into specific skill needs? Is there any need for both standardized diagnostic silent reading tests and IRIs in a classroom? in a clinic? What information other than insights into reading levels and skills could be obtained from administering an IRI? Do you agree with Johnson and Kress that an IRI is a "clinical device"? Can you learn to administer an IRI by reading this article?

WHAT IS AN INFORMAL READING INVENTORY?

Basic Concepts

The term informal reading inventory is one in our language which with three words expresses three fundamental concepts. Consider first the basic noun in the title. This technique of evaluating a child's performance is an inventory in the sense that it is a detailed study of his whole performance in the

---

Reprinted from *Sociological and Psychological Factors in Reading*, 21st Annual Reading Institute, Temple University, 1964, pp. 47-60, by permission of Marjorie S. Johnson, Roy A. Kress, and The Reading Clinic, Temple University.

reading area and those language and thinking functions related to reading. The second major concept is that of reading itself. In the label informal reading inventory, the function reading is widely conceived. The interest is not in mere pronunciation of words, but also in the manipulation of ideas which are represented by these words. Finally, the technique is an informal one in that specific methods are not standardized, and no norms have been established for performance compared with what other students can do. Instead evaluations are made in terms of absolute standards. A child's performance is judged against virtual perfection rather than by comparing it with what the majority of children might do given the same job.

An informal reading inventory therefore offers the opportunity of evaluating a child's actual reading performance as he deals with materials varying in difficulty. While an appraisal is being made of these specific reading abilities, opportunities are also present to make informal evaluations of his expressive and receptive abilities in the oral language area.

Specific Purposes

A number of very specific kinds of information can be obtained from careful administration of an informal reading inventory. Accomplishing of these purposes is inherent in the administration of the informal reading inventory provided a competent examiner makes the evaluation. Because the information to be gotten is dependent on accurate observation of the individual's performance in the testing situation, and interpretation based on these observations, only a competent examiner can accomplish the purposes.

The informal reading inventory can serve as a means of appraising achievement levels in reading. To be more exact in this statement, careful administration of such an inventory can determine the level at which the child is ready to function independently, that point at which he can now profit from instruction, the level where he reaches complete frustration with the material, and his hearing comprehension level. Three of these levels have special every day significance for the teacher. It is imperative that he know the level of material the child can handle adequately when he is working on his own. A great deal of the child's school work and certainly that reading which will make of him a mature and avid reader are done on an independent basis. Unless materials at the proper level are provided, the child can hardly be expected to do an adequate job in independent work and thereby establish for himself high standards for performance. In the same fashion all instructional work must be provided at a level where the child meets sufficient challenge to learn and yet has adequate readiness for learning. This means that he must achieve well enough to be able to absorb the instruction which is being given. However, to give instruction in materials which the child could handle virtually independently would be foolhardy. Finally, for oral activities, it is important to know_the child's hearing comprehension level. Too often the false assumption is made that if material is read to the child, he will be able to understand it regardless of the level of complexity it represents. For profitable listening activities, one must know the hearing comprehension level.

A second purpose to be served by the informal reading inventory is the determination of the child's specific strengths and weaknesses. Only in terms of such analysis of specific skills and his adequacy of achievement in these skills can a suitable instructional program be planned. Teaching at the right level is not enough. The teaching must be directed toward the overcoming of any specific weaknesses which exist. It must also be given in areas where the child has adequate readiness for learning.

A third purpose of the inventory is to help the learner himself become aware of his levels of achievement and his specific strengths and weaknesses. As he works with materials of increasing difficulty, he should be able, with the aid of the examiner, to detect those points at which he functions well and those at which he demonstrates a need for assistance. In the same fashion, he should be able to develop an awareness of the kinds of thinking and word recognition which he is capable of handling and those in which he needs to improve himself. Without adequate learner literacy the task of instruction becomes an exceedingly difficult if not an impossible one.

A final area of purposes to be accomplished by an inventory is that of evaluation of progress. Repeated inventories at periodic intervals should make it possible to determine changes in levels and in the handling of individual skills and abilities. In this way a true measure of the child's growth can be obtained.

Criteria for Levels

One of the problems in the determination of independent, instructional and hearing comprehension levels is the variability which exists in the criteria used for judgment. It would seem safe to say that all too often the criteria are quite low. Consequently the level at which a child's performance is judged adequate for independent work often turns out to be one at which he is meeting many problems. Instead of doing a virtually perfect job with the material, he is perhaps operating at something close to the old seventy-percent-passing level. In the same fashion children are often considered ready for instruction when they have a great many deficiencies in their operating patterns at a particular level. Experience has shown that when there is too much to be accomplished through instruction, the child does not perform adequately in terms of profiting from instruction and retaining those things which are taught. In order to overcome these weaknesses, high standards must be used for judging the achievement levels. In the following paragraphs each of the levels previously noted is discussed in terms of the specific criteria to be applied.

Independent Level. This is the level at which a child can function on his own and do a virtually perfect job with the handling of the material. His reading should be free from observable symptoms of difficulty such as finger pointing, vocalization, lip movement, and other evidences of general tension in the reading situation. Oral reading should be done in a rhythmical fashion and a conversational tone. Materials, in order to be considered to be at an independent level, should be read with ninety-nine percent accuracy in terms of word recognition. This does not mean merely final recognition of the words in the selection. Rather this means that even in a situation of oral reading at sight the child should be able to handle the material accurately, making not more than one error of even a minor nature in one hundred running words. In terms of comprehension the score should be no lower than ninety percent. Whether the reading has been done silently or orally at sight, the child should be able to respond with this degree of accuracy to questions which will test factual recall, ability to interpret and infer, and to handle any other comprehension ability which happens to be required for full understanding of the material. He should be able to respond adequately to humor, for instance, or to follow any sequence of events involved in the material. In addition the child should be able to make adequate applications of information and ideas to other situations.

Attention to the independent level can be a key point in the determination of progress in reading. The child, his teacher, his parents, and the librarian should all be concerned with this level. All are involved in the process of selection of materials for his independent reading. Books bought for his own reading, his personal library, should be ones he can read well. References suggested to him by the librarian, as she helps him get resources for carrying out a project, must be ones he can use successfully. Homework assignments should be ones he can read without the need for someone to help him. It is through wide reading at the independent level that the child has opportunities to apply the abilities he has acquired, to learn through his own efforts, to increase the rate and flexibility of his reading — in short, to bring his reading ability to the point that it provides him with real satisfaction. Only through his independent reading will an individual become a "spontaneous reader," one who reads as a natural part of his living.

Instructional Level. This is the level at which the child should be and can profitably be instructed. Here again the child should be free from externally observable symptoms of difficulty. Again as at the independent level, he should be able to read rhythmically and in a conversational tone. However, one would expect that certain difficulties might arise in the course of oral reading at sight. When he has a chance to read the material silently, most of these difficulties should be overcome. Consequently, oral rereading should be definitely improved over oral reading at sight. In order to be able to profit from instruction, the child should encounter no more difficulty than can reasonably be expected to be overcome through good instruction. In terms of specific criteria in word recognition, this means that he should be able to perceive accurately at least ninety-five percent of the words in the selection. In terms of comprehension, he should have the ability to attain a seventy-five percent level of understanding of the material without instructional aid. When this is true, he in all probability will be able to reach, with teacher help, the same high levels of performance as were indicated as criteria for the independent level. In general, one should strive in instruction to have the child handling the material independently by the time the lesson is completed. If he begins the lesson with less adequacy than indicated in these criteria, there is very little likelihood that he will overcome all of his problems.

Certain other evidences of ability to profit from instruction can be observed at this level. The child should know, for instance, when he is running into difficulty. He should be able to profit from minimal clues offered by the examiner to help him overcome his difficulties. He should also know when he needs to ask for direct help because he does not have the skills necessary to solve his problem. Here, as at the independent level, the child should be able to set continuing purposes for reading once he has been helped to develop an initial readiness.

It is in his guided work at the instructional level that the child will have the opportunity to build new reading and thinking abilities. Building on the foundation of his previously acquired skill, he can profit from teaching and thus extend his concepts, his word analysis skills, and his specific comprehension abilities. Their extension, through both increased range of abilities and greater depth in their applicability, is the purpose of instruction. If it is to be accomplished, knowledge of the child's instructional level is essential to the teacher.

Frustration Level. The point at which the child becomes completely unable to handle reading materials is of more clinical than classroom importance. For the classroom teacher, however, knowing this level may serve two purposes. Information on the frustration level may give the teacher some guidance about the kinds of material to avoid for this child's work. It may also give him some indication of the rate at which the child might be able to progress when he is taught at his proper instructional level. If a child is ready for instruction at one level and completely frustrated at the next, there is clear cut evidence that he has many problems to be overcome through the instruction at the appropriate level. The likelihood is not that this instruction will progress rapidly because of the complexity of problems to be met. On the other hand, if there is a considerable spread between the instructional and the frustration levels, there is a better chance for fairly rapid progress. There is evidence that he can continue to use his reading abilities with fair effectiveness when he meets more difficult material than that truly appropriate for instruction. This fact would seem to indicate that the needs to be met at the instructional level and somewhat above are not terribly serious or complex ones. Consequently, he might be expected to solve his problem relatively rapidly with good teaching to help him. Specific criteria for the frustration level are these: comprehension of fifty percent or less and word recognition of ninety percent or less. Failure to meet the other criteria already described for independent or instructional levels would also be indicative of frustration.

Hearing Comprehension Level. This is the highest level at which the child can satisfactorily understand materials when they are read to him by the examiner. The hearing comprehension level can serve as an index to the child's current capacity for reading achievement. It indicates, in other words, the kinds of materials that he would be able to understand if his reading levels were at this moment brought to a maximum point. Criteria for judgment of adequacy of hearing comprehension are parallel to those for the establishment of the instructional level. The child should be able to understand at least seventy-five percent of the material when it is read to him. A second measure and a very important one is the index given by his own speaking vocabulary and language structure. He should, in responding to the material, show an oral language level which is comparable to the language level of the material which has been read to him. The necessity for the examiner to translate questions down in language level or for the child to answer in a lower level of language would indicate that he is not comprehending fully at this point.

All instructional activities involving listening should take into account each child's hearing comprehension level. Whether materials are being read to the class or spoken, there can be no real profit to an individual if they are beyond his hearing comprehension level. He may simply tune out when he finds himself failing to understand. Knowing the appropriate levels for oral language activities can lead, then, to better classroom attention and thus to greater learning.

The hearing comprehension level has one other kind of significance for the teacher. It gives him an indication of the level at which the child *should be reading*. The criteria in terms of comprehension are the same for the instructional reading level and the listening level. One should not feel completely satisfied until the child can do as well with the material when he reads it himself as when it is read to him. Therefore, a goal to aim for is equivalence of the reading instructional and the hearing comprehension levels.

Materials

The types of materials to be used in an informal reading inventory are dictated by the purposes of the inventory itself. Because the establishment of levels is one of the expected outcomes of the administration, it is obviously necessary that the materials represent a variety of levels. In a clinical instrument, for instance, it is usual to have the difficulty level of the material progress from preprimer level to the highest point that one is likely to need. These materials may sample a variety of subject areas and types of writing. However, if one were interested primarily in the achievement levels of the child in the science area, then materials relevant to this content field should be used for the inventory. Because an evaluation of competency in handling specific skills and abilities is the desired outcome, the materials of the inventory must present the opportunity for evaluating this competence. Obviously, not every ability which is a part of reading comprehension could be tapped in the course of each inventory; however, an adequate sampling should certainly be made.

The length of materials must be controlled sufficiently to allow the inventory to be administered without undue fatigue on the part of the child. In general, selections of increasing length can be handled as the difficulty level of the material increases. Specific materials and arrangement of them for the inventory depend, to some degree, on whether the evaluation is to be in an individual or group situation. For an individual inventory, most frequently used on a clinical basis, two selections, preferably connected, should be chosen for each level, from preprimer to the highest level to be tested. One of these is used for oral reading at sight and the other for silent reading. Oral rereading ability is evaluated by having the child reread aloud a portion of the material designed for silent reading.

Ideally, the materials chosen for the inventory should parallel as closely as possible those materials which will be used for instruction. However, they should not be materials which the child has actually encountered in his instructional program. The inadequacies of material which had been used for instruction seem obvious. There would certainly be the real possibility that the child would respond in terms of what had gone on in the classroom rather than in terms of what he was reading at the moment.

PROCEDURES FOR ADMINISTRATION

The total process of an individual informal inventory of reading ability may be divided for convenience into four major sections. These might be labeled pupil and examiner readiness, the word recognition test, the reading inventory, and the listening inventory. All four must be included if a thorough and competent job is to be accomplished.

Pupil-Examiner Readiness

Two major purposes are to be accomplished during this period. There is, of course, a need to enlist the cooperation of the person being examined if the inventory is to give valid and reliable results. Consequently, this period must be one during which rapport is established, both with the examiner and with the examining technique to be used. It is important that the pupil have at least a minimum degree of literacy about the method which is to be used to evaluate his accomplishments and needs in the reading area.

During this period, the examiner has an opportunity to appraise the child's oral language facility in many different ways. As they engage in informal conversation, he can pick up any actual defects in speech, appraise the degree of spontaneity in informal situations, determine the child's ability to respond to specific questions, and get some measure of the maturity level of the child's vocabulary, sentence structure and pronunciation. Likewise, there will be some reflection of the child's ability to concentrate on oral language activities and to respond appropriately. While all of this is going on, a great deal can also be learned about the child's attitude toward himself and the reading process. All of this material is significant in the total evaluation of his strengths and weaknesses in the reading area.

With the information gained in the course of this period and any previous data on the child, the examiner should also be able to estimate the possible level at which to begin with the word recognition test. The materials which the child is currently using for instruction, for instance, may give some clue. His own evaluation of the problems that he faces in reading may be indicative of the kinds of needs which will be uncovered, and may well dictate that testing should be begun at a very low level.

One guiding theme in the course of this period should be the attempt to get the child as serious and yet relaxed as possible about the job which faces him. He should understand that he is going to face tasks of increasing difficulty, so that he may go as far as his abilities will allow him to reach at this particular time. He should become aware of the fact that, if it is at all possible, the examiner will begin with materials which are quite easy for him, so that he will be able to demonstrate those things which he has accomplished in the reading area.

Word Recognition Test

To appraise the child's immediate recognition vocabulary and use of word analysis skills, words are presented in isolation. Lists of words from pre-primer at least through sixth should be available for this testing. In a clinical word recognition test, these lists should be samplings of common vocabulary at the various levels. For classroom use, however, the sampling is more often from the specific instructional materials. Twenty to twenty-five words appear to constitute an adequate sampling at each of the reader levels.

For actual test material, these lists of words should be typed clearly, at least double-spaced, so that they can be flashed with a manual tachistoscopic technique for immediate recognition purposes. Clear, readable type should be provided so that there is no possibility of difficulty which results from the vagueness of the visual stimulus rather than from the child's inability to handle the particular word recognition task required. From each list of words two scores will be derived, one representing the child's immediate recognition of the words (flash presentation), and the second, his performance in working words out in an untimed situation. In each case, the percentage of words correct is the score. On the flash test, only those correct responses which are given immediately are counted in the basic score. If corrections are made spontaneously, without a re-exposure of the word, credit is given for independent correction, but the basic score does not change. Thus, if a child, on a list of 20 words, pronounced 19 correctly and one wrong, his basic score would be 95%; if he made an immediate correction of the twentieth word without seeing it again, a plus one would be added to the record of the scoring. The 95% + 1 would indicate, then, that he had corrected his one error without examiner aid.

The manual technique for flashing the words to the child is a relatively simple one, but requires practice so that it can be executed smoothly. Two cards (3 x 5 index cards suggested) comprise the materials needed. To flash a word to the child, the two cards are held together immediately above the word form. The lower card is moved down to expose the word; the upper card is then moved down to close the opening between them. This complete series of motions is carried out quickly so that the child gets only a flash presentation of the word. However, it is important that the word be exposed completely and clearly. A tendency in inexperienced examiners is to follow the lower card with the upper one, thus never really giving a clear exposure of the word. If a child responds correctly on the flash presentation, the examiner goes on to repeat the performance with the next word. If, however, an incorrect response is given, the word is re-exposed by pushing up the upper card so that the word can again be seen. No clues are given to its recognition, but the child has the opportunity to re-examine the word and to apply whatever word analysis skills he has at his command.

Immediate responses are recorded in a flash response column. The responses for re-exposures of the word appear in the untimed column. The untimed score is the basic sight vocabulary plus all corrections made without examiner help. It is important that responses be recorded immediately, so that there is complete accuracy in the record of the performance. Delay in writing down the child's response for even a few seconds may lead to confusion and incorrect reporting on the part of the examiner.

The word recognition test is continued, moving from level

to level until the point at which the child is no longer able to function adequately at any given level. Unless the situation is extremely frustrating to the child, it is advisable to continue the test until the child is able to recognize only a very few of the words in the list at the level then being administered.

The example on page 197 shows two levels of one boy's word recognition test as his responses were recorded. A check indicates a correct response; zero, no response; d.k., a statement that he did not know the word; separated letters, a naming of the letters. Single letters or phonetic symbols represent attempts to reproduce the indicated speech sound. Where an incorrect response was recorded and followed by a check, Robert made a spontaneous connection. A zero preceding a word or a check mark indicates an unusual delay before responding.

The seventy-five percent score, plus one, at preprimer level, for example, indicates that Robert had fifteen words of the twenty correct initially, during the flash presentation, and made one spontaneous correction without seeing the word again. His eighty percent untimed score represents credit only for sixteen words which were gotten at flash because Robert made no additional corrections during the untimed presentation. At primer level, however, he worked out three in the untimed exposure. Here, his untimed score represents forty percent finally gotten correct during the flash presentation plus an additional twelve points for those three corrected when he had unlimited time to consider the word.

The Reading Inventory

A wise procedure for starting the reading inventory is to begin at least one level lower than that at which the child first encountered difficulty in the word recognition test. The one situation in which this might not be suitable would be that in which the child has definitely revealed in his conversation or in his past history severe difficulties with comprehension. In this case, it would be best to begin at the very lowest level in order to present as few comprehension problems as possible on the initial selection.

Once the starting level has been determined, the procedure at each level is the same. Before any reading is done a definite readiness for the particular selection should be established. In

The Reading Clinic, Department of Psychology
Temple University, Philadelphia, Pennsylvania

Individual Word Recognition Test C

Name _Robert_   Age __9__   Date _1/2/64_

(The following is a random sampling of words taken from the
Daniels' READING VOCABULARY STUDY)

--------Pre-Primer Level--------   ---------Primer Level----------

Stimulus	Flash	Untimed
1. little	✓	
2. you	✓	
3. can	✓	
4. Play	✓	
5. said	o	(something)
6. Want	o	o
7. come	✓	
8. it	✓	
9. comes	(came)	o
10. Come	✓	
11. for	✓	
12. see	✓	
13. play	✓	
14. It	✓	
15. I	✓	
16. to	✓	
17. in	m ✓	
18. Big	✓	
19. not	(down)	o
20. big	✓	

75+1   80%

"only four wrong!
I did good.
I'm reading."

Stimulus	Flash	Untimed
1. Good	o-o-dog?	o (what story was it in)
2. Run	✓	
3. are	(can)	o-o and
4. like	(little)	o
5. one		
6. Away	(never saw that word)	o
7. All	o	(dk)
8. duck	o	b-b-b/o
9. yes	y-e-s ✓	
10. get	o	o
11. She	her	✓
12. make	o	m-m/o
13. my	✓	
14. No	o-o ✓	
15. This	o	they
16. am	it-at	o
17. red	✓	
18. run	✓	
19. Do	✓	
20. he	d-remember	o
21. yellow	✓	
22. will	what	✓
23. home	✓	
24. went	o	o
25. they	o	came ✓

36+1   52%

the course of this readiness, a purpose for reading should be brought out. The examiner must be careful not to reveal so much in the way of vocabulary used in the selection or ideas contained that he gets no opportunity to measure the child's actual reading performance. Instead, some orientation should be given which will give the child a reason for reading, and a set in the right direction. As soon as this is accomplished, the selection designed for oral reading at sight is read aloud by the child in order for him to accomplish the established purpose. The examiner keeps a careful record of the exact way in which the selection was read. Each hesitation or error is recorded for example. If there is need for examiner help with pronunciation of words, this is given, but the amount is very carefully checked. As soon as the reading has been completed, the comprehension check is administered. The examiner must keep in mind that his purpose here is to evaluate the child's comprehension, and not to teach him. If a question is answered incorrectly, this does not mean that the examiner should help the child arrive at the right answer. Instead, he should go on to the next question. Responses to the comprehension questions should be recorded verbatim wherever this is possible. If such recording is not done, the immediate reaction to the adequacy of the response is oftentimes in question.

When the check on the reading of the first selection is completed, readiness for reading the second selection should be established immediately. Again, a purpose must be set for the reading. This time, the child reads the second selection at the same level silently. While this reading is being done, the examiner should observe carefully, keeping track of the time required for the reading as well as any signs of difficulty or specific reactions to the material. The comprehension check on the silent reading should be administered in the same fashion as was that for the oral reading at sight. When this has been completed, a new purpose should be established for re-reading a portion of the selection orally. Here, the performance should be recorded exactly as was done during the oral reading at sight.

This same procedure is followed at each level until a frustration point has been reached. When this occurs, the reading inventory itself is discontinued.

The example on page 199 is one child's performance on oral reading at sight at primer level. The notations indicate that

Primer –
Oral at sight   AT THE BARN
56 words

Bob and his father came out of the house.

They went to the big red/barn.   sec. 28) 3360   *120 WPM*

They were going to get some milk.   28 / 56

"You can help me," said Mr./Black.   56) 2.00   *.0357% error*

"I will get the cow!" called Bob as   1 58 / 320 / 280 / 40

he ran on into the barn.

"Don't go ~~too~~ so fast," called Mr. Black.   *good rhythm Expressive WR – 96%*

"You will make her jump."

✓ How do you know Bob and his father had not been outside? *came out of the house*

✓ Where had Bob and his father been? ✓

✓ Where were they going? *to the barn*

✓ What did they want to get? *milk*   *80% comp. Quick, natural response*

✓ In what were they going to put the milk? (picture clue) *a bucket*

0 What was Bob's last name? *I forget – it told his father's name but I forget.*

✓ Did Bob expect to milk the cow? How do you know? *yes* *He went right to the barn (0) to milk the cow.*

→ ✓ How did Bob feel about being allowed to help? How do you know? *I guess he liked it. most boys would. (0) He ran right away (0) when his father*

✓ What warning did Mr. Black give Bob? *not to go real fast.*

✓ How do you know Mr. Black was afraid Bob might scare the cow? *told him he could help* *He yelled at him to slow up or she'd jump.*

Ques. not really To push for thinking What did he do? (then?)

Recapitulation

WR   **96**   Oral Comp. **80**   ORR: Time _____

Oral WRM **120**   Silent Comp. _____   Correct? _____

Silent WPM _____   Avg. Comp. _____   Rhythm _____

---

he hesitated twice during the reading, apparently to give some thought to the words. Two actual errors were made. He read *cows* for *cow* and repeated to correct the error. He read *so* for *too* and apparently never noticed his error. Generally, he showed good fluency with the rest of the selection.

On the comprehension check, he responded freely, and showed ability to handle various types of questions. He forgot one bit of necessary information for the inference about the boy's name — the father's name. However, he made it clear that, had he remembered this, he would have been able to make the inference. His other error seemed to be one of failing to realize that the boy showed no signs of expecting to help until he was told he could and then went to bring the cow to his father rather than milk her himself.

All in all, indications are that the performance certainly meets the criteria for an instructional level. This is not to say that he might not also meet these criteria at a higher level or demonstrate similar needs at a lower level.

The Listening Inventory

The process of determining the highest level at which the child can understand materials read to him is usually begun at the next level following the one at which frustration was reached. In this process, the examiner again develops a readiness for the handling of the selection, and sees that a purpose is established just as it was for the reading of the materials by the child himself. In this case, however, the actual reading is done by the examiner. When this has been completed, listening comprehension is evaluated in a manner similar to that used for measuring the child's reading comprehension. This process is continued at successively higher levels until the child fails to maintain a level of 75% accuracy in comprehension.

When difficulties with understanding are at the root of the reading problem, the child may be able to do no better in the hearing comprehension test than when he was doing the reading himself. In such cases, it may be necessary to use alternate selections at lower levels to establish a hearing comprehension level.

INSTRUCTIONS FOR SCORING

The effectiveness of the evaluation made by informal inventory techniques depends on the adequacy of the observations which are made. Considered judgments based on these observations are required. It is essential, therefore, that the examiner have an accurate record of the examinee's total performance. Only with complete information available can he really analyze the child's performance, comparing what happened in one situation with what happened in another, and arrive at reliable conclusions. For this kind of evaluation, no examiner can depend on his memory. Too many things happen too quickly for him to recall them. Therefore, complete recording must be achieved and accurate scoring and interpretation done on the basis of this record.

Recording

Teachers using informal reading inventories will find it helpful to develop a 'short-hand' for use in recording all significant elements of the behavior noted during the administration. Unlike the word recognition test, where ample time for recording can be taken whenever needed, in the inventory proper the child's reading of a selection is never interrupted for recording purposes. At the independent and instructional levels, where symptoms of difficulty are at a minimum, the examiner usually experiences few problems in recording behavior. However, as the selections become more difficult for the examinee these symptoms multiply and it becomes an increasingly complex task for the examiner to keep pace with the reader and still note all of the errors made.

In addition to the above, all other pertinent behavioral symptoms and comments should be noted. The following example will serve to indicate one clinician's method of recording the oral reading.

In this case the examiner, following the establishing of a purpose for reading, asked the child to locate the story "about a farm" in the book — the resultant method employed is noted. The actual reading began with a substitution of *Bill* for *Bob*, a slight pause and then an initial consonant attack on *father*, followed by correct pronunciation of the word. Next came two substitutions which were corrected by repetition after a two second pause. No pause occurred at the end of the first sen-

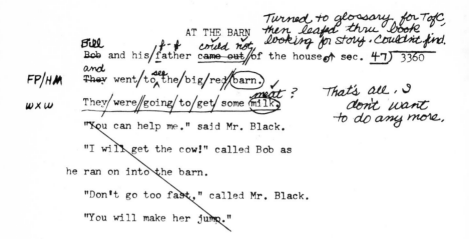

tence. Both finger pointing and head movement were evidenced during the reading. In the second sentence, in addition to inappropriate pauses and a substitution, *see* was inserted and, after an extended pause, the word *barn* was given by the examiner. By the third line the child's rhythm had deteriorated to a word by word performance. He further substituted *meat* for *milk*, but in a questioning tone, and the examiner told him the word. The entire line was then repeated with the final word correctly recognized in this reading. This was followed by the refusal to continue indicated in the margin of the illustration. The entire performance, from the initial substitution to the final repetition, consumed forty-seven seconds.

Scoring

The objective criteria suggested for identifying the various levels of a child's reading performance are based upon measurement of word recognition and comprehension abilities. The former is computed, in the individual inventory, for the oral reading at sight, while the latter is found for both selections used at each level of material. Although nearly all the behavioral symptoms suggested as indications of difficulty with a selection are positively related to word perception skills, only four of these are usually counted in computing the word recognition score — substitutions, insertions, omissions and requests for examiner aid. The clinician should count the number of such errors and compute a percent score by dividing this number by the total number of words in the selection (see sample, page 199). When the resultant quotient is subtracted from 100, a percent correct score for the selection is obtained. This should be recorded in the recapitulation table at the bottom of the page for each oral reading selection employed in the administration.

Similarly, the comprehension score for *each* selection at every level of materials used may be computed by dividing the number of questions answered correctly by the total number of questions asked.* When questions are included which require multiple responses, partial credit is usually given and included on a fractional basis in this total. These scores should be recorded in the spaces provided in the recapitulation box and averaged for a total comprehension score at each level of material.

The computation of words-per-minute scores for both oral and silent reading is facilitated when advanced provision has been made for this in the preparation of an inventory. In the sample shown, an appropriate dividend for division by the elapsed time in seconds taken for the reading has been included. This dividend represents the product of the number of running words in the selection and sixty (seconds). Thus, the quotient obtained when the division has been completed is a words-per-minute score. The score for both the oral and silent selections should also be recorded in the recapitulation table.

Evaluating Oral Rereading

The oral rereading mission in an informal reading inventory serves three specific purposes: It provides (1) a gauge of the child's ability to skim for the re-location of specific information; (2) another measure of his ability to read for a specific purpose and stop when that purpose has been satisfied; and (3) an index of his ability to profit from his previous visual contact with the material and thus improve, essentially in accuracy and rhythm, his oral reading performance here over his oral reading at sight. Improvement in rhythm is to be expected, if it was not originally good, in all selections ranging between a child's independent

---

* Assuming that each question rates the same numerical value in the inventory being employed.

and his frustration level. When this is not the case, such non-improvement is often interpreted as a sign of the need for the use of multi-sensory materials for word learning. The level recapitulation box provides a place for recording the ORR performance appropriate to these three purposes.

Recapitulating the Results

The Recapitulation Record shown on page 205 is suggested as a means of summarizing the objective data obtained in the administration of an informal reading inventory. In Part I the percent scores in word recognition from both the *Individual Word Recognition Test* and the oral reading at sight (context) are recorded for each level tested. Similarly, comprehension scores for reading and listening activities are summarized. Successful or non-successful completion of the oral rereading task and some indication of the improvement or non-improvement of rhythm should be noted at each level given. Finally, the words-per-minute scores for both oral and silent reading should be recorded.

From examination of the summarized data and inspection of the recorded performance at each of the levels tested, the examiner will be able to assign a reader level for each of the "Estimated Levels" in Part II. The criteria suggested for each of these levels must be kept constantly in mind when one is drawing conclusions on the basis of the data obtained.

Parts III and IV provide space for a summary of specific needs in word recognition, comprehension, conceptual development, etc. and for brief statements of pedagogical techniques to be tried or materials to be used. Any observations made which indicated the need for further testing or referral to specialists in related disciplines should also be reflected in appropriate recommendations here.

CONCLUSION

The individual informal reading inventory is a clinical device. It is designed to reveal extensive information about a child's reading strengths and needs as well as to establish the levels at which he can function independently and with instruction. The results obtained from administration of such an inventory are as good as the examiner, no better. Specific criteria for the

Informal Reading Inventory

Recapitulation Record

Name _____ Date _____ Grade _____

Case No. _____ C.A. _____ Examiner _____

I. Test Data

Level	Word Recognition Isolation			Comprehension					WPM oral/silent
	Flash	Untimed	Context	Hearing	Oral	Silent	Average	ORR	
PP	100%	100%	99%		100%	90%	95%	✓	123/157
P	95+1	100	99		95	85	90	✓	128/149
1	75	95	96		80	75	78	✓I	114/138
2	60+1	80	93		65	70	68	✓I	90/110
3	20	50	89		60	45	58	✓NI	67/72
4				90%					
5				78					
6				62					
7									
8									
9									

II. Estimated Levels

Independent _____ P _____

Instructional _____ 1 _____

Frustration _____ 2 _____

Hear. Comp. _____ 5 _____

III. Recommendations

Modified experience appr.
Utilize interest in animals
Parents read content mater.
  to him for awhile
Discontinue formal spell.
Have nurse check vision
  & refer if necessary

IV. Summary of Specific Needs

Retarded three years in rdg.
        achv't.
Phonics needs:
  bl, str, long vowels, final e,
  vowel digraphs, diphthongs
Syllabication:
  compound words, prefixes
    suffixes, varient endings
Uses context clues well,
  especially pictures
      (over dependence)
Broaden interest & experience
  from animals to other areas.

No knowledge of T. of C.

establishment of levels have been indicated. However, the powers of observation and the standards of judgment of the examiner are the final determinants of the adequacy of the information gained.

WALLACE RAMSEY

The Values and
Limitations of Diagnostic Reading
Tests for Evaluation in the Classroom

Analysis and evaluation are as important as depth and breadth of knowledge for anyone striving to be a true professional. But who has the time, knowledge, and energy to scrutinize and weigh the plethora (welter?) of available reading tests? We must frequently rely on experts like Ramsey to do some of the job for us, as he does in this unique and outstanding discussion. But eventually we must use the tests and decide for ourselves, not rely totally on somebody else's opinions.

How do the listed criteria differ from those typically suggested for evaluating diagnostic instruments? Can you truly understand the values and limitations listed by Ramsey without examining and administering the tests? How do you respond to the fact that in Ramsey's opinion all tests have several distinct limitations? Can diagnostic test results be analyzed in the ways Ladd recommends in the next article in this section? Should they be? Does Ramsey believe that diagnostic reading tests should supplement or supplant typical standardized achievement tests in the classroom? How would you use them?

The classroom teacher who seeks ways to evaluate the reading potential and ability of the children under her care will find an almost bewildering array of published tests and other instruments to assist her. In fact the number available and the variety of abilities appraised by them make a wise selection very difficult.

Each of the available instruments has its shortcomings, so much so that it is the writer's impression that very few reading

From *The Evaluation of Children's Reading Achievement*, Thomas C. Barrett, ed. (Newark, Delaware: International Reading Association, 1967), pp. 65-77. Reprinted by permission of Wallace Ramsey and the International Reading Association.

clinics use one, or even a few, of these in their diagnosis. On the contrary, the informal reading inventory and various other teacher-made and clinician-made instruments seem to be very popular in the centers whose main activity is the careful diagnosis of reading problems.

Nevertheless, the classroom teacher who lacks the training or the time to construct or administer informal instruments will find certain standardized measures of substantial value in helping her gain insight into the reading strengths, weaknesses, and potential of her pupils. The greatest advantage in using such instruments lies in the fact that they have been, for the most part, constructed by persons of substantial training, experience, and reputation. Such people as Donald Durrell, Marian Monroe, Arthur Gates, George Spache, Guy Bond, Morton Botel, and their colleagues have great insights into the nature of reading and the ways that reading disabilities manifest themselves. Their experiences in clinical reading qualify them to construct instruments designed to be most revealing about areas of concern.

The writer is not well acquainted with all of the diagnostic reading tests currently available. This prevents a complete and exhaustive discussion. The following are the most widely used tests of this nature and the discussion in this paper will be largely restricted to them:

1. Botel Reading Inventory
2. California Phonics Survey
3. Developmental Reading Tests: Silent Reading, Diagnostic Tests
4. Diagnostic Reading Tests
5. Durrell Analysis of Reading Difficulty
6. Gates-McKillop Reading Diagnostic Tests
7. Gilmore Oral Reading Test
8. Gray Oral Reading Test
9. McCullough Word-Analysis Tests
10. McKee Inventory of Phonetic Skills
11. Monroe Diagnostic Reading Examination
12. Spache Diagnostic Reading Scales

Trella has recently described six of the foregoing tests in terms of the skills they analyze *(16)*. More comprehensive discussions have been made by Bond and Tinker *(12)*, Harris *(13)*, and Zintz *(17)*.

GENERAL VALUES OF DIAGNOSTIC TESTS

The diagnostic reading tests discussed in this paper have numerous general values for the classroom teacher. Several of the tests provide a series of unfamiliar but carefully graded paragraphs for oral and silent reading testing. The paragraphs usually have been especially prepared for the test (and are therefore likely to be unfamiliar to the child) and the levels of difficulty have been carefully determined. The use of the paragraphs, following the procedures prescribed in the test manual, or following the teacher's own procedures which she may use because her expectations concerning reading performance are different from those of the test maker, is likely to reveal much valuable knowledge about the child's reading. For reasons to be noted later in this paper, this may be their most valued advantage.

In addition, some of the tests provide graded lists of words to use in determining the size and level of a poor reader's sight vocabulary and his word analysis ability. The words on such lists are usually very carefully chosen and grade level established according to discrete and important criteria.

Some of the tests include special sections designed to reveal information about reversals, word blending, and other specific word analysis skills. Some items of this type are ingeniously devised and their construction calls for more creativity than many teachers have.

Most of the tests have norms for many of their subtests so that it is possible to determine how a given student's performance compares with that of other students of various ages and grade levels. Such information is highly useful in communicating test results to other teachers, to parents, and occasionally to the child himself.

An ultimate value of several of the tests is that they present a model for systematic analysis of reading skills, a model devised by an authority in reading, a model likely to be more nearly all-inclusive of the skills needing testing than a procedure derived by the average classroom teacher. The use of or even acquaintance with the test will stimulate the teacher to make a more comprehensive analysis of reading abilities than she might otherwise make. For this reason, if for no other, such tests are worth buying and studying very carefully.

In the diagnosis of reading there is a need for instruments to evaluate *many* abilities in reading. A battery of minimum value will include measures of oral reading, silent reading, and word perception skills, including sight vocabulary and phonics. A measure of reading potential, either an individual intelligence test administered by a trained person or a listening test that has been skillfully constructed, well standardized, and carefully administered, is highly desirable. Tests of such word perception skills as use of context, reversals, and structural analysis are certainly useful. There is no one diagnostic test that will do all these things. There are some that do *most* of them, and it is always possible to put together a collection of tests to do the job.

DESIRABLE CRITERIA FOR DIAGNOSTIC TESTS

There are several criteria that should be met by diagnostic reading tests. Some of these that are especially important are listed and explained below. Each has been given a label which will be used in referring to it in discussing specific diagnostic tests in remaining sections of this paper.

The *reality* criterion is of primary importance. If a test meets this criterion it will test an ability in much the same manner as the ability is used in real reading. If it is not met, then an accurate appraisal of a specific ability by the test in question is not possible and conclusions drawn concerning student responses may not be valid. Examples of conformity or the lack of conformity to this criterion will be given later. It should be noted that it is not always possible for all items in a test to meet this criterion completely while meeting all those listed below.

The *guessing* criterion is met when it is *not* possible for the student to *guess* the correct answer to an item. The purpose of diagnosis is to make possible corrective teaching that is specific to the student's needs. Therefore, the examiner should not be forced to entertain the possibility that the student can guess the correct answer to an item. The possibility of guessing can never be eliminated but the nature of the desired response to an item can reduce the possibility of guessing. Poor readers will quite often guess wildly on multiple-choice tests. They have usually had trouble with tests and have learned that they have little to lose by guessing. They frequently inflate their test scores by such behavior.

The *active* criterion is met if the desired response demands some overt, observable behavior from the student as he reacts to an item. This is necessary so that the examiner can clearly discern the nature of the student's response. Tests of ability in phonics especially need to meet this criterion as well as the *specificity* criterion. The latter criterion is met if an item measures a specific ability rather than a constellation of abilities.

The *comprehension* criterion is especially important in tests of oral and silent reading. The criterion is met if items checking the understanding of what is read actually test *comprehension* and *interpretation* rather than pure *memory* of what has been read. Some poor readers can remember very well what they read but understand little of it. A student whose teachers have stressed remembering rather than understanding will tend to read to attain that objective. It would be foolish to contend that memory is not involved in understanding but understanding involves many more — and more important — abilities. Thorndike's study *(15)* of reading as reasoning established this principle almost fifty years ago.

No one test could completely meet all of the above criteria, due to differences in the abilities to be tested and the kinds of responses that are possible. In some cases one criterion may be intrinsically at odds with another. In such cases arbitrary decisions are necessary concerning which criterion shall be met.

COMPLETE DIAGNOSTIC BATTERIES

There are four batteries of diagnostic reading tests that contain material and directions for comprehension evaluation of reading abilities. These are the Durrell, Gates, Monroe, and Spache Diagnostic Tests. All must be given to one child at a time.

The Durrell, Gates, and Monroe tests constitute three of the oldest complete batteries of diagnostic reading tests. Each of the three, with its component parts, tends to give a complete picture of a child's strengths and weaknesses. The Durrell evaluates both oral and silent reading, a desirable attribute. The Monroe and Gates evaluate oral reading only. Recent revisions of the first two tend to make them more up-to-date than the

Monroe. The Monroe does not evaluate as many abilities as the Gates or Durrell and its lack of recent revision makes it less popular.

The Gates test provides a set of reading paragraphs which increase in difficulty and tell a continuous story, but there is only one paragraph at each level in the test booklet and there are no comprehension questions. This condition plus the lack of a test of silent reading greatly reduces the effectiveness of the battery. However, the battery is probably more suitable than the Durrell test for diagnosing the problems of the severely retarded reader.

The Durrell provides tests of both oral and silent reading, but neither the oral nor the silent reading paragraphs tell a continuous story. The comprehension questions in the oral section are almost exclusively of the memory type — there is almost a complete absence of questions evaluating the ability to draw inferences, get the main idea, note the sequence of ideas, or draw conclusions from what is read. There are no questions over the silent reading (except some *optional* ones referring to imagery), but the student is asked to tell what he *remembers* of the selection. Credit in comprehension depends upon the number of ideas remembered and repeated.

The oral reading tests of the Gates, Durrell, and Monroe, as well as all of the oral reading tests described in this paper, can be very revealing if a careful recording and analysis is made of pupils' oral reading errors on the tests. Several systems for manual recording of pupil errors have been devised. All of them provide for crossing out, underlining, and writing in by the examiner on a copy of the material being read.

Classroom teachers who have not had much practice in doing this are likely to find that their marking cannot keep pace with the student's reading. Such marking is distracting to the student and may tend to influence his performance negatively. Therefore, it is recommended that the student's oral reading of the test material be tape recorded. This can be made less distracting than written recording and is likely to render the errors more amenable to careful analysis.

Oral reading is suitable for noting word recognition errors and not much else of major importance. It is true that phrasing ability and attention to punctuation can be noted. These in themselves are unimportant, unless one uses oral reading much more extensively, or for more important purposes than the usual person does — except as indicators of obtained meaning. Because the oral reading task is so complex, the presence or absence of attention to phrasing and punctuation do not necessarily indicate whether or not the meaning is being understood.

In many schools there is an overemphasis on oral reading and sounding out of words. Students get the impression that this is all there is to reading and are concerned with nothing else. Many fluent oral readers have trouble in understanding what they read.

There is some evidence that the oral and silent reading selections in most standardized reading diagnostic tests are too short for perceptually handicapped children. Shedd *(14)* has indicated that the children with specific perceptual motor disabilities with whom he has worked in the Berea (Kentucky) project do not mobilize as rapidly as normal children and therefore make many more mistakes in the first paragraph they read than they do in later paragraphs. Given the great degree of distractibility of such children and their tendency to inattention and hyperactive motor discharge, effective diagnostic testing of them is extremely tedious and difficult and not possible for most classroom teachers.

Silent reading performance is much more valid for testing comprehension than is oral reading. Careful questioning after silent reading, which utilizes many types of questions (main idea, detail, inference, sequence, background, vocabulary, etc.), is the best way of assessing understanding. Most, if not all, of the standardized reading diagnostic tests do not provide for this kind of questioning. Most are tests of memory for what is read, in itself of importance but not of exclusive importance.

Both the Gates and Durrell provide tests of sight vocabulary using a hand tachistoscope. The use of such a device provides a highly artificial way of testing such vocabulary and may distract some children to such a degree that it keeps them from giving a true indication of what they know. Nevertheless, it seems to be a *fair* way of evaluating sight vocabulary if it is preceded by a short session orienting and accustoming the child to the device. The Durrell method of tachistoscopic testing is much more convenient than the Gates, and the word list used is more extensive and more carefully graded.

On both tests children are given unflashed (untimed) tests of word analysis. On the Durrell a child is asked to analyze a word only if he cannot recognize it when flashed. This seems to be a better procedure than that used in the Gates, a test in which a child might recognize as sight words most of the words to be "analyzed."

The Gates tests the child's recognition of phrases; the Durrell does not. Both test the ability to name letters. Both have tests which ask the child to indicate which letter spells the first sound of a word, or which word begins like a word pronounced by the examiner. Both fail to meet the criterion of *guessing* and are subject to the same defect as that found in the McKee Phonics Tests, namely, that testing the ability to identify the way a spoken sound is spelled is not testing the same ability as that called for in supplying the sound of a letter appearing in writing. The Gates Nonsense Word Test is subject to the same limitation. The auditory blending part of the test is valid only if used with children who have been taught phonics by a synthetic (sound blending) method. The same can be said of the Durrell Sounds of Letters test.

The Durrell test, Learning to Hear Sounds in Words, is a very useful one, as is the Test of Listening Comprehension, except that the latter utilizes questions that are largely of the memory type. The tests of spelling (Gates and Durrell), and Durrell's handwriting test are only of general interest and value in a reading analysis.

Spache's Diagnostic Reading Scales is a fairly comprehensive battery of diagnostic reading tests of recent origin. It is designed for individual administration, contains tests of both oral and silent reading, and has six short supplementary phonics tests. A multi-level word recognition test of 130 words, spanning grade levels one through six, can be used to test sight vocabulary and establish a starting level for the oral and silent reading. A series of 22 reading passages at various grade levels from primer to eighth grade can be used for oral and silent reading testing. These range in length from thirty words at early first grade level to over two hundred at eighth grade level. Comprehension questions, with seven or eight questions per passage, are given for checking understanding. The questions do not meet the *comprehension* criterion since they are chiefly of the variety that test *memory* for what is read, rather than testing understanding. The paragraphs themselves seem to be carefully written and the difficulty carefully established.

Norming of the test appears adequate, although establishing validity by showing high correlation with one specific reading survey test seems questionable. The survey test used sets individual reading levels significantly higher than other similar tests of high repute. Directions are given for establishing "reading potential level" using the 22 paragraphs. This is done by determining the highest level at which the pupil understands the paragraphs when they are read to him. The lack of questions evaluating the various *kinds* of comprehension reduces the usefulness of this part of the test.

The phonics tests do not meet the *reality* criterion and call for responses that would be normal only for a child taught phonics by synthetic methods.

Despite the limitations noted, all of the tests described above, especially the Spache and Durrell, are highly useful tests. They have been carefully constructed, are fairly comprehensive, and will prove very valuable to one who administers them carefully. They are time consuming, but their results are worth the time.

BOTEL READING INVENTORY

The Botel is discussed apart from the others, because it is partly a group test and samples fewer abilities than those previously treated. It consists of four parts: (a) tests of word recognition on grade levels 1-4, (b-c) word opposites, a test of reading and listening comprehension, and (d) a phonics mastery test. The word opposites and phonics mastery tests may be given as group tests; the test of word recognition is an individual test. It is designed chiefly for pupils reading at levels up to fourth grade.

Colleagues at the University of Illinois, Saint Cloud (Minnesota) State College, and the University of Massachusetts have reported that they teach the use of this inventory in their classes for preservice and in-service teachers. We have used it in the Reading Center at the University of Kentucky and have found it to be a useful instrument for teacher education in reading. We have been disappointed in its value for use with children. The results obtained have not been discrete enough for individualized remedial reading work. It cannot be said to what extent the inventory would detect group weaknesses.

The value of the use of Word Opposites Test as a test of listening comprehension is based on the idea that a pupil's listening ability is a direct indication of his reading *potential*. The writer has no quarrel with this idea, but the Botel test seems to be only an incomplete test of listening vocabulary. It does not meet the *guessing* criterion. Even if it did, a much more comprehensive test of listening ability would be needed.

The phonics mastery test is by far the most useful and valid test in the battery. It tests the major phonic abilities by determining the child's ability to *spell* certain sound combinations. By testing the abilities in this way it fails to meet the *reality* criterion, since the ability to spell certain sound patterns is not the same as the ability to supply sound equivalents for patterns of print. Nevertheless, it is superior to most phonics mastery tests.

The Test of Word Recognition appears to be a valid test of sight words *in isolation* (as they seldom appear in real reading). However, it should be pointed out that they are tested in an untimed situation where they may be analyzed, if the child wishes. Since the words are taken from a standardized grade list, the child may or may not have had a chance to learn them as sight words. This test seems to fail to meet the criterion of *reality*.

The Word Opposites Test used as a test of reading comprehension is an unusual test. It purports to test comprehension by measuring the pupil's ability to select a word that is the opposite of another word. It is, to the writer, more of a test of reading vocabulary and not a particularly valid test at that. A child might do poorly on it because he did not recognize the words; another child might do well on it and still have difficulty in comprehending phrases, sentences, and paragraphs.

ORAL READING TESTS

The Gray Oral Reading Test is a recent revision — actually a rewriting — of the traditionally useful Gray Oral Reading Paragraphs and Check Tests. It consists of thirteen reading selections that range in length from twenty to fifty words, and vary in levels of difficulty from preprimer to adult level. For each selection there are four questions which can be correctly answered by oral reproduction of the words of the text or by paraphrasing it. The questions do not meet the *comprehension* criterion. The selections appear to be carefully graded — all are of a narrative variety but do not tell a continuous story. In scoring the test the word recognition errors must be recorded, and the time taken to read each selection must be carefully noted. There are four different forms of the test. The test is very valuable for noting weaknesses in word perception. The norms seem quite high — the test tends to underestimate children's instructional reading levels. The reading selections are too short for establishing instructional level in a dependable way.

The Gilmore Test consists of a series of ten paragraphs that range in length from 26 to 250 words and in difficulty from preprimer to grade eight and tell a continuous story. The five comprehension questions that accompany each story ask chiefly for direct recall of the material. The selections are interesting and seem to be well graded. Their greater length makes them more useful than the Gray paragraphs.

Either the Gray or the Gilmore are satisfactory for use in determining word perception strengths and abilities — insofar as this can be done through oral reading. Neither has a test of the specific abilities of phonics. Since both are only oral reading tests their usefulness is limited.

HIGHER LEVEL DIAGNOSTIC TESTS

The battery named The Diagnostic Reading Tests, published by the Committee on Diagnostic Reading Tests, is one of the few batteries designed for use with average readers in high school. The Committee also publishes similar batteries for use with children in grades one through eight. The diagnostic battery consists of seven separate tests: one each of vocabulary and comprehension, tests of oral and silent word attack, and three tests of rate. All are designed for group administration. Each test takes from twenty minutes to an hour to administer.

The test would have many different uses for teachers of reading or content subjects to determine general *class* strengths or weaknesses. Several criteria for diagnostic tests are not met. The student can have a field day guessing on the tests. The tests do not meet the *specificity* criterion. In many cases an error on a particular item might mean any one of several things.

The vocabulary tests have too small a sample of vocabulary from any one field — although not as small as some of the more widely-used survey tests. They violate the *specificity* criterion since a person may miss items because he cannot pronounce the words on the test rather than because he does not know word meanings.

The writer has the highest regard for the comprehension section of the test. It requires the student to read material from several different subject fields and answer multiple-choice questions of several different types. By analyzing the student's responses some impression of his ability to comprehend material in different subject fields may be obtained; there are no directions to assist the examiner in doing this. A good test of *listening comprehension* (therefore, of reading potential) of subject matter in different content fields can be given by using one of four forms of the comprehension test, reading it to students and having them answer the comprehension questions.

The rate tests have in the past been withdrawn from sale for revision or restandardization. They would be useful to determine pupils' rates of reading in general reading material, social studies material, or science material.

The word attack (silent) test is more a test of auditory discrimination than of word attack. It is doubtful if an analysis of errors on it would help a teacher determine what word attack weaknesses a student had. The word attack (oral) will fill the same role as the Gray Oral or the Gilmore except that it contains selections of higher difficulty — up to and including grade twelve.

The tests seem to be expensive but the possibility of reuse reduces the per student cost. However, the test booklets are not very sturdy and do not seem durable.

The tests are misnamed: they are not diagnostic tests in the strictest sense but are actually survey tests that do a more extensive job than the usual survey test — and are therefore possibly more reliable than most survey tests.

TESTS OF WORD ATTACK

The California Phonics Survey, the Bond-Clymer, the Mc-Cullough Tests, and the McKee Tests are all instruments designed to evaluate word attack abilities.

As the title indicates, the California is designed for use as a *survey* test from grade level seven through college and is included here because of its uniqueness. It is intended for group administration: all items have multiple-choice answers. The student *listens* and marks his booklet to indicate if a pronounced sound cluster is spelled out, or if a pronounced word is spelled out in his test booklet, etc. By testing phonics abilities in this way it violates the criterion of *reality*. Using the given directions, errors on the California may be readily analyzed to determine the student's weaknesses in various areas of phonics. It is doubtful that remedial teaching could be adequately planned, even after an analysis of test results, without more information concerning students' abilities in phonics.

The Bond-Clymer is a group test utilizing the multiple-choice format. According to the manual, it is designed for children reading at third grade level and above, but it would not be useful with readers above grade level eight. The California might be more appropriate above that level.

The Bond-Clymer purports to test twelve different word attack abilities in the areas of sight recognition, phonics, use of context, and structural analysis — syllabification and root words. The test seems to be carefully constructed and fairly comprehensive. All sections violate the *guessing* criterion because of the multiple-choice format. Some areas violate the *reality* criterion — including the "Locating Elements," e.g., the word *entirely* is printed under the picture of a tire; the student is expected to "find that little word in the big word below the picture." "Word Synthesis" is when words are broken at unnatural places at the end of a line of print, e.g., *stick* is broken ST-ICK with the second part located below and to the left of the first. The tests of the use of context and reversals are unique and useful portions of the battery. The test might be useful in some *corrective* reading classes; however, the writer has found that the level of teacher knowledge in corrective reading techniques must be exceptionally high if he is to make practical use of Bond-Clymer test results.

The McCullough Word-Analysis Tests contain seven subtests, five concerning phonics abilities and two measuring structural analysis abilities. The phonics subtests utilize the multiple-choice format and therefore violate the *guessing* criterion; two of these ask the child to *listen* and choose letters that spell the initial consonant or medial vowel sound. These violate the *reality* criterion. One subtest is a sound-matching exercise (letter combinations spelling the same sound combinations are matched) — a test of auditory discrimination, one important ability in learning phonics.

A fourth phonics subtest asks the student to scrutinize trios of letter combinations and decide which, if any, spell actual words. This seems to the writer to be a valid test of letter sounds. A test measuring the ability to use a dictionary pronunciation key rounds out the phonics tests. Except for the fact that it utilizes multiple-choice items, it seems to be a valid test of the ability.

Dividing words into syllables is tested by having the students do just that. However, the words would be familiar as sight words to many intermediate grade children and could be divided without the child's possessing knowledge of the principles of syllable division.

The final subtest requires the child to circle affixes in words. This seems to be a valid test and meets most of the criteria for a good diagnostic test.

All things considered, the McCullough Test would be useful with a group of children in intermediate grades, even though the multiple-choice format reduces its effectiveness. In cases where it violates the criteria of a good diagnostic test it is no worse than several others measuring the same abilities.

The McKee Test has been included in the teachers' manuals of the McKee Reading Series for a number of years and is also available in printed form apart from the manuals. It is designed to evaluate phonics skills such as initial consonants and knowledge of vowel principles, and some structural analysis skills such as inflectional endings and affixes. It utilizes a multiple-choice format and is thus susceptible to guessing and requires children to listen and choose the response that contains the same initial sound (or syllable), final sound, or medial vowel as the one spoken by the teacher. This ability is, of course, different from that required in actual reading, in which the child is confronted by symbols and must supply sound equivalents.

In a study directed by the writer, 43 poor readers in grades five and six were given the McKee Test along with two individually administered tests: one was a nonsense syllable reading test and the other a specially constructed test. The latter utilized words from the Dolch list and required students to pronounce words constructed by changing one element in a Dolch word to make a new word. The changed element was written in cursive writing so that the form of the new word would be unfamiliar. All three tests tested the same basic elements. It was found that if the nonsense word test was used as a criterion, the McKee Test detected only 13.7 percent of the children's individual weaknesses in phonics. If the Dolch-Changed Element Test was used as a criterion, the McKee detected 16.7 percent of the weaknesses in phonics.

Since the McKee Test detected so few of the potential trouble spots in the word recognition abilities of the children, its use is inadvisable. It might be useful in detecting *group* weaknesses but in view of the fact that it utilizes the multiple-choice format, the word perception weaknesses of poor readers are likely to be inaccurately evaluated by it.

SUMMARY

Standardized diagnostic reading tests are likely to be useful to the classroom teacher, especially as models for the diagnostic procedures to be followed. Ideally such procedures will evaluate *many* aspects of reading and the tests used will need to meet most of several important criteria. Very few batteries that evaluate all the important phases of reading and also meet the criteria of a good test are available. Various published tests have specific strengths and weaknesses and are useful in different ways in different situations. A careful examination of several of the tests is recommended before any test is purchased for use in evaluating the various aspects of reading.

[An enlightening list of criteria for selecting diagnostic tests is given by Priscilla Hayward in "Evaluating Diagnostic Reading Tests," *Reading Teacher*, 21 (March 1968), 523-528.]

REFERENCES

Tests

1. Bond, Guy L., Theodore Clymer, and Cyril J. Hoyt. *The Developmental Reading Tests*, Silent Reading Diagnostic Tests. Chicago: Lyons and Carnahan, 1955.

2. Botel, Morton. *Botel Reading Inventory.* Chicago: The Follett Publishing Co., 1961, 1962, 1966.

3. Brown, Grace M., and Alice Cottrell. *California Phonics Survey.* Monterey, California: California Test Bureau, 1963.

4. Durrell, Donald. *Durrell Analysis of Reading Difficulty.* New York: Harcourt, Brace and World, 1955.

5. Gates, Arthur I., and Anne S McKillop. *Gates-McKillop Reading Diagnostic Tests.* New York: Bureau of Publications, Teachers College, Columbia University, 1962.

6. Gray, William S. (Helen M. Robinson, Editor) *Gray Oral Reading Test.* Indianapolis, Ind.: The Bobbs-Merrill Co., Inc., 1963.

7. McCullough, Constance M. *McCullough Word-Analysis Tests.* Boston: Ginn and Company, 1960, 1962.

8. McKee, Paul. *The McKee Inventory of Phonetic Skills.* Boston: Houghton Mifflin Co., 1962.

9. Monroe, Marian. *Monroe Diagnostic Reading Examination.* Chicago: C.H. Stoelting Co., 1928.

10. Spache, George D. *Diagnostic Reading Scales.* Monterey, California: California Test Bureau, 1963.

11. Triggs, Frances, *et al. Diagnostic Reading Test: Upper Level,* (Grade 7-College Freshman Year). Mountain Home, North Carolina: The Committee on Diagnostic Reading Tests, 1952, 1958.

Other References

12. Bond, Guy, and Miles A. Tinker, *Reading Difficulties, Their Diagnosis and Correction.* New York: Appleton-Century-Crofts, Inc., 1967.

13. Harris, Albert J. *How to Increase Reading Ability.* New York: David McKay Co., 1961.

14. Shedd, Charles. "Specific Perceptual Motor Disabilities," speech delivered at NDEA Institute in Reading, University of Kentucky, July 29, 1966.

15. Thorndike, E.L. "Reading as Reasoning: A Study of Mistakes in Paragraph Reading," *Journal of Educational Psychology, 8* (June 1917), 323-332.

16. Trella, Thaddeus M. "What Do Diagnostic Reading Tests Diagnose?" *Elementary English, 43* (April 1966), 370-372.

17. Zintz, Miles V. *Corrective Reading.* Dubuque, Iowa: William C. Brown, 1966.

ELEANOR M. LADD

More than Scores from Tests

*How are standardized test scores used? Is it "file and
forget"? Ladd contends they are a veritable gold mine of
diagnostic information, but they must be correctly mined.
Classroom teachers, remedial teachers, and administrators at all
levels can profit equally from this discussion of practical
techniques.*

*What happens to test scores in your school? What are some
feasible ways of finding time and personnel to item analyze large
numbers of tests? What kinds of abnormal behaviors have you
observed from children taking tests? Why is there a band (dark
lines) in the illustration of the bivariate distribution? How many
different uses can you think of for a bivariate distribution?*

There is more information in the results of standardized tests
than is ordinarily used. Even the orthodox suggestions of the
test makers are often ignored and valuable information is lost.
Perhaps more important, there are unorthodox techniques
which yield diagnostic information from the standardized test of
particular value to the reading teacher. Through the use of
these suggestions a teacher will add to her store of knowledge
regarding the reading behaviors and skills of her students. An
investment of time is required but no additional money is
needed.

The recent trend has been toward centralized scoring of
achievement tests. The delay in the return of the results even by
a few weeks makes the use of the data less pertinent to the
instructional program. Furthermore, data provided are often
inadequate for application of some of the suggested techniques.

Reprinted from *The Reading Teacher*, 24 (January 1971), pp. 305-311, by
permission of Eleanor Ladd and the International Reading Association.

Teachers who are interested in teaching to the weaknesses and strengths of their students find it difficult and self-defeating to wait and then perhaps to receive only printouts of scores rather than the tests themselves. The author finds many teachers scoring their own tests before sending them to central headquarters. Administrators should routinely investigate the current feelings of their teachers on this matter — especially in the primary grades — and, where necessary, make provision for this local scoring even if the tests are subsequently sent for central processing.

To reduce as much as possible the time lapse between the testing and the use of the results and to give maximum opportunity for effective use, the tests should be administered toward the beginning of the school year. The prospect that the results will affect the instructional program is much greater if this practice is followed.

Among the techniques through which it is possible to gain additional information from the administration of standardized reading tests are (1) an item analysis, (2) an analysis of patterns of performance, (3) the observation of student's behavior during the taking of the test, (4) an untimed performance score, (5) the Durost reading reinforced by hearing technique, and (6) the use of a bivariate (two-way) distribution chart to show the relationship between two scores simultaneously, which may yield a clearer picture of the reading performance of a classroom or a school. Some of these may be applied to test scores. Others require additions to the prescribed testing procedures. All, however, require more than perusal of a profile sheet.

ITEM ANALYSIS

Much diagnostic information can be gained through analysis of the correct responses and errors produced by students. First, each test item must be examined as to its intended purpose. Often publishers give a skills chart in which each item is identified relative to a particular skill. Sometimes these charts are not in the usual "Directions" or "Manual" but have to be separately obtained. When a new test is being given, such charts should be requested, routinely. By itself, this analysis of the purpose of each item can be an enlightening experience.

Mysteries of the construction of the test are often revealed which may explain the apparent lack of "fit" of the test to the population under consideration

After each item has been analyzed and categorized as to its purpose, the items testing similar skills are grouped or coded so as to yield information relating to the mastery of skills. When separate items or groups of homogeneous items are so evaluated and a judgment made as to the quality of the response, the action is closely related to the presently "in" process called criterion-referenced test interpretation since it focuses upon the level of mastery of individual items (Prescott, 1971; Johnson and Kress, 1971).

When the correct responses and errors of all students are charted, the teacher has information regarding the mastery of particular skills of the class as a whole as well as of the individual child. Instruction then can be adjusted to the strengths and weaknesses revealed. Valuable instructional time can be saved when the tests show certain understandings are already mastered. The errors constitute instructional guidelines which assist the teacher in providing for individual differences.

PATTERNS OF PERFORMANCE

Inspection of the spacing of right and wrong responses will often reveal additional information concerning a student. Standardized tests generally are arranged so that the items are in order of difficulty from easy to hard to measure the range of power in the area to be tested. A student who is appropriately tested most often answers a certain number of questions more or less correctly at the beginning of the test, after which the correct responses are scattered or cease altogether. Most students, when they reach this point in the test, stop.

The distribution of correct responses oftentimes reveals with startling clarity when a student has stopped answering the questions from his knowledge and has started to guess — sometimes on the basis of partial information and sometimes randomly (Fry, 1971). For example, if a perforated scoring key is placed over the answer sheet, it is easy to see that the first part of the test shows high concentration of correct responses which subsequently tend to get less and less concentrated. If a child has attempted all of the items and has missed the very large proportion of them beyond a certain level, this is almost positive evidence of guessing toward the end of the test. Students as a general rule do not guess and should not guess. Test taking should not be an exercise in educational roulette. However, the directions for many standardized tests encourage children to guess with the result that oftentimes the test score is invalidated.

One technique which is very effective in avoiding this trouble is the inclusion among the choices of a "don't know" response. This type of response, pioneered in the *Metropolitan Achievement Tests* published in 1958 particularly in Arithmetic and Language, has proved subsequently to be very effective, especially if accompanied by directions which urge the children to take the attitude that the test is a sharing of information with the teacher and that it is just as important for the teacher to know that a child does *not* know the answer as it is for him to know that the child does know the answer. Guessing contributes nothing to anyone, neither pupil nor teacher, which is helpful in improving instruction.

Occasionally, the subject of some particular selection in the reading comprehension test will be of great interest to a child and will relate to his previous experience. In such instances, the child may answer a series of questions correctly concerning that paragraph and this, too, will be revealed by studying the pattern of the child's responses. In other words, a cluster of items, somewhere farther along in the test than you would normally expect the student to work, appears as a series of correct responses. Some consideration of the nature of the paragraph in question can be helpful to the teacher in identifying an area of interest for the child which may not have been previously suspected.

OBSERVATION DURING THE TESTING

The teacher's own attitude toward the testing procedure is vitally important. It should be matter of fact, almost casual, and yet rigorous in adhering to directions and time limits. If this kind of testing atmosphere has prevailed, the behavior of the students during the testing will reveal to the alert teacher much significant information. Testing situations too often are tension producing. The extreme cases of tension are often observable through non-verbal behavior. Nervous twitching of the face or body, repetitive movements, scratching, biting lips or pencil, erasing often, etc., may be clues to the cost of the effort being made by the student and should not go unnoticed. Symptoms of nervousness may change from sub-test to sub-test. The number and degree of tension symptoms exhibited by a student should be noted in order that comparisons can be made from performance in one sub-test to another.

The more astute the teacher in observing the behavior of the students, the more diagnostic the information gathered will be. However, the teacher has to be aware of the usual behavior of the student before he can evaluate the abnormal reaction. All wrong responses have meaning, but errors made under extreme pressure are more likely to be an indication of the frustration the child is experiencing than of the specific nature of his problem.

Testing should not be a frustrating experience for a normal child. If it is, the teacher has every reason to believe that the test is inappropriate and the paper should be so marked. As a general rule this is not the fault of the test so much as the fault of the person deciding to give the test. The problem is not a simple one. If promotion is on the basis of chronological age and the child is really not functioning at the grade level in which he is placed, he should be tested (or retested) on a more suitable instrument. The situation also works in reverse. Some children who are very able will not be adequately tested by the test appropriate for the grade. Such children should be given a more difficult level.

Test makers can determine only what the typical curriculum is grade by grade and make their tests accordingly. Astute teachers will know what children should be excused from the test or given a more suitable level. Administrators should be sympathetic with this need while, at the same time, wary of the effect on the distribution of scores and the average performance of a group with the removal of any considerable number of children from the tested group.

UNTIMED SCORE

To get more information some of the students may be allowed to continue to work for an "untimed" score after the reading test has been administered according to the time limits set by the test designer. This can easily be done by giving those who have not finished the test during the time limits a different pen or pencil, producing a different color, to mark their test booklets without the pressure of time. They can be told to continue marking as many items as they can: This procedure yields a score which, when compared with the timed score, reveals whether "speed" is a problem for the student. If students can handle the content when not timed, they may need assistance in correcting their inefficient reading habits.

If the tests are to be optically scanned, the items answered after time is up must be marked by an optically "clear" pencil or felt-tipped pen. The only generally safe color in such cases is a light blue. The publisher or machine processor (Measurement Research Center, for example) should be able to suggest a generally available instrument. If processing is done locally on an IBM 1230 or Digitek scanner, a quick experiment with various colors will show which ones are safe to use.

DUROST READING REINFORCED
BY HEARING TECHNIQUE

The Durost reading reinforced by hearing technique yields a measure of potential to compare with the achievement score gathered under standard conditions (*Metropolitan Manual for Interpreting*, 1962). It appears to be effective with all students having a reading problem. Whole grade administration is not recommended after the third or fourth grade as the reading speed of the majority of the students at this level and higher often is faster than the speaking speed of the administrator. Under these circumstances a substantial portion of readers are bothered by the teacher's voice instead of being assisted.

Subsequent to the administration of a reading test under standard conditions, an equivalent form is administered with the teacher reading aloud all the items and possible answers while the pupil reads silently. In this way, the student is assisted with the difficult words and a measure of his understanding of the content of the materials is obtained. Both tests are scored as usual. When the test administered "under conditions of rein-forcement" yields a considerably higher score (three stanines) than the test administered under standard conditions, the student should be suspected of having greater ability than the present level of achievement in reading and of being a good candidate for a corrective or remedial program.

There is some advantage in readministering the same form under conditions of reinforcement with the child using a different marker for the second administration. However, most children of average or better reading ability gain more than one stanine when this is done and the three stanine rule must be closely adhered to.

As coordinator of the Upper Pinellas (Florida) Corrective Reading Program, the author found the use of the reading reinforced by hearing technique to be economical of time and money. It yields comparative data of a diagnostic nature from a group testing situation. Coupled with teacher nominations, the technique proved to be a powerful screening device for the selection of students for corrective work. It identifies for the classroom teacher those students who can understand content through listening when the fear of reading the words is negated. As listening comprehension is one of the most important indicators of ability, measurement of this skill in an objective fashion is of great assistance to the teacher.

BIVARIATE DISTRIBUTION

Plotting on graph paper the potential (mental ability stanine based on score) of a student on one axis and the reading achievement stanine on the other axis will assist a teacher or administrator in visualizing the performance of a group of students. When used for one class, each student is given a number and his performance is plotted on one axis and his capacity as measured by an ability test is plotted on the other axis. If the total grade tested is plotted first, this provides a most suitable frame of reference for the special cases identified by number or letter. The students who have more ability than they are using are easily identified by inspection. Grouping for a number of purposes is suggested when inspecting data in a bivariate distribution.

A sample bivariate distribution is shown for one community on which has been superimposed the numbers to label selected cases previously considered for inclusion in a remedial reading program (Figure 1). From the chart, it can be seen that

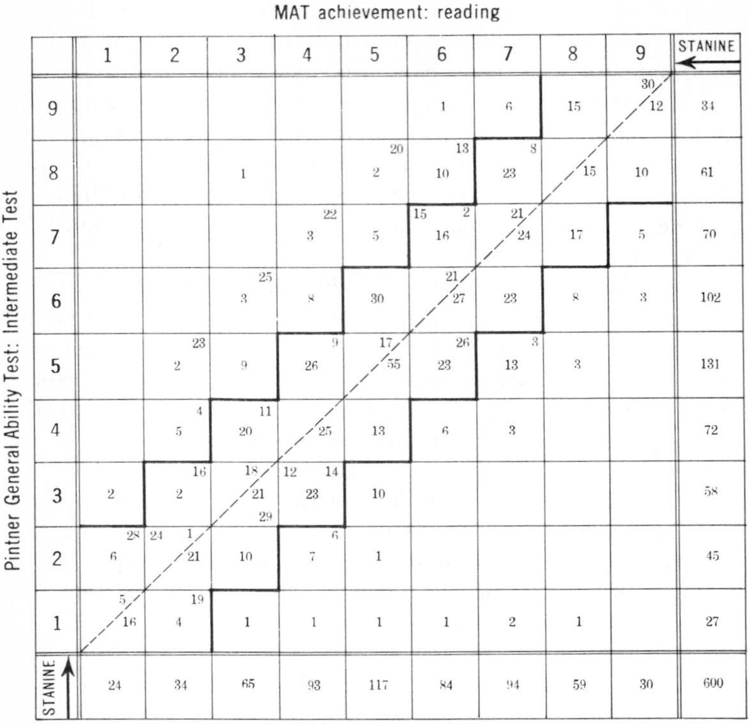

MAT achievement: reading

Pintner / MAT	1	2	3	4	5	6	7	8	9	STANINE
9						1	6	15	30/12	34
8			1		20/2	13/10	8/23	15	10	61
7				22/3	5	15 2/16	21/24	17	5	70
6			25/3	8	30	21/27	23	8	3	102
5		23/2	9	26	9/17/55	26/23	3/13	3		131
4		4/5	11/20	25	13	6	3			72
3	2	16/2	18/21/29	12 14/23	10					58
2	28/6	24 1/21	10	6/7	1					45
1	5/16	19/4	1	1	1	1	2	1		27
STANINE	24	34	65	93	117	84	94	59	30	600

Pintner General Ability Test: Intermediate Test

Correlation of General Ability and Reading: .79
Percent of cases in Mid-Stanine Range: .79

Figure 1. Hypothetical data showing the possible distribution
of thirty cases suspected of having reading difficulties superimposed on a base of 600 actual cases
representing a single community.

there were fifty-five students who ranked at the fifth stanine
level in reading achievement and also registered at the fifth
stanine level in general ability. It can also be seen that one of
these students (number seventeen) was selected for inclusion in
a remedial reading program. The data would indicate that the
student is a poor choice for corrective reading.

Inspection of these data reveals a number of students
working at capacity level who were suspected of having reading
problems. It also reveals a number of students with more
potential than reading ability who should have been considered.

SUMMARY

Within the limitations of the standardized testing situations are a number of opportunities to secure more than the usual information. Of course, whenever the tests are manipulated in ways other than the standardization procedures indicate, the results must be interpreted with caution. Familiarity with the procedures could result in securing three measures of abilities related to reading from a single test: reading achievement, reading speed, and listening comprehension ability. The acumen of the teacher in observing non-verbal behavior and patterns of performance within the written test adds to the knowledge of the child's learning problems. The item analysis and bivariate distribution chart yield important information from the organization of data in observable patterns.

REFERENCES

Durost, W. N. *Metropolitan manual for interpreting*. New York: Harcourt, Brace, Jovanovich, Inc., 1962.

Fry, E. R. The orangoutang score. *The Reading Teacher*, 1971, 24, 360.

Johnson, Marjorie Seddon, and Kress, R. A. Task analysis for criterion-referenced tests. *The Reading Teacher*, 1971, 24, 355.

Prescott, G. A. Criterion-referenced test interpretation in reading. *The Reading Teacher*, 1971, 24, 347.

LYMAN C. HUNT, JR.

Do We Have Diagnostic Measures of Reading Comprehension?

One aim of diagnosis is to specify relative strengths and deficiencies in reading skills. We can do this quite reliably for sight words, word attack skills, and some study skills. Hunt asks whether standardized tests give meaningful comprehension subtest scores that are valuable for diagnosis.

What does Hunt believe distinguishes one comprehension skill from another? Could there be other factors as well? What does he mean by saying that our tests give "quantitative" results? What advantages are there to the author's new approach? what limitations? What commercially available tests give separate subtest scores for supposedly different comprehension skills or encourage that kind of classification and analysis?

Do we have tests which measure different aspects of reading comprehension? Are the tests currently in use as diagnostic measures of reading comprehension *truly diagnostic*? I am not convinced that they are. Let's take a good look.

We See Three Profiles. George's score on the vocabulary test indicated a relative weakness. He appeared to grasp the central thought and do fairly well in retention of clearly stated details but less well in drawing inferences from context. His interpretation of contents was about average. George's total score on the test was approximately average with respect to the norm group.

Virginia, according to the first section of the test, was a slow reader. Comprehension and index usage scores were high,

---

Reprinted from *The High School Journal*, 39 (October 1955), pp. 44-48, by permission of the University of North Carolina Press.

advertising reading and poetry comprehension were relatively high, sentence meaning and general vocabulary fair, while paragraph meaning was relatively low. Virginia's total score was somewhat above average.

Hiram is less fortunate — he has his troubles with reading. But where? First, he took a survey test. His rate of reading seemed adequate, but vocabulary was low and comprehension very low. He was then given diagnostic reading tests of reading comprehension — both silent and auditory. The results of the auditory test showed a substantially higher performance in listening comprehension than in silent reading comprehension. Results on both tests showed better comprehension of details than of main ideas and conclusions which reached approximately the same low point.

The test results for these three hypothetical young people have been used for illustrative purposes only. We have been trying to illustrate practices common in both classroom and clinic. Both teacher and specialist use so-called diagnostic tests to determine strong and weak areas of reading comprehension for individual students.

Is This Procedure Sound? The diagnostic procedures described above have been fairly common for the past decade or two. Regardless of good intentions we may have been operating under false colors. Let us re-examine the fundamental issues carefully.

The most fundamental question follows: Does the reader in the usual or natural reading situation use mental processes which are sufficiently different to reflect described differences in reading comprehension? Does George use a different mental process in grasping the central thought than he does when he makes interpretations from the contents? Are you sure? As students of the reading process we can classify and define several different processes associated with comprehension. But unless these differences exist in the mental functioning of the reader we will merely be dealing with two names for the same process.

We Must Make an Assumption. Of course we must make the assumption that George, Virginia, and Hiram do use different thought processes within the total comprehension process, otherwise our measure would necessarily be one of "general comprehension" (total test score). Yet the difference in the thinking process during the reading act must be more than a use of different words or symbols used in such thinking. The difference must be in the actual thought process.

Unless we think clearly about the subtleness of the differences in the mental thought processes used in reading comprehension we may be dealing with differences that exist only on paper.

Virginia did relatively well in comprehension yet not so well in paragraph meaning. Are the items which follow the longer passage in the comprehension test sufficiently different from the items which follow the series of unrelated paragraphs to cause Virginia to use different thought processes?

Is there a real measurable difference between comprehension and paragraph meaning? The selection and assembling of items designed to measure a given comprehension process becomes a critical step in determining the answer to this question.

How Do We Assure Ourselves of Measuring Different Comprehension Processes? When we say that Hiram did equally poorly in main ideas and conclusions are we in effect talking of item groups which measure highly similar or truly different processes? How valid a measure of main ideas is each item within the comprehension item group? We must find out. This question is as important as whether a main idea item is a true measure of "main ideas."

We Use Item Analysis. The statistical technique of item analysis must be used to determine if real differences exist among groups of items assembled to measure allegedly different comprehension processes. If we have assembled items for two tests — say main ideas and conclusions — we must proceed to establish that each item in the main ideas group is highly similar with all other items in this group but likewise highly dissimilar to items used as a measure of conclusions. The item validity must be high with respect to the total score for main ideas and item validity must be low for total score for conclusions.

In his doctoral research this writer used differential item analysis with items designated to measure six processes related to reading comprehension. The results of the analysis showed that five item groups measured equally well each of the five designated processes. Stated in another way this is saying one common function "comprehension" is being measured by five allegedly different item groups. A sixth item group "vocabulary" was found to be measuring a somewhat — but not distinctly — different process of comprehension.

We Use Intercorrelations and Reliabilities. Another statistical test which should be applied whenever the claim "diagnostic" is made relates to intercorrelations among the various separate measures and the reliability of each measure.

If two item groups designed to measure two different processes of comprehension are correlated we obtain their interrelationships. If, on the other hand, the two item groups are measuring essentially the same process we have in effect a measure of consistency or reliability. Thus by having the intercorrelations among the various measures presented with the item group reliabilities, inspection can give some clue to whether measures are truly different. This information should always be given for any group of tests purported to be diagnostic. When such statistics have been subjected to factor analysis the task of interpretation is made a good deal easier. Factor analysis should be used for any group of tests when the claim diagnostic is made.

For example, if the intercorrelation between the item groups of main ideas and conclusions is .6 and the reliabilities for the two item groups are .7 and .5 we must exercise caution in assuming that the item groups measure different processes.

It is highly questionable whether it is a legitimate practice to include items grouped under labels such as main ideas, sentence meanings, details, paragraph meanings, within a larger test unless it is established that such differences are truly reflected in measurement.[1] Establishment of these validly

---

[1] The example used in the discussion of interrelationships and reliabilities of main ideas and conclusions may strike a familiar note with those who use the "Diagnostic Reading Tests." The development in this article is for illustration purposes *only* and nothing derogatory is intended. In fact the Committee on Diagnostic Tests is to be commended for the following statement: "There is one total score. . . . As was indicated earlier, the Committee's research, as well as the research done by other workers, does not justify presenting sub-scores which would break down 'comprehensions' into main ideas, details, and conclusions."

different measures is the burden of the test constructor. In most instances this has not been done. Therefore, it seems quite clear that George, Virginia, and Hiram may or may not have the specific difficulties or strengths their test profiles indicate. What meets the eye on the profile may or may not be real.

What Are We to Do? Are we on the right track when we use test scores for diagnosis? Can a quantitative approach — the number of items right — ever give us real insight into how an individual reader does with sentence meaning, paragraph meaning, or interpretations from context?

The basic proposition has previously been that recording and studying variations in the number of responses (raw scores made comparable) made by the individual reader is sufficient evidence of relative strengths and weaknesses in his ability to comprehend in reading. Can an analysis of the number of correct or incorrect responses prove to be sufficient?

To this writer only one possible hope exists for those who persist in using standardized test scores. The procedure used by the Committee on Diagnostic Reading Tests is that hope. The Diagnostic Reading Tests include a survey test as well as a series of independently constructed diagnostic tests which pertain to several aspects of the reading process. The use of a survey test to be followed by the use of one or more of the appropriate diagnostic tests may have merit. However, except in one or two instances (e.g., Sec. IV: Word Attack, Oral), diagnosis is made according to the number of correct responses. The approach remains quantitative in nature.

The Committee on Diagnostic Reading Tests should be encouraged to pursue their particular path. However, their road may be an endless one. Others must seek solutions to the problem of utilizing different, perhaps unique, approaches.

McCullough in her most delightfully written article, "What's Behind the Reading Score" (*Elementary English,* 30: 1-7, January 1953), suggests we analyze the reader's response to each particular item of the test. The important consideration becomes "what does this individual's responses to these items mean?" The total score is not important. But is there not a fallacy in this approach? It seems to this observer that a teacher or test user who can gain insight into an individual's reading pattern by analyzing in detail his response to test items can gain similar insights through a less arduous and tedious process. A possible merit of McCullough's approach to this problem, however, is that it is qualitative rather than quantitative in nature. McCullough suggests a fresh approach to the problem.

A Possible New Approach. Perhaps diagnosis is an individual matter. Perhaps appraisal of complex and subtle thought processes involved in reading comprehension must be made in informal observational situations rather than in the formalized test situation. Perhaps we have tried to take short cuts we cannot take.

This writer would suggest exploring the use of individual observation and interrogation. Following a survey measure of reading comprehension the examiner or teacher would conduct an interrogation with the student. In this interview the student would respond orally to sets of items based on carefully selected reading passages. The student would indicate his reasons for selecting each particular response, correct or incorrect. This information would be recorded, and specific errors made by the reader with respect to the meanings involved in the reading material studied. Diagnosis would thus be accomplished by analysis of errors in thinking made by the individual reader. Much of the thinking would be verbalized aloud. Herein lies the uniqueness of the approach.

This writer, using passages and items from some currently used diagnostic tests, feels he has attained some degree of success in this approach. Admittedly it is a subjective procedure. However, there is not sufficient evidence to show that measures based on "objective scores" provide the useful kind of information that is desirable to ascertain the individual's understanding of different aspects of reading comprehension. It is not reasonable to consider test criteria such as objectivity, scoring ease, etc., if in the final result we do not find out what we want to know about any particular individual's specific ability to comprehend in reading. If we really want to help George, Virginia, and Hiram we may have to listen to them think.

RUTH STRANG

Informal Tests in Each Subject

The upper levels of reading demand the ability to cope with materials written for specific content areas. These materials contain writing patterns different from those found in general reading and reading at lower levels of achievement; therefore, they demand special reading skills. However, standardized tests typically neglect or slight such skills. Strang offers some specific and practical suggestions for appraising these unique skills and abilities.

In what ways are these inventories similar to the IRIs described by Johnson and Kress in an earlier article in this section? Would it be helpful to construct, administer, and revise a try-out inventory first? Would there be any value in analyzing the results in ways suggested by Ladd in a previous article in this section? What are some curricular areas other than social studies and science where inventories such as these would be useful? Are there any skills Strang omits that you think should be included if you were to construct such an inventory? Do you agree that student scoring and discussion of these inventories is an important integral aspect? What cautions must be exercised in interpreting the results of these inventories?

Every subject teacher needs to find out how well the students in a new class can read the books he expects them to read. He wants to know: What is their purpose or purposes in reading a given selection? What is being communicated to them — what have they learned and remembered from reading this section of the text or reference book? How well can they communicate orally or in writing the ideas gained? An informal "teaching test" in each subject will answer these questions.

These teaching tests have several advantages: They are closely geared to instruction, whereas a formal diagnosis is too often divorced from instruction. The test results are easy for the teacher to apply in his daily instruction. The free or unstructured response shows how students approach a reading assignment, what they remember from reading it, and how well they communicate the ideas in it. These tests also promote student self-appraisal. By encouraging the student to take the initiative in analyzing his own reading process, they motivate learning. A series of similar tests followed by a discussion of progress made enables the student to assess his ability to profit from instruction.

Informal tests are fairly easy to construct and administer. The teacher selects a section of about a thousand words from a text which the students have not read. The student reads the selection and computes his speed. He may time himself or the teacher may write the time on the board in ten-second or larger intervals, erasing each number as the next comes up. As soon as the student finishes reading, he looks up and writes the number that he sees. This figure is his reading time in seconds.

He then answers the questions without referring to the selection. Thus retention as well as comprehension is tested. This is a student's most natural response after reading an assignment.

The first question calls for a free or creative response. It may ask simply for information: What did the author say? Or it may ask for information plus opinion: What did the author say? What did the author mean by this? Or it may combine information, opinion, and consideration of the author's motive: What did the author say? What did he mean by this? Why did he say it? After obtaining answers to the first question only, the teacher will be amazed at the wide range of responses in a single class.

The free response may be supplemented by short-answer or objective questions. Some of these test the reader's ability to recognize the main ideas and supporting details; others, his ability to draw inferences and conclusions, to define key words, and to appreciate humor, character portrayal, or other qualities of literary style. The test exercises can be varied to serve different purposes, such as to see how well students can answer questions they have formulated before beginning to read, or how effectively they can extract ideas relevant to a particular topic.

Some students in a heterogeneous class will do very poorly on this kind of informal test. The text for the grade is obviously too difficult for them. But they can learn to get some ideas from it, and they usually want to have the same book as their classmates.

As students participate in the class discussion of one another's answers to the questions, they see more clearly why their free response rated only 1 or 2, whereas others deserved ratings of 9 or 10. They become aware of the reasons why some definitions of words are more precise and clear than others. They learn how to get the main idea more quickly by analyzing the ways in which paragraphs are built.

The informal reading test may be expanded into an informal group reading inventory and into a comprehensive, integrated, diagnostic self-appraisal teaching procedure.

GROUP READING INVENTORY

The group reading inventory is used to determine the reading proficiency of every student in a given subject class. The most important part of the inventory is the informal test already described. To this are added questions on study skills, location-of-information skills, and other skills needed in reading the particular subject. Ability to apply the ideas gained from the passage to current events or to personal problems may also be appraised in this informal group inventory.

Students mark their own papers to see for themselves their strengths and their difficulties in reading. Junior high school students are especially interested in themselves as persons and like to know about their reading efficiency. When the student has corrected his inventory, he tabulates the results on the front page, for example:

> Parts of book
> Speed of reading
> Vocabulary meaning
> Contextual meaning, and so on

A check may indicate either skills in which the student needs instruction and practice or, if preferred, the skills he has mastered.

The grade level at which the student is able to read is not so important as the analysis of his reading skills. If, however, a student scores 65 per cent below the grade level, he should be given an individual reading inventory.

Detailed directions for making group reading inventories for social studies and science classes were worked out for teachers by Dr. David Shepherd when he was serving as reading consultant at the Norwalk (Connecticut) High School. They are reproduced here with his permission. Permission for reprinting parts of the social studies and science inventories was also obtained from Harper & Row (Shepherd, 1960). *

SOCIAL STUDIES: GROUP READING INVENTORY

Directions for making a group reading inventory using the social studies textbook:

1. Use 26 to 30 questions.
2. Write questions designed to measure the following reading skills in the proportions as shown below:
   (1) Using parts of the book (5 questions)
   (2) Using resource (library) materials (4 questions)
   (3) Using maps, pictures, charts, etc. (4 questions)
   (4) Vocabulary (3 questions)
   (5) Noting the main idea (3 questions)
   (6) Noting pertinent supporting details (3 questions)
   (7) Drawing conclusions (3 questions)
   (8) Noting the organization of the material (1 question)
3. Choose a reading selection of not more than 3-4 pages in length.
4. Have questions of skills — (4) through (8) — vocabulary, main ideas, details, conclusions, and organization — based on the reading selection.
5. Explain to the pupils the purpose of the test and the reading skills the test is designed to measure. As the test is given, let the pupils know the skill being measured.
6. Read each question twice.
7. Write the page reference of each question on the blackboard as the question is read.

---

*The social studies and science inventories were adapted by Ruth Strang from the following publications: David L. Shepherd, *Effective Reading in the Social Sciences,* Row, Peterson Co., 1960, pp. 20-22. David L. Shepherd, *Effective Reading in the Sciences,* Row, Peterson Co., 1960, pp. 22-24. Reprinted with permission of David L. Shepherd.

8. A pupil is considered to be deficient in any of the skills if he gets more than one question in any of the skills wrong. For example, if a pupil gets two vocabulary questions wrong, he will be considered deficient in vocabulary. If he gets only one vocabulary question wrong, he will not be considered deficient.

Form of Test (Sample)

Parts of book

1. On what page would you find the map that shows (name of map). (tests use of map table found in front of book)
2. On what page does Chapter ____ begin? What is the title of the unit of which it is a part? (use of table of contents)
3. How can the introduction on pages ____ help you in your study? (shows understanding of unit introduction)
4. Of what value are the questions, activities, and vocabulary shown on pages ____ to you for the understanding of the material of the textbook? (shows understanding of specific textbook study aids)
5. In what part of the book would you look to find the page references of this topic? ____ (purpose of index)

Use of resources

6. What library aid will tell you the library number of the book ____, so that you would be able to find it on the shelves? (knowledge of function of card catalogue)
7. What is a biography? (shows knowledge of a type of reference)
8. Name one set of encyclopedias. How are the topics in them arranged? (shows knowledge of a type of reference material)
9. Name a library guide that will help you to find a specific magazine article ____. If you were to give a report in class and you knew that most of your information would be in current magazines, what guide would you use that would tell you what magazine to use and what issue of it to use for information on your topic? (shows knowledge of a type of library guide to research)

Use of maps, charts, etc.

10. What does the map on page ____ show you? (shows an understanding of fundamental idea of map)
11. What do the black areas (or some other special feature)

shown on the map on page____represent? (shows ability to
read information from a map)

12. Turn to page_____. Ask for some specific bit of information
that is shown by the chart. Example: "What are the three
branches of our Federal Government?" (shows ability to
understand diagrams)

13. Turn to page_____. Ask for some specific bit of information
that is shown by the picture. Ask also for interpretation.
Example: Picture showing sod house on the prairie: "What is
the settler's house made of? Can you tell why that type of
building material is used?" (shows ability to understand and
interpret picture)

Vocabulary

Read pages_____.

14. Define_____ _____ _____.

15. What did "So and So" mean when he said_____
_____(word or term to be defined from the comment must
be pointed out to the pupils)? (contextual meanings)

16. What is a____ _____?

Noting main ideas

17. Questions to ask for only the main points of
18. information — main ideas of the longer
19. important paragraphs.

Noting details

20. Questions to ask for specific bits of
21. information about the principal characters
22. or ideas of the material.

Drawing conclusions

23. Questions, the answers of which are not completely in the
24. textbook. Questions beginning with "Why," making com-
25. parisons, predicting events, usually measure drawing conclusions. Example: "Why did the pioneers brave the dangers
to move westward?"

26. Each author follows an outline in writing the information in
your textbook. In looking through the chapter (one from
which the reading selection was taken) write down the
author's first main topic.

or

If you were to outline the material that you have read, what
would be the 1-2-3 main topics (headings) of your outline?

SCIENCE: GROUP READING INVENTORY

Directions for making a diagnostic test using science text-book:

1. Use approximately 30 questions.
2. Write questions designed to measure the following reading skills in proportions as shown below:
   (1) Using parts of the book (4 questions)
   (2) Using resource (library) materials (3 questions)
   (3) Vocabulary (meaning from the context) (4 questions)
   (4) Noting the main idea (4 questions)
   (5) Noting pertinent supporting details (4 questions)
   (6) Following directions (3 questions)
   (7) Drawing conclusions (3 questions)
   (8) Applying theoretical information (3 questions)
   (9) Understanding formulas and equations (3 questions)
3. Choose a reading selection of not more than 3-4 pages in length.
4. Have questions on skills (3), (4), (5), (7), (8) — vocabulary, main ideas, details, conclusion, application — based on the reading selection. Items (6) and (9) may require student to refer to the textbook.
5. Explain to the pupils the purpose of the inventory and the reading skills the inventory is designed to measure. As the inventory is given, let the pupils know the skill being measured.
6. Read each question twice.
7. Write the page reference of each question as necessary on the blackboard as the question is read.
8. Have pupil score his own paper.
9. A pupil is considered to be deficient in any of the skills if he gets more than one question in any of the skills wrong. For example: If a pupil gets more than one question in any of the skills (two vocabulary questions) wrong, he will be considered deficient.
10. Form of Tabulation

Name of Class _____ Section _____ Teacher _____

Name of Pupil	Parts of book	Resource material	Vocabulary	etc.

_____

_____ (state wherever the pupil is deficient) (See page 130.)

Form of Test (Sample)

Parts of book

1. On what page would you find the chapter called____? (tests ability to use table of contents)
2. Of what value to you are the questions under the chapter section called____? (shows understanding of specific textbook aids)
3. How are the chapters arranged or grouped? (shows knowledge of organization of textbook)
4. What sections of the book would you use to find the page reference of the topic_____? (shows knowledge of the purpose of the index)

Library

5. How are topics arranged in a "reference book"? (shows knowledge of organization of reference book under consideration)
6. What is a biography? (shows knowledge of a type of reference material)
7. Explain the difference between science fiction and science factual materials. (shows knowledge of important types of science reading materials)

Vocabulary

8. These questions test two ways of defining words:
9. One — through the context — turn to page _____.
10. How is the word used by the author?
11. Two — recall — what does the word mean? Use it in a sentence or give the definition and ask for the appropriate word.

Main ideas

12. Questions to ask
13. for main points of information —
14. for main ideas of the longer important paragraphs
15. (chapter headings, subheadings, marginal headings, introduction and summary).
16. Summary of an experiment.

Details

17. Questions to ask for specific bits of information about the

18. principal definitions and laws, aspect of a process, ap-
19. plication of law, principal steps in an experiment, a life cycle.
20. Use words that select the relative importance of details —
    how author shows the importance of specific details. All
    similar details are grouped around one main idea — each
    main idea has its qualifying details.

Following directions

21. Questions to show sequence of steps or ideas
22. for solving a problem or performing an
23. experiment. Chain of events.

Drawing conclusions

24. Questions, the answers to which are not completely found in
    the textbook.
25. Questions beginning with "Why," asking for the significance
26. of a finding, the value of the finding of an experiment, or the
    implication of a description of some species, or natural
    phenomena, cause and effect. What happens if certain
    natural conditions were present, comparing two or more
    types of living organisms or inanimates, etc.

Application

27. Questions asking for examples of how scientific laws and
28. principles can be put to practical use. Example: Explain the
29. relationship of photosynthesis to the conservation of plant
    life.

Formulas, symbols, etc.

30. Questions showing meanings attached to
31. symbols as given in the text.

The summary chart shown on page 247, with names of
students to be listed along the left-hand side and types of
reading difficulties enumerated across the top, summarizes the
information for a class. When read horizontally, it describes the
individual students; when read vertically, it shows which difficulties are common to the class. Thus the teacher sees the
instruction needed by the whole class and the special help
needed by individuals.

Name of class _____ Section _____ Teacher _____

Name	Use of parts of book	Vocabulary	Meaning	Contextual meanings	Synonyms and antonyms	General knowledge	Word recognition	Syllabication	Accent	Prefixes and suffixes	Part of speech	Comprehension	Main ideas	Supporting details	Drawing conclusions	Sequence of ideas	Skimming	Speed in wpm	Comments
John Jones	✓	✓	✓	✓	✓	✓	✓	✓	✓	✓	✓				✓			194	(Check wherever pupil is deficient)
Robert Brown				✓	✓	✓								✓	✓			150	

Summary Chart

For students whose comprehension score is below 50 per cent or above 95 per cent, Shepherd recommends administering the individual inventory (described in Chapter 10). Appropriate instruction should follow the giving of the inventory; this, indeed, is its main purpose. When the inventory is repeated at the middle and at the end of the semester, both teachers and students get a sense of accomplishment as they see improvement in reading skills.

DIAGNOSTIC SELF-APPRAISAL TEACHING PROCEDURE

The instructional value of these informal procedures is brought out more fully by the integrated procedure developed by Melnik (1960) for improving the reading of social studies in junior high school. This procedure

> starts by asking students to state their aims or goals in reading a social studies assignment. Most students of this age are vague about their reasons for reading and about the reading method that would be most appropriate. They are then asked to read a selection from a social studies book that is typical of the material the students will be expected to read in their classes. After reading the passage they answer two types of questions — creative response or open-end: What did the author say? and a number of multiple-choice questions that are designed to furnish evidence of the student's ability to get the literal meaning, to see relations, draw inferences, make generalizations, and understand the meaning of key words.
>
> As soon as the student has answered the questions, he has data before him for self-appraisal. He marks his own paper. He grades his free response on a ten-point scale, and analyzes the kinds of errors he has made in the multiple choice questions (each choice represents a certain kind of error). Instruction immediately follows this self-appraisal, while the students are specifically motivated to learn how to get the right answers and to avoid the same errors next time.
>
> There is a next time; the whole procedure is repeated with another similar selection. After the second exercise is completed and analyzed, the students are able to note the progress they have made. A third repetition of the procedure makes further improvement possible.

This testing-teaching-evaluating procedure bridges the gap between the hurriedly-made teacher test and the standardized test. It relieves the teacher of some of the burden of making instructional material; at the same time it gives him a concrete model for further testing-teaching-evaluating based on the text or reference books used by his particular class (Strang, 1961, pp. 386-387).

REFERENCES

Melnik, Amelia, *The Improvement of Reading through Self-appraisal: A Procedure for Teaching Reading in Junior High School Social Studies.* Unpublished doctoral project, Teachers College, Columbia University, 1960.

Strang, Ruth, "Evaluation of Development in and through Reading," *Development in and through Reading*, Nelson B. Henry, ed. Sixtieth Yearbook of the National Society for the Study of Education, University of Chicago Press, Chicago, 1961, chap. 21.

PAUL M. HOLLINGSWORTH

Diagnosis and Prognosis:
An Interdisciplinary Approach

Educators for years have generally accepted a multiple-causation theory of reading disability, no single factor being individually responsible. We must translate this belief into practice in both diagnostic and remedial phases of our work. Hollingsworth outlines six levels of diagnosis, each progressively broadening the information base, and then he describes the operation of an interdisciplinary program based on this rationale.

Is it necessary for all children to be diagnosed at all six steps of diagnosis? Review the titles in Part Two. Are there any aspects of diagnosis you consider important that Hollingsworth slights or omits? How does his approach relate to Robinson's proposal about auxiliary services in Part Six? What changes would be necessary in your program to make it interdisciplinary? If we have interdisciplinary diagnosis, what ramifications has it for remediation?

Reading teachers, clinicians and reading specialists throughout the United States have supported the theory that reading disabilities are caused by many different facets of the learning process. Yet, this has not led these same reading experts toward an approach for diagnosis and prognosis that reflects the multiple-causation theory of reading disability. If this theory is tenable, an interdisciplinary approach to diagnosis and prognosis is essential.

Very often the diagnosis of a student with a reading problem consists chiefly of tests to determine the extent of

A paper presented at the 1970 convention of the International Reading Association. Reprinted by permission of Paul M. Hollingsworth.

reading disabilities or to evaluate the student's performance in reading. An attempt to determine the causes of this disability beyond the reading achievement level is often neglected. If the diagnosis does go beyond the reading performance level it often goes into visual or auditory screening and intelligence testing. The results of this type of a diagnosis is not an attempt to uncover the multiple causes that many reading experts claim cause reading disabilities. It is an inadequate diagnostic study which can only lead to an inadequate remedial program for the student.

A questionnaire sent to the Connecticut Association for Reading Research, was reported by Criscuolo *(1)*. The respondents indicated that the determination of whether a child has a reading disability should involve the concerted effort of the classroom teacher, principal, reading specialist, guidance counselor, psychologist and school nurse. The respondents felt that this approach was necessary because of the multiple-causation factor in reading disability.

LEVELS OF DIAGNOSIS

In the International Reading Association's Target Series Book Three — *Treating Reading Disabilities: The Specialist's Role (3)*, levels of diagnosis are discussed. Four levels of diagnosis are pointed out. These were:

1. Description of performance.
2. Behavior affecting reading performance.
3. Specific analysis of reading process.
4. Determination of mental ability.

These four areas are indeed a vital and important part of any extensive evaluation of a student's reading problem; however, more information is needed concerning his learning problems if an interdisciplinary approach is really functional. Added to the above four levels should be:

5. Evaluation of medical problems affecting learning.
6. Family attitudes contributing to learning problems.

In the first level of diagnosis, the reading performance of the child is observed by the classroom teacher. Strengths and weaknesses in vocabulary, word recognition skills and comprehension are determined through observation, informal teacher-made tests and group standardized tests. The classroom teacher should also observe the child's performance in other academic areas. Special attention should be given to the pupil's functioning in communication areas such as listening, speaking and writing as well as reading. The method in which the child attacks thought problems in any area of the curriculum would also be helpful in the diagnosis.

At the second level of diagnosis, the student's attitudes toward reading are evaluated. This is accomplished through classroom observation and by the use of attitude and personality tests. This may point out his attitudes toward reading and poor work habits. An interest inventory and autobiographical sketch written by the child would be most helpful in an interdisciplinary approach to the reading disability.

On the third level of diagnosis the remedial reading teacher or reading specialist becomes involved. At this level, the reading specialist makes a more specific analysis of the process of reading by determining association, assimilation, analysis and evaluation which lead to motor, visual or vocal output. The reading specialist's use of standardized tests of specific skills as well as informal tests and observation will aid in the interdisciplinary approach to diagnosis.

The fourth level of diagnosis involves testing procedures that require the trained abilities of a psychologist or clinician. The child's mental abilities, memory and his association and reasoning abilities are determined. Standardized tests such as the Wechsler Intelligence Scale for Children, and memory and associative tests are available for diagnosis at this level. Along with standardized tests, informal tests and observation are also essential at this level of the evaluation.

The fifth level of diagnosis adds medical information to the interdisciplinary approach to reading diagnosis. At this level the medical evaluation would entail examinations by the family doctor or pediatrician, the ophthalmologist, orthoptist, otologist and neurologist. Possibly a psychiatrist may also be consulted. Since reading disability is a complex problem with many possible etiologies, this level combines the medical and educational evaluation to the interdisciplinary approach for diagnosis.

At the sixth level of diagnosis family background and parental attitudes are evaluated as possible contributing factors to the child's learning difficulties. From the parents, birth information, developmental and medical history, school history, home background, behavior, interests and attitudes are obtained. After this information is received from the parents it should be compared to the reports from the classroom teacher and the school for similarities and differences. Also information received from the parents is valuable for the complete diagnosis because much of this information is not observable in a classroom or clinic situation.

THE READING SPECIALIST IN AN INTERDISCIPLINARY APPROACH

In instances where an interdisciplinary approach to diagnosis for reading difficulties has been implemented, the reading specialist's work and responsibilities have been increased immeasurably. It is quite apparent that the reading specialist, with his training in the areas of psychology, child development, educational methods, communication skills, learning problems and specifically reading, would be the individual who would direct and coordinate the interdisciplinary approach to reading diagnosis. The reading specialist is probably more capable than other area specialists in interpreting the various reports and evaluations from this team approach and directing the team efforts to the problem of teaching the child to read. This is certainly no easy task because when experts from the various disciplines discuss diagnosis from their particular point of view, there is difficulty in communicating with one another.

AN INTERDISCIPLINARY PROGRAM

An interdisciplinary approach to reading difficulties is operating on an experimental basis in Reno, Nevada (2). The personnel at the University of Nevada's Reading Clinic, the Washoe County School District and the Medical Facilities in the Reno area have combined their disciplines into one comprehensive diagnostic program. It was felt that by combining the available medical and educational disciplines of the community into one program, the children who have severe reading problems would be better served.

Upon discovery of a severe reading disability, the classroom teacher may refer the child to the program after consulting with the principal, reading teacher, school nurse and the school counselor. The first level of diagnosis, description of performance, and the second level of diagnosis, behavior affecting reading performance, are usually accomplished at this time by the classroom teacher, principal and possibly the reading teacher or school counselor. Observational reports, interest inventories, school nurse's records, school cumulative files, standardized and informal tests concerning the child referred are collected and forwarded to the University of Nevada's Reading Clinic.

The next step in this program is taken when the parents, referred by the school personnel, take the child to the Reading Clinic. (A physician may also initiate referral to the program.) At the Reading Clinic, the third level of diagnosis, specific analysis of the reading process and part of level four, determination of mental abilities, are completed at the Clinic. Also assisting in the level four diagnosis are personnel from the Washoe County School Districts. These psychometrists measure various mental abilities and give other specific learning tests. An informal psychological examination for emotional problems is also given each child by a psychologist from the Washoe County School District.

At level five, evaluation of medical problems affecting learning, the child is examined by the family doctor or pediatrician, the ophthalmologist, orthoptist, and neurologist. The neurological examination may require an electro-encephalogram (EEG). Depending upon the findings of the school psychologist and the medical examiners, a psychiatrist may be consulted. The child is given an audiogram which is administered by an otologist in the Speech and Hearing Clinic at the University of Nevada.

While the evaluation is in progress at the Reading Clinic, the parents are interviewed concerning the child's home background and his attitudes and interests. An additional parent questionnaire is completed by the parents and mailed to the Clinic to further clarify certain family attitudes that might contribute to learning difficulties. Parole officers and social workers may also contribute to this sixth level of diagnosis, family attitudes contributing to learning problems.

Reports from the entire work-up in all six levels of diagnosis are channeled to the Reading Clinic at the University of Nevada, where an Evaluation Board meets for a final analysis of the individual child's problem. Basically, the Board consists of a medical doctor, a representative from the Reading Clinic and a representative from the Washoe County School District. This group analyzes and incorporates all of the reports, tests and materials of the child into one case study. Specialized professional people may be called in as deemed necessary at any particular time during the final analysis.

Once the evaluation is made, the appropriate referrals for treatment are made. This may be remedial reading started, medical problems corrected, emotional problems handled, home environment aided, etc. The Evaluation Board and especially the reading clinician continues to assist in the therapy for these children who are referred for this program.

SUMMARY

The comments in this paper concerning the interdisciplinary approach to diagnosis and prognosis has mentioned only a few ideas that people from various disciplines involved in the child's learning process may aid one another in an integrated and more comprehensive and complete diagnosis. There are many other ways an interdisciplinary approach could be organized. If one truly acknowledges the multiple-causation theory of reading disability, then it follows that one needs a multiple-discipline approach in solving the reading disabilities of children.

The interdisciplinary approach focuses attention on the individual child and his learning problems. Many factors must be considered before an adequate explanation can be made of the child's inability to read effectively and by utilizing the many discipline experts in this explanation, it will do much toward solving this problem for the individual child.

REFERENCES

1. Criscuolo, Nicholas P., "Seven Crucial Issues in Reading," *The Reading Teacher*, 23 (November 1969), 156-158.
2. Hollingsworth, Paul M. and Donald K. Mousel, "One Community's Approach to Dyslexia," *Journal of Pediatric Ophthalmology*, 6 (August, 1969), 125-127.

3. Smith, Carl B., et al., *Treating Reading Disabilities: The Specialist's Role*. Newark, Delaware: International Reading Association, p. 16.

4

Creating
A Learning Environment

A good carpenter cannot build a sound house without quality materials, and quality materials cannot create a sound house for a bad carpenter. Both must be good or the product cannot be. A good teacher must work knowledgeably with the best material to create a true learning environment

Prevention and correction must not be simply a repetition of a classroom developmental program that has already failed. Materials selected after diagnosing the problem must be coordinated with appropriate methodology. Materials do not exist in a vacuum but are, hopefully, an integral part of an organized, systematic program. They must be carefully matched with causal factors and methodology on an individual basis.

Currently there is unanimous agreement that the key element in any successful reading program is the knowledgeable, competent teacher, especially when children are having reading difficulties. Some situations, such as teaching the inner-city child, demand unique qualities, outlooks, and capabilities, and any teacher who grossly lacks them may be foredoomed to frustration and failure. But all teachers, in classroom or clinic, apparently can make some progress just by talking with, and relating to, children. Children with reading difficulties have the same needs as all other children, plus additional ones. Being unable to read as well as other children is truly a traumatic experience that produces profound negative effects. Not only do these children need the best professional reading instruction possible, they also need large doses of reassurance, empathy, acceptance, success, recognition, praise, and love. Our attitudes, particularly as manifested in our talk, apparently can either facilitate or inhibit both the child's reading progress and his self-concept. We must make certain that what we say and how we say it are positive, not detrimental, influences. No books or teacher's manuals can help us attain these goals. Only day-by-day intentional practice followed by rigorous and candid self-analysis and renewed efforts can move us in the desired direction.

DOROTHY CHENOWETH KLAUSNER

Screening and Development
of the Remedial Reading Teacher

This article develops the well-documented idea that per-
sonality traits strongly affect the success of the reading-
improvement teacher. It also suggests some informal methods
that can be used by teachers in developing healthy states of
mind.

What personality traits do you consider most important for
a reading teacher? Which are least important? How would you
appraise your strengths and weaknesses against a list of im-
portant traits? What are some principles of mental hygiene? If
feasible, develop an outline for an in-service plan related to
mental health and personality development.

Why did Johnny gain three years in a remedial reading course
from Miss X and then lose one and one-half years in a second
course from Miss Y — both teachers using the same methods?
The next ten years will certainly include research on the causes
of this recurring problem of varying success of different
teachers of reading *(22)*.

Attention may well be directed both to the fact that the
teacher's personality is important to her success in teaching
remedial reading and to the specific personality traits which are
helpful. Methods of developing such desirable personality traits
— both in teacher-training and in teachers already serving —
will surely follow.

Relatively few reading teachers have had the personality
screening required by such programs as Columbia's *(3)* for the
Diploma of Reading Specialist, which states that "The Diploma

Reprinted from *Journal of Reading,* 10 (May 1967), pp. 552-559, by permission of Dorothy Klausner and the International Reading Association.

is granted only to those who do a high quality of work, *and possess personal and professional aptitudes essential for success in this field."* Many are English teachers or elementary classroom teachers who have been assigned to teach remedial reading without special training or personality qualifications. Others are teachers who have had some instruction in the teaching of remedial reading, varying from in-service sessions to correspondence, extension, and university courses. But almost none have had an opportunity to consider their own personalities in relation to effective reading improvement.

What personality traits are considered important? Mackie and Engle *(20)* list the following:

1) Sympathetic and understanding attitude
2) Warm, approachable, and friendly manner
3) Spirit of cooperation and helpfulness
4) Genuine love of and interest in people
5) Faith in the dignity and worth of a person regardless of social position or handicap
6) Enthusiasm
7) Optimistic, idealistic, yet practical attitude
8) Keen-thinking, intellectually alert mind
9) Emotional maturity
10) Tolerance, kindness, patience, and tact

To which experienced teachers would add a sense of humor, perseverance, courtesy, and a strong stomach. Certainly these personality traits would be helpful to any teacher. Why are they especially needed by teachers of reading improvement?

First, because it's harder to develop the necessary good relationship with most disabled readers than with the average student. Each is different, of course, but more than 70 percent of disabled readers show some degree of personality maladjustment. *(26)* The remedial reading student usually has a history of failure. He is discouraged, apathetic, or hostile, according to *his* personality. He thinks the teacher doesn't want to and/or can't help him, or that he himself doesn't want or need help. His pride has suffered, not only from failure, but from being put into this special classification. He is afraid — that maybe he really is "dumb," or of the new situation, new teacher, reading machines, diagnostic tests *(7) (28)*. He is under pressure from himself, his family, his teachers. He often has physical and neurological problems which affect his behavior and his appearance. His personality may be thorny and unpleasant. Habits of wiggling and squirming, spitting when he speaks, picking off scabs and pulling out his hair, neglected runny nose, frequent belching, and rude or sarcastic remarks may make him very difficult to like *(23)*.

Spache *(26)* described "five patterns among elementary retarded readers — the hostile, adjustive, defensive, solution-seeking, and autistic or withdrawn. For each of these groups he suggested logical adjustments of the teacher-pupil relationship and the climate of the remedial reading program." Obviously the teacher needs to be emotionally mature, and to have a warm, cooperative, sympathetic, tolerant, yet enthusiastic attitude to get through the wall created by such disabled readers. If, as Roswell *(23)* says, developing a good relationship is achieved through "total acceptance of the child as a human being worthy of respect" and "encompasses a collaborative spirit within a planned structure, compassion without overinvolvement, understanding without indulgence, and above all, a genuine concern for the child's development," then the teacher needs a personality strong in such traits as those listed by Harris *(13)*; optimism, enthusiasm, good cheer, creation of a calm, relaxed atmosphere, kindness, praise, sensitivity to emotional needs, appreciation, respect, friendly interest, building up of self-confidence and self-respect. "Appearance, dress, age, speech, theoretical knowledge, experience — all these are less important than a genuine fondness for children as they are, complete with their faults and annoying habits." Just as "reading cannot be regarded as separate from the behavior of the individual" *(7)*, so success in the teaching of reading improvement cannot be regarded as separate from the personality of the teacher.

Causes of reading problems may be neurophysiological (inferior learning capacity, defective vision or hearing, speech difficulties, deficiency in language and motor functions, poor health), psychological (lack of interest, instability of temperament interfering with attention, passive or antagonistic attitude toward learning), educational (inadequate habit formation in the mechanics of reading, insufficient practice), sociological (inadequate background, foreign-language background, poor home training, population mobility) *(17)*, or a combination of these. The teacher may attempt remediation with methods based on the phonics approach *(2)*, *(14)*, *(15)*, *(27)*, *(30)*, kinesthetic tracing *(9)*, visual-perceptual-motor training *(10)*, language experience approach *(1)*, neuropsychological principles *(4)*, *(29)*, basic sight word vocabulary *(6)*, or a combination of these and others. Neither diagnosis nor remediation methods, however, but the teacher's personality will get over to the disabled reader the essential message, "I like you. I *can* help you," which is basic to success in remedial reading *(23)*.

Second, the remedial reading student must often follow procedures which at best are strange to him, and may often strike him as babyish or useless, unrelated to reading. And again it is the teacher's personality traits of understanding, enthusiasm, cooperation, and faith in the student's dignity and worth rather than his knowledge of procedure that makes the difference in the student's effort and cooperation. If he is to practice drawing lines from left to right *(19)*, tracing words with his finger while saying the word aloud *(9)*, sounding out nonsense syllables *(30)*, or trying to read words flashed on a tachistoscope *(21)*, he must believe that it will help him and that it is not some incomprehensible busywork which will demean him.

Third, the development of good work habits and the ability to persevere, never easy to teach, is doubly difficult and doubly necessary with the disabled reader. He has been cajoled, reprimanded, subjected to all sorts of training methods, and gotten progressively more frustrated. The reading teacher's real interest in him as an individual, understanding, patience, enthusiasm, and emotional maturity in acceptance of his slips and starts will be more effective in helping him develop acceptable work habits than will knowledge of the underlying causes or methods of remediation. As Roswell *(23)* says: "A teacher needs to have confidence that she can help, but she needs to realize also that she is not personally responsible for lack of progress. She must understand that…it is simply a reality to be remedied. When…her own status is not threatened…she can then recognize the child's ultimate potentialities, not his present achievement."

And fourth, tests of all kinds are administered much more frequently by the reading improvement teacher than by subject teachers. Diagnostic tests and progress tests are an integral part of the reading improvement program. Validity of the tests may depend on the teacher's personality traits — understanding the student and his fears, recognizing the peripheral influences affecting him and his day-to-day progress, securing his confidence and trust so that his test performances reflect his reading skills as accurately as possible.

Diagnostic testing may be done outside the classroom *(26)*, but there are still progress tests and the informal testing of teacher observation. If the reading teacher has established good rapport with the student, such informal testing will yield much helpful information about his attitudes, working habits, reading skills, and reading needs. His interests, distractibility, speed, dependence on listening for a substitute become a part of the sum total which helps the teacher help him. "Each adds another tentative bit of information about the child's present reading behaviors, his progress, and his future," says Spache *(26)*. But if the teacher's lack of warmth, sincerity, and faith in the individual have prevented development of a good relationship, if the student is still afraid or apathetic or hostile, test results may very well lack validity.

Besides the relationships with the student, the reading improvement teacher is more closely involved with parents, with administrators and other teachers, and with the community in relation to her work than is the average classroom teacher. And personality traits will strongly influence the success or failure of these relationships. Widespread interest in reading and equally widespread lack of information about methods and techniques of improving reading create the situation where reading teachers "find themselves required constantly to defend the modern reading program rather than being engaged in explaining it" *(26)*, or, as Schick and Schmidt *(24)* put it: "Whether he wishes it or not, the teacher of reading is forced into the role of publicist, advocate, and explicator of reading instruction."

Parents who are worried, critical, hostile, or uncooperative, well-intentioned administrators who become critical of what seems to them to be slow progress *(23)*, fellow teachers who feel that reading is not their concern nor related to their subjects, and community organizations and representatives who believe that reading problems wouldn't exist if only the "good old-fashioned methods" had been used — how does the reading improvement teacher affect these people? With knowledge, certainly, of causes of disability and techniques of remediation — but for that knowledge to affect others, with personality traits of tact and diplomacy, patience and understanding, willingness to listen and cooperate, and enthusiastic belief *(5), (28)*.

If we accept the dictum that personality traits strongly affect the success of the reading improvement teacher, what can we do about it? Personality improvement courses and personality screening may be provided as part of teacher-training for new teachers. But what of teachers now in the field?

"To prescribe 'maturity,' 'serenity,' or 'interest' as requirements for good teaching, without helping teachers to remove their inner impediments to these healthy and desirable states of mind, is to burden them with assignments for which they have no adequate preparation" *(7)*. Personality tests? The questions are often not effective and sample only certain facets of personality. It is doubtful that persons respond truthfully and objectively. And they are usually complex in scoring and interpretation, requiring extensive training of the examiner *(26)*.

Assessing one's own personality in relation to the traits listed might be a first step. Most teachers possess these traits in some degree, or they would not be teachers. But with thoughtful analysis most of us could discern a need to develop more tact, or real belief in the fundamental dignity and worth of every person, or more patience, or a better understanding of other people's motives, etc. At the same time, a realistic appraisal of one's personality strengths and the types of pupils with whom these would be most successful would be helpful. Gates *(12)* says, "The fact is that teachers, like pupils, have specialized abilities and disabilities.... Thus the ideal remedial program involves a teacher-pupil-method totality."

Using the basic principles of mental health as a second check might follow. "The majority can improve their relationships with children greatly, by studying principles of mental hygiene and trying to incorporate them into their everyday relations with children," according to Harris *(13)*. Such books as *Mental Hygiene — A Manual for Teachers (11)*, *Mental Hygiene in School Practice (8)*, *The Psychology of*

Adjustment (25), The Psychology of Personal Adjustment (16), and *Psychology in the High School (18)* are among the many that offer helpful information and bibliographies leading to other reading in this field.

In-service training related to mental health and personality development would be valuable not only to reading improvement teachers but to all teachers. With recent recognition that reading is taught by *"every* teacher, at every level, from the early grades throughout college and adult classes" *(24),* in-service training has greatly increased. It has been designed to acquaint subject-teachers with the reading improvement program and techniques, as well as to convince them that good reading habits will make their students more effective, require less of their time in drill and repetition, and in effect help them to do a better job of teaching their subjects.

Perhaps such in-service training might equally well offer help in personality improvement to all teachers. In many schools, the in-service training program is developed by the reading improvement teacher. According to Schick and Schmidt *(24),* as he passes on to his colleagues the knowledge and skills he has acquired, he "learns more and more about theory and practice and results . . . . He enlarges his own stature while assisting his fellow-teachers." By the same token, if the reading improvement teacher were to include information on good mental health practices and development of optimal personality characteristics in a program of in-service training, he might very well at the same time learn how to improve his own personality.

Until the next decade's research and methods of personality screening and development are available, perhaps we can make a start with informal methods such as these.

REFERENCES

1. Anderson, Irving H. and Walter F. Dearborn. *The Psychology of Teaching Reading* (N.Y.: The Ronald Press Co., 1952), pp.259-266.

2. Bond, Guy L. and Miles A. Tinker. *Reading Difficulties:Their Diagnosis and Correction* (N.Y.: Appleton-Century-Crofts, 1957), pp. 420-422.

3. Columbia University. *Programs for Reading Specialists and Supervisors* (N.Y.: Teachers College, Columbia University, 1957), p.1.

4. Delacato, Carl H. *The Treatment and Prevention of Reading Problems* (Springfield, Ill.: Charles C. Thomas, 1961).

5. D'Evelyn, Katherine. *Individual Parent-Teacher Conferences* (N.Y.: Teachers College, Columbia University, 1958).

6. Dolch, Edward E. *Helping the Educationally Handicapped* (Champaign, Ill.: Garrard Press, 1950); and *A Manual for Remedial Reading* (Champaign, Ill.: Garrard Press, 1945).

7. Ephron, Beulah Kanter. *Emotional Difficulties in Reading* (N.Y.: The Julian Press, 1953), pp. 7, 27, 275.

8. Fenton, Norman. *Mental Hygiene in School Practice* (Palo Alto, Calif.: Stanford University Press, 1943).

9. Fernald, Grace M. *Remedial Techniques in Basic School Subjects* (N.Y.: McGraw-Hill, 1943), pp. 35-55.

10. Fostig, Marianne. "Corrective Reading in the Classroom," *The Reading Teacher* (April, 1965); and *The Fostig Program for the Development of Visual Perception* (Chicago, Ill.: Follett Co., 1964).

11. Griffin, Laycock, and Line. *Mental Hygiene — A Manual for Teachers* (N.Y.: American Book Co., 1940).

12. Gates, Arthur I. *The Improvement of Reading* (N.Y.: Macmillan, 1955), pp. 132, 486-487.

13. Harris, Albert J. *How to Increase Reading Ability* (N.Y.: Longmans Green, 1954), pp. 250, 249, 250.

14. Hay and Wingo. *Reading with Phonics,* rev. (Chicago, Ill.: J.P. Lippincott, 1954).

15. Heilman, Arthur W. *Phonics in Proper Perspective* (Columbus, Ohio: Charles E. Merrill, 1964).

16. Heyns, Roger W. *Psychology of Personal Adjustment* (N.Y.: Dryden Press, 1958).

17. Hildreth, Gertrude and B. C. Wadell. *Identifying Reading Difficulties (N.Y.: World Book Co., 1959), pp. 3-4.*

18. Jersild, Arthur T. and Kenneth Helfant. *Psychology in the High School* (N.Y.: Teachers College Columbia University, 1953).

19. Kephart, Newell C. *The Slow Learner in the Classroom* (Columbus, Ohio: Charles E. Merrill, 1962).

20. Mackie and Engle. *Directors and Supervisors of Special Education in Local School Systems* (Washington, D.C.: U.S. Government Printing Office), pp. 40-41.

21. Pollack, M. F. W. and Josephine Piekarz. *Reading Problems and Problem Readers* (N.Y.: Van Rees Press, 1963).

22. Albert J. Harris *(13)* says: "A few people seem to be naturally

endowed with warmth, tact, and sympathetic understanding. Such people usually get good results, even if the methods they employ are far from the best." Arthur Gates *(12)* insists that "It is imperative that first meetings develop in the pupil a feeling that the teacher is a good sort and will surely help him." Ruth Strang *(28)* adds: "Emotional relations in the classroom affect learning" and "There is no substitute for an adequate understanding of the individual (and) a sensitivity to his needs." George Spache *(26)* concurs: "In our opinion, the reason for the moderate success that almost any remedial approaches achieve lies in the type of interpersonal relationship established between the pupil and the remedial teacher."

23. Roswell, Florence C. and Gladys Natchez. *Reading Disability: Diagnosis and Treatment* (N.Y.: Basic Books, 1964), pp. 142, 65, 66, 178-79.

24. Schick, George B. and Bernard Schmidt. *Guidebook for the Teaching of Reading* (Psychotechnics Press, 1966), pp. 44, 43, 47.

25. Shaffer and Shoben. *Psychology of Adjustment* (N.Y.: Houghton Mifflin Co., 1956).

26. Spache, George D. *Toward Better Reading* (Champaign, Ill.: Garrard, 1963), pp. 298, 120, 299, 263, 204, 121; and *Good Reading for Poor Readers* (Champaign, Ill.: Garrard, 1966), p. 4.

27. Spalding, Romalda Bishop and T. Walter. *The Writing Road to Reading* (Whiteside Inc. and William Morrow, 1957).

28. Strang, Ruth. *Reporting to Parents* (N.Y.: Teachers College, Columbia University, 1957); *Understanding and Helping the Retarded Reader* (Tucson, Arizona: University of Arizona Press, 1965); Strang, McCullough, and Traxler. *Problems in the Improvement of Reading* (N.Y.: McGraw-Hill, 1955), p. 70.

29. Stuart, Marion Fenwick. *Neurophysiological Insights into Teaching* (Palo Alto, Calif.: Pacific Books, 1963).

30. Terman, Sibyl and Charles S. Walcutt. *Reading: Chaos and Cure* (N.Y.: McGraw-Hill, 1958).

ADDITIONAL SOURCES

Abraham, Willard. *A New Look at Reading — A Guide to the Language Arts* (Boston, Mass.: Porter Sargent, 1956).

Blair, Glenn M. *Diagnostic and Remedial Teaching in Secondary Schools* (New York: The Macmillan Company, 1946).

Blumfield, Leonard and Clarence L. Barnhart. *Reading, A Linguistic Approach* (Detroit: Wayne State University Press, 1961).

Bond, G. L. and Eva Bond Wagner. *Teaching the Child to Read,* 3rd edition (New York: The Macmillan Company, 1960).

Brogan, Peggy and Lorene K. Fox. *Helping Children Read* (Holt, Rinehart, & Winston, Inc., 1961).

Cleary, Florence Damon. *Blueprints for Better Reading* (New York: H. W. Wilson Company, 1957).

Durkin, Dolores. *Phonics and the Teaching of Reading* (New York: Teachers College, Columbia University, 1962).

Haring, Norris G. and E. Laken Phillips, *Educating Emotionally Disturbed Children* (New York: McGraw-Hill Book Co. Inc., 1962).

Hovious, Carol. *Following Printed Trails* (Boston, Mass.: D. C. Heath and Co., 1936).

Kottmeyer, William. *Handbook for Remedial Reading* (St. Louis, Missouri: Webster Publishing Company, 1947).

Miller, Helen R. and John DeBoer. *Creative Reading* (Graessle-Mercer Company, 1951).

Scheifele, Marian. *The Gifted Child in the Regular Classroom* (New York: Teachers College, Columbia University, 1953).

Stagner, Ross. *Psychology of Personality* (New York: McGraw-Hill Book Company, 1961).

Witty, Paul. *Helping Children Read Better* (Chicago, Ill.: SRA, 1950); *Streamline Your Reading* (Chicago: SRA, 1949); *How to Become a Better Reader* (Chicago: SRA, 1953); *How to Improve Your Reading* (Chicago: SRA, 1956).

A.A. ROOT

What Instructors Say
to Students Makes a Difference!

Education suffers from a research gap*! Researchers have a warehouse full of information about how children learn, but appallingly little of it gets translated into educational practices. Researchers who eschew application of their findings are at fault, but so are educators who ignore or fail to apply known psychological findings. Children with reading difficulties bring a superabundance of unmet needs to school and not until many of these are moderately satisfied can they wholeheartedly engage in learning to read better. Much recent experimentation has convinced many people that the way teachers respond to and talk with students can facilitate or impede learning. Root beautifully bridges the* research gap *by integrating Maslow's hierarchy of need with Flander's and Amidon's concepts of interaction analysis to show how such a simple thing as how a teacher talks to students can promote more and better learning.*

Do any children you know have outstanding unmet lower-level (maintenance) needs? Does this hierarchy of motives help you understand why some children you know haven't learned as well as their cognitive functioning has led you to expect? Does this hierarchy help you better understand how to motivate certain children? Have you ever recorded twenty to thirty minutes of your interaction with students and then categorized your responses as either "direct" or "indirect"? Do you understand how indirect teacher responses can help meet students' needs better than direct ones? Will reading this essay cause you to interact differently with children in the future?

Reprinted by permission of the American Society for Engineering Education and A. A. Root. Reprinted from *Engineering Education,* 60 (March 1970), pp. 722-725.

Let us suppose that a student stopped to talk with his instructor after class, and in a halting, uncertain manner, said something like this:

> "You know, I'm having an awful time with stuff we're supposed to be learning in this course — and in some of my other courses too. I don't think I'm stupid, but — well, a lot of people told me I should go into engineering because I was good at math in high school — but now I don't know. You're doing a good job with this material, but I wonder if I shouldn't drop this course."

Most instructors would like to be helpful to a student, at a time like this — to say the "right thing."

How would *you* respond? Below are seven responses that might be made to this student. Read the statements carefully and select the one which is closest to what *you* would be likely to say, in order to be *most* helpful. At the same time, mark an *x* beside the statement that you think would be *least* likely to be helpful. (Actually take the time to mark the responses — the *most* and the *least* likely to be helpful!)

1. "What do you think you should do?"
2. "I've watched what you have been doing and am convinced that you'll be able to make it if you keep trying. Engineering is a profession well worth working for."
3. "Now, in spite of the advice people have given you, you're not sure that engineering is the right thing for you."
4. "Hmm — it certainly would be a shame if you were to quit after all the time and effort you've put in. I hope you'll think seriously before you give it up."
5. "Uh-huh. Hmm."
6. "This has been bothering you for some time, and — now, you're really not sure what is best.
7. "I recommend that you talk with a counselor who can help you decide what you are best suited for."

In almost any group of instructors, there are some who choose each of these different responses. They give many different reasons *why* they selected the response they did, and almost always the motives behind their selections are laudable. Most instructors truly *want* to help a young man experiencing this kind of uncertainty.

CATEGORIES OF CONVERSATION

Before commenting on the merits and shortcomings of different answers, let us examine a scheme for categorizing the different kinds of things an instructor *can* say to a student. With a moderate amount of training, almost anyone can learn to listen to another person's conversation and classify each statement he makes, labeling it with one of the category numbers from Figure 1 (page 272).

We are going to be using these categories of conversation repeatedly in the material that follows, so it would be worthwhile for you to read them carefully. Let us pause a bit, so that you can become acquainted with them — right now.

Now, go back and re-read the different replies you might have made to that uncertain student, and next to each statement write down the number of the conversational category to which it belongs. (There's one statement for each category, so don't duplicate yourself.)

The "correct" categorizing of these seven statements is printed, upside-down, below. When you've marked each statement, check yourself.[1]

When instructors find their responses labeled in this manner, they sometimes feel a little uncomfortable, because they may not have intended to appear in quite that way to the student. Unfortunately, the student has no way of knowing the instructor's intentions — he can only hear the words.

About this time, someone usually points out that any one of these statements can be completely changed by changing the tone of voice used to say the words — and that is absolutely right. The instructor could say, "You're uncertain," as a gentle category 1, to express genuine concern for the feelings being expressed — or could say, *"You're un-cert-ain!"* and have it come out as a strong category 7, with sarcastic criticism. For the moment, let us assume that an instructor's tone and facial

---

[1]

Statement 7: category 6 (give direction)
Statement 6: category 1 (label feeling)
Statement 5: category 2 (encourage)
Statement 4: category 7 (mild criticism)
Statement 3: category 3 (reflect ideas)
Statement 2: category 5 (opinion)
Statement 1: category 4 (question)

Figure 1. Categories of Conversation.

The Instructor	*Indirect (Inter-personal)*	1. Identify and label *feelings*. Tell him how you think he feels. Sense his emotional state and put that into words.	"This really upsets you." "You wonder if ——." "If you just knew ——."
		2. *Encourage and assure*. Indicate that what he does is acceptable. Nod, say "Uh huh," or "I see."	"Hmm —— yeah." "Uh huh, go on." "I see. Tell me more."
		3. Identify and reflect *ideas*. In your own words, tell him what you heard him say. Demonstrate your understanding.	"As you see it, this ——." "You're saying that ——." "Your idea is ——."
	Content	4. *Ask question*. With the intent that he answer, ask any kind of question which urges him to answer. Inquire.	"Where is ——?" "What kind of ——?" "Why do these ——?"
		5. *Give information* or opinion. Introduce new data or add something which the other has not said. Lecture. Present ideas.	"The solution is ——." "I'm sure that ——." "Another point is ——."
	Direct (Organizational)	6. *Give directions*. Give instructions which the other is to follow. Tell him what to do. Inform him of procedures.	"Do these problems ——." "Go talk with ——." "After that, then ——."
		7. *Criticize or correct*. Indicate an error with the intent that he change his behavior. Either mild criticism or harsh scolding.	"No, the right way ——." "How could you ——." "Damn, you didn't ——."
The Student		8. *Responds*. He answers you or follows instructions or implied direction. He stays on the subject.	"Yes, I did ——." "The answer is ——." "Well, when I ——."
		9. *Initiates* new idea. He goes beyond the previous information. Brings up new material. Asks or suggests novel item.	"I think that ——." "But, how about ——." "Another way would be ——."
		10. *Silence or confusion*. There is no structure to the conversation. This may be constructive silence or bedlam.	

expressions match his words — as they usually do. In repeated experiments using these categories to record classroom interactions, it is observed that an instructor's verbal behavior corresponds closely to his nonverbal performance — a kind of consistency most people develop.

Before going back to comment on the helpfulness of the different statements considered earlier, several other ideas will be presented to help put these statements into perspective. The next two basic ideas are: (1) a framework for analyzing the things that attract or disturb people, i.e., their "motives," and (2) a set of suggestions for how to respond to a person in order to be most helpful. After this last set of suggestions, the meaning of each response will become more apparent.

SENSITIVITY AND RESPONSIBILITY

Instructors often feel caught in a bind between responsibilities to subject-and-schedule and to the individual student. The pressure to "cover" the material in the course is real and demanding. At the same time, instructors often want to be understanding and friendly with their students. One instructor phrased this conflict, "How can I be understanding and sensitive with students without giving up my responsibilities for the everyday business of life?" There is no simple answer to such a question. The best answer seems to come from an examination of the different types of motives that must be dealt with.

One way of representing the interests, motives and needs of man is shown in Figure 2, where different classes of needs are shown in a "hierarchical" structure. The "stair-step" form indicates that there is a kind of progression in which the higher levels build upon the lower ones. The lower left represents the needs of man for physical survival. When these are threatened, they generally take precedence over any other need (for example, try to stay under water for ten minutes while thinking "beautiful thoughts"; the demand for air will trigger most people to violent exertions). When survival is reasonably well assured, one next becomes concerned for the security of a home, good health, adequate pay, life insurance, a regular job, and the regularity of a reliable environment. When these physical and organizational needs are moderately satisfied, affiliation and social needs begin to become of major im-

Figure 2. Actions, Motives, and Incentives of Man

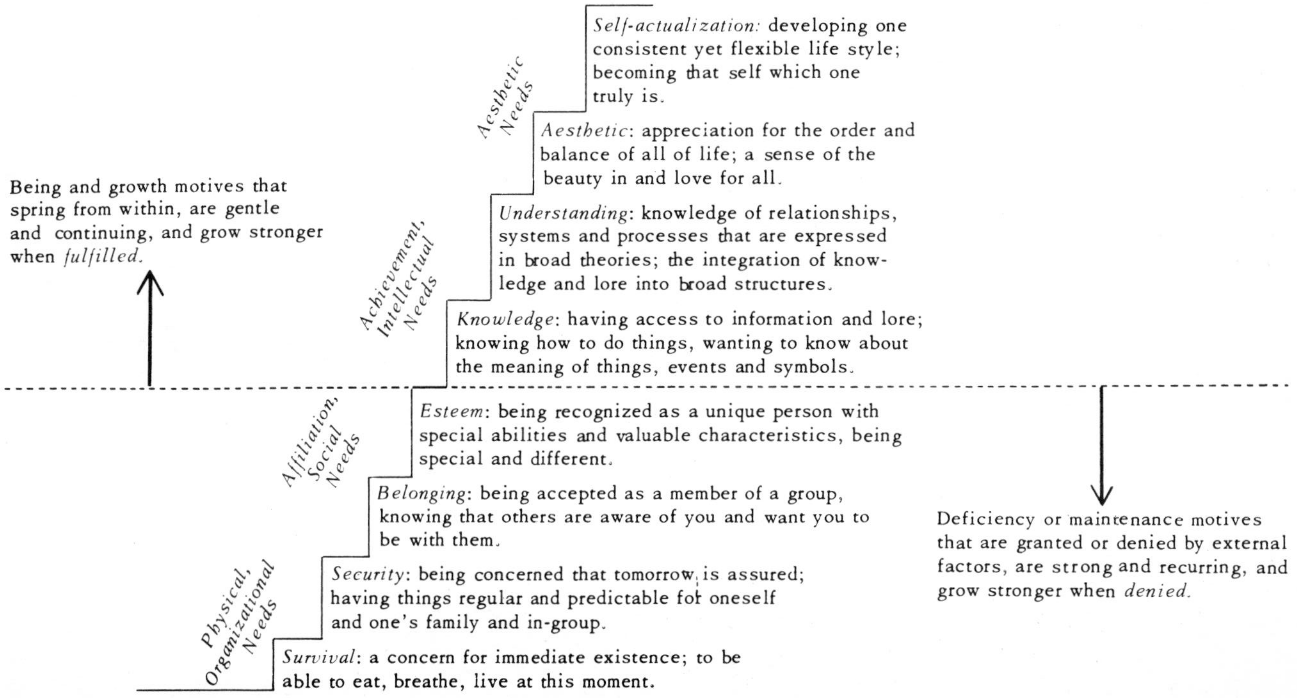

Being and growth motives that spring from within, are gentle and continuing, and grow stronger when *fulfilled*.

Physical, Organizational Needs

Affiliation, Social Needs

Achievement, Intellectual Needs

Aesthetic Needs

Survival: a concern for immediate existence; to be able to eat, breathe, live at this moment.

Security: being concerned that tomorrow is assured; having things regular and predictable for oneself and one's family and in-group.

Belonging: being accepted as a member of a group; knowing that others are aware of you and want you to be with them.

Esteem: being recognized as a unique person with special abilities and valuable characteristics, being special and different.

Knowledge: having access to information and lore; knowing how to do things, wanting to know about the meaning of things, events and symbols.

Understanding: knowledge of relationships, systems and processes that are expressed in broad theories; the integration of knowledge and lore into broad structures.

Aesthetic: appreciation for the order and balance of all of life; a sense of the beauty in and love for all.

Self-actualization: developing one consistent yet flexible life style; becoming that self which one truly is.

Deficiency or maintenance motives that are granted or denied by external factors, are strong and recurring, and grow stronger when *denied*.

portance, i.e., the desire to be accepted by others and to have a special place in their regard. These four, lower level needs are sometimes called deficiency or maintenance needs as they seem to be the necessary human requirements a man must receive before he can be productive and give — rather like inhaling before one can exhale. An interesting feature of these needs is that they grow stronger when *denied* by one's environment. This is in contrast to the higher level growth needs (intellectual and aesthetic) which grow stronger when *fulfilled*.

The achievement and intellectual needs are concerned with an individual's desire to know enough about this environment to be able to influence it and, eventually, to understand how significant decisions can be made to achieve important goals. At the highest levels of this hierarchy are the aesthetic needs — the need to appreciate the order and balance of life and to find a unique, yet consistent, style of relating to the environment out of a sense of belonging to all of life.

PRINCIPLES BASED ON MAN'S NEEDS

Out of an understanding of this general structure of man's needs and motives come three related principles which are applicable to education, business, family life, and other activities where men work together to achieve important goals.

PRINCIPLE 1: *Human motives are ordered in a hierarchical structure such that when lower level motives are excited, they are stronger and take precedence over higher ones.* (Examples of self-sacrifice by persons very high on this hierarchy are rare and do not affect the general principle.) This principle would suggest that a student worried about money or failing grades ("security" deficiencies), and who is socially ostracized or lonely ("social deficiencies"), would have a hard time functioning at the intellectual or achievement level. A similar thing is expressed in Principle 2.

PRINCIPLE 2: *Strong emotions may produce "internal noise" which prevents the reception of other stimuli and, therefore, the functioning of higher level reasoning.* Some persons appear to generate their own emotional "noise," such as the young man at the beginning of this article. Efforts to help such a person lead to a third principle.

PRINCIPLE 3: *If one can demonstrate that he hears,*

understands, and accepts what the other person says and does, the other person will be most likely to hear and understand him, and become able to make constructive decisions.

Based on these principles, with the accompanying hierarchy of motives, it seems best to provide someone who is worried about grades with an environment which, at least temporarily, provides for his deficiency needs. It is important for an instructor to learn to control his own behavior (both verbal and nonverbal) so as to reduce the intensity of these lower level drives. He can do this by following a sequence such as:

1. Whenever you sense that the student is reacting to strong internal emotion, identify and reflect your understanding and acceptance of these feelings. Continue doing this until the intensity of these feelings has decreased, say something like, "You're really not sure that this is right for you." This kind of a statement can do much to meet both his security and social needs — because a significant person in the organization has thought enough of him to listen and respond, sensitively, to his immediate problem.

2. When the student's emotion has decreased in intensity, identify and reflect the content or *ideas* he has expressed, without adding anything new. Such a statement can show further evidence of your acceptance of him as a person-of-worth (positive social relations) and begins to lead up to the intellectual domain, starting with his own ideas as suggested by Principle 3.

3. When the student knows you've heard him, then you can begin to add some *new material* that he has not mentioned. The first new ideas you add should be as noncontroversial as possible, e.g., "Something you didn't bring up was the fact that . . . . ." Add controversial topics only when he is able to consider new ideas without getting emotionally involved again, e.g., "On the other hand, the way I see it is . . . . . ."

4. Arrange for some specific *actions* both for the student and for yourself, including who will do what, by when, e.g., "Why don't you do . . . . .I'll do . . . . . ., and we'll get back together again on . . . . . ." Only as a last resort issue ultimatums about what *must* be done, as this drops back to exert force in the organizational-security level of the motivation hierarchy.

Now, look back at Figure 1 and identify the category of

conversation you would be using at each of the above four steps. The correct classification is printed, below and upside-down.[2] After analyzing each of these four types of statements, check yourself.

Now we have a basis for recommending which of the first seven possible responses to the uncertain student would be most likely to be helpful. As you can see, almost every statement has *something* to recommend it. What is most likely to help the student come to that solution which is best for him is a sequence of things you could say to him. Following the four steps recommended above, you'd probably be most helpful responding as follows:

     6. "This has been bothering you for some time."

     3. "In spite of advice, you're not sure engineering is for you."

     2. I've watched you, and think you'll make it. What do you think?"

     7. "Let me help you get in touch with a counselor who can help you."

And you notice that this arrangement has avoided using any Category 7. Also, during any such conversation, there should be a liberal sprinkling of Category 2. (All of us use this on the telephone, when we want the person on the other end to know we're still there, listening).

APPLICATION TO TEACHING

But, are these categories of conversation applicable to what students and instructors say in classrooms? Absolutely! They were originated in order to study the kinds of things said in educational settings. Some of the best data on good vs. poor teaching has come from research studies based on this kind of analysis of verbal interaction in classrooms. In the discussion that follows, one basic diagram summarizes the conclusions of a number of research studies. Finally, the research data are

---

2

First, category 1 (identify feelings)
Second, category 3 (reflect ideas)
Third, category 5 (add ideas and opinions)
Last, category 6 (directions for action)

considered in relation to the ideas of motivation discussed above.

The data in Figure 3 were obtained from a study of many mathematics teachers. Their classes were arranged in rank order according to their average scores on a standardized test of mathematics achievement. This list was divided into thirds, so that the researchers could talk about the "high," "moderate," and "low" achievers. At the same time, observers visited all of these classrooms and recorded the category of conversation *every three seconds,* for extended periods of time. These observers had been carefully trained in the use of these categories, and were shown to be "reliable" observers (multiple observers would record the same categories, while observing the same activities), but they did not know which classes were the high, moderate, or low achievers.

Tallies Per 1000

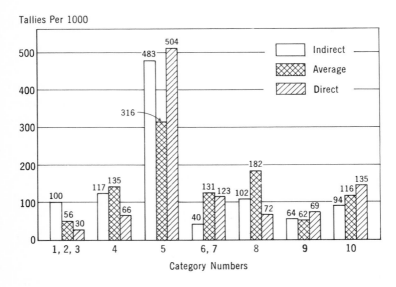

Figure 3. Influence Patterns of Most Indirect,
Average, and Most Direct Mathematics Teachers

When observers' records were separated according to levels of achievement, as shown in Figure 3, there were significant differences. The instructors of the high achievers used significantly more "indirect" behavior and less "direct."

The reverse was observed for instructors of the low achieving classes, where there was significantly less "indirect" and more "direct" teacher behavior. It is interesting to note that all of the teachers used approximately the same amount of Categories 4 and 5, asking questions and presenting information (lecturing).

In a parallel study, almost identical results were obtained when classes were arranged in rank order according to attitudes toward school and the specific course. Evidently, students are aware of and respond to differences in the patterns of instructors' verbal behavior in the classroom. What instructors say to students makes a difference!

SUCCESS OF INDIRECT BEHAVIOR

There are at least two reasons why instructors who use more indirect types of behavior have students who perform better and have more positive attitudes: (1) as described above, students whose lower level organizational and social needs are met, rather than excited, are free to function at the intellectual level, to be curious and to strive for the achievement of significant goals, and (2) instructors who learned to provide reinforcement and feedback to students for their efforts tend to have students who try harder and like the classroom environment. Thus, both reasons tend to be "motivational" explanations.

It is common for instructors to say that they want to "motivate" their students, yet it is uncommon for instructors to know how to provide the kind of "indirect" environment that achieves the result they want. Many programs to develop "effective teaching" have concentrated on the analysis of what instructors say to students. Teachers can learn to control their own verbal behavior and, when they do, students can tell the difference. For those who wish to learn more about "interaction analysis" and who may want to work with others to modify their own classroom behavior, the references listed below should provide an introduction to a challenging and valuable new experience.

REFERENCES

1. Amidon, E. J., and Flanders, N. A., *The Role of the Teacher in the Classroom*. Association for Productive Teaching, 1040 Plymouth Building, Minneapolis, Minnesota, 1967.

2. Amidon, E. J., and Hough, J. B., *Interaction Analysis: Theory, Research and Application.* Addison-Wesley, Reading, Mass., 1967.

WAYNE OTTO
RICHARD McMENEMY

A Point of View
for Remedial Teaching

A large proportion of children with reading difficulties have greater emotional problems than children who have made normal reading progress. Thus, reading teachers are faced with a dual responsibility: improving reading and building emotional stability. Even though Otto and McMenemy caution the teacher to avoid playing "amateur psychiatrist," they do encourage him to become more aware of certain counseling principles that teachers can use to benefit children with reading and emotional difficulties, as well as the parents and themselves.

To what degree do you think you already possess the attributes necessary to establish an adequate counseling relationship? Which characteristic will you have to work hardest to establish with the students you work with? Which of the listed techniques have you used successfully? Do you think role playing might help you improve acquisition of the needed characteristics and techniques? In what ways do these suggestions repeat Root's theme in the preceding article?

All disabled learners are not emotionally maladjusted nor are all emotionally maladjusted pupils disabled learners. Yet success in the basic skills — especially reading — is an essential step in normal development, for failure precludes the sequential acquisition of the higher level academic skills and learnings. Failure in the basic school subjects, then, is likely to interfere with adequate adjustment. To attempt to decide whether an individual pupil's learning problems were caused by emotional problems or vice versa is less important than to recognize the probability that many learning disabilities will be accompanied by varing degrees of emotional maladjustment.

Many children with severe emotional maladjustments need intensive psychotherapy before they can respond to remedial teaching; every attempt should be made to secure competent professional help in such cases. But in the majority of cases it is up to the remedial teacher to deal with emotional problems along with learning problems. Mastery of diagnostic and remedial techniques provides the teacher with a means for outlining a plan of instruction, but success in remedial teaching is often as dependent upon meeting emotional needs as upon meeting instructional needs. This does not mean that remedial teachers must be highly trained counselors, but it does mean that teachers who can establish relationships that communicate acceptance and understanding with their pupils are more likely to be successful than those who depend entirely upon the manipulation of diagnostic and remedial techniques.

Successful remedial teachers have more than a collection of techniques; they have a way of working with children. From our observations, it appears that their success is often based upon an ability to establish relationships with their pupils. Although they may not be formally trained as counselors, they have what we shall call a counseling point of view, for the relationships that they establish are essentially counseling relationships. In the pages that follow we shall very briefly describe the basic elements of the counseling relationship and discuss some applications of what we shall call a counseling point of view. We feel that a remedial teacher who has a basic understanding of the function of counseling and the counseling relationship and who utilizes some of the common techniques of counseling is in a position to work more effectively with disabled learners.

THE FUNCTION OF COUNSELING

Because counseling is a complex process it is difficult to state what it is or what it does very concisely. It has been said, admittedly rather vaguely, that the function of counseling is to unchain the giant that resides within every individual; but counseling does not tamper with the giant. Perhaps counseling is best conceived as a positive expanding process. The purpose is not to bring about a complete personality change but, rather, to make changes and modifications of attitudes. Counseling stresses the positive growth of the individual toward greater self-understanding, self-reliance and self-respect, which can help him to work through his own problems and to make his own decisions. Thus, counseling enables an individual to help himself.

THE COUNSELING RELATIONSHIP

The foundation of the counseling process is the relationship established between the counselor and the client. (We shall use the terms "counselor" and "client" in discussing the counseling relationship. In the present context, "remedial teacher" and "pupil" would be equally appropriate.) The counseling relationship has certain characteristics that are similar to the interactions between close friends and relatives, but it is different in that two conditions are present that are not generally found in other relationships: It is structured in a psychological framework and the client is always positively accepted by the counselor. The details of establishing and maintaining the relationship vary widely — from play therapy with young children to directive and nondirective approaches with adults — but good relationships have certain characteristics in common. Again, because of the complexity of the counseling process — which is due in no small part to the fact that a number of things must happen concurrently — it is difficult to focus upon basic characteristics one at a time; but we shall do so for discussion purposes.

One of the characteristics of the counseling relationship, *uniqueness,* is paradoxical: While certain general statements can be made about the relationship, each relationship is unique because individuals are unique. Thus, a counselor must know and understand himself, have a generally positive feeling toward human beings, and be flexible enough to adapt basic counseling techniques to the particular needs of each client. The paradox is not a new one for teachers who know from experience that what works with one child does not necessarily work with another.

The counseling relationship also contains the paradox of *objective thoughts* and *emotional feelings.* A counselor must maintain an intricate balance between these two diverse positions. In order to apply the scientific principles of human behavior to what the client is presenting, the counselor must remain, to a degree, removed or detached from the remarks. He must not react to them personally. However, he must, at the same time, be emotionally involved with the client so as to communicate that he is sensitive to and aware of the feelings the client is expressing. This also enables the client to remain emotionally involved. If the counselor becomes too detached, he takes on the characteristics of a computer; but if he becomes too emotionally involved, he loses his objectivity and starts reacting personally. Thus, the counselor must strive to be both emotionally involved in and objectively detached from the counseling situation. This simultaneous dual role makes counseling both an art and a science.

The counseling relationship must also be *real*; it must be genuine, sincere, and honest. People carrying on conversations in everyday life mask their true feelings with small talk; but if such a facade is maintained in the counseling relationship, then conversation instead of counseling takes place. But a counselor cannot merely say, "I am interested in you"; he must show it by his behavior. As the counselor communicates his realness, the client is able to remove his mask and drop his defenses.

Beginning counselors are sometimes unable to differentiate between a friendly relationship and a warm relationship. Being friendly is nothing more than a superficial aspect of a warm relationship; a big smile, a slap on the back, or a friendly remark are trite ways to convey warmth. The client is able to see through such actions as readily as a used-car buyer is able to see through the actions of the friendly salesman. A counselor — by his behavior, his manners, his facial expressions, his awareness, his consideration for the client — is able to transmit an atmosphere of warmth. Most of the successful remedial teachers we have seen have mastered the art of establishing warm, real relationships with their pupils.

Another important characteristic of the counseling relationship is *acceptance* of the individual by the counselor. To accept is to value an individual for his characteristics of infinite worth and dignity, to place extreme value on a human being for having an inner self, for being unique, for producing original thoughts and ideas. The counselor's acceptance tells the client that he is valued for his unique self and that he has the qualities necessary for positive development; thus, the client is better able to accept himself.

Sympathy is not a part of acceptance. A counselor who expresses sympathy is saying, "I agree with your suffering — you must feel awful — let me help you." Sympathy teaches the client to be dependent; instead of learning to operate independently, he learns to rely on the counselor. A counselor must feel *with* a client, which is empathy, not *for* a client, which is sympathy. Remedial teachers who do not guard against dependent relationships may find that children who have learned to function effectively during remedial sessions cannot do so when they return to the classroom.

Nor is judgment a part of acceptance. A counselor must completely accept the client; to judge is to express like or dislike, to present a personal evaluation of good or bad. Nonjudgmental acceptance is necessary if the client is to feel safe and free enough to express himself honestly and fully. In an accepting atmosphere the client gains a deep sense of freedom, which is seldom found in other interpersonal relationships; he is then able to drop his defenses and to experience being his true self.

(It should be interjected here that remedial teachers who have agreed that they can and should function as counselors up to this point often feel that they cannot realistically implement nonjudgmental acceptance. Their feeling is that because they are primarily tutors they must make judgments about a child's work; work that is incorrect or inferior cannot be accepted as equal to work that is correct and superior. Certainly this is a legitimate observation. It must be clear, however, that in an already paradoxical relationship the remedial teacher who operates with a counseling point of view must cope with still another paradox. The roles of teacher and counselor may at times seem to be at odds. The point to be made here is that a remedial teacher can continue to accept a child as a person even when it is necessary to evaluate his academic performance. Acceptance supersedes judgment. We shall return to this point later.)

A final characteristic of the counseling relationship is *understanding*. It follows acceptance and makes acceptance meaningful. To understand a client means to appreciate, by a process of intellectual thought and sensitive feelings, the significance of his remarks. To truly understand a client is to perceive his private world through his frame of reference, to see things as he sees them. This is a difficult task, for the counselor must leave his world and enter the world of the client. In making the transition the counselor leaves behind his ideas, perceptions, values, and feelings and bridges the gap to the thoughts and feelings of the client. At this stage the counselor is not outside looking in but rather inside seeing the meanings that the client gives to the experiences of his life.

TECHNIQUES

Listed below are some basic techniques of counseling that can be adapted by remedial teachers; brief explanations are given. The techniques are simply fragments that must be skillfully combined to make up an integrated whole which is more than the sum of the parts; and, because the techniques are general in nature, their use depends upon the individual and the situation. As he attempts to implement the techniques, the remedial teacher must keep in mind his paradoxical role as tutor-counselor. The suggested techniques are useful in building interpersonal relationships, but adaptations must be made to fit the teaching situation as well.

1. Drop the authoritative teacher role. Be an interested human being.
2. Communicate by transmitting attitudes and feelings. Do this by being real; it is more effective than simply to use words.
3. Arrange the physical setting so as to be close to the pupil. Do not sit behind the desk, but rather share the desk by having the pupil sit at the side. This is a technique that good remedial teachers have long applied.
4. Talk only about one-third of the time when the pupil discusses his problems. This gives him the opportunity to do most of the talking and shows that you are interested.
5. Ask questions that cannot be answered with yes or no. Instead of saying, "Do you like to read?" say, "What do you dislike about reading?" Or, instead of "Do you get along with your mother?" say, "Tell me about your mother."
6. Ask questions using the declarative tone of voice. Otherwise you may sound like an interrogator.
7. Do not interrupt the pupil when he is talking. This communicates

that what he has to say is important. However, if he digresses from the subject, focus him back on the subject by saying, "How does this apply to the subject we started talking about?" or "What does this mean to you?"

8. Give the pupil silence in which to think. Realize that there will be periods of silence during which the pupil is thinking. This may take practice, for in normal conversation silence produces a feeling of awkwardness.

9. Move the focus from intellectual thought to emotional feelings when feelings are being discussed. Ask such questions as, "What does this mean to you?" and "How did you feel about that?" (See the following three techniques.)

10. Observe and interpret nonverbal clues. Notice when the pupil moves his body or cries or drums his fingers. It is important to understand the relationship between his nonverbal clues and the subject being discussed.

11. Be alert to notice a change in the rate of speech, a change in the volume of speech, or a change in the pitch or tone of the voice. Such changes may indicate that there are emotional feelings connected with the subject being discussed and that the subject needs further exploration.

12. Point out what is currently happening. Say, "I notice your eyes are moist. What kinds of feelings do you have?"

13. Use brief remarks. Do not confuse the pupil with long, complicated questions or comments.

14. Pause before talking. The pupil may wish to make additional remarks; a pause of a few seconds enables him to continue.

15. Don't give lectures on ways to behave. Ask the pupil to suggest alternatives and let him make the decision. Help him to examine the consequences of his alternatives. Information, possibilities, and alternatives may be presented, but only for his consideration. There is a big difference between telling a person what to do and suggesting alternatives.

16. Avoid talking about yourself and your experiences. Do not use "I" and avoid personal anecdotes. Focus on the pupil and *his* problems.

17. Clarify and interpret what the pupil is saying. Use such remarks as, "It seems to you that your mother wants you to go to college." At other times, make a summarizing remark. But make these brief interpretations *after* the pupil has presented his ideas.

18. Do not be alarmed at remarks made by the pupil. Instead focus on the reason behind what was said or done.

19. Do not reassure the pupil that things will be all right. This will be recognized as superficial. Look for ways to demonstrate change and progress.

20. Do not make false promises. Instead communicate a feeling for the pupil and a desire to see and understand his problem; but do not appear to be overly concerned or to assume his problem.

21. Do not make moralistic judgments. Instead focus on what is behind the pupil's behavior; ask yourself, "What is there about this person that causes him to behave in this manner?" As a remedial teacher, do not blame the student for his failures; try to understand why he has failed.

22. Avoid undue flattery and praise. Instead focus on why the student asks for an undue amount of praise. If a pupil constantly asks such questions as "Do you like this dress?" say, "Yes, but why do you ask?" or "Do *you* like it?"

23. Do not reject the pupil through your remarks or nonverbal clues, but instead attempt to accept him. Try not to show impatience; do not threaten or argue; guard against any act that might appear to belittle.

24. Refer "more serious" cases. A more explicit definition of "more serious" cases cannot be given here. The remedial teacher must sense his own limitations and seek additional help when he seriously questions his own competence.

We suggest the above techniques as a means whereby a remedial teacher can implement a counseling point of view without denying the paradoxical nature of his roles as tutor and "counselor." Children who are underachievers are not simply problem learners; they are learners with problems, many of which are emotional as well as academic. We feel that to adopt a counseling point of view is not to usurp the role of a professional counselor, but to be pragmatic in seeking a way of becoming a more effective remedial teacher.

APPLICATIONS

Application with Pupils. A counseling point of view can be extremely beneficial to a remedial teacher's efforts in working with children. A warm, positive, accepting relationship created by the teacher can enable a pupil to be more receptive to remedial teaching. As a student who has met defeat and failure in one or more school subjects experiences the teacher's positive attitudes of acceptance and understanding, the foundation for improvement is laid. Then, when remedial work is geared to the unique needs of the student, the stage is set for him to experience success, perhaps for the first time in his school experience. Motivation is created as the remedial teacher is able to give honest, genuine compliments, praise, and encouragement. This, in turn, produces a greater degree of self-confidence, additional educational goals, and forward movement. Just as failure tends to beget failure so, too, can success beget success.

The remedial teacher should understand that the acceptance and understanding inherent in a counseling relationship do not necessarily imply that he must use a permissive approach with all pupils. There is, for example, no incompatibility between the counseling point of view and the highly structured learning situation needed by some hyperactive children. Even a Marine Corps drill instructor could be warm, accepting, and understanding — if he should happen to be so inclined — without sacrificing any of the rigors of boot camp.

A counseling point of view can be useful, too, as the remedial teacher attempts to deal with the disturbances that may be causing or contributing to a learning disability.

For example, if a student has a physical symptom such as poor hearing, headaches, or frequent upset stomach, the teacher can ask questions like, "How do you sleep at night?" or "What kinds of pain do you have?" Such questions may aid in focusing upon the student's physical health; but, equally important, they serve the function of communicating to the student that the teacher is interested in him as a person. The teacher can also secure information that may lead to a referral for a medical examination.

Or, a disabled lerner may frequently cause disturbances in the classroom. To get at causes for the misbehavior, the remedial teacher should not talk about his own personal experiences or give advice but, instead, listen to the situation as presented by the pupil. It may become apparent that the student's behavior is following a recognizable pattern because he does not know an appropriate way to behave. If this is so, the teacher can say, "Is there any other way you might act?" and give the student a chance to come up with alternatives. If he has no ideas the teacher should make no direct suggestions but, instead, ask him questions along the lines of, "Could you follow this course of action?" or "What might happen if you acted this way?" By presenting additional and more appropriate forms of behavior the remedial teacher may lead the pupil to try to learn other ways of behaving. Changed behavior can reduce the conflicts in a disabled learner's life and enable him to concentrate more upon his school work and upon the remedial teaching.

Finally, a student may have personal problems that cause him to feel depressed, rejected, fearful, or guilty. Again, the remedial teacher should listen to the student describe his feelings and the events which bring about the feelings, ask questions, and make clarifying statements, such as, "If I understand you correctly, you are having some difficulty with your father," or, "How do you feel about your father doing this to you?" Thus, an attempt is made to enter into the private world of the student in order to see his situation from his frame of reference. Then, as the student relates to the teacher and talks out his feelings, the emotional level is reduced and the student is better able accurately to perceive the world around him. When he is freed from concentrating primarily on his emotional problems, he is more able to respond to remedial teaching.

Instead of merely "treating" a learning problem and occasionally inquiring later as to the reason for the disability, a remedial teacher with a counseling point of view can often facilitate a long-term solution to the learning problem. The counseling relationship can help to reduce or eliminate a student's reluctance to learn; then the specific remedial program can insure success and accomplishment; and finally the praise and confidence of the teacher can be instrumental in promoting motivation and further growth. The counseling point of view, then, combines with the effective teaching of skills to result in optimum learning.

Applications with Parents. Parents, too, will generally respond in a favorable manner when they encounter a warm, sincere, honest, accepting, and understanding atmosphere. A teacher should recognize the fact that many parents are reluctant to visit school. They may, for example, feel inferior to an "educated" teacher; or they may be afraid that the teacher will criticize their method of raising children. When parents are apprehensive, their defenses are raised. A counseling point of view can help the teacher to help parents feel more at ease and drop their defenses.

At times parents come to a conference with feelings of hostility and antagonism toward a school policy, the administration, or the teachers. It is very easy for a teacher in this situation to react by defending the school and attacking the parents. However, to argue with a parent tends to be extremely unproductive, for each party simply defends his position. Then the major purpose of the conference — to help the child — is lost. A preferable procedure would be to let the angry parents express their negative feelings while the teacher neither agrees nor disagrees, attacks nor defends a position. After a period of time, the parents' anxiety may be reduced and then a successful conference can be conducted.

As parents express negative feelings the teacher can take an active part by using some of the following questions and remarks:

"If I understand correctly, you seem to have strong feelings about. . . ."

"How do you account for these feelings?"

"What is your understanding of. . .?"

"How do you help Clyde study at home?"

"What did you say when he brought home his last report card?"

"What you are describing happened in the first grade. How might we help Clyde now?"

"What do you see ahead for your child?"

"This is the information we have about your child. How realistic does your goal seem?"

It is important to notice that the above remarks do not give in or surrender, nor do they attack. On the other hand, a neutral attitude is not maintained, for the teacher shows his interest by asking clarifying questions. Thus, the counseling point of view is utilized.

Two additional points need to be made. First, a conference can create a feeling of frustration if the teacher makes suggestions which the parent cannot completely understand or carry out. When parents fail, they feel frustrated and they transmit their anxiety to the child. As a result, the child is exposed to additional pressure; and, instead of helping the child, the teacher and the parents have compounded the problem. If suggestions are given to parents, they should be specific, concrete, and practicable. Second, in interacting with parents, or at a later time, with students, a teacher should never reveal information which was received in confidence. Individuals will not be open with a teacher if they have reason to suspect that their remarks will not be kept in confidence.

A parent conference should conclude on a positive note. The parents should feel that they have gained additional information, received new insights, and expressed their reactions and feelings. Occasionally, it may be desirable to suggest additional conferences. Successful implementation of a counseling point of view should help parents to consider conferences as valuable and meaningful; when this is so, they will feel free to return whenever additional conferences seem desirable.

Application for the Teacher. A remedial teacher must submit to careful self-scrutiny before he can adopt a counseling point of view and make it an operative part of his personal orientation. What a person *is* dictates what he *does*. Thus, the rational thoughts, emotional feelings, beliefs, and self-awareness of a remedial teacher determine his actions, attitudes, methods, and — ultimately — his results. The function of self-scrutiny is to help a person to examine himself in order to increase his self-awareness; for only when a person knows who and what he is can he hope to establish significant relationships with others in any predictable manner. Through self-examination a person can begin to discover the false fronts, the masks, the facades he employs in his day-to-day interactions. He may discover, too, that he often reacts as he *feels he should* instead of as he *feels he wants to* react. When a person gets to know himself — to see his "real self" — he is in a position to change and to develop in a positive way.

Self-examination that leads to change requires courage; it may cause apprehension, discouragement, and pain; it may require giving up complacency and comfort. But change is challenging and ultimately worthwhile. The teacher who knows himself and is comfortable with change does not teach the same lesson for thirty years, nor is his life dull, narrow, shallow, constant.

The following sets of questions are suggested as guides to introspection. The first set deals with a specific incident in which a teacher has experienced disturbing emotional feelings.

1. What did Clyde say and do? How did he react? What feelings and attitudes did he transmit to me?
2. How did I behave? What did I say and do as I observed Clyde's reactions?
3. What caused *me* to react as I did? What was I feeling inside?
4. What did I wish to accomplish? Did I succeed?
5. Would I want to change my behavior if a similar incident came up in the future? If so, how?
6. What does looking at my behavior in this incident tell me about myself?

The second set of questions is more general.

1. How much have I changed in the past several years?
2. Do I have many "right" answers? If so, how come?
3. How safe do I really need to be?
4. How do I feel about change?
5. In what small area could I begin to change? What would it take on my part?

The capacity for change resides in each individual; but without self-awareness change is unlikely. If the procedures in a chemistry experiment are not changed, the results of each replication of the experiment will be the same. Similarly, the teacher whose inappropriate behavior leads to undesirable results will continue to get the same undesirable results until he changes his behavior. But when he becomes aware of his behavior pattern and, consequently, able to vary his approach, then the results will be different. The future does not have to be the same as the past. Self-awareness can lead to change, improvement, growth, and greater satisfaction. The teacher who is comfortable with change is one who can apply a counseling approach in his teaching because it is a part of his life.

A FINAL WORD

An understanding of the function of counseling, the creation of the counseling relationship, and the application of basic techniques can become an integral part of the general attitudes and techniques of the remedial teacher. However, it should be clear that every attempt was made to keep the present discussion (1) general in nature — not limited to any school or philosophy of counseling — and (2) pragmatic. Obviously there is much more to counseling. However, our purpose is not to transform remedial teachers into counselors but to borrow some useful concepts and techniques from counseling. Many teachers perceive counseling as something reserved entirely for specially trained personnel, like counselors, psychologists, and psychiatrists; as complex in nature, somewhat mystical, and far beyond their scope or ability; and as having negative or harmful results if performed to any degree by them. These perceptions are false and, fortunately, they are being corrected. For example, one important aspect of the current national mental health program is the concept that untrained or partially trained personnel such as clergymen, family physicians, teachers, probation officers, sheriffs, scoutmasters, public welfare workers, and others can readily acquire the additional skill of mental health counselors. The moderate amount of training proposed consists of short courses and consultation on the job. *(4)*

By projecting a counseling point of view, remedial teachers can contribute to more positive learning situations by creating rewarding interpersonal relationships. Rogers *(9)* was speaking of such relationships when he wrote, "As I think back over a number of teachers who have facilitated my own learning, it seems to me each one has this quality of being a real person. I wonder if your memory is the same. If so, perhaps it is less important that a teacher cover the allotted amount of curriculum, or use the most approved audiovisual devices, than that he be congruent, real, in his relations to his students."

REFERENCES

1.*Brammer, L. M., and Shostrom, E. L., *Therapeutic Psychology: Fundamentals of Counseling and Psychotherapy* (Englewood Cliffs: Prentice-Hall, 1960).
2.*Dinkmeyer, D., and Dreikurs, D., *Encouraging Children to Learn:*

*Recommended reading.

the Encouragement Process (Englewood Cliffs: Prentice-Hall, 1963).

3.*Johnson, W. F., Stefflre, B., and Edelfeldt, R. A., *Pupil Personnel and Guidance Services* (New York, McGraw-Hill, 1961).

4. Joint Commission on Mental Illness and Health, *Action for Mental Health* (New York: Basic Books, 1961).

5.*Maslow, A. H., *Toward a Psychology of Being* (Princeton: Van-Nostrand, 1962).

6.*Ohlson, M. M., *Guidance, an Introduction* (New York: Harcourt, Brace and World, 1955).

7. Orwell, G., *Animal Farm: A Fairy Story* (New York: Harcourt, Brace and World, 1946).

8. Rogers, C.R., *Client Centered Therapy* (Boston: Houghton Mifflin, 1951), p. 442.

9. Rogers, C.R., *On Becoming a Person* (Boston: Houghton Mifflin, 1961), p. 287.

10.*Tillich, P., *The Courage to Be* (New Haven: Yale University Press, 1952).

11.*Tolbert, E. L., *Introduction to Counseling* (New York: McGraw-Hill, 1959).

12.*Tyler, Leona E., *The Work of the Counselor* (New York: Appleton-Century-Crofts, 1953).

LEATRICE EMERUWA

The Teacher of Reading
and the Inner-city Child

Regrettably, inner-city children — particularly those of minority ethnic groups — are and will continue to be the ones in our society with the greatest reading problems and needs. The teacher of these children is probably of much greater importance than are methods and materials. What kind of person do these children need as teachers? What can teachers expect of these children and their schools? Emeruwa is compassionate, insightful, straightforward, and honest as she "tells it like it is."

Look around at the members of your reading class. How many truly understand and can wholeheartedly accept these children in their environment? In what ways are reading-methods classes and textbooks such as this one almost totally inadequate for preparing the ideal teacher described by Emeruwa? How generalizable to non-inner-city situations are the teaching-learning conditions described in this article?

"He who would slay dragons must first know their habits." But he who would cope successfully with the reading problems of students in urban schools must first know his own habits, as well as those of his students. It is the purpose of this paper, therefore, to focus on those habits and attitudes which the urban reading teacher needs to cultivate. To complete the analogy, this paper concerns itself with two inter-related aspects of teaching reading: the first with those whom the reading teacher would rescue from the dragon of reading disability; and the second with those who are the strategists on the battlefields.

That this concern is focused in the proper direction can best be deduced from the fact that U.S. Commissioner of

A paper presented at the 1970 convention of the International Reading Association. Reprinted by permission of Leatrice Emeruwa.

Education James E. Allen, at the inception of the new year, issued a call for a national drive for reading improvement in the 1970's. This call comes despite the fervid and frenetic activity during the 1950's and 1960's to upgrade reading instruction.

Such activity has embraced either alternately or concomitantly the "Why-Johnny-Can't Read" and phonics vs. the look-say controversies, experience charts, Fernald methodology, Initial Teaching Alphabet, Color cues, Words-in-Color, programed textbooks, eye cameras, reading slides, films and filmstrips, SRA reading laboratories, individualized vs. basal texts reading programs, SQ3R and other formulas, NDEA reading-teacher training institutes, tachistoscopic training, listening posts, perceptual development studies, talking typewriters, reading-task forces, tutorial programs, compensatory education plans, in-service training, and presently even culturally-valid basal readers and trade books. Much "hue and cry" has accompanied each new study, each new method, each new panel of experts, each new piece of hardware and each new text. Yet after sixteen years — the span of International Reading Association's existence — there is a forty percent (40%) high-school dropout rate for black inner-city students and a seventy percent (70%) reading retardation rate for those black youth who do remain and complete high school. (To say nothing of the percentages for other disadvantaged groups.) Obviously something is wrong!

PUBLIC REACTION

Columnist Carl T. Rowan on December 7, 1969, in a nationally syndicated column (*The Plain Dealer,* Cleveland Ohio) drew an ominous picture of the plight of this country's urban schools. He stated:

> The public schools of America's cities are in a mess. And growing worse. They are populated by children who do not or will not learn and burdened by the teachers who cannot or will not teach. They are plagued by racial and ethnic hostilities and by violence flowing out of an assortment of emotions. Some schools in our greatest cities are graduating classes in which three diploma holders out of four cannot truly read or write and are utterly unprepared to go on to higher education, or to cope with the problems of earning a living.

Obviously new directions must be sought!

Although it is axiomatic that knights should map out their winning campaigns, and planners of viable urban reading programs should do the same by becoming thoroughly familiar with the "lay of the land," it is not within the province of this paper to deal with the smoke and flames of the socio-economic-political reports which are belched forth steadily each day by communications media. It should be sufficient to say that for this nation, Armageddon may be the next campaign. The plethora of sociological tracts and learned statistical reports which describe the physical and emotional climate of today's city pin-point the teaching problems that middle-class, wasp-oriented instructors face — whatever their race. These reports indicate, also, to the discerning teacher that preliminary skirmishes are already under way in urban settings.

EDUCATIONAL CLIMATE

By connotation the term "urban school" is synonymous with "inner-city" school and conjures up a vivid image of an antiquated physical plant, overcrowded, with a basically non-white student population which is both intellectually and financially impoverished. (The jargon is "disadvantaged" or "culturally deprived.") Accompanying this idea is the horrendous vision that within the school walls, one finds wild scenes of mayhem — unruly classroom behavior, violent language, drugs, robberies, beatings, assaults, rapes, and even murders. As a result of these criminal occurrences, there is much unrest resulting in student confrontations, parental demonstrations, and striking teachers.

In the immediate environment outside the school, one visualized hunger and deprivation in the community, rat and roach infested, over-peopled, dilapidated housing, bloody scenes of police shoot-ins and shoot-outs, accelerating crime rates, spontaneous riots and blatant militant demands for community control of schools. The picture — more often than not — is for real! And it is with this reality that the urban reading teacher must cope. Again, it should be sufficient to say that any holier-than-thou, missionary-type teacher who ventures into a large city school to teach reading — or any other subject for that matter — without having first armoured himself in the sociology of that school and its environs will end up as frustrated and ineffective as Don Quixote in his battles with windmills.

DISABLED READER SYNDROME

Moreover, it matters not whether the reading teacher is in grade school, secondary school, adult education, dropout programs or remedial courses in the two-year college. The same identifiable disabled reader syndrome appears. This syndrome reveals itself to a greater or lesser extent according to the individual. However, its general features can be discerned by any sensitive teacher. In short, the observer will find poor readers who manifest attitudes of negative self-concepts and low esteem for their individual and group abilities. These students will exhibit passive despair and quiet hopelessness or aggressive, angry unconcern in reading situations. Their mannerisms will show signs of nervousness and anxiety. Their individual and/or collective behavior may be overtly hostile. An aura of fearfulness will enshroud those who still have varying degrees of hope left. But all these poor readers — whatever their rank, whatever their behavior, and whatever their verbalization — scream in quiet desperation: "I am hopeless. I want to read well whatever I desire to read!"

Of course, while attitudes cannot be measured accurately, and the reading teacher must sense them, he should be able to diagnose objectively that these retarded readers are deficient in a multiplicity of reading skills: conceptualizing, interpreting, analyzing, word attack, comprehension, rate adjustment and vocabulary power, as well as deficient in the other communication skills of speaking, writing, and listening, i.e., standard usage in language power. However, the ability to read well is of paramount importance, not only to the readers themselves, but also to their parents and the members of the larger community.

THERAPY

Like the disability syndrome, a workable therapeutic approach for reading remediation at all grade levels appears. It, too, seems to manifest similar characteristics for reading success irrespective of the readers' ages. To get to the "nitty gritty" of this approach for the improvement of reading instruction in ghetto-ized American city schools, reading teachers should be aware that there are generally recognizable conditions the successful teacher must meet. These conditions are the same which any good teacher meets to ensure the success of learning objectives at even the most prestigious upper-class private schools. Namely, the teacher needs to:

1. Know the subject matter thoroughly
2. Possess skill in the latest methodology
3. Be familiar with the intellectual and physical background of the students
4. Use a wide variety of relevant instructional materials and resources
5. Be accessible and responsive to the parents
6. Be enthusiastic and able to arouse enthusiasm for learning
7. Be warm and flexible, relating both humanly and humanely to meet the individual and group needs of students

But there are broader dimensions to coping with the urban students' reading problems, dimensions which go far beyond the usual psychological concepts expounded in the typical "silent-majority-based, how-to-do-it" methods courses. The specialist who resolves meaningfully most of the learning problems of his disadvantaged students is of a special breed. It has been stated earlier that he is an expert in the sociology of his school and its community — and is knowledgeable of the peculiar socio-economic political data pertinent to his particular teaching situation. This ideal reading teacher, further, is a master instructor well abreast of his pedagogic homework. For it is a fact, that the onus of today's chaotic public educational climate is due in great part to the tradition-bound, conservative, and ill-prepared teacher who neither understands what he should teach, how it should be taught, nor whom he teaches!!

THE IDEAL READING TEACHER

To explicate, in addition to the gifts of social and pedagogical omniscience, the successful reading teacher has other attributes. One characteristic is that he is thick-skinned and immune to the possible enmity of his colleagues. For if they are typical, they will evince the same middle-class attitudes, misunderstandings and prejudices as the larger dominant community does toward poor non-white readers. Also if the reading teacher is experiment-minded and multi-talented — which he ought to be; if the reading teacher is creative and indefatigable — which he should be; if the reading teacher is sensitive to the present needs and future aspirations of his disabled students — which he must be; then that teacher also must be cognizant that he may incur the resentment of his less involved co-workers — unless he is a master politician. With the single-minded aim to improve the reading capabilities of his students, the teacher invariably "steps on toes" as he goes to battle for personal lesson planning time, community-resources involvement, laboratory assistance, individual student time, more space, the latest reading materials, and human dignity for "those people" whom he teaches. In essence, when the administration is conservative, the dedicated reading teacher still tries to "do his own thing." He forgets an administrative fight. However, when the administration is favorable, the teacher is even "more together," but he does not forget his colleagues. The ideal situation, of course, is one wherein both administration and staff are emotionally geared and materially enabled to ameliorate the entire range of learning problems evidenced by the students. Such utopias are seldom found in today's city schools, however.

Still another personality attribute that the teacher of reading needs is that of being impervious to the hostility, open or latent, of his students. At the same time he manifests a monolithic dedication to his students' welfare, he is sympathetic to their personal and group needs. Intellectually the urban reading teacher recognizes that the institutionalized racism inherent in the American educational system has perpetuated a mythopoeic philosophy and curriculum that has served to "enwhiten" two generations of black people.

It is the rejection by today's militant black youth of this educational stance which has set the stage for urban school battles. It is this awareness by black students and black parents of the instructional failures of educational institutions which has caused the cry for community control of schools. And it is the disillusionment for most black people with the reality of the American nightmare that has ignited flames across urban skies. The perceptive teacher, thereby, in urban schools knows that the discontent is contagious — causing infection in other alienated ethnic and poor white minority groups, and/or causing polarization along ethnocentric lines.

Consequently, the reading teacher who would be successful at any grade level has another important attribute to his make-up. He deems it important — in addition to the proper attitude, pedagogical preparation, and sociological consciousness — that he be familiar with the ethos of the students with whom he interacts. He knows that he must operate within a carefully constructed framework built upon respect for and knowledge of the history, culture, cultural contributions, and present life-styles of the students, their families, and their ethnic group within the larger community. He is aware that despite all his other talents, his ability to sympathize and empathize with the physical and psychic needs of his inner-city students will influence their learning success. In the final analysis, it will be the reading teacher's demonstration of all the previously mentioned attitudes plus his ability to utilize black literary models, black folkways/lifestyles, and black linguistic idioms as sources for instructional materials and inspiration that will determine instructional success. It will be, too, the reading teacher's exploitation of the resources of the larger community and his capacity to make his teaching relevant to the needs of this community which will sustain success.

If teachers of reading would deal meaningfully with problems in urban schools, then they must believe as does Dr. Richard Worthen, who in a recent address to the College section at N.C.T.E.'s Annual Convention (November 29, 1969, Washington, D.C.) stated:

> Every student, regardless of any other consideration, is driven to seek intellectual encounter and is worthy of being taught to cope with symbols successfully. . . .Teachers must recognize that literature must be used in all ways that are relevant to the students and that the needs of the students must be paramount, rather than the predilections of the instructor.

In 1968 Sister Aretha Franklin sang a best seller on the Soul Hit-Parade entitled "Respect." Although she is singing to her lover, there is one significant line which every reading teacher in urban schools needs to heed. She spells out the word *respect* and urges her lover to find out what it means to her. She expands this theme in the refrain by noting that a little bit of respect is all she needs.That is what the revolution in urban schools is about in part: "R-E-S-P-E-C-T" and what it means not only to black students, but also to Chicanos, Native-Americans, Eskimos, Appalachians, Puerto Ricans, Portuguese, Hawaiians, or whoever.

To conclude, the urban teacher who hopes to meet the reading needs of his students must be an extraordinary instructor. He realizes that one of his biggest tasks is to get out of the "narrow Anglo ethnocentric bag of middle-class America." He must rethink and revise methods and objectives even at the expense of hostility possibly from his administrators, co-workers or students. He is willing to utilize cultural data and to use his imagination, creativity, and ingenuity to make the reading classroom the relevant and exciting place of learning it can be. If he needs help to ease his conscience at being caught between the dilemma of serving either the dominant culture or meeting the special needs of his students, he remembers that relevant education is this country's best means for keeping alive the goal of a viable democratic society. As Dr. Worthen said, "Barbarism threatens if communication becomes untenable."[1] The reading teacher today in urban schools must be committed to keeping open the channels of communication — and in the rhetoric of the revolutionaries — "by any means necessary." For the reading teacher is the last hope before the academic-political barbarism or totalitarianism that threatens.

---

[1] Aarons, Alfred C., Barbara T. Gordon and William A. Stewart, eds. *Linguist-Cultural Differences and American Education.* North Miami Beach, Florida: The Florida Fl Reporter, Spring, Summer 1969.

IRA AARON

Maintain the Gains

Learning to read is a psychomotor task that occurs most quickly and efficiently if certain principles drawn from research on learning are followed. We run the risk of slow, erratic, and quickly lost gains if we do not incorporate these principles into our instruction with all children. By ignoring these principles, we may create reading problems where none would otherwise exist, and we may unduly retard the improvement remedial readers would otherwise make. Aaron speaks both to classroom and remedial teachers and says, in part, "Love is not enough; neither is discussing the story in the basal reader. There is no substitute for psychologically sound, systematic, organized instruction."

How does this article relate to Storer's and Schell's articles later in this section? After reading the selections in Part Five, you might profit from rereading this article and seeing how these principles are applied in the different approaches described in that section. You might take a sheet of paper and write the principles listed by Aaron on the left side, leaving the right side blank. Then try to fill in the right side with ways you have applied or can apply each of these principles to your teaching situation.

At one time or another every teacher has experienced the frustration of discovering that a reading skill he has taught was not learned or has been forgotten. Maintaining gains is one of the major problems of teaching children to read.

Many different factors are involved in learning to read. Among these are the quantity and spacing of instructional

---

sessions, the learner's motivation, the extent to which the learner receives feedback on his efforts, the degree to which instruction is aimed toward transfer, the organization of the learning task itself, and the extent to which the teacher assesses progress. All of these factors and many others operate both in original learning and in practice for maintenance of previously learned skills and abilities.

The major purpose of this chapter is to suggest some actions that will help the teacher maintain — and add to — the gains children have made in reading. Six guides, each with several related and sometimes overlapping suggestions, are presented. These guides for action presuppose that reading teachers, in keeping with good teaching practices, will recognize and adjust to the individuality of each child insofar as this can possibly be done.

The suggestions presented are based largely upon conclusions drawn from learning research. However, they are supplemented by reports of what teachers of reading have found useful in their classes.

SCHEDULE PERIODIC REVIEWS OF READING SKILLS THAT HAVE BEEN PREVIOUSLY INTRODUCED

Teaching a child a reading skill gives no assurance that at a later time when he needs the skill he will still possess it — unless there is further teaching for maintenance. It is only through periodic reviews that skills previously learned can be maintained at their original response level.

Teach for overlearning of important reading skills and abilities. The mature reader knows the reading skills so well that he uses them automatically. This overlearning will not be achieved unless the learner periodically encounters reading situations involving use of what has been taught previously.

The degree of original learning, the depth of learning, is a major factor influencing retention. Skills and understandings that are overlearned will show less loss over periods of time than those learned only to the point of recall. Therefore, it is essential to teach for thorough learning of important skills and abilities from the beginning stages of reading instruction. With experience the teacher will learn to estimate the number of practice sessions necessary for the desired degree of learning to occur. The development of certain reading skills will, of course, require constant instruction over a long period of time.

Growth in the use of reading skills is sequential, with the use of more complex skills and abilities building on, or growing out of, those that are less complex. For instance, facility in locating a dictionary definition of an unknown word in a sentence involves knowing alphabetical sequence, how to use guide words, how to open the dictionary near the entry word, how to select the appropriate meaning from among several possibilities, and so on. Each of these skills and abilities will have been practiced separately at some time in the instructional sequence, but in location of a definition they are combined into a larger, more complex ability. As subskills and abilities become clustered or merged into a more complex ability, separate practice on the subskills is not needed for maintenance. Practice on the more complex ability will maintain the lower-order reading skills.

Space the reviews in terms of the level of learning at the time of reviews. To say precisely how often reviews are needed for maintenance of reading skills and abilities is impossible in view of the many factors influencing learning. Nevertheless, general statements can be made about the needed frequency of reviews. Practice should be frequent in the early stages of teaching a reading skill until the desired level of response is approached. Gradually the reviews may be spaced further and further apart as learning progresses.

All children do not need the same amount of practice, and the teacher must be flexible in making decisions about how much practice is needed. The amount of practice should be geared to the personal needs of the children involved.

MOTIVATE THE CHILD TO PRACTICE
WITH AN INTENT TO LEARN

If practice is to be effective, the pupil must be motivated to learn. To be sure, learning can occur when the child has very little motivation for tackling the task at hand, but practice with a strong intent to learn will lead to better results. In fact, repetition of a previously learned reading skill will not in itself necessarily reinforce that skill. What the repetition does is to make it possible for additional learning to occur. Not much effective learning is likely to occur in practice sessions in which the child is listless and uninterested.

As in the case of most aspects of learning, many factors influence a child's attitude and performance in a given task.

Make practice meaningful to the child. If practice is meaningful to the child, then learning is likely to occur. Mentioning to the child that a review exercise in reading is a check on what he remembers about previously taught skills will serve to tie the current activity immediately into his previous experiences and thus facilitate learning. Also important is the extent to which the learner understands why practice is needed. The child who knows why a skill or understanding is being reviewed tends to apply himself more actively to the task, and more effective learning usually results.

Establish a good relationship with the child. The relationship between the teacher and pupil has many facets: the positive or negative feelings the child has toward the teacher, the teacher's feelings toward the child (as perceived by the child), the extent to which the teacher expects the child to achieve, and so on. If the child perceives that the teacher respects him and expects him to respond favorably toward practice sessions in reading, he will usually try to meet this expectancy. The personal relationship between teacher and pupil is as important in reading instruction as the techniques the teacher uses in teaching.

The child's own personality also affects his ability to learn. Some children, because of traits developed long before entering a particular teacher's classroom, immediately devote their energies to learning. In contrast, other children need much encouragement; their experiences have not led them to value school achievement. Motivating them to practice with an intent to learn is often difficult.

Reinforce practice by means of appropriate techniques. In the practice of skills and abilities in reading — in fact, in all learning — the manner of reinforcement is important. Though research does not support specific guides to be followed with all types of learners in all types of settings, some general statements can be made about reinforcement in learning. Praise is usually more fruitful than verbal reprimand, and verbal reprimand — which must be used with extreme caution — is usually better than neutral statements about a child's progress in reading. Reinforcement should be keyed to the individual child. For instance, praise should be appropriate for the child receiving it; what a six-year-old considers to be praise may produce a different reaction in an eleven-year-old.

GIVE THE CHILD IMMEDIATE FEEDBACK
ON THE EFFECTS OF HIS PRACTICE

If practice is to be effective in maintaining gains, children must have confirmation or correction of their performances. If the child is permitted to practice a wrong response, the teacher has the added problem of helping the child unlearn the incorrect response before he can learn the correct one.

Check exercises as soon as possible. When paper-and-pencil practice sheets are used, the teacher should check the exercises as soon as possible after completion and give the results to the children. Pupils in upper primary grades or higher, except for the poorest readers, can do a great deal of their own checking if a key copy is provided. The teacher needs to discuss items that the children have missed in order to correct any misconceptions they may have. Spot-checking of the self-corrected exercises may, occasionally, be necessary to determine the children's accuracy in correcting their responses. If exercises are appropriate to the child's current level of achievement, the teacher usually need not be concerned about the possibility of student cheating.

Aim feedback on effectiveness of practice toward the individual child. The reading teacher must consider the effect of his method of giving feedback on practice sessions. Of course, he needs to help the child diagnose strengths and weaknesses. In addition, he needs to make the feedback as specific as possible. A comment such as "You're now getting all the main-idea questions; this is good, but you need a little more work on getting the details" serves to motivate the child to better efforts than a "satisfactory" or "good" with no elaboration.

HAVE CHILDREN PRACTICE SKILLS
IN A VARIETY OF SETTINGS
AND IN A VARIETY OF WAYS

A child learns to speak in such a way that he can understand and create sentences he has never heard before. In like manner he must also learn to read in such a way that he can recognize whole sentences and words he has never seen before. If effective learning has occurred, the child can use what he has learned in a variety of situations. This transfer is more likely to occur if many different kinds of materials are provided for practicing skills.

Let children practice the same skill using different kinds of materials to assure transfer. One of the teacher's goals is teaching pupils to read for implied meanings. Children need to practice this comprehension skill using several different types of material — fiction, biography, factual material, and so on.

Another example of the importance of practicing in a variety of settings may be noted in the self-contained classroom, where the teacher separates developmental reading instruction from instruction in the content areas. Unless the teacher teaches for transfer, some children may use a skill in the reading class but not necessarily in reading a social studies text. Teaching for transfer involves helping pupils see how a skill learned in one setting also can be applied in a different setting.

Use variety in practice sessions to maintain pupil interest. Children soon tire of doing the same thing over and over. They may go through the steps of practice with little or no learning occurring unless they are actively involved in the practice. Shifting the types of practice exercises — sometimes using discussions around a chalkboard, again using a paper-and-pencil exercise, later using discussion of a selection being read — will help maintain children's interest.

The teacher must use careful judgment in selecting items for practice, making sure that the variety facilitates, rather than hinders, learning. It is not essential to make each practice setting different. In fact, too much shifting could interfere with effective learning. The first practice after the initial introduction of a reading skill should be in a format related to that of the child's initial introduction to that skill. However, as the child improves his performance on the skill, the teacher should be alert to flagging interest — an indication that it's time to modify the practice activity.

ORGANIZE THE PRACTICE SESSION
TO FACILITATE LEARNING

If the task to be learned is well organized, a greater degree of learning is likely to occur. Factors involved in organization include the extent to which the task is made clear to the learner, the conciseness and clarity of teacher instructions or printed directions, the sequence in which skills are introduced, the relationship of the current task to previously learned tasks, and the number of elements involved in the task.

Help the child understand clearly what he is expected to learn or to practice. The pupil should know what he is to learn and why he needs to practice. Teachers may say, "We now are going to review the prefixes we studied yesterday. Do you remember the ones we learned?" Or they may say, "I want you to read this story to note the order in which the main events happened. When something important occurs, try to remember what led up to it. This will help you know why it happened. We'll discuss the causes when you finish your reading." Both in initial learning and in practice for maintenance, the teacher must lead the child to an understanding of what the learning task is.

Present clear and concise directions for practice activities. Clear and concise directions help children organize their own thinking about the practice activity. When they know what is to be accomplished, boys and girls can expend their major energies toward getting the job done instead of puzzling over what they are expected to do. The teacher must have a thorough knowledge of what is to be learned and how to set the stage for effective learning; then he is in a position to give clear and concise directions for the reading task. It is equally important that printed directions meet criteria of brevity and clearness.

Know the skill sequence being followed. The sequence in which reading skills are introduced also influences learning. Though research does not support a particular sequence for introducing all reading skills, studies do give support, in broad terms, to introducing lower-order, less complex skills before introducing higher-order skills that involve the lower-order ones. More important than the specific sequence being followed, however, is the fact that a sequence gives the teacher a systematic way to introduce all important reading skills.

Relate the current learning task to what the child already knows. Relating a current task to what children already know facilitates learning. This statement applies both to the introduction of a new skill and to practice for maintenance of a previously learned skill. When a new skill that involves lower-order skills previously learned by the children is introduced, the lower-order skills should be reviewed before the new element is added. The extent of the review is determined by how well the children know the lower-order skills. Practice sessions, in which nothing new in the way of skills is involved, may well begin with a brief discussion of what was done in the last practice period.

Keep the size of the learning task within manageable limits. Ease of learning is determined in part by the number of elements in the learning task whether the task is aimed toward introducing a new skill or reviewing one previously introduced. Children must not be expected to learn or to review too many facts, skills, or relationships in one package. Reading teachers need to analyze the task to see that it is suited in complexity to the learner. A given exercise may well concentrate on one reading skill to be taught or reviewed; when clusters of reading skills are involved, they should be related.

APPRAISE CHILDREN'S GROWTH CONSTANTLY TO DETERMINE NEED FOR PRACTICE

The previous five guides have dealt mainly with learning and its relationship to practice for maintenance of reading skills and abilities that children have learned. This guide concerns the teacher's appraisal of reading growth. An effective teacher constantly assesses children's achievement to ascertain strengths and weaknesses so he can help pupils maintain the skills and abilities they possess and assist them in overcoming their weaknesses. Such assessment of children's growth in reading may be done in a variety of ways.

Observe children's silent and oral reading. The teacher can determine strengths and weaknesses by observing children as they read silently and orally. To guide the observations, a check list of skills might be used. The teacher then assesses each child's performance periodically in terms of skills taught or reinforced at a given reading level. Thus each child's reading is appraised in relation to the knowledge and skills appropriate for his reading instructional level.

Determine suitability of materials by means of informal reading inventories. Another useful method of assessing reading achievement is through informal reading inventories. An informal inventory appraises the individual pupil's level of competence without reference to what others do. Many patterns for inventories are offered in the literature on the teaching of reading. The most frequently used ones are based on a series of selections approximately 100 to 150 words in length that have been graded for readability. The teacher has the child read a relatively easy selection silently, answer the comprehension questions provided, and then read the selection orally. This procedure is followed for several increasingly difficult selections until the child reaches a level that is obviously too difficult for him. The teacher observes and records the child's reading habits and his skill strengths and weaknesses and, on the basis of the silent and oral reading and the responses given to the questions, determines the level at which the child can best be instructed. Such an inventory, then, serves the dual purpose of determining a child's placement and diagnosing his particular needs.

Check children's progress on specific skills by means of teacher-made tests. Though teacher-made tests often are crude measures of achievement, they can be helpful in determining the status of children's growth in specific skills and abilities. Test items can be aimed directly toward checking specific skills and understandings on which instruction has been given; later, review or reteaching sessions may be scheduled. Maintenance practice sessions may well be spaced, perhaps every three or four weeks, whereas reteaching sessions will be scheduled more frequently.

Assess acquisition of recently taught skills by using prepared assessment exercises. Among the most useful skill-assessment aids to the teacher are periodic assessment exercises. These serve both to review previously taught skills and information and to diagnose further instructional needs. In fact, an individual practice exercise may be considered in the same light; it reviews skills and provides diagnostic data. To reap the greatest benefit from these exercises, the teacher must be thoroughly familiar with the specific skills and abilities covered.

Evaluate pupil progress in reading through pupil conferences. Through conferences with children, the teacher gains knowledge about their interests and attitudes toward reading, as well as about their knowledge of skills. Although all teachers have pupil conferences, the teacher using a personalized reading approach perhaps bases more of his evaluation on information gained in such conferences. If conferences are to serve as a basis for practice and assessment, they must be purposeful and organized. The face-to-face teacher-pupil conference can glean information about the child's individual knowledge and preferences in reading that often cannot be obtained in any other way.

Assess learning of important skills taught. Assessment tests designed to check achievement at the end of a given level serve to review skills for maintenance as well as to determine if the child has learned the skills and abilities taught at that level. These tests assist the teacher in establishing areas of strength and weakness in reading.

Evaluate long-range reading growth by means of standardized reading tests. Standardized reading tests of the types usually used in assessing reading achievement help answer questions about overall reading achievement. However, they often give little information about the specific strengths and weaknesses of individual children. As a rule they are administered only once a year. The common standardized reading tests, though useful in long-range assessment of growth, do not help the teacher in day-to-day or week-to-week assessment of children's growth in reading.

IN SUMMARY

To become a mature reader, the child must learn the reading skills so well that he can use them automatically. Success in reading will not occur unless skills and understandings, once taught to the point of adequate pupil performance, are practiced periodically.

If gains in reading are to be maintained, the teacher of reading must be concerned with motivating his pupils to practice with an intent to learn. He must make the practice as meaningful as possible to the child. He must also be concerned with his relationship with the child and with adequate techniques for reinforcing learning.

In order to help children get the most from practice, the teacher needs to give immediate feedback through such activities as having exercises checked as soon as possible and having children keep records of their own reading achievement.

Skills and abilities should be practiced in a variety of settings and in a variety of ways in order to facilitate transfer of learning and maintain pupil interest. However, variety should be introduced in such a way that it does not interfere with effective learning.

Organization is important in both the introduction and practice phases. The effective teacher helps the child understand what he is expected to learn, presents directions clearly and concisely, knows well the particular skill sequence he is using, relates the current learning task to what the child already knows, and keeps the size of the learning task within manageable limits.

Children's growth in reading should be assessed regularly. On the basis of the assessment, the reading teacher plans for reviews of known skills and for reteaching of skills and abilities not developed sufficiently.

The problems of maintaining gains actually are the problems of teaching. The teacher who wants success must teach for success. Otherwise, what appears to be learned at one time may disappear at a later date. Maintain the gains in reading by teaching for success!

JO M. STANCHFIELD

Boys' Reading Interests as Revealed Through Personal Conferences

From 75 to 90 percent of all children with reading difficulties are boys. Because interest is vital both in preventing and in correcting such problems, it is imperative that we learn the reading *interests of these children and then supply materials that match their interests. This is one of a few studies to investigate this topic in depth.*

Are materials that meet these criteria generally available? What materials other than books seem appropriate? Do typical basal readers meet these criteria? What implications do these findings have for teachers using the language-experience approach with disabled readers? How are Stanchfield's findings evident in the criteria and materials listed by Storer and Colton in the next article? Do reading teachers have a responsibility to raise and broaden interests as well as to cater to the status quo?

He ate and drank the precious words,
His spirit grew robust;
He knew no more that he was poor,
Nor that his frame was dust.
He danced along the dingy days,
And this bequest of wings
Was but a book. What liberty
A loosened spirit brings. —

Emily Dickinson

This poem by Emily Dickinson expresses with beauty and clarity what reading can mean to the individual. There is a sense of personal joy in reading a book and a creative reaction which

Reprinted from *The Reading Teacher,* 16 (September 1962), pp. 41-44, by permission of Jo M. Stanchfield and the International Reading Association.

cannot be replaced by motion pictures, television, or radio. Reading remains a critical element in much analytical thinking, in the accumulation of knowledge, and in the transmission of thoughts and ideas.

What role does interest play in developing reading abilities? It is generally agreed that interest is highly significant in the motivation of human behavior. Dewey emphasized the dynamic quality of interest when he wrote of interest as being active, projective, and propulsive. Many other authorities have recognized the "magic" of interest and have conceded that interests may not only be created, but may also be discovered and measured. Much has been written about children's reading interests during the last thirty years. Many studies have shown that relationships exist between reading interests and such factors as intelligence, chronological age, sex, socio-economic background, and reading achievement. A review of these investigations has indicated that the relationship between reading interests and reading achievement has not been widely studied. Many people have tended to assume, without supporting facts and evidence, that reading achievement affects reading interests. The author felt that this vital question of the effect of reading achievement upon reading interest needed to be scrutinized more closely and therefore conducted an intensive study in this area. The problem of this study was that of discovering the current reading interests of elementary school boys, grades four, six and eight, and in relating these interests to grade-level reading achievement.

SELECTION OF BOYS

To secure a statistically adequate sample, 153 boys were interviewed, 51 at each grade level studied. Within each grade level there were three sub-groupings; superior readers, average readers, and poor readers. The group of interviewees was limited to boys because boys, throughout the nation, have far more frequent and severe reading problems than girls. The boys were chosen from Los Angeles City Schools, selected to provide a cross section of socio-economic levels, ranging from lower-middle class to upper middle class. The study was further delimited to American-born families, in order to assure an English-speaking background. The range of I.Q. extended from

90 to 120. The boys were carefully checked to eliminate those with emotional disturbances or physical problems.

INTERVIEW TECHNIQUES

In order to study boys' reading interests with depth and intensiveness and to secure the most valid responses possible, it was considered necessary to talk at length with each boy. The personal conference of over an hour for each boy had advantages over the questionnaire procedure in that the researcher was able to clarify meanings for the interviewee, stimulate his thinking processes, and encourage him in the articulation of his responses. Establishing rapport and a cooperative attitude at the beginning of the conference was essential.

After building a good feeling tone for the interview in the introduction, the writer attempted to avoid emotional blocks in the area of reading, which might be a problem with the low achievers, by first exploring the free-time activities of the boys and gradually approaching the questions about reading. In answering all the questions, the boys were first encouraged to talk without interference or restriction in a "free-response" situation. Then the interviewer suggested other possible responses; and the boys, after careful thought, decided on their final answers.

ANALYSIS OF THE DATA

Preferences in categories of reading interests. There were two general areas to investigate with respect to fifty categories of reading interests: first, describing the interests by grade level and by reading ability; second, determining which, if any, of the categories received significantly different ratings by different subsamples. In the first area, rank-order correlation coefficients were computed for the grade levels and for reading achievement levels. In the second area, a two-way analysis of variance was performed for each of the fifty categories, the dimensions of these analyses being the three grade levels and the three levels of reading achievement.

The coefficients of correlation indicated a strong similarity among the preferences of all three grades. The coefficient between the choices of the fourth and sixth graders was a

positive .92; between the fourth and eighth graders, a positive
.94; and between the sixth and eighth graders, a positive
.89. An even greater similarity of preferences was shown in the
choices made by the three groups of achievers. The coefficient
between the selections of the high achievers and the average
achievers was .93; between the high achievers and the low
achievers, .92; and between the average achievers and the low
achievers, .93.

The preferences of all the boys indicated that "outdoor
life" was the most highly preferred of all fifty categories.
"Explorations and expeditions" and "sports and games" were
close second and third choices. The topics of "science fiction,"
"sea adventure," and "fantasy" tied for fifth place. "Historical
fiction" and "humor" ranked seventh and eighth in interest. The
categories of "everyday life adventure of boys" and "outer
space" were given a rank of nine. "Mystery" and "war" also held
great appeal for the boys. The relatively small range of thirteen
points among the first twelve categories showed that the boys
were highly interested in all of these areas.

The boys, as a group, appeared to be less interested in the
categories of "cowboys and westerns," "transportation,"
"fables," "Bible stories," "teenage romance," "riddles and
puzzles," "weather and climate," "mathematics," "birds and
insects," "occupations," and "fairy tales." The topics which
elicited the least interest included "plants," "music," "plays,"
"art," "family and home life," and "poetry."

No significant differences were found in the choices of the
boys who were reading above grade level, at grade level, and
below grade level. As for the differences by grade levels, there
were ten categories which received significantly different
ratings. These differences appeared to be in the expected
direction of changes in tastes with increasing age and maturity.

Preferences in characteristics of reading interests. The
same procedures used with the Categories of Reading Interests
were employed with the Characteristics of Reading Interests.
Here, again, the rank-order coefficients of correlation between
the choices of all three grades approached a positive 1.0, so that
it was evident that there was a high degree of similarity among
the preferences of the grade levels. The coefficient of
correlation between the choices of the fourth and the sixth
graders was a positive .92; between the fourth and eighth

graders, a positive .94; and between the sixth and eighth graders, a positive .89. The high, average, and low achievers showed an almost identical degree of similarity in their choices, as evidenced by a coefficient of correlation of a positive .96 in all comparisons.

Of twenty characteristics of reading interests, "unusual experiences" was the most highly preferred. The characteristic of "excitement" was a close second choice. "Suspense," "liveliness and action," and "surprise or unexpectedness" also evoked great interest as indicated by ranks of three, four, and five. There appeared to be little difference between the boys' enthusiasm for "fantastic, fanciful, or weird elements" and for "funny incidents." "Physical courage," with its implications of strength and bravery, also held great appeal.

The boys exhibited a moderately decreasing amount of interest in "frightening or scary incidents," "moral courage," "friendship and loyalty," "ridiculous or exaggerated elements," "information," "happiness," "hardships," and "heroism and service." The boys showed a consistent and almost identical pattern of least preference for "sadness," "family love and closeness," "qualities such as anger, hate, cruelty, fighting, or brutality," and "familiar experiences." It was evident that the boys were highly interested in unusual, action-filled experiences and not very much interested in familiar, commonplace happenings.

The two-way analysis of variance performed on each of the twenty characteristics of reading interests revealed no significant differences in the preferences of the boys with differing reading abilities. The analysis by grade levels, however, showed five categories with significantly different ratings: "friendship and loyalty," "moral courage," "liveliness and action," "qualities such as anger, hate, cruelty, fighting, brutality," and "ridiculous or exaggerated elements."

IMPLICATIONS FOR THE TEACHERS

All of the boys interviewed showed an overwhelming preference for exciting, suspense-filled, dramatic stories with emotionally charged vocabulary. Over and over again, when asked why they liked certain books or stories, the boys would remark, "Lots of action," "Full of excitement," "Something going on all the time." Conversely, the boys stated that they did not like other books and stories because "Nothing much happened," "Just ordinary things you do every day," "All about pets and a family."

As teachers understand the nature of boys' reading interests, they should be better able to use these interests as motivational forces in reading, and to encourage and expand these interests. It would appear that some of the free-reading books and materials in the readers, especially at the primary level, not only do not motivate boys to read, but actually alienate boys' reading interests.

Throughout the interviews, there was a striking similarity between the reading interests expressed by the superior, average, and poor readers, a similarity confirmed by the statistical analysis of the data. The boys who read poorly commented thus: "Sure I like to read books about outer space, but I can't pronounce the words." "The books that I can read are too silly and babyish."

All of this would seem to imply an urgent need for easy-to-read books on a variety of topics and subjects.

One of the strongest impressions the writer gained from conferences with the boys was the increasing hostility and defensiveness of the low achievers as they progressed from the fourth to the eighth grade. In view of the apparent cumulative effect of frustration in not being able to read up to grade level and the heightened result at the junior high school, it would seem imperative that the boys learn the necessary reading skills before leaving the sixth grade. Hence, an essential part of the elementary school program should be one of becoming increasingly aware of reading problems at the third and fourth grades and of beginning a concentrated program to analyze deficiencies and to develop reading skills.

ELDON L. STORER
MARJORIE COLTON

Selecting Elementary
Remedial Reading Material

A frequently asked question is, "What materials are desirable for remedial reading instruction?" There is probably no single listing on which there would be unanimous agreement. This essay reports on materials used at the reading clinic in Topeka, Kansas. In the editor's viewpoint, although materials for remedial instruction must encompass more than commercially published books, workbooks, etc., students of remedial reading surely need to be thoroughly familiar with the ever-increasing horde of prepared materials. But unless a teacher uses some definite criteria to evaluate potential purchases, he may collect a splendid hodgepodge without rhyme or reason. Storer and Colton address themselves to two questions: What materials *and* why.*

Does it surprise you that the criteria do not explicitly deal with qualities inherent in the material (for example, size of type and interest)? In what ways do the authors' criteria for material selection become an integral part of both the diagnostic and the instructional phases? How are these criteria related to Cohen's "Taxonomy of Instructional Treatments" in Part Five? How does the authors' philosophy of remedial reading instruction become evident as they include material for reading in the content fields and literary anthologies as well as traditional phonic workbooks; high-interest, low-vocabulary books; and comprehension materials? In what ways could this list become the basis for a program of prevention of reading difficulties as well as for remedial instruction?

An original article written for this book by Eldon L. Storer and Marjorie Colton.

Learning to read depends upon the mastery of the developmental process of decoding and understanding a symbolic language. Most children develop satisfactory reading skills through a systematically developed reading curriculum while others experience difficulty. The success of one program over another probably depends more on the ability of the teacher using the program to cope with individual differences rather than on inherent attributes of the program. Materials, carefully and specifically chosen, play a key role in a reading program and offer maximum opportunity for a teacher to augment her creative efforts in teaching reading.

Our primary concern is to offer help in choosing and using success-oriented instructional material for elementary remedial reading programs. Some important criteria to be considered in selecting remedial reading material are (1) the child, (2) teacher knowledge of the reading process, (3) modality aspects of children's learning, (4) instructional techniques, and (5) availability of published material.

THE CHILD

The child is of primary concern in choosing material. Too often teachers look at material without knowledge of students' particular backgrounds, abilities, ages, attitudes, or basis for motivation.

Within a remedial reading class will be found a wide range of both reading levels and skill difference which make it necessary to adjust teaching procedures and material. For example, three fourth-grade students who have 75, 100, and 125 I.G. scores would have expected levels of about 3.0, 4.0, and 5.0. If all three students' reading scores were 2.5, one might assume they could all be placed in second semester, second-grade material.

Something happens in the process of development that brings about differences in these youngsters. In the first place their rates of learning and progress will vary. Other factors include cultural and language background, auditory and visual perception and discrimination ability, interests and drive (acceptance of the need and willingness to read), personality and emotional differences, home-and school-fostered variables, as well as specific reading disabilities.

Obviously, a variety of materials is required to cope with the needs of children, and it is important that materials and teaching techniques relate to the specific skill being treated.

KNOWLEDGE OF READING PROCESS

The teacher must understand the reading process, and be able to transmit this knowledge to students. It is not enough to simply follow the scope and sequence of a particular "series." Based upon diagnostic findings, a reading program should be designed first, then materials can be found to fit the design. Too often committees simply review books and arbitrarily decide which book "appeals." Remedial students show greatest progress when materials are chosen which make use of the learner's strengths and experiential background.

Reading skills could be listed in one of the following classifications: (1) Word attack skills, (2) Comprehension skills, and (3) Study skills. A balance must be maintained among them, rather than deciding which is most important. In diagnosing, one can find which skills are deficient and trace them to the most elementary skills to begin remedial work. An example would be:

	Word Attack	*Comprehension*	*Study Skills*
Readiness	Ability to hear and see likenesses and differences, identification of what a word is, ability to move from left to right.	Ability to repeat or originate ideas in sentences, understanding of vocabulary such as *below, over, under,* etc.	Ability to attend to a task for sufficient time, ability to screen out distractions, interest in learning to read, ability to listen, etc.
Reading	Sight vocabulary, initial consonants, blends, digraphs, long and short vowels, letter patterns, affixes, syllabication, accent.	Identify main idea, retell stories in sequence, interpretation, relate details to main idea, etc.	Study habits, locational skills, etc.

Many sequences can be developed, depending upon the approach to be used. It really matters little whether vowels or consonants are taught first, or whether main idea or generalizations, so long as there is logical sequence and one skill augments the teaching of the next step.

Once a sequence is established, a variety of techniques will be used, depending on the progress of the child, as the remedial student's program is in a constant state of revision. Selection of materials needs to consider both the different classifications of reading skills and an instructional sequence for each one.

MODALITY ASPECTS

Children learn in many ways. It is not difficult to determine the modality strength of the partially sighted or hard of hearing child. Yet we frequently overlook the modality strength of the poor reader who is otherwise apparently normal.

Vision screening is important. A child unable to see or whose sight skews the image will have difficulty learning to read. A more difficult problem occurs when a child seemingly is unable to contain a visual image (visual perception). The image seems to disappear when the stimulus is removed, and he does not relate to it when it reappears.

Auditory acuity plays an important role, and, like visual acuity, makes for easier learning, One can hear the intensity of sound, however, and be unable to distinguish among sounds. Compare a stereo player with 12-inch speakers with a transistor radio with 2-inch speakers. Each can be turned to the same intensity (volume), but the 12-inch speakers will be able to separate certain frequencies, making them more easily understood. Auditory discrimination within an ear can be thought of in like manner. It is not unusual for children to confuse th and wh; sh and ch; ĕ and ĭ; etc. These pairs of sounds are easily confused because they are made in very similar manner. A high level of discrimination is needed to differentiate them.

The old adage of learning by doing causes many teachers to insist that children "write" their new words. This is another modality which seems to work when visual or auditory methods fail. Brain-damaged children are one group who seem to learn better by this kinesthetic-tactile method.

Most teachers combine methods and techniques for the

three modalities when presenting lessons. Most children can learn through all, but remedial students often learn more rapidly and thoroughly through one sense modality. Tests can be bought or made for teaching words by each method to see which yields best and lasting learning. Depending on the nature of the modality strength, children can usually be taught to use all modalities, but sometimes can make swiftest improvement through the strongest one. A child whose visual modality is strongest should be taught by visual methods, introducing other methods when he is able to handle them and relate to them.

Nearly any "book" can be taught by any technique, but in contrast it appears that programed material, placed before a child for individual seatwork, would be a mistake if he is an auditory learner, and a taped phonics lesson would baffle the visual learner.

TECHNIQUES

Techniques must be developed from the standpoint of both immediate and long-range goals. Then they must be placed in context for the child, considering his interests, age, abilities, background, etc.

For example, John knew initial and ending consonants, initial and ending blends, and was ready for consonant digraphs (ch). Through testing it was found that he could handle only one item at a time, he had a tendency to forget the next day, and he learned better by listening (sometimes he overlooked letters he knew because he paid more attention to context). He remembered ideas, both general and specific, and could tell a story back very well. He was distracted by people moving about, and showed continual interest in pictures, etc., on the wall. He reacted by turning his head, fidgeting, and appearing ill at ease when one tried to work with him. His interests were varied and he seemed to respond to most any subject. He was tired of worksheets.

Simply to find pages from workbooks with "ch" would yield minimal results. The following recommendations might be made:

1. John needs to be where there are as few visual distractions as possible, by isolation, study carrels or particular placement in the room.

2. Assignments must be short, precise, and auditorily oriented.

3. The use of a dictaphone, card reader, or tape recorder should be used.

4. Lessons should be presented quickly, without physical distractions (arm waving, walking, etc.).

5. He should be asked to repeat sounds and examples.

6. Material to be used:

   A. Phonics charts (using only "ch")

   B. Flash cards using "ch" in beginning and ending position

   C. Reader (possibly *Basic Reading,* 1^1, Lippincott) which introduces and uses "ch" in a story

Materials for another day might consist of records, games, and contrasting "sh" and "ch" exercises, leading quickly to reading stories.

The use of a single book or method tends to teach too generally, whereas specifically designed lessons give emphasis when needed.

The technique, therefore, becomes the psychological environment as well as the particular reading lesson. An intense study of the child's responses is helpful. Reinforcement must be used and can consist of a pat on the back, praise, points, stars, and candy, which is about as tangible as one can get.

Techniques will determine the type of material most useful (programed, text, workbook, charts, machine, etc.) Materials selected must also depend on the techniques used to cope with the child's interest, attention span, and learning rate, as well as motivational needs.

AVAILABILITY OF PUBLISHED MATERIAL

The first mistake made by many remedial reading programs is to buy a single program which is supposed to solve all problems. The second mistake is made by many educators who have well-chosen material but then misuse it or use only one book because "everyone needed this." This makes for easier teaching; at least individual assignments need not be made daily. However, it is professionally questionable.

In selecting material for an elementary remedial reading program, one should first concentrate on books containing interesting reading material. Too often we teach a child to read and then don't allow him to read. Two or three copies of any title are enough. If five children are all at the same level, two can read *Dan Frontier,* two read *Jim Forest,* and the other can work on audio recordings, or individual assignments.

A second need is material for word attack skills. An assortment of several series is needed. Remedial students are likely to need exercises providing more reinforcement than is usually contained in one book.

Games are very useful. They often provide motivation as well as a means for the group to work together.

Machines provide good motivation, and are useful to the degree in which teachers consciously plan for their use. The overhead projector (for both students and teacher use), a tape recorder, and a tape card player are basic equipment requirements in a remedial program.

The typewriter can be an asset for the student whose motor control or directional orientation makes it difficult for him to present an acceptable lesson.

An ample supply of tagboard for flashcards, chalk or paper for experience stories, and reinforcement gadgets such as picture puzzles, word puzzles, readiness and developmental material are also needed.

For an elementary remedial reading program, material above the fifth grade is seldom used. There will always be some children needing instruction at beginning first-grade level or below, but most material needs to be at the second and third grade level.

In beginning a program, a minimum list might include:

Folder for each child (5 students per class)
File cabinet (other standard furniture)
Bulletin board, chalk board, display table
Phonics charts
Several word games and flash cards
Tape recorder
    Listening program (EDL, SRA or other)
    Blank magnetic tapes (3)
Tape card player/recorder
    Blank tape cards
    Published tape cards

Overhead projector — with transparent rolls

Plastic overlays (to be used on workbooks)

Marking pencils (grease pencils, crayons)

SRA Reading lab

SRA Pilot Library (or other kit)

Phonics workbooks (3 series)

Reading practice books (Gates-Peardon, Barnell Loft, etc.) (3 or 4 series including all titles and levels)

High Interest-Low Vocabulary Books (10 sets with 2 or 3 copies of same title at 2.0-3.0 level)

Reader's Digest (assorted)

Comic books and/or paperbacks

Three or four well-chosen text series with workbooks

Since new published material is placed on the market weekly, compiling a complete list is impossible. The Topeka, Kansas, Reading Clinic, Centers, and Services, has reviewed and used many materials over the past several years. This list is compiled with annotations from their experience. Other worthwhile materials are available, but exemplary materials can be chosen from this list.

Books, Workbooks, Visual Aids

Publications	Level	Content	Skills
American Education Pub. Education Center Columbus, Ohio 43216			
Reading Success Series	2 – Jr. High	Sports oriented	Phonics (6 books) Structural analysis Word meaning
Know Your World	Easy Intermediate	Current events	Crossword puzzles, phonics and word analysis review, comprehension, vocabulary
		These weekly newspapers are objective and appeal to youngsters. Other papers and magazines are available for content subject, as well as phonics workbooks, word puzzles, etc.	
Barnell Loft, Ltd. and Dexter and Westbrook, Lts. 111 So. Centre Ave. Rockville Centre, N.Y.			
Specific Skill Series Available either individually or in complete specimen sets, 42 books include seven titles at six different levels each, self-correcting is optional	1 – 6	Seven reading skills: Locating the Answer, Following Directions, Using the Context, Getting the Facts, Working with Sounds, Drawing Conclusions, Getting the Main Idea	
		Mature format with combination of curriculum-oriented and factual materials makes material acceptable to any age.	

Publications	Level	Content	Skills
Barnell Loft, Ltd. (Cont.)			
The Picto-cabulary Series Set of 36 Books (12 titles) and related materials	Intermediate +	High-interest booklets stressing illustrated words	Direct vocabulary instruction
Instructional Aid Kits	1 – 6	Each kit contains 50 cards plus answer sheet in the areas of reading, social studies, and English. Titles include Time for Sounds, One Too Many, Riddle Riddle Rhyme Time, We Read Sentences, Pronoun Parade, Fun with Words, Oral Reading Series, Word Shapes and Word Parts.	
Benefic Press 1900 N. Narragansett Ave. Chicago, Ill. 60939			
Invitation to Adventure 9 hardbound titles, workbook, activities, cards	PP – 6	Multi-ethnic true-to-life stories, highlights poetry	Interpret social values
World of Adventure Series 8 titles	2 – 6	Adventure	Comprehension, vocabulary and review of skills
	Teacher's guide and activity book available – longer stories appear more difficult than reading level indicated.		

Series	Level	Description	Purpose
Dan Frontier Series 11 titles, new companion recording	PP – 4	Frontier life and social studies concepts	Interpretation, vocabulary, word perception
Button Family Adventures 12 titles	PP – 3	Blue collar family stories	Recreational reading
Cowboy Sam Series 15 titles - workbooks available	PP – 3	Western adventure	Vocabulary and comprehension
Sailor Jack Readers 10 titles	PP – 3	Real-life sea experiences – action and humor	Drill and practice in phonics and vocabulary
Butternut Bill Series 8 titles (records available)	PP – P	Light-hearted escapades of mountain boy and his pet	Controlled vocabulary Recreational
Animal Adventure Books 12 titles (records available)	PP – 1	Wild animal stories based on facts	Further interest and understanding of animals
The Moonbeam Series 10 titles	PP – 2	Fun-filled adventures of space-bound chimp	Highly interesting for recreational reading
Easy to Read Books 5 Titles	PP – 1	Antics of various birds and animals	Amusing recreational reading

Additional series include: Space Age Books, Tom Logan Series, Tommy O'Toole Books, Outdoor Adventure Series, Pioneer Series, Our Native American Books, Cowboys of Many Races, Space Science Fiction, Sports, Mystery, and Mystery Adventure.

Publications	Level	Content	Skills
Benefic Press (Cont.)			
Study Scope Programs fit into cylinders for self-correcting responses	1 – 4	588 programs directed toward individual problems	Reinforcement of basic skills
Bowmar 622 Rodier Drive Glendale, Calif. 91201			
Bowmar Reading Incentive Program, 12 titles – hard or soft cover	Begins at Level 3	High interest, low vocabulary stories depicting activities related to cars, dune buggies, horses, surfing	Recreational reading, comprehension, creative writing
		Also available in multi-media Kits including 10 soft cover books of the same title, records, filmstrips, and manual.	
Bowmar Language/Communication Program (An adjunct to the Reading Incentive Program.) Two titles, *Drag Racing* and *Horses*, each include workbook, manual, picture dictionary, study print set and record	Level 3 +	Workbooks develop basic communication skills, comprehension, vocabulary, critical thinking. Humor and art work are highlighted.	

Source	Title / Description	Grade	Type	Skills
Century Consultants 6363 Broadway Chicago, Ill. 60626				
	Shapes Around Us Series	1 – 3	Curriculum-oriented	Comprehension, word recognition, vocabulary
	Appreciate Your Country Series	1 – 3		
	Learning to Read While Reading to Learn	4 – 9		
Collier McMillan 866 Third Avenue New York, N.Y. 10022				
	Individual Phonics Wall charts, flash cards, and ditto masters	Primary	Phonics presented with photographed pictures	Complete phonics program stressing diagnostic placement
The Continental Press, Inc. Elizabethtown, Pa. 17022				
	Wordland Phonics Series A program of phonics in carbon masters for liquid duplication and individual pupil books	1 – 5	Phonics	Reading Readiness, visual discrimination, auditory perception, word recognition and word analysis

Publications	Level	Content	Skills
The Continental Press (Cont.)		Also available are the following materials for use in regular classes or special remedial programs: Reading Readiness Series; Reading-Thinking Skills; Crossword Puzzles; Reading-Writing Skills; Reading-Study Skills; Phonics and Word-Analysis Skills; Long and Short Vowels; Varient Vowel Sounds; Transparencies, and It's Your World.	
The Economy Company 1901 North Walnut Oklahoma City, Okla. 73125			
Phonetic Keys to Reading	1 – 3	Adventure stories using natural language patterns	Strong word attack program including comprehension skills
Keys to Independence in Reading	4 – 6	,,	,,
Field Educational Publications, Inc. 609 Mission Street San Francisco, Calif. 94105			
The Checkered Flag Series 8 titles and Teacher's Manual, also available in classroom Reading Kits containing filmstrips, records, tapes or cassettes and Teacher's guide	2.4 – 4.5	Low vocabulary-high interest stories of sports cars, motorcycles, antique cars and dune buggies in competition	Comprehension, vocabulary

Title	Level	Description	Skills
The Jim Forest Readers 12 titles with consumable practice books	1.7 – 4.1	Low vocabulary-high interest stories in setting of forest preserve with conservation concepts, suspense and humor	Comprehension, vocabulary
The Morgan Bay Mysteries Teacher's manual includes many suggestions for using books, 8 titles	2.3 – 4.1	Low vocabulary-high interest, tales of suspense spiced with humor	Comprehension
The Wildlife Adventure Series, manual includes scientific information on animal habits and habitats, 8 titles	2.6 – 4.4	Low vocabulary-high interest stories of man and his relationship with animals	Comprehension and reinforcement exercises
The Deep-Sea Adventure Series, Teacher's manual provides excellent motivational material, 8 titles	1.8 – 5.0	High interest-low vocabulary stories of sea divers, frogmen, sharks, submarines, treasure	Comprehension and skills development
The Kaleidoscope Readers, 8 titles	2.5 – 9.5	Topics relating to today's issues	Study skills and varied writing styles
The Cornerstone Readers 5 titles	1 – 4	Enrichment for science, social studies, and literature	Development of basic skills
Cyclo Teacher Learning Aid School Kit Machine with study wheels, response sheets and manual	Multi-level	Programed, curriculum lessons	Individualized review, practice, and reinforcement or enrichment of skills

Publications	Level	Content	Skills
Garrard Publishing Co. Champaign, Ill.			
Dolch Books			
First Reading Books 16 titles	1	Animal folklore and true stories	Basic 220 words
Basic Vocabulary Books 10 titles	2	True stories, folklore	Basic 220 words
Folklore of the World 11 titles	3	Stories from different old countries	Basic vocabulary
Pleasure Reading 7 titles	4	Retold classics	
My Puzzle Book I and II	1 – 3	Crossword puzzles	Sight vocabulary
	Other Dolch teaching aids available such as sight word and phrase cards, picture cards, vowel and consonant cards, bingo-type word games, consonant and vowel lotto.		
Junior Science Books 26 titles	3	Topics from animals to astronomy	Supplementary sciences

Sports Biographies and Histories 10 titles	4	Biographies	
Americans All 13 titles	4	History	
		Many other books at 4th and 5th level with topics including rivers and countries	
Ginn and Co. 125 2nd Ave. Waltham, Mass. 02154			
Ginn Word Enrichment Program (workbooks, records and tapes available)	Primary	Word analysis and vocabulary (self-evaluation)	Complete word analysis – modern trends in linguistics
Word Study Charts (20" x 25" charts)	Primary	Phonics and word study skills – development and remedial Texts and enrichment materials available.	
Harcourt, Brace and World 757 Third Ave. New York, N.Y. 10017			
Speech to Print Phonics Boxed kits, manual, practice cards, pupil response cards	Beginning	Phonics	A systematic developmental approach to application of phonics in whole meaningful words

Publications	Level	Content	Skills
Harcourt, Brace and World (Cont.)			
The Palo-Alto Reading Program, Sequential Steps in Reading, paperbound books, workpads, and other teaching aids	Primary	Phonics and word study	Development of decoding skills
Harper and Row Evanston, Ill.			
Reading In the Subject Matter Areas		A supplementary reader which is *excellent* in developing study skills in all content areas for remedial or regular classes	
From Elephants to Eskimos	1		
From Fins to Feathers	2		
From Bicycles to Boomerangs	3		
From Codes to Captains	4		
From Actors to Astronauts	5		
From Coins to Kings	6		
Holt, Rinehart & Winston 383 Madison Ave. New York, N.Y.			
Sounds of Language Readers	K – 6	Each book an anthology of poetry, stories, and articles emphasizing total linguistic experience and language exploration. Fully annotated teacher's edition	
The Owl Program The Kinder Owl Books 20 books	Pre-school – 1	All of these books are individualized reading, science, math, literature, and social studies	

The Little Owl Books 40 books	1 – 2	
The Young Owl Books 40 books	2 – 4	
The Wise Owl Books 20 books	4 – 6	
	Other beginning material and books are available.	
Houghton Mifflin 110 Tremont Street Boston, Mass.		
Key-Lab Box containing 10 trays of die-cut letters and picture cards	Primary	Self-correcting spelling program
		Sound-to-letter correspondence
	Also available: other basic readers, games, kits, records, and trade books.	
Initial Teaching Alphabet Publications, Inc. 20 East 46th Street New York, N.Y. 10017		
The Early-To-Read i/t/a Program Readers, workbooks, teacher's manuals, using an augmented Roman alphabet as a symbol for each of 44 English sounds	Level 1	Language arts approach to skills program
		Sound-symbol relationship

Publications	Level	Content	Skills
Lyons & Carnahan 407 E. 25th Street Chicago, Ill. 60616			
Curriculum Motivation Series, 6 titles designed for marginal readers	1.6 – 4.1	Varied curriculum-oriented content	Stimulate interest in reading without undue written work
Pacesetters 6 titles	PP – 8.3	Language Arts oriented. Each book spans several reading levels and includes informal reading inventories	Communication skills are reinforced through teacher's manual
Phonics We Use	Intro. to the Alphabet A Readiness B 1 – 2 C 2 – 3 D 3 – 4 E 4 – 5 F 5 – 6 G 6 or higher	Phonics	A complete word recognition program providing intro., reinforcement, testing and review of phonic skills
Phonics We Use Learning Games Kit	1 – 6	Ten assorted games with teacher's manual	Reinforcing phonics principles
	Can be used effectively with any basic series. Easily understood by children and include meaningful tasks. Directions are clearly stated.		

McGraw-Hill
330 West 42nd Street
New York, N.Y. 10036

Dr. Spello Second Edition	4 – 9	Spelling General Phonics Revision of a corrective program for language essentials.
Time for Phonics	K – 3	Phonics Complete phonics program
Reading Clues	4 – 6	Techniques for word attack Continued word attack skills
Programmed Reading	K – 3	Programmed linguistic approach for beginning or remedial Available are: Placement tests, student response booklets, ditto masters, filmstrips, correlated story books, vinyl overlays.
Reading for Concepts Soft or hard bound	1 – 6 (high interest)	Short selections for comprehension, critical reading, drawing conclusions, making inferences
New Practice Readers Books A – G	2 – 8 (high interest)	Short stories with vocabulary development and comprehension check Direct and implied details, meaning, opinion, synonym, antecedent of words
Conquests In Reading	Remedial workbook for 4 – 9	Phonetic and structural analysis, reading and spelling

Publications	Level	Content	Skills
McGraw-Hill (Cont.)			
New Webster Word Wheels (63 word wheels in box)	3 – 8	Phonics or structural analysis. Beginning blends, digraphs and affixes	
		Filmstrips, transparencies, teachers' handbooks, ditto masters and tests also available.	
Read for Fun (10 titles)	1 – 3	Colorful adaptions from European stories	
The Skyline Series (4 titles)	1 – 4	Stories of culturally underprivileged urban child, emphasizing values to overcome disadvantages	
The Everyreader Series (20 titles – paperbacks)	4	Adapted classics	
Reading Incentive Series (5 titles – hard cover)	3 – 7	Supplementary stories	
Webster Classroom Reading Clinic	4 – 9	Comprehensive kit of remedial material including: Dr. Spello, Conquests in Reading (10 or 20 copies); Teacher's Guide (Kotmeyer), Skill Cards, Answers, Word Wheels, Everyreader Series, games, sight vocabulary. *May be purchased separately as listed.*	
The Macmillan Co. 866 Third Avenue New York, N.Y. 10022			
The Macmillan Reading Spectrum, non-graded multi-level color-coded booklets	4 +	Self-correcting, self-directing lessons, at 6 levels for each skill	Word analysis, reading comprehension, vocabulary development

in a display box, Teacher's Guides, placement tests and pupil's record books

The Spectrum of Books Set A, Set B, (includes 30 books and Teacher's Guide)	2 – 6 (A) 3 – 8 (B)	Enrichment to accompany Macmillan Spectrum	
Decoding for Reading, 2 readalong books with accompanying records, Teacher's Guide	4 +	Audio-instructional phonics program for remedial readers	From sounds through listening and speaking vocabulary to meaning
The Bank Street Readers, urban-centered basal readers, also useful in supplementary and remedial situations	1 – 3	Literary material related to urban children with varied cultural backgrounds	Emphasis on firsthand experiences, oral language and vocabulary in a program of skills development
		Skill practice books, duplicating masters, cards, photographs and Teacher's Guides available.	

Charles E. Merrill Pub. Co.
1300 Alum Creek Drive
Columbus, Ohio 43216

New Reading Skilltext Series, text-workbook format, teacher's edition with over-printed answers	K – 6	Review and diagnostic lessons	Getting information, understanding ideas, organizing ideas, making judgments, studying words

Publications	Level	Content	Skills
Charles E. Merrill Pub. Co. (Cont.)			
New Phonics Skilltext Series, text-workbook format, teacher's edition with over-printed answers	1 – 6	Reading skills lessons in 2-page units	Structure of words, understanding of words, sounds of words
New Diagnostic Reading Workbook Series, text-workbook format, answer keys available	1 – 6	Reading selections with exercises	Systematic checking and rein-forcement of basic reading skills
	Also available are programmed box kits, Building Reading Power at 5th grade level, and Building Language Power, text-workbook, levels 3 – 8.		
Merrill Literature Program	K – 9	Literature appreciation	
Phonovisual Products, Inc. P. O. Box 5625 Washington, D.C. 20016			
The Phonovisual Method Based upon 2 scientifi-cally planned pictorial charts (consonant and vowel), game-like pro-cedures and supporting aids	K – primary	Phonics	Supplemental phonics program

Publisher / Title	Level	Description	Skills
Prentice-Hall Englewood Cliffs, N.J. 07632			
Be A Better Reader Foundations A, B, and C, Teacher's Edition, Individual Progress Kits (boxed answer cards)	4, 5, 6	Paper-bound books in major subject areas; literature, social studies, science, and new mathematics	Word attack, comprehension, interpretation, vocabulary and study skills
	Also available are Books I through VI covering reading level 7 through 12. Valuable in improving basic skills and developing special skills.		
Reader's Digest Educational Division Pleasantville, N.Y. 10570			
Reading Skill Builders	1 – 3	Stories adapted to 1 – 3 reading level, exercises and tests	Word analysis and concepts, comprehension and evaluation
Reading Skill Builders, high-interest format, digest size, Teacher's editions	4 – 6	Realistic stories with exercises and tests	Word study, comprehension-interpretation, and study skills
	(Also available are Pegasus Storybooks, Science Readers, and Practice Pads for skills reinforcement. May be ordered in kits or individual books.)		

Publications	Level	Content	Skills
Scholastic Book Service 904 Sylvan Avenue Englewood Cliffs, N.J.		Multi-level paperbacks available.	
Science Research Associates, Inc. 259 East Erie Street Chicago, Ill. 60611 *SRA Reading Laboratory*	Multi-level Sets Ia, Ib, Ic, – primary Sets IIa, IIb, IIc, – intermediate	Reading selections Each laboratory spans a number of ability levels and is designed so that students begin at their present level. Contains Power Builders and Rate Builders with answer keys, teacher's handbooks with Listening Skill Builder selections, student record books and colored pencils.	Vocabulary, comprehension, word-attack skills

Reading Laboratory 1: Word Games, includes 44 word games, one phonics survey, Teacher's handbook, student record book and check test pads	1 – 6	Color-coded word-building games	Phonics
Pilot Library Series 72 paperback selections, Teacher's Handbook, Key booklets and student record books	Multi-level Set IIa – level 2 – 7 Set IIc – level 4 – 9	Excerpts from noted literature	Supplementary reading

Also available are other materials and equipment, including the Reading Accelerator (pacing device useful in deterring regressive eye movements).

Scott-Foresman
1900 E. Lake Ave.
Glenview, Ill. 60025

New Linguistic Block Series	Primary and Intermediate	Letters, words, pictures on 1-inch plastic blocks	Arranging words into meaningful thought units
The Talking Alphabet	Primary	Consonant and vowel sounds presented on LP records and pictures	Records Pictures Work sheets

Other material available including basal text series, games, charts, pictures and recordings.

Publications	Level	Content	Skills
Spoken Arts, Inc. 59 Locust Ave. New Rochelle, N.Y. 10801			
The Road to Reading 33 tapes 33 activity sheets ditto master 33 scripts Teacher's Edition custom boxed	Beginning	Sounds presented in stories Useful for listening and motivation. Used as supplementary.	Beginning sounds, long and short vowels
Steck-Vaughn Co. P. O. Box 2028 Austin, Tex. 78767			
The Human Values Series			
Values to Learn *Values to Share* *Values to Live By*	4 5 6	A supplementary series designed to help each child attain a realistic sense of his own value and the dignity of others. Eight values developed via reading-discussion: affection, respect, skill, well-being, wealth, power, enlightenment, rectitude. Especially useful for children with adjustment problems.	

348

Equipment

Many items of equipment and accompanying materials are not included in this list. Such things as tape recorders and overhead projectors can be purchased through local dealers. Only those items actually used by the authors are included.

Publications	Level	Content	Skills
Bell & Howell Co. 7100 McCormick Road Chicago, Ill. 60645			
Language Master Audio-visual instruc- tional device	Multi-level	Tape-cards with tracks for both instructor and student	Phonics program
Central Scientific Co. Cenco Center 2600 S. Kostner Ave. Chicago, Ill. 60623		Complete catalogue of educational equipment including a reading pacer, lesson rolls, pro- jector reader and tachistoscope and overhead projector.	

Publications	Level	Content	Skills
Craig Research Division of Craig Corp. 3410 So. La Crinega Blvd. Los Angeles, Calif. 90016		Program for speed and comprehension printed on cards for use in the Craig Reader.	
Educational Developmental Laboratories, Inc. Division of McGraw-Hill 3242 Holmes Street Kansas City, Mo. 64109			
Aud-X Sight-sound synchronization, workbook, which may be used with transparent overlays	R to adult	Lessons by filmstrips and disc recordings	Writing, word-building, sentence completion
Tacb-X (Projector which flashes at various speeds	R to adult	Pictures, numbers, letters, symbols	Details, L-R direction, visual memory
Flasb-X Circular, metal tachistoscope for individual use	R to adult	Curriculum-oriented discs, each with 40 exposures	Concentration, accuracy of perception

Product	Level	Description	Skills
Controlled Readers Filmstrips, study cards and Teacher's Guide, projector	R – 14	Stories with vocabulary and comprehension exercises	Visual coordination and comprehension
EDL Study Skills Library Self-directed reading activities; science, social studies, and reference kits	3 – 9	Curriculum-oriented folders with related worksheets	Interpretation, evaluation, organization, reference
EDL Listen and Think Self-contained lessons using reel or cassette recordings with lesson books, Teacher's handbook	1 – 9	Lessons providing for alternating listening and responding	15 comprehension skills on each level
Learning Through Seeing, Inc. Sunland, Calif. 91040			
Tachist-O-Film and Tachist-O-Flasher		Speed-i-o-scope (Flash attachment to fit controlled reader or film strip projector)	
		Tachistoscope presentation of letters, phonics principles and words	
Rheem Califone Division of Rheem Mfg. Co. 5922 Bowcroft Street Los Angeles, Calif. 90016		Listening centers with response books and student activities.	

LEO M. SCHELL

Meeting Individual
Differences in Reading Skills

Even the limitless availability of commercial materials cannot adequately meet the infinite variety of skill needs of children in classroom or clinic. This article suggests some possible approaches to meeting these individual differences.

What are the advantages and disadvantages of autopsy charts? of skills files? Isn't a basal-reader workbook really just a bound skills file? If so, why "unbind" them? Are the two suggested tools primarily for prevention or remediation of reading difficulties? Are they classroom or clinic?

Historically and perennially teachers are exhorted and admonished to "Meet Individual Differences!" Unfortunately, the exhorter/admonisher typically fails to specify precisely how this can be accomplished. In teaching reading, the teacher must cope with twenty-nine bundles of energy at varied levels of achievement in such widely diverse skills as phonics, context clues, dictionary usage, and reading-study skills. The same basal reader and workbook for each child — even for those within a reading group — is wholly insufficient, even when a teacher has limitless time, energy, knowledge, and ditto masters!

Dividing the pupils into three, four, or even five reading groups will not alone insure satisfactory attention to individual strengths and weaknesses in reading skills. Woestehoff (6) concluded that "there is little justification for the assumption that a given level of general reading ability will necessarily be accompanied by an equivalent level of competency in specific reading sub-skills." She felt her findings lent "emphasis to the belief that if children are to develop optimum reading ability,

---

An original article written for this book by Leo M. Schell.

their instruction must not be determined by a process of inference, but rather through a careful diagnosis of their specific sub-skill needs. As difficult as it may be, from an instructional standpoint it becomes vital to consider specific learnings rather than a generalized ability." Teachers must know the individual needs of pupils and occasionally group for *skills* instruction, as well as grouping for *reading* instruction.

This discussion will not describe how to discover skill needs. It is assumed that teachers know how to use available diagnostic tests, can find patterns in repeated oral reading errors, can analyze performances on practice materials, and have access to specialized diagnostic personnel. This article will try to tell what to do once the skill needs have been discovered.

USE AN AUTOPSY CHART

A listing of reading sub-skills forms the heart of an autopsy chart. All basal-reader publishers have skills scope and sequence charts that list the various skills included at each reading level. Most curriculum guides contain similar charts, and Wayne Otto at the Center for Cognitive Learning, University of Wisconsin, has produced a quite usable one *(4)*. It is simple to convert such charts into an autopsy chart — for individual pupils, a reading group, or a class — as shown in Figure 1 (see p. 354).

The teacher determines each pupil's level of performance on each appropriate sub-skill, codes the chart, locates appropriate practice materials, and groups children for instruction.

The obvious questions most teachers raise at this point are, "What shall I use for practice materials? And where can I get them?"

BUILD A SKILLS FILE

A primitive skills file is nothing more than pages torn from various grade-level skills books (a 1970 euphemism for "workbooks") that are grouped according to skills and filed sequentially by grade level. When a teacher discovers that Johnny needs additional practice with medial vowel sounds (or use of guide words or notetaking), she can merely go to the file, pull out one or more skills sheets at the correct level of dif-

Figure 1. Sample Autopsy Chart

	Adam	Bob	Cindy	Doug
Sight Words				
Dolch's 220				
Relational words (these, where)				
Phonic Analysis				
Initial consonant sounds				
Final consonant sounds				
Initial consonant blends				
l-blends				
r-blends				
Long vowel sounds				
Short vowel sounds				
Vowel digraphs				
Vowel diphthongs				
Structural Analysus				
Inflected forms				
Plural forms (s, es)				
Verb endings (s, d, ing)				
Comparative endings (er, est)				
Affixed forms*				
Syllabication*				
Accent*				

*Each area can be subdivided into appropriate subskills.

Pupil performance code:

I — No skill; needs introduction and teaching
R — Weak; needs review and reinforcement
S — Satisfactory for grade level; regular program adequate
M — Has mastered skill; no more practice necessary

ficulty, and assign them to Johnny. Admittedly, this won't guarantee that Johnny will thereby automatically improve his mastery of medial vowel sounds; teaching is usually essential also. But with a skills file, at least the teacher has something to teach with and from at her fingertips. With a skills file teachers cannot complain that appropriate practice materials are lacking.

Gilliland *(3)* points out that when several different kinds of skills books are available, most teachers make little or poor use of them because they don't have the time to find the pages that would meet the needs of each student and they have no way of keeping track of exactly what exercises are available in each book. But when these same skills books are converted into skills files, they are used much more effectively and frequently.

Commercial and teacher-made dittoed skills sheets can be mounted on oak tag so that they can be used repeatedly. And if pupils cover them with acetate and use a grease pencil for writing, prolonged use is possible. Each sheet can be labeled (or coded) for convenient use with the following information: reading level, skill, worksheet number. They can be made self-checking either by pasting an answer sheet on the back of the oak tag or by having an answer sheet in a separate folder. Not only can they be self-checking, they can also be self-directing. For example, a note at the bottom of the answer sheet can say, "If you made 3 or more errors, do the next sheet in this series. If you made only 1 or 2 errors, see me." There should be multiple copies of each worksheet so that several pupils can work simultaneously on the same skill.

One beauty of skills files is their ease of expansion and elaboration. Teacher aides or volunteer parents can readily mount and label pages, make answer sheets, or even make ditto masters. An ambitious teacher can easily find ways to include learning activities other than worksheets in a skills file. Games, devices, transparencies, and even filmstrips and audio tapes can be prescribed and used individually or in small groups without teacher supervision.

A group of teachers at a single grade level could cooperate to establish a central file that they could all use. Obviously, this could be extended to several grade levels, a wing of a school, or even the whole school. In the last case, the file could be housed in the instructional materials center. (The same advantages and disadvantages exist for room vs. central skills files as for room vs. central school libraries. Obviously, having materials in both locations is desirable, and a satisfactory arrangement is easy to work out.)

To provide for individual differences in all the varied reading skills, teachers must have differentiated practice material. Macmillan has tried to provide this somewhat with its *Spectrum of Skills (5)*, Houghton Mifflin offers material for several skill areas in their *Reading Skills Lab (1)*, and Harcourt, Brace & World has organized phonics materials this way *(2)*. But commercial material is only a drop in the bucket; teacher initiative in establishing skills files would be a major breakthrough toward making individualized instruction a reality.

REFERENCES

1. Durr, William K., *Reading Skills Lab*. Boston: Houghton Mifflin Company, 1968.
2. Durrell, Donald D., *Durrell-Murphy Phonics Practice Program*. New York: Harcourt, Brace & World, 1968.
3. Gilliland, Cleburne Hap, *Materials for Remedial Reading and Their Use*. Billings, Montana: Reading Clinic, Educational Division, Eastern Montana College, 1965, 97.
4. Otto, Wayne, *Overview of the Wisconsin Prototypic System of Reading Instruction in the Elementary School*. Madison, Wisconsin: Wisconsin Research and Development, Center for Cognitive Learning, University of Wisconsin, 1968.
5. Weinberg, Joel S., *Word Analysis, Macmillan Reading Spectrum*. New York: Macmillan Company, 1964.
6. Woestehoff, Ellsworth S., "The Specific Reading Proficiencies of Pupils Having Normal and Accelerated Reading Growth." Paper read at the 1969 International Reading Association Convention.

EDWARD FRY

Developing a Word List
for Remedial Reading

A universal deficiency of children with reading difficulties is a small and uncertain sight vocabulary. Children must know commonly used words so that such words do not become reading problems and so that they can read material containing a high percentage of these words.

Examine the first hundred words. Would you teach them in isolation or in context? The following are in the first hundred words: they, then, their, there, them, three, what, that, who, how. *What learning problems might such words present to children with and without reading problems? Do you agree that these words deserve to be called "instant words"?*

One of the important tools in every remedial teacher's "bag of tricks" should be a list of the most frequently used words in reading. Children and adults who have failed to learn to read properly from regular instruction frequently have a very spotty reading vocabulary. They know some relatively uncommon words while they do not know some of the words which appear most frequently. Furthermore, some of the most frequently appearing words are difficult to teach by context or word analysis.

By using a graded list of the most frequently appearing words, the remedial reading teacher or for that matter any reading teacher can locate and correct specific weaknesses.

For diagnostic purposes the child might be asked to read the list aloud or he might be asked by the teacher to mark the words he knows.

From *Elementary English,* 34 (November 1957), pp. 456-458, reprinted with the permission of the National Council of Teachers of English and Edward Fry.

For teaching words from the list, methods which emphasize the individual word might be favored — methods such as flash cards, kinesthetic approach, tachistoscopic drill, completion sentences, spelling tests, and word games such as bingo or rummy. Of course, the final test in learning the word would be proper use of it in reading and writing.

In attempting to develop a word list for remedial reading, several criteria were kept in mind.

1. Select the most frequently used words first so that the child would achieve the greatest flexibility in reading.
2. By editing, avoid the pitfalls of the purely mechanical word counts such as including easily recognized variants (like, likes, liked) and nouns of restricted use (Thanksgiving, Washington).

In achieving these critera two standards were used:

1. Several scientific word counts of millions of words which yielded the most frequent words.
2. Personal experience as a remedial teacher plus a sort of subjective logic. For example, the scientific word counts included in their first 500 words all the numbers — "one" through "ten" except "nine." I arbitrarily added "nine." I also omitted "babyish" sounding words like "daddy" and "candy" out of deference to high school remedial readers.

The scientific word counts used were the Thorndike-Lorge First Five Hundred based on millions of words of reading material; the Rinsland List, which groups words in groups of 100's, based in the children's writing; and the Faucett list, which combines the most frequent words on the Thorndike Count and the Horn list. Further reference was made to studies done by Fitzpatrick and to Dolch's word list.

My list, which I have chosen to call the "Instant Words," because they should be recognized instantly, is divided into groups of twenty-five words for teaching facility. Several of the previously mentioned lists are divided into groups of 100 or more; but I felt that this was too large a group for the teacher to handle. This does not mean that 25 is an ideal lesson size — it might be much smaller and, in some cases of review, much larger. Perhaps it would have been best to divide the words into smaller groups or into serial order but the way the words were presented in the scientific word counts did not permit this.

Several statements can be made as to the frequency values of the list of 600 Instant Words. The first part of the list is much more valuable and accurate than the latter part. That is, the first group of 25 words is definitely more frequently used than the second group of 25, the first 100 more frequent than the second hundred; the first half (300 words) more frequent than the second half. There is high agreement on all the scientific word counts for the first part of the list.

Conversely, it is doubtful if the 23rd group of 25 words is much more frequently used than the 24th group or even that some of these words should be included in a list of the 600 most common English words. But let me hasten to add that almost all the words on this list, including the words in group 24 (the last group of 25 words) appear in either the Thorndike-Lorge first 500 or Rinsland's First 600, and usually on several other lists also.

This list of 600 Instant Words is particularly valuable for remedial reading because of the editing, combining, grouping, and supplementary studies used.

Instant Words
(See footnote, p. 363)
First Hundred

Group 1	*Group 2*	*Group 3*	*Group 4*
1. the	he	go	who
2. a	I	see	an
3. is	they	then	their
4. you	one	us	she
5. to	good	no	new
6. and	me	him	said
7. we	about	by	did
8. that	had	was	boy
9. in	if	come	three
10. not	some	get	down
11. for	up	or	work
12. at	her	two	put
13. with	do	man	were
14. it	when	little	before
15. on	so	has	just
16. can	my	them	long

First Hundred *(Continued)*

Group 1	Group 2	Group 3	Group 4
17. will	very	how	here
18. are	all	like	other
19. of	would	our	old
20. this	any	what	take
21. your	been	know	eat
22. as	out	make	again
23. but	there	which	give
24. be	from	much	after
25. have	day	his	many

Instant Words
Second Hundred

Group 5	Group 6	Group 7	Group 8
1. saw	big	may	ran
2. home	where	let	five
3. soon	am	use	read
4. stand	ball	these	over
5. box	morning	right	such
6. upon	live	present	way
7. first	four	tell	too
8. came	last	next	shall
9. girl	color	please	own
10. house	away	leave	most
11. find	red	hand	sure
12. because	friend	more	thing
13. made	pretty	why	only
14. could	eat	better	near
15. book	want	under	than
16. look	year	while	open
17. mother	white	should	kind
18. run	got	never	must
19. school	play	each	high
20. people	found	best	far
21. night	left	another	both
22. into	men	seem	end
23. say	bring	tree	also
24. think	wish	name	until
25. back	black	dear	call

Instant Words
Third Hundred

Group 9	Group 10	Group 11	Group 12
1. ask	hat	off	fire
2. small	car	sister	ten
3. yellow	write	happy	order
4. show	try	once	part
5. goes	myself	didn't	early
6. clean	longer	set	fat
7. buy	those	round	third
8. thank	hold	dress	same
9. sleep	full	fall	love
10. letter	carry	wash	hear
11. jump	eight	start	yesterday
12. help	sing	always	eyes
13. fly	warm	anything	door
14. don't	sit	around	clothes
15. fast	dog	close	though
16. cold	ride	walk	o'clock
17. today	hot	money	second
18. does	grow	turn	water
19. face	cut	might	town
20. green	seven	hard	took
21. every	woman	along	pair
22. brown	funny	bed	now
23. coat	yes	fine	keep
24. six	ate	sat	head
25. gave	stop	hope	food

Instant Words
Fourth Hundred

Group 13	Group 14	Group 15	Group 16
1. told	time	word	wear
2. Miss	yet	almost	Mr.
3. father	true	thought	side
4. children	above	send	poor
5. land	still	receive	lost
6. interest	meet	pay	outside
7. government	since	nothing	wind
8. feet	number	need	Mrs.
9. garden	state	mean	learn

Fourth Hundred (*Continued*)

Group 13	Group 14	Group 15	Group 16
10. done	matter	late	held
11. country	line	half	front
12. different	remember	fight	built
13. bad	large	enough	family
14. across	few	feel	began
15. yard	hit	during	air
16. winter	cover	gone	young
17. table	window	hundred	ago
18. story	even	week	world
19. sometimes	city	between	airplane
20. I'm	together	change	without
21. tried	sun	being	kill
22. horse	life	care	ready
23. something	street	answer	stay
24. brought	party	course	won't
25. shoes	suit	against	paper

Instant Words
Fifth Hundred

Group 17	Group 18	Group 19	Group 20
1. hour	grade	egg	spell
2. glad	brother	ground	beautiful
3. follow	remain	afternoon	sick
4. company	milk	feed	became
5. believe	several	boat	cry
6. begin	war	plan	finish
7. mind	able	question	catch
8. pass	charge	fish	floor
9. reach	either	return	stick
10. month	less	sir	great
11. point	train	fell	guess
12. rest	cost	hill	bridge
13. sent	evening	wood	church
14. talk	note	add	lady
15. went	past	ice	tomorrow
16. bank	room	chair	snow
17. ship	flew	watch	whom
18. business	office	alone	women
19. whole	cow	low	among

Fifth Hundred *(Continued)*

Group 17	Group 18	Group 19	Group 20
20. short	visit	arm	road
21. certain	wait	dinner	farm
22. fair	teacher	hair	cousin
23. reason	spring	service	bread
24. summer	picture	class	wrong
25. fill	bird	quite	age

Instant Words
Sixth Hundred

Group 21	Group 22	Group 23	Group 24
1. become	herself	demand	aunt
2. body	idea	however	system
3. chance	drop	figure	lie
4. act	river	case	cause
5. die	smile	increase	marry
6. real	son	enjoy	possible
7. speak	bat	rather	supply
8. already	fact	sound	thousand
9. doctor	sort	eleven	pen
10. step	king	music	condition
11. itself	dark	human	perhaps
12. nine	themselves	court	produce
13. baby	whose	force	twelve
14. minute	study	plant	rode
15. ring	fear	suppose	uncle
16. wrote	move	law	labor
17. happen	stood	husband	public
18. appear	himself	moment	consider
19. heart	strong	person	thus
20. swim	knew	result	least
21. felt	often	continue	power
22. fourth	toward	price	mark
23. I'll	wonder	serve	president
24. kept	twenty	national	voice
25. wall	important	wife	whether

BIBLIOGRAPHY

Dale, Edgar, *Bibliography of Vocabulary Studies.* Ohio State U., Columbus: 1949.

Dolch, Edward W., *The 2000 Commonest Words for Spelling.* Garrard Press, Champaign, Illinois: 1955.

Faucett, Lawrence, *A Study of English Word Values.* M. Sanshodo, Tokyo, 1932. (Contains a ranking by groups of the commonest words as determined by Horn & Thorndike lists)

Fitzgerald, James A., *A Basic Life Spelling Vocabulary.* Milwaukee: Bruce Publishing Co., 1951.

Rinsland, Henry D., *A Basic Vocabulary of Elementary School Children.* New York: The Macmillan Co., 1945.

Thorndike, Edward L. and Irving Lorge, *The Teachers Word Book of 30,000 Words.* New York: Bureau of Publications, Teachers College, Columbia University, 1944.

EDWARD FRY

Judging the Readability of Books

Matching child and book begins by establishing his reading level, continues by determining his reading interests, and ends by locating a book suitable in both topic and level. Prior articles have discussed the first two steps: this one completes the process.

To see whether you have confidence in Fry's technique, check the readability level of several books of known reading level. How many different uses could you find for this graph? Would you find graded library books helpful? Have you ever used such a formula when adopting textbooks?

Selecting the right reading material for his pupils is one of a teacher's most important jobs. If he gives a student material that is too hard for him, the student will become bored with it and may stop reading, or his comprehension of the material will be poor. Even if he does struggle through it, it will take an excessive amount of time. On the other hand, if the student is given material that is too easy, he may find it "babyish" and again become bored and stop reading.

The basic interest in the subject itself is of course an important factor. Given a very high interest, the student may work through very difficult material. But on the average, given only a normal amount of interest in the subject matter, if the material is too difficult the student will stop reading. And most teachers would agree that it is very important for students to read, and read widely and frequently, if they are to be properly educated.

Adapted from *Teaching Faster Reading* (New York: Cambridge University Press, 1963), pp. 135-140, and reprinted by permission of Cambridge University Press and Edward Fry.

Hence, this article is concerned with a specific method of judging readability. Some teachers may say, "Oh, I can tell from looking at a book how difficult it is." This may be true in a few instances, but most teachers cannot. Studies have shown that readability formulae, for all their faults, are more reliable than teachers' judgments. Readability formulae tend to be stiff and mechanical and often those who love English prose distrust them. But teachers who love children and wish to see them learn at a maximum rate might well give heed to readability formulae as an important aid to their judgment.

The use of a readability formula is valuable only if the teacher knows the reading ability of the student. Unfortunately, teachers do not always know the reading ability of each student. The teacher should use standardized oral or silent reading tests. If no standardized tests are available, there are many reading textbooks which will tell the teacher how to make his or her own.

You can teach reading (and every other subject) much better if you have books at the right level of difficulty; in fact, if you can get a student reading by giving him easy interesting materials, and if you simply keep him reading, gradually increasing the difficulty of the material, you will have gone a long way towards having a very good reading program. Do not worry about the material being too easy, especially where students have difficulty with reading; they will gradually seek more difficult material. Too many teachers start with difficult material and then wonder why students hate to read and avoid it at every opportunity.

DIRECTIONS FOR USING THE FORMULA

1. Select three 100-word passages from near the beginning, middle, and end of the book.
2. Count the total number of sentences in each 100-word passage (estimating to the nearest tenth of a sentence). Average these three numbers (add together and divide by three).
3. Count the total number of syllables in each 100-word sample. There is a syllable for each vowel sound, e.g., cat (1), blackbird (2), continental (4). Do not be deceived by word size, e.g., polio (3), through (1). Endings such as -y, -el, or -le usually make a syllable, e.g., ready (2), bottle (2). Average the total number of syllables for the three samples.

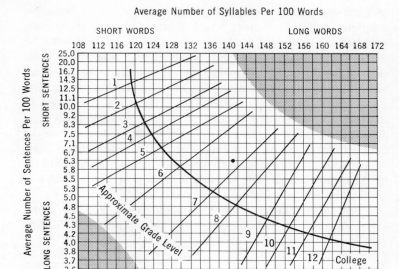

Figure 1. Graph for Estimating Readability

4. Plot on the graph the location of these two points to determine the grade level of the material.

5. Choose more passages per book if great variability is observed and conclude that the book has uneven readability. Few books will fall in the gray area, but when they do, grade level scores are invalid.

Example

	Syllables	Sentences
1st Hundred Words	124	6.6
2nd Hundred Words	141	5.5
3rd Hundred Words	158	6.8
Average	141	6.3

Readability — 7th grade (see dot plotted on graph)

CONCLUSION

This formula can be used as an aid in determining the difficulty of reading material. It is not intended to replace the judgment of an experienced teacher but rather to act as a valuable supplement. Other factors which contribute towards making material easier to read are large clear type, familiarity with the subject matter, and helpful illustrations. But these considerations should not override the consideration of the more basic factors of vocabulary difficulty and sentence structure.

Every school library should have at least one shelf of books that have been graded according to difficulty. The level of difficulty should be marked on every book graded, inside the back cover or on the binding. Often the teacher can train several of his older students to work the formula on new library books as they arrive. The formula might also help teachers and administrators in selecting textbooks.

For further information and validity data, see the April, 1968, *Journal of Reading* and the March, 1969, *Reading Teacher*.

5

Putting It All Together

The significance of individual differences becomes evident when the teacher must select instructional approaches appropriate for the child, his background, and his reading needs. Remedial instruction is not a group of children seated constantly at a variety of electronic devices; neither is it endlessly "doing" pages in workbooks. Procedures must be selected on the basis of *all* the information unearthed during diagnosis. Trite though it may sound, in preventive and remedial instruction, "needs should determine methods."

Noticeable and notable advances have been made in recent years in the number and range of approaches especially geared for remedial instruction. Some are derived from disciplines such as behavioral psychology and psychotherapy, others are based on conceptions about the development and functioning of certain human senses, and still others are designed to remedy deficiencies typical of a certain group of children. Most are remarkably sound, educationally and psychologically, and in tune with the general principles of remedial instruction.

Special procedures are often necessary and valuable for several reasons. Some children learn better by one approach than by another and we need to know their idiosyncracies. Also, a sharp break from familiar methods may provide just the spark needed to ignite latent motivation. Remedial instruction should not be mere repetition — in a more intensive, one-to-one situation — of methods by which the child originally failed to learn. Such conditions may account for our miserable failure with many disabled readers.

Procedures successful in remedial situations have potentially broader application than mere clinical use; many are equally useful in the classroom as preventive measures. After validating them by pilot projects in clinics with disabled readers, we should incorporate them into an enlarged and enriched developmental reading program better able to provide for the myriad individual differences of children.

Even though materials, methods, techniques, and programs may be vitally important in preventive and remedial instruction, the success or failure of such instruction ultimately depends upon a creative, hard-working, competent teacher able to devise, organize, and administer a systematic, individualized instructional program. Teachers of children with reading difficulties must face the challenge of the instructional task before them. What progress do these children make — or fail to make — toward the generally accepted instructional goals? We dare not delude ourselves about such vital questions. Rose-colored glasses are not for remedial reading teachers! If we fail to recognize the difficulties inherent in remedial instruction, we fail to plan appropriate programs, we terminate instruction too early, we do not have the necessary follow-through, and ultimately we doom the child to a minimum of reading progress. Delusion can lead only to despair and apathy; realism should lead to determination and perseverance. Hopefully this section will help teachers formulate an appropriate and adequate attitude toward the challenge presented. We hope to suggest some instructional approaches not treated in most reading textbooks, to whet the reader's interest in exploring new avenues, and to increase his awareness of such possibilities.

ASHER CASHDAN
P. D. PUMFREY

Some Effects of the
Remedial Teaching of Reading

We know we must determine whether children receiving special instruction improve as a result of this instruction. But we may be less cognizant of even more important questions: Do these children continue to progress independently after remedial instruction is ended? Are their attitudes toward reading improved? and What instructional schedule provides the best results? This unique study suggests some eye-opening answers. Though they are hardly reassuring, they give us some insights that should be helpful in designing and implementing realistic remedial programs.

Do the results depress you, surprise you, or confirm what you previously suspected? Are the authors optimistic or pessimistic about the long-term effect of such instruction? What specific and practical revisions do you think are justified in remedial instruction in the light of the results of this and similar studies? Do you believe the same general results would be obtained with your students, in your school? Why or why not?

Since 1944 many LEAs have set up Remedial Education services to assist children who, while remaining within the normal school, fail to learn to read. A considerable amount of research has been concerned with the short-term and long-term effects of treatment on attainment and on the child's social and emotional adjustment (see Chazan, 1967, for a useful review). Substantial short-term gains in reading attainment of two-three months of reading age per month of remedial treatment are frequently found. However, these gains are usually recorded on Word

Reprinted from *Educational Research,* 11 (February 1969), pp. 138-142, by permission of the publishers, National Foundation for Educational Research in England and Wales, and by the author.

Recognition tests; on Reading Comprehension tests, gains are rather smaller. Follow-up studies for varying periods up to three years after treatment have indicated little or no difference between children who had received remedial education and those who had not, in terms of their attainment. The relatively rapid progress made during remedial education is not continued when treatment ends. This failure of the remedial teaching of reading to improve children's attainments in the long-term is naturally somewhat disappointing to remedial teachers.

Some slight evidence exists that the longer the remedial teaching of reading continues, the greater the children's gain in terms of attainment (Cashdan, Pumfrey and Lunzer 1967). To return children to the situations which precipitated their initial failure and selection for remedial education is likely to result in some falling off in their progress. And remedial groups which have become too large and are taken by peripatetic teachers also cease to benefit the children.

Pringle (1962) has stressed the importance for some children of remedial education as an "emotional re-education"; this is hard to measure and in Dunham's (1960) study his attitude scale brought out no improvement in the children studied, although their reading attainment had increased.

This article summarizes a small, but fairly well-controlled experiment in which both attitudes to reading and changes in reading attainment were examined in three groups of retarded junior school boys. Special features of the study are the comparison of once-weekly with twice-weekly teaching, comparisons between different reading tests, and the use of an improved version of Dunham's (1960) attitude scale. The aims of the experiment were to answer the following five questions:

1. Would second year junior school boys failing in reading make greater progress in attainment if given remedial help twice-weekly compared with a matched group given remedial help once a week?
2. At the end of the initial two-term treatment period, would the groups receiving treatment have significantly higher reading attainments on two criterion tests compared with a control group receiving no remedial help?
3. Would a differential practice effect favoring the boys' attainments on the Burt-Vernon Graded Word Reading Test (hereafter called the Burt test) compared with their attainments on the Standard Test of Reading Skill be found after two terms of remedial treatment?

4. Would any significant differences in attainment in reading be found between the three groups two years after the end of the initial treatment period?

5. Would any significant differences in attitude to reading be found between the treated and untreated groups two years after the initial treatment period?

THE INVESTIGATION

Twelve boys were selected from sixteen backward second year junior school children who were taught in groups of four as part of the practical work of a university diploma course. Two other groups of twelve boys were matched individually with the university group. The thirty-six boys chosen to take part in the investigation were of low average ability as measured by the Moray House Picture Intelligence Test. All had reading ages on the Burt test at least two years behind their chronological ages, and came from the Registrar General's socio-economic groups four and five.

The three groups were named A, B and C. The twelve boys in Group A were given remedial teaching in reading in groups of four twice-weekly for 30-60 minute sessions at the university. All the teachers engaged in the work were qualified and experienced in remedial or Special education. Members of Group B were taught in groups of from four to six children for sessions of similar length once-weekly by teachers of the local authority's remedial education service. Group C was a control group of children selected from the records of the remedial centers, and receiving no special help in reading. Some characteristics of the three groups are set out in Table 1.

There were no significant differences between the respective group means.

The initial experimental period lasted for two terms. At the end of the second term (Spring 1964) all thirty-six boys were tested on the Burt test as well as on the Daniels and Diack Standard Test of Reading Skill. Twenty-two months later (Spring 1966) as many of the subjects as could be found were tested again with the Burt test and with the Neale Analysis of Reading Ability, which allowed assessments for accuracy, comprehension and reading speed to be obtained. The boys were also tested on a Thurstone-Chave attitude to reading scale constructed by Williams (1965), a development of Dunham's (1960) scale. The Williams attitude scale contains twenty-five statements with scale values ranging from 0.5 for the most positive attitude to reading to 10.5 for the statement indicating the most negative attitude.

As the investigation was based on the organization of a functioning educational service, the boys continued with remedial treatment for varying lengths of time after April 1964.

Table 1

Characteristics of the Groups at the Start of the Investigation

Group	N	Mean CA	SD	Moray House Picture Intelligence Test		Burt-Vernon Reading Test	
				Mean IQ	SD	Mean RA	SD
Group A (University)	12	8.6	0.40	89.5	4.97	5.4	0.86
Group B (Remedial Service)	12	8.6	0.37	90.3	4.57	5.5	0.57
Group C (Control)	12	8.6	0.26	89.6	5.78	5.7	0.73

RESULTS

The general school attendance of all thirty-six children during the two-term period was checked. There was great individual variation but no group differences. The mean number of remedial attendances for the two experimental groups was also examined. The university group, who attended twice weekly, should have made twice the number of attendances that were registered for the remedial service group. In fact, the discrepancy was even bigger — Group A (university) had a mean attendance of 37.1 and Group B (remedial service) of only 14.1, the discrepancy being due to absences and to organizational differences. These attendance differences were statistically clearly significant.

On the Burt test, the mean gains at the end of two terms were: Group A. 1.24 years, Group B, 1.25 years, and Group C

(Control), 0.86 years. There was no significant difference between the groups, though the controls did appear to have made fractionally less progress than the other two groups.

Because gains in reading attainment attributed to remedial education might have been due to practice effects on the Burt test, the boys were also tested on the Daniels and Diack Standard Test of Reading Skill at the end of the initial experimental period. Scores obtained by the three groups are given in Table 2.

The small mean discrepancies between the tests for each group indicate little practice effect in the Burt test result. There is more indication in Group B than in the other groups, but even here it is slight. There was no significant difference between the groups in the numbers of children gaining higher scores on the Burt test than on the Standard Test of Reading Skill.

Although the initial experimental period ended in May 1964, all the boys in Group A continued to receive remedial treatment until July 1964, and six boys in this group received remedial help for a further twelve months. Most of Group B also received help until July 1964, and two members of this group continued to receive treatment after that date. The mean length of remedial treatment was 14.8 ms. for Group A and 9.5 ms. for Group B. The mean chronological age for all three groups at follow-up was 10 years 11 months. Because of extensive rehousing, only 32 of the original 36 boys could be located.

Table 2

Group Mean Scores on the Burt Test and on the
Standard Test of Reading Skill,
Obtained after Two Terms

Group	N	Burt Test Mean Score	SD	Standard Test Mean Score	SD
Group A (University)	12	6.65	1.27	6.40	0.94
Group B (Remedial Service)	12	6.73	0.78	6.03	0.72
Group C (Control)	12	6.57	1.37	6.33	1.18

Burt Test Results

The mean gains of the three groups on the Burt test over the 22 months of the follow-up period were: Group A, 2.52 years, Group B, 1.46 years, and Group C, 2.50 years. There were no significant differences between the groups.

The mean rates of progress of the three groups on the Burt test were calculated in months of reading age per month of follow-up period. The results for the three groups were: Group A, 1.36, Group B, 0.80 and Group C, 1.36.

Burt Test Results Compared with the
Neale Analysis of Reading Ability Results

In order to see whether any tendency towards a differential practice effect favoring the boys' performance on the Burt test existed, the results obtained by the three groups were compared. None of the mean differences were significant. The scores of the three groups are given in Table 3.

Attitude to Reading

The boys' attitudes to reading were assessed, using the Williams' (1965) attitude scale, in which a high score denotes a "poor" attitude. The means for the three groups were 4.33 for Group A, 3.95 for Group B and 3.72 for Group C. The difference in scores between the groups was not significant. The correlations between attitude score and final reading ages were also not significant.

DISCUSSION

In the light of our results we can now look at the five questions raised earlier.

The suggestion that boys in Group A receiving remedial teaching in reading twice-weekly would make greater progress in reading attainment than boys in Group B helped only once-weekly, was not supported at the end of the initial seven-months experimental period. The mean gains of these two groups did not differ significantly, although Group A boys attended almost three times as many remedial sessions as those in Group B.

The second possibility, that at the end of the initial treatment period the groups that had been given remedial teaching in reading might have significantly higher reading

Table 3

Group Mean Reading Ages at Follow-up

	N	Burt-Vernon Test		Neale Analysis of Reading Ability					
				Rate		Accuracy		Comprehension	
		Mean	SD	Mean	SD	Mean	SD	Mean	SD
Group A	10	9.17	1.87	8.69	1.44	8.68	1.14	9.03	1.64
Group B	11	8.20	1.19	8.08	0.92	8.17	0.76	8.25	0.90
Group C	11	9.07	2.33	8.63	1.57	8.79	1.59	9.26	1.90

attainments than the controls on both the Burt test and the Daniels and Diack test, was not confirmed. However, an initial spurt in progress of the groups receiving remedial teaching (found by many other researchers) was indicated in the differing rates of increase in scores between the groups on the Burt test.

The continuation of remedial help might have maintained the different rates of increase in reading attainment found in the three groups, thus producing significant differences favoring the treated groups in time. Other work by Cashdan, Pumfrey and Lunzer (1966) and by Lytton (1967) and Morris (1966) has shown that the continuation of remedial help in reading brings continuing improvement.

It seemed possible that a differential practice effect favoring the boys' scores on the Burt test might be found. This has been suggested by other researchers, including Curr and Gourlay (1960). But, comparison of the three groups' scores on the Burt test and on the Daniels and Diack test at the end of the initial seven months of remedial treatment lends no support to this hypothesis.

The differential practice effect was also not found when the Neale Analysis provided a measure of comprehension which could be compared with the Burt test scores for the three groups.

The hypothesis that twenty-two months after the initial two-term period significant differences in reading ability would be found between the groups was also not supported. Thus, the findings agree with the somewhat depressing evidence produced by both Collins (1961) and Lovell (1966), although it may not be reasonable to expect short-term improvements in children's attainments to be maintained if the children are returned to the initial situation. The need for continuing compensatory education for children who fail to acquire reading at the junior level must again be emphasized (see Morris, 1966).

We also investigated whether, on follow-up, any significant differences in attitude to reading would be found between the groups. None in fact were, although the groups' mean attitude scores were towards the favorable end of the continuum. Attitude to reading is probably less easily improved than reading attainment, at any rate with poor readers in the junior school (Dunham, 1960). It must also be noted that the attitude scale used in this investigation was of a relatively coarse grading and to some extent its purpose must have been visible to the children to whom it was administered. Georgiades (1968) suggests an alternative technique which may have considerable promise in the measurement of attitude to reading.

CONCLUSION

The remedial teaching of reading to retarded junior school boys in two experimental groups did not improve reading attainment or attitude to reading when the groups were compared with a control group. The "natural" improvement of the control group, which seems at first sight to be largely maturational, may be misleading. Very often, one suspects, the "untreated" children get indirect help in the form of advice to their teachers from the Remedial Service, relief of pressure if some of their classmates are being helped, and so on. These are suggestions, rather than firmly established facts, which may help to explain awkward results. A more likely general conclusion is that the kind of children we are concerned with require a far more continuous program of remedial treatment as an integral part of their normal school activities if they are to enter secondary education as literate children.

BIBLIOGRAPHY

Cashdan, A., Pumfrey, P. D. and Lunzer, E. A. (1967). "A survey of children receiving remedial teaching in reading," *Bulletin of British Psychology and Sociology,* 67, 17A.

Chazan, M. (1967). "The effects of remedial teaching in reading: A review of research," *Remedial Education,* 2, No. 1, 4-12.

Collins, J. E. (1961). *The Effects of Remedial Education*. London: Oliver and Boyd (for Birmingham University Institute of Education).

Curr, W. and Gourlay, N. (1960). "The effect of practice on performance in scholastic tests," *British Journal of Educational Psychology*, 30, 155-67.

Dunham, J. (1960). "The effects of remedial education on young children's reading ability and attitudes to reading," *British Journal of Educational ·Psychology*, 30, 173-5.

Georgiades, N.J. (1968). "The testing of reading today." In: Downing, J. and Brown, A. L. eds. *The Third International Reading Symposium*. London: Cassell.

Lovell, K. (1966). "The aetiology of reading failure." In: Downing, J., ed. *The First International Reading Symposium, Oxford 1964*. London: Cassell.

Lytton, H. (1967). "Follow-up of an experiment in selection for remedial education," *British Journal of Educational Psychology*, 37, 1-9.

Morris, J. M. (1966). *Standards and Progress in Reading*. Slough: NFER.

Pringle, M. L. Kellmer. (1962). "The long-term effects of remedial education: A follow-up study," *Vital Humanities*, 5, 10-33.

Williams, G. M. (1965). "A study of reading attitudes among nine-year-old children." Diploma dissertation. University of Manchester.

ROBERT M. WILSON
LOUISE F. WAYNANT

Success —
An Urgent Need in Remediation

Is it possible that in our eagerness for improvement we have preached but not practiced and have not seen the forest for the trees? Wilson and Waynant present a generally unorthodox view of remediation. (It is unorthodox only because we have usually ignored the obvious; it is not unorthodox in that it is esoteric or radical!) It is refreshingly simple, to the point, and totally feasible. Yet how many of us would ever have thought it up — or how many of us have ever practiced it?

Is the relationship between the rationale of this discussion and those of Root's and of Otto and McMenemy's in Part Four obvious? How does such a diagnostic orientation affect the teacher's attitude toward remediation? How does it affect the teacher's attitude toward the child? Do you agree that "one must avoid the temptation to teach a skill via a frontal attack"? Does it seem reasonable that this approach would have beneficial effects far beyond actual reading improvement?

Traditionally, remediation has been based upon diagnostic results which identify the weaknessess children demonstrate in testing situations. The literature is replete with statements such as, "Teach to the needs of the child" and "Correct the child's deficiencies." However, available evidence indicates that traditional remedial reading programs often result in *short term gains (6)*. Yet, while children may be able to demonstrate improvements in the areas of deficiencies, they may also choose not to *use* their newly acquired skills. Therefore, some writers suggest that remedial programs produce children who see themselves as failures in scholastic situations *(1)*. For this

An original article written for this book by Robert M. Wilson and Louise F. Waynant.

reason, a fresh approach is needed in remedial reading. Perhaps this approach should stress the development of positive self-concepts and self-esteem along with the development of skills. Such a program might well instill both the desire to read and the ability to read.

A positive approach to remedial reading must be based upon philosophical premises needed to explain it:

Children MUST see themselves as accepted and respected learners.
Learning environments must be supportive, yet stimulating . and challenging.
Teachers must focus upon children's strengths.
Success must be clearly and dramatically illustrated to the children.

Authoritative support for these premises adds respect to the immediate acknowledgement of their desirability.

The following statements illustrate the importance of acceptance and respect:

" . . . to feel that one is deeply valued regardless of how one looks or acts, is to have a haven of safety in case of failure . . . ." *(5)*
" . . . if a person is accepted and valued and esteemed, he becomes an inquiring person and he actualizes himself . . . ." *(7)*
" . . . provide an environment that accepts children's feelings and thought . . . ." *(8)*

These show the need to develop a supportive learning environment, to teach to strengths and to illustrate successes.

" . . . the more supportive the climate, the more the student is willing to share, the more learning will take place . . . ." *(2)*
" . . . tolerance for failure is best taught through providing a background of success that compensates for experienced failure . . . ." *(3)*
" . . . in a remedial program, the child's first instruction should be at a level we are certain will result in a successful satisfying experience . . . ." *(10)*
" . . . reinforcement is important . . . it is generally found that positive reinforcements . . . are to be preferred to negative . . . ." *(4)*
" . . . pupils who have had little success and almost continuous failure in school tasks are in no condition to think, to learn, or even to pay attention . . . ." *(9)*

Authoritative support from such a diversity of sources shows the amount of considered thought which many have given to the stated problems.

To this authoritative support must be added proof that such a program can be developed and that its implementation is indeed practical.

First, how is diagnosis involved in such a program? A traditional diagnostic report tends to stress what a child *cannot* do, e.g., "Bill does not know his vowel sounds. He fails in all activities at the 2^2 reading level. His comprehension shows no signs of problem solving abilities." Under this new system, diagnosis would state that "Bill has acquired the skills of consonant substitution. He reads well at the 1^2 level and can read with direction at the 2^1 level. His comprehension skills in the area of literal understanding are well developed." Note that both diagnostic reports refer to the same child. However, the positive tone in the latter diagnostic report, emphasizing the child's strengths, leads to a remedial program focusing on those same strengths.

Second, how does one start such a remedial program? We have found that the *only way* to start is to teach to the child's strengths all of the time. Making activities both interesting and challenging, while assuring him of success, improves the child's attitude toward future instruction. For example, we discovered one child with intensive interest in living forms. Ants were his interest at the moment. Therefore, an ant unit, developed around his interests and his language strengths, was instituted. As he became knowledgeable of ant living, he was recognized by his peers as a successful learner, one with interesting information to share. Another boy enjoyed drag racing. Model cars, magazines, and experience stories on drag racing stimulated his interest in reading.

Third, how does one get to a child's weaknesses? The answer is that he doesn't! He continues with the child's strengths. One should search for new interests and continue to assess a child's skill status in terms of his strengths, e.g., work on initial consonant substitution develops vowel awareness. Reading for fun at the 2^1 level then develops into reading for skills at the 2^2 level. Also, it legitimately develops a feeling of success, of worthwhileness. . . or of belonging to the group of learning children.

Fourth, what materials should be used? We recommend that the teacher make them. Clinicians who work with few or *no* commercially prepared materials use materials directly related to a child's strengths and interests. By using readily available materials such as comics, cartoons, newspaper headlines, experience stories, and trade books, a remedial program reflects a positive philosophy. Where the teacher relies heavily upon commercial materials, children are limited by interests and skills inherent in the materials, whether they are appropriate or not. Teachers tend to fall into the trap of teaching the materials, not the child. However, when teacher-made materials are used, children's strengths and interests are most often met.

Fifth, when are the skills of reading taught? One must avoid the temptation to teach a skill via a frontal attack, for every remedial reader has experienced the frontal attack again and again. That they are remedial readers attests to the success of such attacks. Instead, let them experience success, lots of success, with mastered skills. Eventually children will ask for specific instruction. At that point, a teacher might make contracts designed to follow the individual child's interests and strengths. Through the contract approach, the child has some voice in the type of skills work being developed, the materials being used, the pacing of the work, and the evaluation of the activities. By involving children in the planning of their own programs, they develop goal awareness. A girl with an intense hatred for phonics activities of all types came to us for remedial help. By working with her strengths and by eventually letting her assist children* with skills which she had already developed, she became concerned about her own needs and asked for instruction in phonics. The clinician obliged her and a successful reader emerged. Each of a child's successes must be rewarded with dramatic emphasis, with letters home, ice cream cones, special trips and privileges, and the like. With success, enthusiasm for learning mounts, at least initially. Intermittent reinforcement starts after success is established. By moving from reinforcement at each indication of success to intermittent reinforcement, the child moves from working for reward to working for the satisfaction of success.

---

*Peer teaching stresses review of instruction developed by the teacher. It is not designed for initial skills instruction.

A look at some results....children involved in remedial programs which stress strengths do approximately as well as do children in traditional programs, that is, the measure of achievement is in terms of skills and test results. However, as we talk with children, parents, and teachers about the program, they note behaviors which are unmeasurable by tests and which indicate attitude and self-concept development. For example,

Children: ...ask to give demonstrations of their proficiencies
             ...tell other children about their reading
             ...desire to help other children instructionally
             ...come to sessions early and leave late
             ...request to make books
             ...request to take books home
Parents: ...state that this instruction is the best thing that ever happened to Bill
             ...indicate that bad dreams have stopped
             ...feel that home life is much better now
             ...remark that the child asks to come to clinic early
             ...say that the child actually reads the newspaper
             ...note that the child is, at last, eager to go to school
Teachers: ...note that the child will try
             ...state that the child moved up one reading group — upon his request
             ...remark that the child contributes much more to total class activities
             ...indicate that classroom behavior is much better
             ...feel that the child smiles more

By seeing every child as beautiful, strong, and developmental in his learning, one can identify successes and use them to help the child want to learn and to read. As the child responds he develops a background of successes which makes learning enjoyable and worth the effort. What better way is there?

REFERENCES

1. Bond, Guy L., and Miles A. Tinker. *Reading Difficulties: Their Diagnosis and Correction.* New York: Appleton-Century-Crofts, 1967, 11.

2. Bowers, Norman D. and Robert S. Soar. "Studies in Human Relations in the Teaching — Learning Process," *V. Final Report: Evaluation of Laboratory Human Relations Training for Classroom Teachers.* Chapel Hill, North Carolina and Columbia, South Carolina, 1961, 11.

3. Cohen, S. Alan. *Teach Them All to Read.* New York: Random House, 1969, 231.

4. Hilgard, Ernest R., and Gordon H. Bower. *Theories of Learning.* New York: Appleton-Century-Crofts, 1966, 563.

5. Prescott, Daniel A. *The Child in the Educative Process.* New York: McGraw-Hill Book Company, Inc., 1957, 358.

6. Silberberg, Norman E., and Margaret C. Silberberg. "Myths in Remedial Education," *Journal of Learning Disabilities,* 2:209-217, April, 1969, 209.

7. Waetjen, Walter B. "Facts About Learning," in Glen Hass and Kimball Wiles (ed.), *Readings in Curriculum.* Boston: Allyn and Bacon, Inc., 1965, 243.

8. Waetjen, Walter B., and Robert R. Leeper (ed.). *Learning and Mental Health in the School.* Washington, D. C.: Association for Supervision and Curriculum Development, National Education Association, 1966, 7.

9. Watson, Goodwin. "What Do We Know About Learning?" in Glen Hass and Kimball Wiles (ed.), *Readings in Curriculum.* Boston: Allyn and Bacon, Inc., 1965, 252.

10. Wilson, Robert M. *Diagnostic and Remedial Reading for Classroom and Clinic.* Columbus: Charles E. Merrill, 1967, 106.

S. ALAN COHEN

The Taxonomy of Instructional Treatments in Reading

Teachers in classroom and clinic who have intensely desired to individualize instruction have frequently been overwhelmed by the management problems involved and the lack of an overall system for organization and instruction. Cohen presents a concise, systematic plan for correlating and organizing the myriad variables that a teacher must be aware of, plan for, and manage.

What kind of a teacher do you think would be most able to operate effectively using this approach? Is the Taxonomy compatible with Wilson and Waynant's recommendations in the preceding article? What relationship do you see between this Taxonomy and the discussions of materials in Part Four of this book? Do you understand and agree with Cohen's distinction between method and system? To what extent do you think this approach could be implemented in a typical classroom? in a clinic? Has reading this article changed your point of view about the simplicity-complexity of remedial reading instruction?

BRIEF DESCRIPTION

The Taxonomy is an analytic tool that helps the teacher match teaching content and style with the diagnosed skill and behavior deficits of individual pupils. The Taxonomy provides criteria for assessing the child's learning styles and how he interacts with a formal instructional stimulus. It aids the teacher in determining which basic skill and related subskills the child must master; at what difficulty level this content can be learned; the communications input that galvanizes maximum reception; the communications output that conducts maximum respon-

Adapted and abridged from an original study sponsored by USOE grant OEG-1-6-062528-2092 to the author and Dr. Abraham J. Tannenbaum. Reprinted with the permission of S. Alan Cohen.

siveness; the instructional media most likely to accommodate behavioral needs; the instructional strategy that the child must use to respond adequately to the stimulus presented in the learning task; and the instructional grouping to provide the most supportive, efficient and effective environment for learning the specific target behavior.

The Taxonomy systematizes the teacher's pedagogical repertoire by classifying behavioral alternatives open to him during the instructional act. To make these alternatives operative, it is necessary to create and assemble instructional materials that will plug appropriate content into every specified teaching style. Once the teacher has determined precisely what behavioral deficits handicap the child, the teacher elects the preferred instructional content and teaching behavior from the array outlined in the Taxonomy. The teacher is then guided to the teaching aids that fit his requirement by the Taxonomy code system which forms the indexing scheme for the materials. The task of the curriculum specialist is to keep the library of instructional aids stocked in such a manner as to fulfill the content and teacher behavior specifications suggested by the Taxonomy. Thus, a diagnosis of individual learning needs is directly applicable to an educational catalogue that provides sources of methods and materials to match the diagnosis. The result is a prescriptive teaching system and a broad diversification of approaches to instruction.

The Taxonomy was developed by the senior author and Dr. Abraham J. Tannenbaum of Teachers College, Columbia University under USOE grant number OEG-1-6-062528-2092 and has more recently been used in a systems approach to reading instruction described in Chapter 11 of S. Alan Cohen's *Teach Them All to Read: Theory, Method and Materials for Teaching the Disadvantaged,* Random House, New York, 1969.

HOW THE TAXONOMY WORKS

Each variable in the Taxonomy is numbered according to the code outlined below in the "Key for the Taxonomy of Instructional Treatments." The Taxonomy of Instructional Treatments can be modified to include or exclude any class of observable behaviors one cares to deal with. Figure 1 is a visually more convenient array of the information included below.

Figure 1

The Taxonomy of Instructional Treatments in Reading

	First Digit: BASIC SKILL	*Second Digit:* BASIC SUBSKILL	*Third* SEQUENTIAL *Digit:* LEVEL

C O N T E N T	1. Word Attack	1. Consonants
		2. Vowels
		3. Word Structure
		4. Sight Vocabulary
		5. Word Meaning
		6. Context Inference
		7. Symbolic Discrimination
			1. Easy/Initial
			2. Average/
			   Intermediate
			3. Difficult/
			   Sophisticated
			4. Ungradable

	2. Comprehension	1. Details-Main Ideas 2. Sequence-Relations 3. Follow Directions 4. Sentence Structure 5. Paragraph Structure 6. Recreational Reading	
	3. Study Skills	1. Dictionary 2. Maps and Graphs 3. References & Texts	

	Fourth Digit: COMMUNICATION	*Fifth Digit:* COMMUNICATION OUTPUT
CHANNEL OF COMMUNICATION	1. Auditory 2. Visual 3. Kinesthetic 4. Auditory/Visual 5. Visual/Kinesthetic 6. Auditory/Kinesthetic 7. Visual/Auditory/Kinesthetic	1. Oral 2. Motoric 3. Oral-Motoric 4. Non Observable Output

	Sixth INSTRUCTIONAL *Digit:* MEDIA	*Seventh* INSTRUCTIONAL *Digit:* STRATEGY	*Eighth* INSTRUCTIONAL *Digit:* GROUPING

S T R A T E G Y	1. Visual-Projector
	2. Auditory-Recorder
	3. Skill-Drill Text
	
	4. Games-Role Playing
	5. Books
	6. Cards (Kits)
	7. CAI
	
	8. Teaching Machine
		1. Play-Chance
		2. Play-Competition
		3. Play-Puzzle
		
		4. Test-Response
		5. Exploration
		6. Programmed Response
		7. Creative Problem
		   Solving
			1. Teacher/Large Group
			2. Teacher/Small Group
			3. Teacher/Individual/
			   Student/Tutor
			4. Student/Small Group
			5. Student/Large Group
			6. Student/Student Team
			7. Individual Self
			   Instruction

KEY FOR THE TAXONOMY
OF INSTRUCTIONAL TREATMENTS

Basic Skills

For the sake of simplicity, the many skills related to the act of reading have been generally grouped under three main headings called Basic Skills. They are coded as follows:

> 1 — Word Attack
>
> 2 — Comprehension
>
> 3 — Study Skills

Basic Sub-Skills

The Basic Skill areas have been further refined into Sub-Skill that has to be taught. The Sub-Skills are coded as follows:

Basic Skill — 1 Word Attack	Basic Skill — 2 Comprehension	Basic Skill — 3 Study Skills
Sub-Skills	Sub-Skills	Sub-Skills
1 — Consonants	1 — Details-Main Ideas	1 — Dictionary
2 — Vowels	2 — Sequence-Relationships	2 — Maps and Globes
3 — Word Structure	3 — Following Directions	3 — Reference-Texts
4 — Sight Vocabulary	4 — Sentence Structure	4 — Listening Comprehension
5 — Word Meaning	5 — Paragraph Structure	
6 — Context Clues	6 — Directed Reading	
7 — Symbolic Discrimination	7 — Inference	

Sequence Levels

The Sequence Levels notation is an attempt to categorize materials according to degrees of difficulty for the target population. The coding is as follows:

> 1 — Easy or initial levels
>
> 2 — Average or intermediate levels
>
> 3 — Difficult or sophisticated levels
>
> 4 — Ungradable

Communication Input

Communication Input refers to the learner's sensory modalities available for mediating the instructional stimuli. The coding is as follows:

1 — Auditory
2 — Visual
3 — Kinesthetic
4 — Auditory-Visual
5 — Visual-Kinesthetic
6 — Auditory-Kinesthetic
7 — Visual-Auditory-Kinesthetic

Communication Output

Communication Output refers to the channels to be used by the student to demonstrate the correctness of processing information received via the Input Channel. The coding is as follows:

1 — Oral
2 — Motoric
3 — Oral-Motoric
4 — Non Observable

Instructional Media

The Instructional Media refer to the alternative designs for "packaging" content in the form of teaching aids. The coding is as follows:

1 — Visual-Projective
2 — Auditory-Recording
3 — Skill-Drill Texts
4 — Games
5 — Books
6 — Cards (Kits)
7 — Computer Assisted Instruction
8 — Other Teaching Machines

Instructional Strategies

Instructional strategies are the transactional styles between the learner and the teaching material. They are coded as follows:

1 — Play-Chance
2 — Play-Competition
3 — Play-Puzzle
4 — Test-Response

5 — Exploration
6 — Programmed Response
7 — Creative Problem Solving

Instructional Grouping

Instructional Grouping refers to the ways of organizing pupils for a formal teaching-learning experience. The coding is as follows:

1 — Teacher directed large group
2 — Teacher directed small group
3 — Teacher-individual-student-tutorial
4 — Student directed small group
5 — Student directed large group
6 — Student-student team learning
7 — Individual self-instruction

USES OF THE TAXONOMY

The first major use of the Taxonomy is for diagnosis. Test data on an individual child are coded according to the Taxonomy on to a Diagnostic Analysis Chart (Figure 2). By referring to the Taxonomy, the chart shows in Content 2, for example, that Tom has a word attack skill problem (Basic Skill 1 in the Taxonomy), specifically in word meaning (Sub Skill 5). He can easily handle sixth-grade materials (Sequential Level 1). Tom can process visual, auditory and kinesthetic inputs (Communications Input 7). He can give a written response (Communications Output 2).

Figure 2
Diagnostic Analysis Chart

Name Tom Smith	Age 11-5	D.O.B. 6-15-55	
School P.S. 148	Class 6-2	D.O.T. 9-30-66	
	Content 1	Content 2	Content 3	Content 4
A. Basic Skills	1	1	1	
B. Sub Skills	2	5	3	
C. Sequential Levels	1	1	1	
D. Communications Input	7	7	7	
E. Communications Output	2	2	2	
F. Instructional Media	1,2,3,4,5	1,2,3,4,5	1,3,5	
G. Instructional Strategy	1,2,3,4	1,2,3,4	1,2,3,4	
H. Instructional Grouping	2,7	2,7	2,7	

Tommy can use any of the five possible ways of presenting materials (Instructional Media 1,2,3,4,5) which employ learning strategies of play-chance, play-competition, play-puzzle or test-response (Instructional Strategies 1,2,3,4) in a teacher-directed small group or individual self-direction (Instructional Grouping 2,7).

The second use of the Taxonomy is for treatment. Published or teacher-made materials are catalogued according to the Taxonomy number system. The teacher uses this Diagnostic Analysis Chart to pull from the catalogue appropriate instructional materials and strategies to meet Tom's needs and learning style. Eventually, the entire process can be automated.

Originally the Taxonomy was designed to implement intensified, diagnostic, prescriptive teaching of reading in Reading Skills Centers. Because it gives the average teacher very specific guidelines for diagnosing learning needs and styles and for analyzing instructional methods and materials, the Taxonomy has been used for teacher training. The use of the Taxonomy forces the teacher to define teaching behaviors and to understand more clearly what professional expertise or techniques he can bring into the classroom.

One of the most important uses of the Taxonomy is as a learning prescription. The teacher enters one or more eight-digit code numbers on a special form for this purpose (Figure 3), indicating what he is going to teach and how he plans to do it. A curriculum specialist helps the teacher create, assemble, and supply the instructional aids that fit the treatment plan. The plan can be made for individuals or for groups, and each pupil can have a cumulative record of the instructional treatments to which he has been exposed all year. This facilitates a systematic evaluation of the program or materials used in the curriculum.

For the author, the most important use of the Taxonomy is to construct a systems approach to classroom pedagogy. Most pedagogy is conceived of as methodology — a methodology being the result of the teacher style, the pupil style and the resources found in the classroom. A pedagogical *system,* on the other hand, dictates the teacher's behavior, the pupil's behavior and the resources needed to control those behaviors. The key difference between a method and a system is best illustrated by the contrasting models in Figure 4. Notice that the vectors go in

Figure 3

Learning Prescription Form Based On Taxonomy

Date 1 – 15   Class 6 – 1   Teacher Brown

General Comments

These kids need code busting, vocabulary, dictionary – low level skills.

Pupil's Names	Content			Communication Channels			Strategy		Teacher Comments
	Basic Skill	Sub Skill	Sequential Level	Input	Output	Instructional Media	Instructional Strategy	Instructional Grouping	
Tommy	1	2	1	4	2	3	4	4	vowels long short a, i, e
Jane	1	2	1	4	2	3	4	4	vowels long short o, i, e
Billy	1	2	1	4	2	3	4	4	vowels long short i, e
Robert	2	3	2	2	2	3	6	7	something like Macmillan Program Dictionary
Kenneth	3	1	2	2	2	3	4	7	dictionary skills from Skilpacers Red-Green-Blue
Peggy	3	4	1	4	2	2	6	7	listening tapes – low level – vocabulary development
Mary	1	3	1	4	2	4	1	7	structural analysis – games
George	1	6	1	1	2	2	6	7	meaning from context on auditory level

(Tommy, Jane, Billy comments bracketed: work together, need at least 10 pages) different directions. In the method, for example, variations in teacher behavior will result in variations in method, leading, of course, to variations in instructional outcomes. But in a system, the system determines the three variables, teacher behavior, pupil behavior and resources. Instructional outcomes are, therefore, controlled.

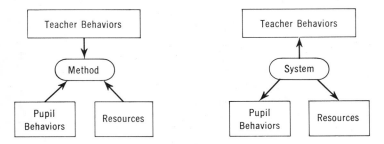

Figure 4. METHOD vs. SYSTEM

In the teaching *system* developed by the author, the curriculum is determined by individual diagnosis. Teaching is personalized for each individual. What the pupil learns, the level and rate at which he learns, is personalized so the instructional grouping is predominantly Taxonomy code numbers 2,3,4,6,7 under Instructional Grouping (Figure 1). Materials are stored in the Instructional Materials Center and drawn daily or weekly on prescription. Thus, the teacher's major job is continuous matching of materials and strategies to individual needs. The teacher becomes diagnostician and prescriber rather than talker or lecturer. And the Taxonomy becomes the guide for diagnosis and prescription. In other words, the pedagogical system is the Taxonomy translated into resources and materials and the strategies required to use these resources and materials.

To construct this system requires the school to purchase various published materials appropriate for every combination of skill, sub-skill, level, channel of communication, medium, strategy and grouping for a defined target population. Thus, the question of what to purchase each year for a classroom is answered by the Taxonomy in relation to the pupils it serves — or more specifically, by the materials gap in the Taxonomy and the pupils' diagnosed needs.

ELIZABETH P. DAVEY

Special Needs of the Culturally Disadvantaged Reader in Corrective and Remedial Classes

Instruction should be individualized as far as possible; each child should be seen as unique. Yet, culturally disadvantaged children may be "more unique" than other children and therefore require a distinct type of treatment. Drawing from personal experiences, Davey delineates some of these major differences and proposes some ways of dealing with them.

Which needs of these children seem to you to be most detrimental? Which ones make diagnosis and instruction difficult or inaccurate? What approaches, materials, and teacher qualities are implied by these special needs? How does this discussion relate to Emeruwa's discussion of attributes of teachers of inner-city children in Part Four? to Edward's suggestions in the succeeding article in this section? to Johnson's "If It's Fun" later in this section?

Every student who comes to a reading clinic must be treated as an individual. His reading weaknesses and strengths have to be diagnosed carefully and remediation planned and carried out to meet his particular needs. In addition to his reading problems, each student has needs that are shared by all students: he desires acceptance, security, and success. We must plan his program in the double framework of both unique and common needs. The culturally disadvantaged student, however, usually has a third set of needs stemming from his background which must be considered in planning his instructional program. In this paper we will concentrate on plans for an instructional program which will take account of these needs.

Reprinted from *Meeting Individual Differences in Reading,* Supplementary Educational Monographs, No. 94, compiled and edited by H. Alan Robinson (December 1964), 133-136, by permission of The University of Chicago Press and the author. ©1964 by The University of Chicago Press.

DEVELOPING POSITIVE ATTITUDES
AND PRACTICAL MOTIVATIONS

Culturally disadvantaged students neither like nor hate school; they are simply indifferent to it. They have attended school without experiencing any personal involvement in its activities. Most of them have attended so many different schools that they feel no identification with any of them. The records of the fifty-seven culturally disadvantaged youngsters who were in our clinic (one of the eight clinics under the Chicago Board of Education) one semester show the average number of schools attended by each child to be three and one-half. Several students have attended as many as ten schools. They have not been in any school long enough to have developed a strong feeling or interest. Instead, they have developed an indifference to learning as they have moved from one school to another. The clinics to which such individuals come for special reading help often appear to them to be just one more school. It is important that their attitude of indifference be changed. The clinic staff should help students identify with it, to become interested in and involved with its work as their own particular enterprise.

The middle-class students who come to our clinic usually feel personal disgrace and often suffer emotionally over their inability to read well. The culturally disadvantaged students who come to the clinic, on the other hand, seldom show any of these feelings. They express little concern over their failure in reading. Their brothers, sisters, and friends have been no more successful. In their society, few learn to read well. When asked why reading has been difficult, middle-class students and their parents usually blame poor instruction, inadequate schools, childhood sicknesses, and similar circumstances. But the lower-class students, who are seldom accompanied by parents, almost invariably say simply, "I didn't get it." They make this statement without blaming the school and without expressing surprise or concern at their failure. This acceptance of failure, and the image of themselves as unable to learn to read, must be changed. They need to develop the belief that they are capable of learning to read. The special reading teacher must feel confident of his ability to help them as well as of their ability to learn. His confidence can change their hopeless indifference to a belief that they can learn to read. Students who attend the reading clinic do make better scores in reading tests; and if the new students are shown these tangible evidences of gains made by others from the same schools and neighborhoods, they will also be helped to build up their belief in their own potentialities and in the clinic as a place to learn.

They must be given reasons for learning to read which they can understand. They must see that reading is of immediate and practical importance to them. Reading for pleasure, or for information, or for self-development has little meaning or appeal to them; but reading for vocational reasons makes sense. Reading must be presented in relation to the real questions which they face. What do they want to be when they grow up? What are the requirements for the job they want? Materials, such as catalogues from the civil service agencies and even from the armed forces, describing job opportunities and requirements prove valuable. From these materials it becomes clear that reading is a skill essential for all the jobs in which they may be interested. The uses of reading in everyday life — reading advertisements, television guides, and newspapers — should also be pointed out. They readily get the idea that being able to read well is a matter of practical importance. Recently, when the heavyweight boxing champion was rejected for service in the U.S. Army, he said, in a television interview, that he was turned down because he couldn't do arithmetic. One of my students interpreted the matter as follows: "Cassius can't read. I used to miss all the arithmetic because I couldn't read the problems. Cassius needs reading help. The best fighter in the world ought to be able to read. How can he understand his contracts?"

But strengthening confidence and developing practical motivations for learning to read is not enough for these students. There are many kinds of personal, family, and social problems which stand in their way. These are not, however, matters with which the special reading teacher has the time or training to cope. The reading teacher who tries to be a parent, a social worker, or a psychologist will find he has no time left for the specific job he is qualified and trained to do — teaching students to read.

One difficulty which seems to be common to all culturally disadvantaged students is learning to cope with the language of most reading materials. Their simple speech patterns do not prepare them for the vocabularies and grammatical constructions they commonly encounter in books. The transition from the language of the streets to the language of books is difficult. In talking to each other, they say, for example, "Dick run good today. Dick run good yesterday. Dick run good tomorrow." Thus they must not only learn to read, but learn to read what is, for them, a different language. Utilizing some of the instructional methods of teachers of foreign languages is helpful: (1) oral reading by the teacher and students so that correct pronunciation, precise enunciation, and proper phrasing can be encouraged; (2) a study of grammar with emphasis on the conjugations of verbs, the uses of pronouns, and the differences between adjectives and adverbs (to mention only a few examples of the things that must be stressed); and (3) the use of machines to develop new language patterns. A simple and useful machine is the Language-Master (Bell & Howell). The student sees cards on which words are printed, hears them pronounced, and then repeats the words himself. He can compare his own performance with the model. Anything which will make the student more familiar with the language he is expected to read should be used.

A closely related area of need is vocabulary building. The culturally disadvantaged students have a meager stock of words; and what is even more serious, they show little curiosity about the structure, derivation, and meanings of words. Many ways of vocabulary building have been tried in the clinic with little success, until recently one approach was found which works well. Being culturally disadvantaged does not mean for these children that they are deprived of all contact with modern communication media. Apparently they are avid television fans, and in the programs they watch, they hear words which they consider important enough to deserve study. We ask students at the clinic to bring to class for study words that they have heard over television. They seem to be becoming more word-conscious through this approach, though the words we study are different from those in the usual vocabulary lists.

ENCOURAGING, REWARDING, AND MEASURING ACHIEVEMENT

All students who come to reading clinics need to experience success, but the culturally disadvantaged students require tangible evidences of their accomplishments to an unusual degree. The progress charts and other symbols of achievement in our clinic are often disliked by educators, and one wishes that successful reading would be a sufficient reward in itself for accomplishment; but these students crave for and respond to extrinsic rewards — stars, 100's and other symbols. In pursuing these symbols of accomplishment, they do develop the skills necessary for the types of reading that are intrinsically rewarding. Two points of caution, however, must be observed: (1) Rewards should be for achievement and not for effort alone. The temptation to reward a student for trying must be resisted. If effective reading skills are to be developed, only correct responses must be rewarded. (2) Encouraging direction toward harder tasks must be given constantly. Otherwise, a student will go on doing the same tasks, happily accumulating symbols of success, without a steady advancement in his reading ability.

It is often said that these students do not do well on standardized tests because they are poor test-takers. To the extent that this is true, it largely reflects a lack of motivation and a lack of experience in taking tests. Many students do not understand the uses and importance of tests in general and of those which determine academic or vocational advancement in particular. They give up quickly when the tests are long or difficult. The development of confidence and motivation for reading has to be carried over to the taking of the tests used to determine progress in reading. It is necessary to spend considerable time in explaining how the tests are designed to measure ability to recognize words, to measure comprehension of the meaning of words, sentences, and paragraphs, and to measure ability to relate and compare ideas. These explanations, with continuous emphasis on what may be called "test-taking techniques," such as deriving the meanings of words from their structure and from the context in which they are used, eliminating obviously wrong meanings, and drawing valid inferences from what is stated, help students to do better on tests and to form the habit of reading with conscious attention to the use of these skills. Always questioning them on their comprehension of a selection helps them form the habit of reading in anticipation of the questions which may be asked. The formation of this habit is a valuable preparation for the taking òf standardized reading tests.

CONCLUDING STATEMENTS

To help culturally disadvantaged students learn to read effectively, we must first motivate them to want to learn; we must build up their confidence in themselves as learners and in us as teachers. Special emphasis must be given to oral reading, language structure, and more particularly, to acquainting them with a language pattern which differs from their ordinary speech. We must use materials in which they find an immediate interest — materials which are concerned with the vocational and practical problems which they face. Finally, we must devote a great deal of attention to explaining the elements of comprehension which constitute effective reading and to helping them see how tests not only measure but may be used to improve their reading ability.

Allison Davis has said, "What we as teachers must always remember is that man is a learner. No matter how handicapped he may be, he still possesses the highest of human capacities, the ability to improve himself by learning. No man, woman, or child is ever so far down that, given the opportunity, he cannot learn his way up."[1] With Davis' injunction constantly in mind, we who are reading teachers must help the culturally disadvantaged see that learning to read effectively is a necessary first step to "improvement by learning." The development of this motivation through emphasis on the practical uses of reading should be our guide in choosing materials and finding ways to deal effectively with language problems, which are the fundamental ones, encountered by this group in learning to read.

---

[1] Allison Davis, "Society, the School and the Student," *Improving English Skills of Culturally Different Youth,* Office of Education Bulletin 1964, No. 5 (Washington, D.C.: U.S. Department of Health, Education, and Welfare, 1964), p. 21.

THOMAS J. EDWARDS

Language-Experience
Attack on Cultural Deprivation

Cultural deprivation not only severely limits reading achievement as Chandler pointed out in Part Two, but also affects perception, cognition, verbal fluency, and academic motivation — all of which, in a truly vicious circle, limit reading achievement. Edwards suggests that in cases of cultural deprivation it is not sufficient to deal with the reading problem alone; related factors must be recognized and treated concomitantly.

Do you agree with Edwards that the language-experience approach is effective at all grade levels? What are some possible outcomes of this approach? What are its shortcomings? Would it be equally effective at other socioeconomic levels? What components of reading might best be promoted this way? Which might be slighted? Can this approach provide for individual differences within a group of children?

Ever-increasing attention is currently being directed toward the student whose family and community background has not prepared him adequately to come to grips with the typical school curriculum. Evidence of this lack of readiness for academic success appears early in his school career, and his early frustrations, understandably, frequently lead to his becoming a school dropout.

PROBLEMS OF THE CULTURALLY DEPRIVED LEARNER

The problems discussed in the following sections are selected from an unquestionably broader array of problems and are

From *The Reading Teacher,* 18 (April 1965), pp. 546-551. Reprinted with permission of Thomas J. Edwards and the International Reading Association.

cited because they bear more directly than others upon the development of communication skills and upon general academic success.

Restricted Background of Experiences and Concepts. The child may not have traveled beyond the confines of his immediate neighborhood, and he is not likely to have derived a great amount of meaning from his experiences even in this restricted environment. No one has guided his perception of the things which he has experienced, and he has not had the opportunity to manipulate verbally his ideas about his experiences.

His adolescent or adult counterpart is also likely to demonstrate the same experiential poverty. True, he may have traveled over a somewhat larger geographical area but he, too, is not likely to have accumulated a significant amount of meaning from his experiences.

The important point is this: It is possible to have experience but for this experience to yield very little in terms of a significant body of meaning or concepts. Mere sensory contact is rarely enough. Rather, this contact must be accompanied by a kind of *directed* perception which will be consummated in the formation of meaningful concepts.

Cognitive Stagnation and the Challenge to Learn. A child who grows up in a severely depressed environment with poorly educated parents and peers is not likely to receive the kind of stimulation to think which would encourage him to flex his cognitive muscles. In a "rich" environment there is frequent dialogue, and language is thus used as the instrument for getting into the thinking processes of the child and stirring them up.

Present-day psychologists and educators are in rather general agreement on the point that cognitive power is quite likely to remain latent or dormant or become stagnant if it is not stimulated *(1, 6, 7, 10)*. Progress in the development of active, precise, and critical thinking ability tends to be slow, erratic, highly specialized, and limited essentially to the very primitive demands of a primitive and highly restrictive existence within depressed communities.

The psychological literature abounds with evidence to support the thesis that there is a disproportionately high number of low I.Q.'s among people from disadvantaged environments *(3, 4, 6, 7, 11, 12, 18)*. The "nature-nurture" debate has diminished considerably, however, since it is generally held that so-called tests of intelligence do in fact measure *functional* rather than *absolute* intellectual capacity. For this reason, responsible educators no longer treat the culturally deprived population as if they were afflicted with wholesale mental deficiency.

Oral Language Deficiency, Receptive and Expressive. His early language experience constitutes another strike against the culturally deprived student when he is confronted with the traditional middle-class curriculum. Generally, the disadvantaged learner comes from an environment in which either an entirely different language is spoken or from one in which a dialect of English is spoken which is at considerable variance with more standard regional dialects of general American English. He has therefore been exposed to a somewhat different system of speech sounds, to a different cultural idiom, to a modified system of labeling concepts (e.g., "tote" for "carry"), and to a system of syntax of considerable simplicity and one which orders words differently within a sentence *(2, 8, 12)*.

The specific language areas in which the disadvantaged student tends to be significantly penalized include auditory discrimination, vocabulary, and syntax. It might be well, then, to see exactly how each of these serves to militate against school success.

Auditory discrimination develops within a special environment in which a special system of speech sounds prevails. One becomes accustomed to hearing and reproducing these speech sounds, but when a new one obtrudes from an alien speech-sound system, there is a tendency toward *perceptual distortion* as one hears and reproduces it in accordance with its nearest equivalent within the more familiar speech-sound system.

This inaccurate perception and reproduction of standard American English speech hampers the culturally differentiated learner in his development of word-recognition skills: he has trouble associating printed symbols with their spoken counterparts because he has never really mastered their spoken counterparts *(5, 11)*. Since decoding is fundamental in learning the highly complex act of reading, the disadvantaged learner very often fails to master not only the basics of reading but also subsequent, more advanced aspects of reading.

Vocabulary problems are likely to relate most directly to the very meager repertoire of concepts which the disadvantaged student has been able to accumulate from his extremely restricted background *(11)*. Beyond this, many of the concepts which he has developed have been assigned special labels (i.e., words) which are unique within his own culture and hence, are not written into traditional curriculum materials *(2, 12)*. An additional vocabulary problem stems from the fact that for many of the concepts which he does have, he has no label at all, since he has not communicated very much about them with anyone *(8)*.

When he encounters a printed word form he has no referent already in his nervous system to which to relate either the *sound* or the *meaning* of this printed symbol. And when the density of unfamiliar words is too great — in either spoken or written learning situations — the linguistically disadvantaged learner is *really* at a disadvantage *(14, 15)*.

Syntax is the third problem area mentioned above. Here we find the sentence structure with which the disadvantaged child is familiar quite at variance with that of the sentences which he hears or tries to read in school *(2, 12)*. Both *word order* and *degree of complexity* of sentences — particularly in textbooks but also in the spoken language of teachers — are likely to overwhelm the disadvantaged student. This, then, represents both a listening and a reading comprehension problem to the disadvantaged learner trying to operate outside of his dialectical milieu.

ONE SOLUTION: THE LANGUAGE-EXPERIENCE APPROACH

The so-called language-experience approach has proved to be an extremely effective technique for approaching the multifaceted problem of culturally deprived students. Very often, unfortunately, its use is limited to very young children at the beginning stages of learning to read. It has been this writer's experience, however, that it works with outstanding effectiveness with adolescents who are potential dropouts, with functionally illiterate adults, in both individual and group situations, and even with illiterate peasants in Persian villages.

The language-experience approach is versatile, stimulating, informal, interesting, fun, and a real challenge to the alert teacher. In essence, it involves the teaching of an array of thinking and language skills in a discussion setting centering around a topic (preferably controversial!) which is anchored directly in the experiences and interests of the group. From the discussion emerges the subject matter which eventually provides the material for the development of skill in handling written language *(9, 13, 16, 17)*.

Array of Possible Skills. Among the multitude of skills which this approach yields are included the following: logical, organized, and critical thinking; oral language facility in terms of fluency, syntax, grammar, critical reasoning, pronunciation, spontaneity, and courteous discussion procedures; expanded background of concepts, coupled with appropriate vocabulary labels; auditory discrimination stemming from increased immersion in more standard general American English; word-recognition skills related to the quick grasp of total word configurations as well as to structural, phonetic, and semantic analysis of words; organizational skills as they apply to listening, speaking, reading, and writing; syntax mastery related both to the grasp of an author's sentence structure or to the structuring of the student's own sentences; composition in the sense both of the student's organizing an array of ideas into a cohesive paragraph or longer selection and also of following the idea arrangement within an author's composition; and reading and listening comprehension, both assimilative and critical.

Suggested Guidelines. The following are a few suggested principles or guidelines for using the language-experience approach. They may be modified and adapted to various age levels and experiential backgrounds, to available teaching aids and resource materials, to individual instruction or to groups of various sizes, and to the teacher's own background and temperament.

Although the language-experience approach is unusually flexible, two very basic considerations must be held inviolate: (1) The basic readiness problems of the culturally disad-

vantaged learner, discussed in earlier sections here, must be
kept in mind by the teacher and attended to before subsequent
learning is required and (2) the array of possible skills described
in the preceding section must be seen as the specific instructional goals of the method, and appropriate material must
be woven skillfully into the learning situation whenever an
opportunity presents itself.

1. Discussion topic. The topic around which the discussion
centers can be anything which is common to the interests and
experiences of the entire group. These may be ready-made
interests and experiences, or they may be ones which the
teacher creates either through planned experiences (e.g., field
trips, projects) or through vicarious experiences (e.g., reading
to the group, films, filmstrips).

2. Teacher's role. Essentially, the teacher's role should be
that of catalyst or devil's advocate to stimulate vigorous
discussion and controversy, a resource person to supply bits of
information missing from the background of the students,
discussion leader to provide reasonable order and logical
pursuit of ideas, and recorder of the mélange of ideas which
should be coming from the group.

3. Sequence. The sequence of steps involved in this approach can carry over for a number of days or even weeks,
subject to the discretion of the teacher. The first step is the
initiation of discussion within the group. (If teacher-created
experiences, such as field trips or projects are desirable, these
should precede the discussion, since they would provide the
topic for discussion.) During the discussion the teacher should
encourage differences of opinion, point out alternative ways of
looking at a given question, and check group members
whenever illogical reasoning becomes evident. The major goals
of this discussion phase are the stimulation of a high level of
motivation and participation, the grooming of logical and
precise thinking skills, and the development by the students of
an easy flow of spontaneous oral communication. At this point
the teacher should *not* stop students to correct grammar or
pronunciation. This might stifle spontaneity. As points are
crystalized at this discussion stage, the teacher records them on
the board without regard to organization.

It is preferable to select one member of the class to copy
what is recorded on the board at this and subsequent stages,

since board space is at a very high premium when this approach is used. Furthermore, it is well to provide each student with his own duplicated copy of the previous day's whole-group work from the board.

The second stage requires that the entire group discuss and decide on the organization in which the randomly recorded ideas are to be arranged. At this point the teacher can explain to the group in a highly functional setting both the logic and the mechanics of outlining. Members of the group should be encouraged to discuss alternative ways of ordering the ideas, giving their reasons, with the teacher guiding the group finally to select the best arrangement.

The third stage involves the construction of paragraphs from the outline which was developed from the initially random ideas. With each student provided with his own copy of the class outline, the group can begin to convert the items in the outline into sentences. Again, very functional use is being made of reading at this point as students refer to their outlines. And much can be taught at this stage about syntactical order and grammar as the final selection is made from among a number of proposed sentences. In addition, the teacher should be alert to the group's need for a new, more precise word to express an idea. Such new words should be supplied by the teacher with appropriate attention given to pronunciation, meaning, syllabication, and spelling.

As the teacher records student sentences on the board and paragraphs evolve, every opportunity should be seized to read them aloud and to have the students read them as they are being discussed.

The final stage involves silent reading of the entire selection after it has been completed and duplicated, followed by oral rereading. Again, each student should have his own copy. His silent reading should be greatly facilitated by the amount of exposure which he has had to each word as the initial random flow of ideas was recorded, followed by the construction of the outline and then the paragraphs. This silent reading serves to reinforce word perception and insure rewarding fluent subsequent oral rereading.

A variety of follow-up activities can be pursued after the whole-group composition has been completed and read by the entire class. For example, students might be asked to take turns giving verbal summaries of each paragraph as an exercise in abstracting the essence and compressing it verbally. Further, the class might be broken down into small groups or pairs, with one student dictating paragraphs from the class composition for the others to write. This will provide motor reinforcement of word-perception and also identify spelling needs. Each student can locate his own spelling errors, make a list of the correct spellings and learn them. Careful visualization, pronunciation, syllabication, and writing practice should be encouraged during these spelling activities.

As still another follow-up activity, students might write independently about additional ideas which they might have on the topic of the whole-group composition. Major attention during this writing activity should be upon the generation and organization of ideas. Points of syntax, grammar, spelling, or other mechanics should be postponed until the entire first draft is completed. The procedure followed previously during the composition of the whole-group selection should be replicated by individual students: initial random free flow of ideas, organization into an outline, and then the construction of paragraphs.

The interest generated during the discussion of the composition topic might entice some students to do follow-up independent reading in the same area. This can lead students to learn to use the library to locate books or to use reference materials. In connection with this independent reading, note taking and summarizing can be taught very functionally, and students might also be encouraged to outline the main points of what they have read and use their outlines as a basis for oral reports to the entire class.

With the background deficiencies and specific learning needs of the culturally disadvantaged student clearly and constantly in mind, any conscientious teacher can use this language-experience approach effectively to reverse the effects of cultural deprivation and arm the discouraged student with increased language facility, learning potential, and academic self-confidence.

REFERENCES

1. Deutsch, Martin. "The Disadvantaged Child and the Learning Process: Some Social, Psychological, and Developmental Considerations." Paper presented at Ford Foundation work conference on curriculum and teaching in depressed urban areas, Teachers College, Columbia University, July, 1962.

2. Dominic, R. Thomas. "Oral Language Sentence Structure and Vocabulary of Kindergarten Children Living in Low Socio-Economic Urban Areas." Unpublished doctoral dissertation, Wayne State University, 1961.

3. Eells, Kenneth. *Intelligence and Cultural Difference.* Chicago: University of Chicago Press, 1951.

4. Haggard, E. A. "Social Status and Intelligence," *Genetic Psychology Monographs,* 49 (1954), 141-186.

5. Harrington, Sister Mary James, and Donald D. Durrell, "Mental Maturity versus Perception Abilities in Primary Reading," *Journal of Educational Psychology,* 46 (Oct. 1955), 375-380.

6. Hebb, Donald O. *Organization of Behavior.* New York: John Wiley & Sons, 1949.

7. Hunt, J. McV. *Intelligence and Experience.* New York: Ronald Press, 1961.

8. Kress, Roy A., Jr. "An Investigation of the Relationship Between Concept Formation and Achievement in Reading," *Dissertation Abstracts,* 16 (Mar. 1956), 573-574. (Temple University, 1955.)

9. Lamoreaux, Lillian, and Doris Lee. *Learning to Read Through Experience.* New York: Appleton-Century-Crofts, 1943.

10. Miner, J. B. *Intelligence in the United States.* New York: Springer, 1957.

11. Nila, Sister Mary, O.S.F. "Foundations of a Successful Reading Program," *Education,* 73 (May, 1953), 543-555.

12. Sexton, Patricia. *Education and Income.* New York: Viking Press, 1961.

13. Smith, Charles A. "The Experience Method in Beginning Reading," *Elementary School Journal,* 38 (Oct. 1937), 96-106.

14. Smith, Henry P. *Psychology in Teaching Reading.* Englewood Cliffs, N.J.: Prentice-Hall, 1961.

15. Smith, Nila B. "Readiness for Reading, II," *Elementary English,* 27 (Feb. 1950), 91-106.

16. Smith, Nila B. *Reading Instruction for Today's Children.* Englewood Cliffs, N.J.: Prentice-Hall, 1963.

17. Spache, George D. *Toward Better Reading.* Champaign, Ill.: Garrard Publishing Co., 1962.

18. Taba, Hilda, "Cultural Deprivation as a Factor in School Learning," *Merrill-Palmer Quarterly,* 10 (Apr. 1964), 147-159.

19. Whipple, Gertrude. "The Culturally and Socially Deprived Reader," *Supplementary Educational Monograph,* No. 92. Chicago: Chicago University Press, December, 1962.

JOAN STAPLES

Using Special Modes of Learning to Improve Reading Instruction in Corrective and Remedial Classes

The question of whether some people learn better through one sensory mode than through another has long been of interest to psychologists and educators. Historically we have acted as though the answer is "no." If the answer is "yes," then we must adapt diagnosis and instruction to these individual differences. Staples presents both rationale and specific suggestions for carrying out such an individualized program.

How good are our diagnostic procedures for discovering such differences? Are deficient modes to be neglected while superior ones are capitalized on? What role may environment play in determining the superiority of one mode over another? In the long run, what mode of learning is of greatest significance in learning to read? How does this article relate to others in this book, such as Storer and Colton's in Part Four and Cohen's earlier in this section?

Several tests have been used in the University of Chicago Reading Clinic to help identify modes of learning. Among these are the Primary Form of the *Monroe Reading Aptitude Tests* (Houghton Mifflin Co., 1935), the Intermediate Form of the *Monroe-Sherman Group Diagnostic Reading Aptitude and Achievement Tests* (C. H. Nevins Printing Co., 1939), the *Gates Associative Learning Tests,* [1] and the revised edition of the

---

Reprinted from *Meeting Individual Differences in Reading,* Supplementary Educational Monographs, No. 94, compiled and edited by H. Alan Robinson (December 1964), pp. 45-48, by permission of The University of Chicago Press and the author. © 1964 by The University of Chicago Press.

[1] No longer published, but xeroxed copies are available from Publications of the Reading Clinic, Dept. of Psychology, College of Liberal Arts, Temple University, Philadelphia. Description of tests may be found in Arthur I. Gates, *The Improvement of Reading* (3d ed., New York: Macmillan Co., 1947).

Learning Methods Tests by Mills (Mills Educational and Testing Center, 1955). Harris and Roswell have developed suggestions for using miniature sample lessons as a diagnostic procedure,[2] but their test is not being used in the clinic. In addition, the *Huelsman Word Discrimination Test* (Alumni Association, Miami University, 1958) and Wepman's *Auditory Discrimination Test* (Language Research Associates, 1958) are used. Several of these tests are designed to evaluate aptitudes, that is, they are concerned with the student's abilities in certain areas before he has been taught to read. The Monroe-Sherman test is an example of an aptitude test. Other tests are achievement tests, that is, they evaluate what the student has already learned about reading. The Huelsman test is an example of this type.

Some of these tests suffer from serious imperfections. For example, the Monroe-Sherman copying test, presumably a motor test, is easier for those children who are able to read and / or hold a visual image. The language or vocabulary section of this test, consisting of groups of four pairs of words, one of which is correct in meaning, uses such words as "coin ropes, coin money, coin monkey, coin cobs," which require adequate auditory discrimination as well as understanding of word meanings. The *Gates Associative Learning Tests* are no longer available and are questioned by Gates himself. We have been experimenting with them to see to what extent they may help us predict the rate of progress a child is likely to make when given appropriate instruction. The *Learning Methods Test* by Mills must be administered over a period of at least five days and cannot, therefore, be used during a one-day diagnosis. At the clinic we are now engaged in adapting the Mills test to the one-day diagnostic situation. Harris' test combines several modes within one method in two of the sample lessons: word family and visual-motor. At the present time, an alert and sensitive clinician or teacher who understands how children learn and who can use a variety of techniques is probably one of the best diagnostic tools we have.

---

[2] Albert J. Harris, *How to Increase Reading Ability* (New York: Longmans, Green & Co., Inc., 1961), pp. 214-17.

PRINCIPLES FOR INSTRUCTION USING SPECIAL MODES OF LEARNING

The following principles for selecting and applying various modes of learning should be kept in mind:

1. Every individual is truly a unique learner. Although some methods are applicable to many students, a given individual probably combines his learning modes in ways quite unique to him. We cannot enter within a student, but our awareness of his individuality may prevent a rash diagnosis. Particular problems may appear to retard reading development in one person, but the same problems may have little or no influence on the reading ability of another. For example, Stanley Krippner describes a four-year-old boy who was a fluent and avid reader but who failed a reading-readiness test because his visual-motor skills were not comparable to those of a six-year-old. [3]

2. If a student appears to learn better by one modality than another, instruction should usually emphasize the introduction of new material through the stronger modality while strengthening the weaker modalities through "readiness" activities. An example of this technique is given by Bernadine Schmidt, who used such activities as the imitation of sounds and sound demonstrations of words and phrases and the introduction of phonetic elements by radio, preceded by oral explanations, to introduce new material to children who were primarily auditory learners. [4] She provided for transfer to visual learning by means of practice activities such as matching words and phrases with pictures, matching words with similar configurations, and selecting printed synonyms.

In some cases it is preferable to work with the weaker modality. To make such judgments, the student's total situation must be taken into consideration and specialists consulted if necessary.

3. Although it is often difficult to separate the various modes of learning for particular words or other reading skills, a

---

[3] Stanley Krippner, "The Boy Who Read at Eighteen Months," *Exceptional Children,* XXX (November, 1963), 105-9.

[4] Bernadine G. Schmidt, "Auditory Stimuli in the Improvement of Reading," *Elementary English Review,* XVIII (April 1941), 149-54. See also Schmidt, "Teaching the Auditory Learner to Read," *Chicago Schools Journal,* XIX (May-June, 1938), 208-11.

single mode should be emphasized, and the student should be given sufficient time to profit from the use of one mode before trying another. However, the teacher must remain flexible in this matter.

4. Whatever mode is emphasized, organization, structure, and consistency should be considered.

5. The timing of methods and activities must be suitable for the individual student's needs.

6. Mode may be cultural and experiential as well as constitutional. For example, Frank Riessman suggests that "culturally deprived" children are oriented toward physical and visual learning rather than aural learning.[5] Sandra Thunander, a student at the University of Chicago, testing the use of various modalities to improve the vocabulary of high-school students, suggests that such students' long experience with visual learning may make the use of other modalities of limited value in improving understanding of word meanings.

7. Much understanding of individual modes of learning can be gained through the student's own insight into his learning process. Students should be encouraged to develop and verbalize such insight.

8. Each activity should have a purpose commensurate with the student's needs in reading and his mode of learning. Gadgets and devices for their own sake should not be used.

9. Walters and Kosowski have suggested that such factors as need for incentive and/or reward and a reduced ability to attend to stimuli may affect a retarded reader's ability to use various modes of learning.[6] They have also found that the retarded reader tends to be less stable in his reaction to learning. The reading teacher might consider these findings in planning instruction for his students.

SUGGESTIONS FOR INSTRUCTION USING VARIOUS MODES OF LEARNING

Various sense modalities can be used in all aspects of reading. Gray, among others, suggests that children learn to glance at

---

[5] Frank Riessman, *The Culturally Deprived Child* (New York: Harper & Bros., 1962).

[6] Richard Walters and Irene Kosowski, "Symbolic Learning and Reading Retardation," *Journal of Consulting Psychology*, XXVII (February, 1963), 75-82.

the full length and general configuration of an unfamiliar word to determine the easiest method of analysis. Familiar parts or syllables of words may be learned by sight through such games as Dolch's *Syllable Solitaire* (Garrard Press). Dolch produced other games that use a visual approach, such as *Popper Words* (Garrard Press) and the *Group Word Game* (Garrard Press). Resourceful teachers can devise similar activities using pictures or context to promote the identification and retention of words.

Accurate articulation and auditory discrimination are desirable before formal phonetic training is attempted. Trunella Stewart, an Illinois classroom teacher, has drawn up an excellent list of activities to improve auditory discrimination. Among them are games such as "Which Is It?"; pairs of words that sound alike are chosen (sweaters, feathers) and then are used in a riddle type construction, such as, "Which grow on chickens? Sweaters? Feathers?" and so on. Or in the game of "Grocery Store" one child might say: "My father owns a grocery store and he sells potatoes." The next child must say potatoes and add another word beginning with *p* (peaches, peas, etc.). This game may be used for practicing a variety of sounds and sound combinations.

The ability to apply phonetic skills by associating the visual element with its sound or sounds as well as blending sounds is often neglected when the emphasis has been on drill of sounds and phonetic generalizations in isolation. Giving the child practice in letting his voice slide from one sound to another is advocated by Marion Monroe. The initial consonant sound may be pronounced with its following vowel and the final consonant sound then added. Both of these activities improve blending ability by helping the student to eliminate extraneous "uh" sounds, thereby making the sounding process as natural as possible. It should be made clear that sounding "bad" as "ba-d" does not mean that students should drill on such syllables as "ba," "da," "fa," "fe," "fu," and the like. The clue to the vowel sound is often at the end of the word rather than at the beginning, and such drill emphasizes meaningless ritual rather than constructive application of knowledge.

Tape recording may also be used for auditory practice and evaluation of word recognition. Reading teachers have adapted Fernald's technique by using sand, sandpaper, or tracing paper for kinesthetic tracing. The chalkboard may be used for tracing and writing activities; the child should be encouraged to use his whole body in his work at the board. Typing and the manipulation of plastic or wooden letters may help a kinesthetic-tactile learner.

For students of all ages, either direct or vicarious experience is essential for the understanding of words. Many children and young people already have experiences from which to generalize word meanings. But the teacher can construct situations to promote meaning. For example, a word such as "furnace" may be clarified by a visit, picture, or film, which are primarily visual experiences. Action words such as "saunter" may be role-played, a kinesthetic experience. More abstract words such as "courage" or "generosity" may be learned through wide reading, films, paintings, sculpture, recorded stories, drama, and music.

Comprehension of sentences may be taught by attention to the rhythmic qualities of both poetry and prose. A visual study of the grammatical structure of a sentence and the meaning of punctuation marks can aid comprehension. Drama is active and social in its appeal to retarded readers, and the reading of drama frequently helps students to become less self-conscious about reading. It is also a purposeful situation for oral reading. Tape recordings of radio plays, including sound effects by students, often bring interesting results. Some of the plays may be made into puppet shows after the reading has been evaluated and improved. Several collections of plays are available.[7] Commercial recordings of stories and plays may help an auditory learner.

Such visual devices as films, slides, diagrams, pictures, and maps may bring vicarious experiences to students. Maps are a great help in aiding the comprehension of adults who may be reading on the junior-high-school level, for example, with limited geographical and historical knowledge, but with an interest in current affairs and the newspaper.[8] Models and

---

[7] Fan Kissen, *The Straw Ox* (New York: Houghton Mifflin Co., 1948) (the first of a series of radio plays for children reading on the third, fourth, and fifth grade levels); Donald Durrell and B. Alice Crossley, *30 Plays for Classroom Reading* (Boston: Plays, Inc., 1957) (plays for intermediate grades with suggestions for expressive and interpretive reading); Lawrence Feigenbaum, *Radio and Television Plays* (new York: Globe Book Co., Inc., 1956).

[8] The C. S. Hammond Company, Maplewood, New Jersey, publishes inexpensive atlases including such titles as *My First World Atlas, Comparative World Atlas, Historical Atlas,* and *American History Atlas.*

concrete objects are both visual and tactile. Field trips may combine learning through all sense modalities. One reading teacher, Mattie McDonald, of Dayton, Ohio, uses a science room to make reading meaningful to young people. Science experiments and experiences are used to provide direct experience utilizing the various sense modalities. She plans activities within this room that will facilitate learning by children primarily through the visual, auditory, or kinesthetic-tactile modes of learning.

CONCLUDING STATEMENT

We have considered the identification and use of special modes of learning to improve reading instruction in corrective and remedial classes. Perhaps some day we may be able to use such differentiated instruction much earlier so that reading difficulties can be prevented.

LEO M. SCHELL

How to Prevent and Correct
Word Identification Problems

There seems to be no reading problem so perpetual, pervasive, and paralyzing as inadequate word identification skills. No words on paper can tell a teacher how to teach; they can only provide stimulation and ideas that must be implemented by the teacher as she works with children. The author presents an overview of some of the more serious word identification problems and some specific suggestions for dealing with them, and hopes readers of this book will apply them in their own teaching.

How systematic are we generally in requiring of ourselves that children master essential words and skills? What material, other than that listed, have you found successful for teaching these fundamental skills? How serious do you believe confused words are? Why do you believe the author is not as specific about which phonic skills to teach and how to teach them as he was about sight words? (For more information on materials to teach these skills, refer to Storer and Colton's list in Part Four of this book.) To what extent do you believe use of the PPAR cycle could help decrease the number of children with word identification problems?

The two biggest problems that teachers face in corrective or remedial situations are (1) small and unreliable sight vocabulary and (2) deficient and inconsistent word-attack skills. All teachers, classroom or remedial, should be cognizant of some basic ways of coping with them.

An original article written for this book by Leo M. Schell.

SIGHT WORDS

Words from three different sources must be recognized quickly and accurately if anything resembling true reading is to occur. These sources are the basal reader, content field textbooks, and service words.

Teachers should make lists of words that pupils, individually or corporately, *repeatedly* miss when reading orally from a basal reader. Specific review time should be provided regularly for concentrated practice on these words, using one or more of the approaches mentioned below.

Some words in content field textbooks are so common that students should recognize them without hesitation. Examples of these words are shown below.

Mathematics — *length, numbers, many, less*

Social Studies — *country, president, forest*

Science — *experiment, electricity, temperature, liquid*

These words can be handled in the same manner as basal words. However, technical or infrequently occurring words such as *acre, plateau, asteroids, oxygen,* and *minuend* should not be considered essential and worthy of review.

Some words, because they occur so frequently in all kinds of material, must be recognized instantly and without confusion if the child is to read independently beyond basal and content field textbooks. Two valuable lists of such service words are Dolch's 220 "Basic Sight Vocabulary" words and Fry's 600 "Instant Words." Dolch's list can be found in the following books:

Dolch, E. W., *Psychology and Teaching of Reading,* Garrard Press, 1951, 507-8.

Dolch, E. W., *Teaching Primary Reading,* Garrard Press, 1960, 255.

Erickson, A. G., *Handbook for Teachers of Disabled Readers,* Sernoll, 1966, 63.

Roswell, F., and Natchez, G., *Reading Disability,* Basic Books, 1964, 239.

Zintz, M. V., *Corrective Reading,* William C. Brown, 1966, 42.

A revision of Dolch's list can be found in:

Johnson, Dale D., "The Dolch List Re-examined," *Reading Teacher,* 24
   (Feb., 1971), 449-57.

Fry's list can be found in the following:

Fry, E., "Word List for Remedial Reading," *Elementary English,*
   November, 1957; 456-58.
Erickson, A. G., *Handbook for Teachers of Disabled Readers*
Schell, L. M., and Burns, P. C., *Remedial Reading: Classroom and
   Clinic,* 2d ed., Allyn and Bacon, 1972. (See Part Four of this an-
   thology — *Editor)*

Children with sight-vocabulary problems need to be tested on
these service words, and appropriate remediation should be
started for any words that are unknown or on which there is
hesitation.

Which Approaches to Use?

Three basic approaches can be used to help children remember
words with which they have problems. These, in rank order for
treating mild to severe problems, are (1) oral rereading, (2)
supplementary practice, and (3) a visual-motor approach.

Troublesome words may be focused on after a basal
selection or context-field passage has been read silently by
asking children to read orally sentences containing these words.
(This procedure assumes the teacher knows or can guess those
words which may present more than average memory
problems.) Prevention, not correction, is the key attribute of
this procedure; it will not help the child who habitually confuses
fill and *full* or who never remembers *that.*

With some children, memory is so unreliable that mere
reseeing is insufficient to embed the visual image deeply enough
for unhesitating recall at a later time. These children must have
their attention focused on a printed symbol while saying or
trying to recall its oral equivalent. For these children, essential
supplementary practice may be provided in at least three ways:
worksheets, games and activities, and tachistoscopic practice.

Three levels of worksheets are possible. The lowest level
would provide as many context clues as possible. For example,
pupils confusing *want* and *went* could work a sheet such as the
following:

WANT   WENT

1. Tom_____to school.
2. Did Rover_____to go?
3. Who_____with Tom?

This worksheet forces the child to write each word while saying it and thus helps him remember minor details in the appearance of the word.

A somewhat more difficult level includes words presented in isolation with some kind of contextual clue such as an illustration or a categorical name.

1. plane   plate   car
2. truck   train   trick

The most difficult level would include rows of words from which children would select and underline those said by the teacher. Obviously, these exercises can be varied in level of difficulty to match the capability of the children.

Write the words that belong together.

Animals		*Buildings*		*Actions*
walk	horse	jump	run	house
fish	school	store	bird	throw

Children who need to study a word before finally recalling its oral equivalent can frequently profit from work with a tachistoscope, of which there are three common kinds. One is homemade from oak tag, has a hand-operated shutter, and should be operated by the teacher. Directions for making two different kinds can be found in the following books:

Bond, G. L., and Tinker, M., *Reading Difficulties,* Appleton-Century-Crofts, 1968, 313.

Durrell, D. D., *Improvement of Basic Reading Abilities,* Harcourt, Brace, and World, 1956, 177.

One advantage of commercial tachistoscopes is that they can be operated by the pupil. And, as with homemade ones, motivation is high and attention excellent. The most widely used model is the *Flash-X*, manufactured by Educational Development Laboratory (EDL), Huntington, New York, which also has extensive word lists at different grade levels to fit into a hand-held device. Most filmstrip projectors can be converted into tachistoscopes by a special attachment with variable speed shutter, or a card held in front of the lens can serve the same purpose. Some suitable filmstrips (and their producers) follow:

The Society for Visual Education (Chicago)
  Speed-i-o Strip Series (10 strips)
  Graded Word Phrases (56 strips)

Learning Through Seeing (Sunland, California)
  Word Mastery (12 strips)
  Phrase Mastery (12 strips)
  Instant Words & Word Phrases (48 strips)

A last resort for children unable to remember words from memory is some kind of a visual-motor approach in which the child traces a word after scrutinizing it intensely. Bond and Tinker discuss several different tracing procedures and conclude that such methods are of primary value to the severely disabled reader and should be used in conjunction with other methods. Harris recommends adaptation of a tracing system and states that it has been highly successful in his Queens College reading clinic. Readers interested in finding out more about this procedure may examine the following:

Bond, G. L., and Tinker, M., *Reading Difficulties,* 471-80.

Harris, A. J., *How to Increase Reading Ability,* McKay, 1970, 353-56.
Otto, W., and McMenemy, R., *Corrective and Remedial Teaching,* Houghton Mifflin, 1966, 166-68.

Roswell, F., and Natchez, G., *Reading Disability,* 82-83.

Attention is called to the fact that the lowest level of worksheet suggested earlier uses a modified visual-motor approach, and the suggestions for coping with severe cases of word confusion on the following pages embody elements of such an approach also. When we consider that much of spelling contains parts of this procedure, it becomes obvious that the approach is a practical way of preventing many sight recognition problems and deserves widespread use in the primary grades.

Even though these three basic approaches provide additional practice for children with problems, all three should be buttressed and supplemented by a painless approach too often overlooked by teachers addicted to the idea of intensive work as the only solution to distinct problems. This painless approach is independent reading of easy and pleasurable material. A book matched to the child's appropriate reading level will, of necessity, repeat many of the words the child has trouble remembering. If selected by the child, it will hold his attention, force him to try to understand it, and demand that he read each word rather than skip or substitute words. Primary-grade teachers have repeatedly reported that independent reading plays too small a role in their total reading program. For many children, perhaps, extensive use of artificial and contrived games, devices, and activities is unnecessary; a natural situation may better provide the necessary review while concomitantly exposing children to quality literature.

What Special Problems to Expect?

Children with a small, unreliable sight vocabulary typically have two special problems: (1) they confuse words of similar configuration and (2) they have exceptional trouble remembering small words with highly abstract meanings.

Almost all children tend to identify a word by looking at the first or last letter of a word while paying little attention to the medial letters. This overreliance on word configuration is the primary cause of children confusing *full, fill, fall; wander, wonder; scare, score;* and numerous other highly similar-appearing words. Teachers have some control over one factor that may contribute to this problem. That is the typical phonics program in basal readers, which introduces initial and final consonant letter sounds early in the sequence but postpones vowel letter sounds until second grade. Vowel letters are almost always the cause of confused words; consonant letters rarely are. It may be that earlier introduction of medial vowel letter sounds might help children focus attention on the internal parts of words, thus preventing later problems. But, just as inoculation does not help children already afflicted with a disease, preventive suggestions do not help pupils already suffering from word confusion; corrective measures are required.

Authorities agree that children with this problem should be presented with situations that demand that they visually scrutinize words that are minimally different, rather than merely relying on the *gestalt* of the word. A sample exercise follows:

We went for a ride in a ＿＿＿＿＿＿.
                                     beet boat.
Then we ＿＿＿＿＿home.
            came come

Following are two excellent sources of practical ideas for practice exercises:

Bond, G. L., and Tinker, M. *Reading Difficulties,* 324-27 and 342-44.
Wilson, R. M., *Diagnostic and Remedial Reading,* Charles E. Merrill, 1967, 127-29.

Not only are there more words highly similar in configuration than we generally realize, but many of these have abstract meanings that seem to compound the problem many children have of remembering them. For example, *there, their, then, these,* and *those* are repeatedly confused or not remembered, as are *on, no, own, how, now,* and *won* and *where, when, were, ever, even,* and *every.* Wilson, the only major author who specifically discusses this common problem, suggests that since these words derive meaning almost totally from context, they should be taught only in context. He recommends three ways to teach these in context: (1) composing an experience story, (2) drilling on prepared phrase cards, and (3) constructing sentences from word cards (4:129-31). The experience story seems equally appropriate as a preventive and as a corrective measure and should be seriously considered by primary-grade teachers. Brown and Loper note that self-illustrated picture cards can be used by a child to build a sight vocabulary even though no publisher could get away with pictures as ambiguous as those children would produce. But, they ask, what difference does it make as long as "the child's illustrations make sense to him — and he learns the words"? (2:94-95)

With severe cases of word confusion, instruction should be as simplified as possible. Teachers should focus on one word at a time and proceed by small steps from easy to more difficult learnings. The following suggested procedure should be adapted to each child's problems and capabilities.

1. Have child *trace* the word.
2. Have child *copy* the word.
   a. from a model.

    b. from memory.
3. Have child *match* the word with similar words.
    a. simultaneously (*while* looking at the confused word).
    b. successively (*after* looking at the confused word).
4. Have child *read* the word in context.
5. Have child *pronounce* the word in isolation.
    a. untimed.
    b. flashed.

After the child has mastered two confused words individually by this procedure, two or more steps can be added to assure absolute mastery.

6. Present two or more similar (confused) words in context to be read orally.
7. Present two or more similar (confused) words in isolation to be pronounced.

Comments

Even children who have no problems learning to read require numerous presentations of words to reach memorization mastery. The procedures mentioned above are merely different ways of repeating the words children have difficulty remembering. Three things seem evident about the repetition of words and the approaches: (1) It seems reasonable that if a child has failed to learn to remember a word by one procedure, correction should not be based solely on the repeated use of that procedure. A change, possibly tentative and temporary, is in order. (2) With children requiring an unusually large number of word repetitions, variety is essential. Several of the described approaches should be used to alleviate monotony and to maintain interest in learning. (3) Even though word repetition is usually successful, mere repetition is insufficient. Children need a variety of ways other than sheer memory for attacking an unrecognized word. The more weapons a child has to attack an "enemy," the shorter the battle, the fewer the casualties, and the surer the victory. Beginning or disabled readers need a whole arsenal of weapons, and teachers who fail to teach phonic and structural analysis, context clues, and dictionary usage are merely handing the child a pop gun while requiring him to storm an enemy stronghold.

PHONIC AND STRUCTURAL ANALYSIS

How to determine which phonic and structural analysis elements to teach and when to teach them is a real and practical problem. For most classroom teachers, an essential tool in answering these questions is the skills chart accompanying the basal reader or in the local curriculum guide. After determining the child's appropriate instructional level, the teacher can use this outline to see what skills were (or should have been) introduced previously and at what level they were taught. This chart provides a rough idea of the skills on which the child most likely is deficient and gives some general clues as to the sequence in which these skills should be taught. Further testing and observation can refine these initial judgments and help zero in on the most deficient and crucial skills. Similar guides can be found in the following sources:

Edward Fry, "A Frequency Approach to Phonics," *Elementary English,* 41, (November, 1964), 759-65.

Bagford, J., *Phonics: Its Role in Teaching Reading,* Sernoll, 1967.

Gray, W. S., *On Their Own in Reading,* Scott, Foresman, 1960.

Heilman, A. W., *Phonics in Proper Perspective,* Charles E. Merrill, 1968.

Without such references, few teachers know the skills taught at earlier levels that must be retaught in a corrective or remedial situation. Thus, such resources play a fundamental role in any remediation program.

How Much Should Be Taught and How?

A fourth grader capable of grade-level reading but performing at a low second-grade level is so far behind, lacks so many skills, and presents so many classroom problems that the temptation is great to present all the missing skills in a short period of time to boost him to his potential level. But if such a temptation prevails, the skills will probably only be presented, not learned. McCullough warned against this temptation by noting, "Rabbits don't become kangaroos by eating carrots faster." (3:4)

It is easy to assume that children with reading skill deficiencies have been malnourished on a meager diet of sight words and have not had a rich, balanced diet of varied word attack skills. Such is usually not the case. Rather, they probably have been presented three balanced, but skimpy, meals daily and have only picked at these and never really cleaned up their plates and have never asked for, or been given, seconds! They require regular meals with large, balanced portions — eaten slowly and thoroughly digested. One way to assure digestion is to use the PPAR cycle, which simply means that one element or principle is *presented, practiced, applied,* and *reviewed* before another one is introduced. Corrective and remedial readers have myriad unrelated bits and pieces of word attack skills floating about in their memory that they are unable to use because they never really gained mastery in applying them in realistic situations. Using the PPAR cycle of skills instruction should transform the unintelligible into the usable by assuring mastery of one element or principle before introduction of another.

In the PPAR cycle, practice should be in a situation structured to assure a maximum degree of success; ease, not difficulty, and definiteness, not ambiguity, should characterize such exercises. Just as we deliberately select reading materials guaranteed to minimize frustration, so should we choose or design practice activities to do the same. Worksheets and other practice activities should be judged by standards similar to those used in an informal reading inventory to determine the proper level of reading materials.

"Mrs. Smith, what's this word?" is a persistent litany in many classrooms and the ubiquitous response is, "Johnny, we worked just yesterday on how to sound out words like that." Phonic elements recently presented and practiced just are not (can't be?) applied. A prime cause of this difficulty may be that practice, of necessity, occurs in an artificial situation, usually on a worksheet or a similar exercise, and there is little or no carry-over of this learning to actual reading situations. Teachers should repeatedly show pupils how learned skills can be used in reading. In introducing words prior to reading a selection, the teacher can select words that embody recently studied elements or principles and ask pupils how they were able to figure out the pronunciations. After reading a selection, the teacher can list, or have pupils find, words that can be attacked using newly learned skills. Not only should this procedure encourage children to actually use their knowledge, but it should also promote their feeling of independence and confidence — major components in reading success. Thus, two birds with one stone.

Children deficient in word attack skills need more than normal repetition and practice to attain satisfactory competency. Varied repetition is highly important for the sake of both learning and motivation. To meet the wide range of individual learning modalities and to reduce the drudgery of what could be boring, repetitive drill, media of all kinds should supplement textual materials. Games, filmstrips, transparencies, audio records and tapes, and programmed materials are all available for providing practice with word attack skills. The best bibliographies of such materials and ideas follow:

Dechant, E., *Diagnosis and Remediation of Reading Disabilities,* Parker, 1968, ch. 7.

Schubert, D. G., and Torgerson, T. L., *Improving Reading through Individualized Correction,* W. C. Brown, 1968, 86-121.

Spache, G. D., *Good Reading for Poor Readers,* Garrard Press, 1970, ch. 7.

An integral part of the PPAR cycle should be periodic, cumulative review of several elements. The memory of the average child is faulty, subject to partial forgetting and inconsistent performance even under the most fortuitous circumstances, so it is not surprising that problem readers respond identically. For best retention, these reviews should stress the application of elements or principles by using unknown words. Reusing words from prior practices facilitates mere recall, a lower level cognitive behavior than application of knowledge. Unknown words more truly correspond to realistic situations children will face in which they must figure out a new word independently. Psychology has unanimously affirmed that the more practice situations resemble use situations, the better the learning will function in the use situations. Ignoring so fundamental a principle only impedes mastery and attests to slovenly, unprofessional teaching.

Undoubtedly, the inconsistent phoneme-grapheme relationship in English spelling is one cause of children's inability to apply word attack skills consistently. One way to have children use these skills in a functional situation is to have them practice in materials containing phonemically regular words, that is, material in which words such as *come, are, once,* and *have* are intentionally omitted or their occurrence is strictly controlled. Most linguistic readers can be used or adapted for this purpose. Some publishers of such readers are Harper and Row; Harcourt, Brace and World; Charles E. Merrill; Science Research Associates; and D. C. Heath. Following are materials written expressly for this use:

Phonics in Rhyme, Teaching Technology, 1967.
Phonic Readers, Wenkart, 1961.
Easy Road to Reading Improvement Series, Marand, 1966.

Concluding Comments

Individual word attack skills cannot function in isolation. Initial consonant letters can be sounded accurately without sounding the following vowel letter; there is no sense in syllabicating a word if the reader can't blend the parts together; and syllabication may produce only unintelligible jibberish without correct accentuation. Since all these skills must work together, instruction cannot focus only on one skill without incidentally incorporating several other facets. The only time skills can be isolated is in a textbook on reading instruction. Piecemeal, unrelated instruction tends to produce highly competent "sounders" who are unable to apply their knowledge functionally in true reading situations, thus negating the ultimate purpose of instruction. A limited program that lacks balance is therefore, in the long run, self-defeating.

REFERENCES

1. Bond, Guy L., and Miles A. Tinker. *Reading Difficulties: Their Diagnosis and Correction.* New York: Appleton-Century-Crofts, 1967.
2. Brown, Don A., and Doris J. Loper. "Word Recognition in the Elementary School," in Marjorie Johnson and Roy Kress (Eds.), *Corrective Reading in the Elementary Classroom,* Reading Aids Series, Newark, Del.: International Reading Association, 1967.
3. McCullough, Constance, "Meeting Individual Needs by Grouping for Reading," Ginn Contributions to Reading No. 19, 1962, 4.
4. Wilson, Robert M., *Diagnostic and Remedial Reading for Classroom and Clinic,* Columbus, O.: Charles E. Merrill, 1967.

LEO M. SCHELL

Some Promising Possibilities for
Improving Reading Comprehension

Compared with word identification problems, relatively few children have difficulty understanding what they read. But correcting problems of understanding is much more difficult and mystifying than are cases of word identification deficiencies. This article pulls together some of the newer and more promising approaches that need to be considered by a teacher of reading both in the prevention and the correction of reading difficulties.

Which of the techniques described are you familiar with? What "fringe benefits" do you see that these procedures might have in addition to possibly improving comprehension? What limitations does each seem to have? Which technique seems to have the greatest possibility for transfer to independent reading situations? Do you agree with the author that "linguistics will eventually make by far the most significant contribution to the improvement of reading comprehension"?

We have been inundated — nay, buried — the past few years in a plethora of resources and techniques to improve children's word identification skills. Some have been merely old wine in new bottles; others have been serious attempts to apply new and different theories and insights. Many of these resources and techniques have been primarily corrective or remedial and tacitly they have asked, "Why not vary the approach during remediation rather than give additional doses of what pupils have already not succeeded with?"

But word identification is only one major component of reading. Where is the flood of materials and strategies for

---

An original paper written for this book by Leo M. Schell.

improving comprehension? Suggestions in major texts on remedial reading instruction do not seem detectably different from those made twenty, thirty, and even fifty years ago! They differ not a whit from those included in any sound developmental text! Recently an eminent reading researcher made the depressing statement that "We cannot reject our present procedures for teaching reading comprehension but we must voice grave doubts about their efficacy" (5:357). Some promising possibilities, the instructional frontier, for improving reading comprehension have surfaced repeatedly in the literature. This article will attempt to describe those that seem most promising and practical.

But some qualifying statements seem warranted. Instruction such as that described here can probably only produce improvement when the reader can quickly, accurately, and fluently read the words on the page. A reader struggling with the mechanics of word identification is no candidate for this kind of instruction. Neither is the child whose understanding of what he is currently reading is restricted by his linguistic or cultural-experiential background. These approaches are no substitutes for programs in oral language or concept formation.

In no case is the rationale for an approach stated or examined, nor is the literature and research reviewed. Readers interested in such aspects are urged to consult the original reports listed in the references.

AUDITORY COMPREHENSION

Listening

The numerous investigations into whether the teaching of listening skills improves reading comprehension has been summarized by Duker *(9)* and Schneyer *(26)*. Both concluded that the findings are inconclusive and inconsistent but that some studies have shown that instruction in listening skills leads to improved reading. As a supplement to other kinds of instruction in reading comprehension, this approach seems to have intriguing and promising possibilities.

Following are some suggestions for implementing listening instruction intended to improve reading comprehension.

1. Only certain kinds of readers may be expected to improve their reading comprehension via this approach. Durrell's

research *(10)* shows there is a huge gap between the listening and reading comprehension of primary-grade children, and it is not until at least grade four or five that this gap is appreciably closed. It seems unreasonable to assume that when this discrepancy is already great, instruction in listening (the superior modality) will not significantly improve reading (the inferior modality). What is needed in such cases is development of fundamental reading skills so that achievement can approach potential.

2. Give instruction at the reader's listening "learning level." Although no research has been done on this topic, it is reasonable to assume that people have a listening learning level just as they have a reading learning level. Material that is too easy will not produce growth; material that is too difficult will stymie or frustrate the listener. Tests such as Durrell's *(11)* might indicate approximate appropriate learning level; even a well-constructed IRI could be administered orally for the same purpose.

3. Instruction must be systematic, organized, and long-term. Ten minutes once a week for ten weeks won't do it. With readers already having trouble comprehending, a reasonable guess seems to be that nothing less than three lessons per week for ten weeks would produce significant, lasting results. But probably only if the material is sequentially slightly more difficult will instruction succeed. And such instruction will need to be reinforced periodically and regularly after the termination of formal lessons. The material must be the same style or content to which transfer is expected to occur. Possibly, even the same comprehension skills intended to be improved in reading should be stressed; for example, main idea, drawing conclusions, and word meanings in context. A variety of skills should be included. Currently available sets of listening tapes seem only partly appropriate for such instruction and must be used cautiously.

Impress Method.

As described by Heckelman *(14)*, the impress method is simultaneous oral reading by reader and teacher. The teacher is seated slightly behind the reader and both hold the book. The child slides his finger under the words as they are spoken with the teacher's voice being directed into the ear of the child.

Hollingsworth *(16)* questioned its value with children making normal reading progress but raised the possibility that it might be effective with remedial readers.

PHRASE READING FILMS

Numerous types of films and filmstrips have been available for years; they are nothing new. But they deserve serious consideration in an instructional effort to improve reading comprehension. Without advertising a specific set of materials, one series nevertheless seems to merit particular attention: *The Iowa Phrase Reading Film Series.* The research done on them by Amble *(1, 2, 3)* has been with subjects of varied backgrounds and reading levels. It has always been well-designed and conducted and has usually resulted in substantial and impressive gains in reading comprehension.

Discrete, unrelated phrases using third-grade vocabulary are flashed on the screen via 16 mm. film, and the reader writes the phrases he sees. Phrases gradually get longer throughout the series of ten films, which are appropriate for children reading at intermediate grade levels. The films are intended to be used in a prescribed manner; detailed directions for use accompany the films, which can be rented or purchased from Audiovisual Center, University of Iowa, Iowa City, Iowa 52240.

Educators interested in such an approach should investigate this and other similar series, paying particular attention to the research available on their value.

THE CLOZE PROCEDURE

In the cloze procedure, words are deleted from a written passage and the reader fills in the missing blanks by using clues available from the remaining context; for example, in the cloze_____, words are_____and the reader must_____them by using the sense of the_____. The reader can either supply the missing words or can choose from among several possibilities the one that best fills the blank as is practiced by several standardized reading tests.

At the present time there are no commercially available materials, even though Rankin mentioned some possibilities over a decade ago and several investigations were reported in the early and mid 1960s *(4, 15, 23, 27)*. Interested teachers must prepare their own materials. Following are some suggestions for preparing and using materials based on the cloze procedure.

1. Begin the reader with a two-item multiple-choice format on material at or below his independent reading level. At the early stages, delete only nouns and verbs. As the reader understands the process better and becomes more adept at filling the blanks, (1) give more items to choose from, (2) eliminate all such answers and force the reader to supply words on his own, (3) and/or delete words in other grammatical categories.

2. When the cloze procedure is used as a measure of reading comprehension, words are deleted randomly according to a predetermined criterion (for example, every fifth or every tenth word). As an aid in improving comprehension, such measures seem questionable; selected deletion appears sounder and more reasonable.

3. Discussion of the process with the reader seems imperative if optimum improvement is to occur. The reader must understand how to delimit a body of feasible options, how to use context to determine whether a word is sensible, and how to use his own oral language, which is an inestimable help.

4. The exact word of the author should not be demanded when using completion-type exercises. Synonyms, definitions, and close guesses should be accepted and reinforced even though the ultimate goal is exact reproduction.

5. Selections should be made self-checking for immediate reinforcement and feedback as well as for easy recording on progress charts.

6. Readers should be able to advance through successively more difficult material as rapidly as possible as long as their accuracy remains at a satisfactory level. (Bloomer *(4)* suggests 95 percent accuracy as the standard to attain before moving to a higher readability.)

7. As with all other procedures, instruction must be systematic, organized, and long-term.

THE REQUEST PROCEDURE

The Reciprocal Questioning (ReQuest) procedure was developed by Manzo *(21)*. It is a one-to-one teaching technique which was tested in a clinical setting with remedial students ranging from seven to twenty-five years of age and was found more effective for improving reading comprehension than was the directed reading activity. Manzo notes that it is a means of teaching (showing) students how to critically think and formulate questions. A condensed outline is given below.

1. Both student and teacher have copies of the selection to be read.

2. Both silently read the first sentence of the selection. The student may ask the teacher as many questions as he wishes about that sentence. He is told to try to ask the kind of questions the teacher might ask, in the way the teacher might ask them.

3. The teacher answers the questions, requiring rephrasing of those questions that he cannot answer due to poor syntax or incorrect logic.

4. After all the student's questions are answered, the second sentence is read, and the teacher asks as many questions as he feels will profitably add to the student's understanding of the content.

5. The teacher should periodically require that the student verify his responses.

6. After reading the second sentence, the teacher should require the integration of the units from both sentences.

7. All through the interaction, the student should be constantly encouraged to imitate the teacher's questioning behavior. The teacher should reinforce such behavior by saying, "That's a good question" or by giving the fullest possible reply.

8. This procedure should continue until the student can (1) read all the words in the first paragraph, (2) demonstrate literal understanding of what he has read, and (3) formulate a reasonable purpose, preferably stated as a question, for completing the remainder of the selection. On rare occasions, reciprocal questioning may continue through a second or a third paragraph, but it may be self-defeating to continue beyond the third paragraph.

9. Upon completion of the selection, any of the traditional followup activities may be used.

Manzo notes that the types of questions that a teacher uses will vary greatly, but for teachers wishing to try ReQuest for the first time, the following types are recommended: immediate reference, common knowledge, related information, open-ended discussion, personalized, further reference, and translation.

The practicality, possibilities, and permutations of this approach seem promising indeed!

LINGUISTICS

The techniques described so far could generally be labeled as "global" approaches to improving understanding what is read. But perhaps a closer scrutiny of what we call comprehension would reveal that it is really comprised of a number of relatively discrete sub-skills which somehow combine to form the larger synthesized whole we term comprehension. One of these seems to be grasping the relationships between words in a sentence and the relationship of successive sentences to each other. Structural and transformational linguistics have made some insights and contributions to these two aspects that seem worthy of exploration and application. Unfortunately, there has been less research and analysis of how linguistics can help improve comprehension than there has been of the other techniques discussed in this paper. Therefore, fewer specific or reliable recommendations can be made. What follows is more speculation and hope than established fact, and it should be treated as such. A comprehensive, in-depth examination of this topic is impossible; only a few of the better understood and accepted ideas and possibilities will be treated.

Sentence Patterns

Even though intonation is viewed by many linguists as fundamental to reading comprehension, this paper will arbitrarily omit any discussion of this aspect and begin with the second level of linguistic application — sentence patterns.

Lefevre points out that a child who learns "sentence function order in familiar sentence patterns will not become a word caller, or a reader of disconnected structural fragments; instead, he will develop a strong sentence sense" (20:80). He recommends that children begin learning these patterns via an "experience chart" approach using the language patterns children bring to school, correcting them only enough to make them correspond to the common patterns of sentence functions and word order. This suggestion seems equally applicable to older readers experiencing certain kinds of comprehension difficulties.

But this is only a beginning; a more conscious understanding and mastery of common language patterns may be needed by certain readers with comprehension problems. Readers interested in gaining fundamental knowledge about the four generally recognized sentence patterns, their variants, transformation, and combinations should consult Lefevre *(20)*, or Wardhaugh *(28)*.

As early as 1952, Center started a case for reader mastery of syntax when she described the task of a reader of complicated sentences. "He must be able to find his way through sentences that are long and often structurally complicated; else he will be lost in a maze of words, words, words. He must be able to recognize the structural elements composing a sentence and the relation of element to element; that is, syntax" (7:50).

And Briggs indicated traditional reading instruction with slighting syntax. He charged that most reading programs are primarily concerned with "widening the semantic background of the student; only incidentally are they concerned with the contributions syntactical skill can make to comprehension" (6:145).

Recently Bormuth *(5)* contributed to the case for better understanding of syntactical structures by the reader when he showed that a large proportion of children were unable to demonstrate a comprehension of the basic syntactical structures by which information is signaled. He concluded that "this deficiency may constitute a serious impediment to the efficiency of instruction" (5:356). Sauer *(25)* reached a similar conclusion. She felt that children who are most able to respond successfully to a variety of sentence patterns and levels of complexity are most likely to succeed in reading comprehension. She suggested that it may be advantageous for teachers to help children become conscious of different sentence patterns and of the way the elements within each are related.

Martin *(22)* pointed out that written English poses special syntactical problems because it is less redundant, more dense, and more formal than oral English. Jenkinson *(17)* supports this. She says that printed materials contain logical and subordinate connectives used with greater frequency and that these permit greater sentence complexity. The intellectual process required for holding ideas in subordination or in apposition may be quite different from those involved in oral communication. Martin concurs and contends that unless a reader can cope syntactically with the structure, he is being asked to hold in mind more isolated ideas at once than he knows what to do with. But he believes that if "the structure is readily understandable to the reader, then what might have been a confusing variable becomes instead a reasonable contributing part of a quite sensible *single* phenomenon" (22:27).

Thus, a substantial case seems to have been built favoring deeper understanding of the structure and patterns of written English as an aid to improved comprehension. The problem now becomes how to impart these understandings to readers in such a way that they mobilize and utilize them when reading difficult-to-understand material.

Lefevre recommends that children not memorize abstract and unreal definitions of sentence functions but rather become conscious of them via inductive experiences that minimize the use of formulas and terminology (20:83-84). Jenkinson cites a doctoral dissertation by Rinne at Stanford that attempted to improve reading comprehension by increasing awareness of written syntactical patterns. Even though no overwhelming improvement was shown, Jenkinson concluded that the data suggested that "the process of comprehension must contain within it a process of recognizing the syntactic relations between words in the written passage" (18:183).

One set of commercial material embodying elements of this approach is published by SRA *(8)*. Sample exercises illustrating this reliance on certain linguistic principles are shown below. They give the flavor of some possible approaches.

Which Sentence Means The Same Thing
As The One On The Left?

The chest was lifted by a boy from New York.

A New York boy lifted the chest.

A boy lifted the chest from New York.

Do The Two Sentences Mean The Same Thing?
A wind from the north froze the pond.
A northern wind froze the pond.

The woman with a dollar bill lighted a candle.
The woman lighted a candle with a dollar bill.

Structure Words

"After intonation and sentence order, the most important clues to reading language patterns of sentences are provided by structure words, or 'empty' words" (20:119). Words such as *the, some, was, out, if, because, why,* and *where* have few referents outside the language system itself and are relatively lacking in meaning or content (as contrasted with "full" words having referents in the real world outside language). Many linguists call these words *markers.* Readers interested in fuller information than can be provided by this paper should consult Lefevre *(20),* or Wardhaugh *(28).*

Lefevre emphasizes the importance in reading of this category of words by showing that 45 percent of Dolch's list and 43 percent of Fry's list are structure words (20:141). Jenkinson (17:185) stated that the exact meaning of structure words demands precision of thinking; confusion as to their exact meaning results in many errors in comprehension. Katz *(19)* studied elementary pupils' understanding of connectives (*because, and, then, but,* etc.) and concluded that even though these were commonly used and heard by children they were not equally well understood. Adversative connectives such as *but* and *although* presented inordinate problems to his subjects. Robertson *(24)* reached similar conclusions with a similar aged group. Six of her seventeen connectives had less than 66 percent comprehension by her fourth- fifth- and sixth-grade subjects. These were *however, thus, although, which, and,* and *yet.* She repeatedly recommended that schools provide systematic training through the reading program to help children understand connectives better at an earlier age so that they could develop greater facility in understanding complex printed sentences (such as this one). Regrettably, these researchers have provided few ideas, insights, or clues as to how to help children better understand and use these words to comprehend what they read.

Lefevre stresses two cautions: (1) Structure words should never be taught in isolation but only as they function in the language that gives them their meaning, and (2) markers identify structure elements as meaningful wholes, delineating larger structures or structure groups (20:119-142).

But he goes beyond these admonitions and suggests that the clause marker (*if, that, now, after, as,* etc.) is the most important one for readers to master because it shows so many different kinds and degrees of structural relationships that reflect myriad meanings. "Reading clause markers quickly and accurately . . . is a first requirement of effective comprehension of meaning" (20:128).

Comments

It is my suspicion that linguistics will eventually make by far the most significant contribution to the improvement of reading comprehension. A quick review of the other approaches described in this paper will reveal that two of them, cloze and ReQuest, embody basic elements of linguistics. Unfortunately, at this time it is far less well understood, researched, and applicable than other techniques. For the sake of readers with comprehension difficulties, it is hoped this situation will change drastically in the near future.

REFERENCES

1. Amble, Bruce, "Phrase Reading Training and Reading Achievement of School Children," *Reading Teacher,* 20 (December, 1966); 210-218.

2. Amble, Bruce R. *Phrase Reading Training with Disadvantaged Students: Four Exploratory Studies 1967-1968.* USOE Contract No. OEC 3-7-062875-3056.

3. Amble, Bruce, and Seigmar Muehl, "Phrase Reading Training and Reading Achievement: A Replication Study," *Journal of Experimental Education,* 35 (Winter, 1966), 93-99.

4. Bloomer, Richard H., "The Cloze Procedure as a Remedial Reading Exercise," *Journal of Developmental Reading,* 5 (Spring, 1962), 173-181.

5. Bormuth, John, et al., "Children's Comprehension of Between and Within Sentence Syntactic Structures," *Journal of Educational Psychology,* 61 (October, 1970), 349-357.

6. Briggs, F. A., "Grammatical Sense as a Factor in Reading Comprehension," *The Psychology of Reading Behavior,* G. B. Schnick, ed. Milwaukee, Wisconsin: National Reading Conference, Inc., 1969, 145-149.

7. Center, Stella, *The Art of Book Reading.* New York: Charles Scribner's Sons, 1952.

8. *Comprehensive Reading Series Workbooks, Level G-L.* Chicago, Ill.: Science Research Associates, Inc., 1967.

9. Duker, Sam, "Listening and Reading," *Elementary School Journal,* 65 (March, 1965), 321-329.

10. Durrell, Donald D., "Listening Comprehension versus Reading Comprehension," *Journal of Reading,* 12 (March, 1969), 455-460.

11. Durrell, Donald D., *Listening-Reading Tests.* New York: Harcourt, Brace and World, Inc., 1969.

12. Early, Margaret, "Reading Instruction and Language Growth: Secondary," *Thought-Language-Reading,* M. S. Johnson and R. A. Kress, eds. Philadelphia: The Reading Clinic, Temple University, 1970, 35-46.

13. Fries, Charles C., *Linguistics and Reading.* New York: Holt, Rinehart, and Winston, 1962.

14. Heckelman, R. G. "A Neurological-Impress Method of Remedial-Reading Instruction," *Academic Therapy,* 4 (Summer, 1969), 277-282.

15. Heitzman, Andrew J., and Richard A. Bloomer, *"The Effect of Non-Overt Reinforced Cloze Procedure Upon Reading Comprehension,"* *Journal of Reading,* 11 (December, 1967), 213-223.

16. Hollingsworth, Paul M., "An Experiment with the Impress Method of Teaching Reading," *Reading Teacher,* 24 (November, 1970), 112-114.

17. Jenkinson, M. D., "Comprehension and Some Linguistic Fallacies," *New Frontiers in College-Adult Reading,* G. B. Schick, ed. Milwaukee, Wisconsin: National Reading Conference, Inc., 1966, 180-187.

18. Jenkinson, M. D. "Information Gaps in Research in Reading Comprehension, *Reading: Process and Pedagogy,* G. B. Schick, ed. Milwaukee, Wisconsin: National Reading Conference, Inc., 1971, 179-192.

19. Katz, E. W., "Understanding Connectives," *Journal of Verbal Learning and Verbal Behavior,* 7 (April, 1968), 501-509.

20. Lefevre, Carl A. *Linguistics and the Teaching of Reading.* New York: McGraw-Hill Book Co., 1964.

21. Manzo, Anthony V., "Improving Reading Comprehension Through Reciprocal Questioning," unpublished doctoral dissertation. Syracuse University, 1969. (Also described in "The ReQuest Procedure," *Journal of Reading,* 13 (November, 1969), 123-126.

22. Martin, R. G., "Decoding and the Quest for Meaning," *Journal of Reading Behavior,* 1 (Fall, 1969), 22-29.

23. Rankin, Earl F., "Uses of the Cloze Procedure in the Reading Clinic," *Reading in a Changing Society.* Newark, Delaware: International Reading Association, 1959, 228-232.

24. Robertson, Jean E., "Pupil Understanding of Connectives," *Reading Research Quarterly,* 3 (Spring, 1968), 387-417.

25. Sauer, Lois, E., "Fourth Grade Children's Knowledge of Grammatical Structure and Its Relation to Reading Comprehension," unpublished doctoral dissertation, University of Wisconsin, Madison, Wisconsin, 1968.

26. Schneyer, J. Wesley, "Instruction in Listening," *Reading Teacher,* 24 (January, 1971), 369.

27. Schneyer, J. W., "Use of the Cloze Procedure for Improving Reading Comprehension," *Reading Teacher,* 19 (December, 1965), 174-179.

28. Wardhaugh, Ronald, *Reading: A Linguistic Perspective.* New York: Harcourt, Brace and World, Inc., 1969.

LEITHA PAULSEN

Developing Reading and Language Arts Efficiencies in the Content Areas in Corrective and Remedial Classes

Research has shown that general reading ability alone is often inadequate for efficient reading in the content areas; there are special skills that must be mastered. Any remedial or preventive program that ignores these skills is subtly but insidiously contributing to continued reading problems as the reading demands upon the child change and increase. These skills are discussed succinctly but cogently in this article.

What obligation does a remedial teacher have to teach students how to read content field materials? How important are these skills to success in the elementary school? the secondary school? What materials listed by Storer and Colton are best suited for such instruction? Do these skills demand more cooperation between special reading teachers and classroom teachers than do the more general reading skills?

Some students in a remedial class will need help in *all* content areas. Others, because of special interests, will read well in some areas but poorly in others. A general reading test will give little indication of a student's particular needs in his assigned content reading; a few standardized tests that measure specific skills required for subject matter reading are available, but even they will not tell you exactly what you want to know. The most direct assessment of needs, therefore, is made through informal tests.

Together, reading teacher and content teacher can examine the skills needed for a particular content area. They

---

Reprinted from *Reading and the Language Arts,* Supplementary Educational Monographs, No. 93, compiled and edited by H. Alan Robinson (December 1963), pp. 92–97, by permission of The University of Chicago Press and the author. © 1963 by The University of Chicago Press.

can draw from their experience for these skills, or, perhaps more wisely, use as a guide one of the lists of skills developed by reading experts. Through such lists classroom teachers are often alerted to important skills they are neglecting to teach. From them, as well as from their own experience, reading teacher and content teacher can decide which of the many skills are most pertinent to the actual assignments the student is required to do.

For each of the skills they select, the reading teacher can then prepare an informal test, using textbook material as well as other subject matter sources from the course. Since one skill is dependent upon another skill, it is probably most efficient to test for only one skill at a time, starting with that which is basic and progressing to higher levels, reteaching or teaching each skill along the way as needed.

Teaching each skill, just as testing each skill, is only effective when it is connected with the real content situation. General reading instruction, that is, the kind of reading instruction common to a basal reading program at the elementary level or to a developmental program at the high school level, will not build the skills unique to the various content areas. Of course, initial instruction of a skill is best done when the teacher uses materials close to the student's interests and abilities. However, unless skills learned through such specially selected or contrived materials are later applied to the actual reading problems being faced in social studies, science, or mathematics, there will be little or no transfer.

DEVELOPING VOCABULARY

Since vocabulary is basic to all comprehension, the problems of word development are of prime importance to the remedial teacher. His first obligation to students in need of vocabulary work is to help them build an *attitude toward words*. With new terms crowded into content subjects, a student may well be failing because he is too satisfied with an "I know what it means but I can't tell you" level of understanding. This may mean only a vague or general understanding of terms; often, however, it means no understanding at all. Many readers, even remedial readers, can pronounce and recite textbook phrases with deceiving glibness; forced to rephrase or translate meaning into their own words, however, they are lost.

Remedial reading teachers should train students to get exact meanings and, in addition, force them to translate these meanings into their own words. The meanings should not only be discussed and clarified in the remedial session but should be used in classroom discussion and related to further learnings. If precision of understanding is thus required, students will soon come to be concerned about the importance of words and their meanings. This "attitude toward words" is essential to success in any subject.

The remedial teacher's second obligation in regard to vocabulary is to give students practical help in building a stock of word meanings. *Pre-teaching* vocabulary is one such help. It can be divided into three steps:

1. Arouse interest. The retarded reader will need to be lured. This may be done with something special, as an object, experiment, or a curiosity-arousing question.
2. Once you have captured his interest, orient the student to the unit. Start with him! Find out what you have to build on. Two questions are paramount: What does the student *already know?* What does he *need to know?*
3. Pre-teach any vocabulary needs you have discovered — needs pertinent to orienting the student or to extending any concepts he presently holds. Now, if possible, push him one step further and draw from him the questions he would like to have answered as he reads. Ask: "What would you like to know about this topic?" Try to induce concern in him about getting something from his reading and thus establish in him a need for further understanding.

Other practical ways for giving vocabulary help at all grade levels involve the use of italics, vocabulary charts, individual word lists, repeated reviews, and context clues.

1. Boldface and italicized types are used to call the reader's attention to important terms. Authors will usually italicize an important term only the *first* time it is introduced. Point out that in any given paragraph, therefore, some difficult and important terms may appear without being italicized. Show the student how to go back to find the meanings of these "repeated" but difficult terms: point out how quickly italics will guide him to their meanings.
2. Help students to become word-collectors. Lift out the key terms of a unit for special study. Placing them on a classroom chart or black-board and adding new terms as the unit progresses are helpful. This

keeps key terms in view throughout the unit and encourages their repeated use in thinking, writing, and speaking. Require students to keep and use their own lists of key terms.

3. Provide opportunities for reviewing new terms. Sometimes an author re-uses difficult words he has introduced, integrating them into the discussion as he proceeds through the chapter; however, in highly concentrated textbooks, a term may be used only once. It is then up to the teacher to bring new terms into focus and continued use. The "key term" charts, individual lists, and individual vocabulary cards may play an important role here.

4. Help students to derive meaning from context. Often a simple word used in a new way puzzles a student more than a new word. Some will not get beyond the familiar meaning; others will deduce the new meaning. Ask *these* students to tell how they arrived at the meaning. Now have all students check with the dictionary. Have them keep their books open and take the sentence to the dictionary rather than bring the many definitions back to the sentence. Of course, there should be similar practice with unknown words, too.

GRASPING THE ORGANIZATION OF THE CONTENT

A second skill common to reading success in all subjects is the ability to grasp the organization of the content. The typical retarded reader reads without any plan or strategy. Therefore, if he reads his assignment at all, he remembers little. Seldom does he realize that textbook reading requires a hard-work, systematic approach. If he has not been taught how to do study-type reading, he may expect the American history or biology book to read as effortlessly as does the hot-rod novel! Students must be helped to recognize that study reading requires a great deal of effort — not only for the retarded reader but for *all readers.* Then they must be shown specific ways to do this type of reading. There are several ways to help students organize content.

1. *The most basic organizational skill is the ability to extract the main idea.* Students should progress from practice in identifying the main idea in a single paragraph, to several paragraphs, to a section, to an entire chapter.

In teaching main idea, the following program has been successful. Figure 1, the Selection Pyramid, is a diagrammatic illustration of this program. It is based on a three-step main-idea

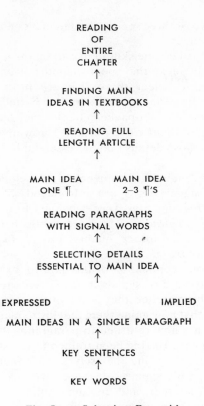

Fig. I. — Selection Pyramid

sequence.[1] The first step is finding key words in a sentence. The second is finding key sentences in a paragraph. The third is deciding upon the main idea. At the very beginning, students must be shown that this is a technique for reaching a broader goal so they will see learning each skill as an important step in a meaningful sequence, as the pyramid indicates.

Students learn to find the main idea in paragraphs with main ideas "expressed" as well as main ideas "implied." They learn to find main ideas in various positions: beginning, middle,

[1] H. Alan Robinson, "Teacher-oriented Reading Instruction," *Controversial Issues in Reading and Promising Solutions,* pp. 125-26. Compiled and edited by Helen M. Robinson, Supplementary Educational Monographs, No. 91. Chicago: University of Chicago Press, 1961.

end, within two or three sentences, and in a combination of first and last sentences.

As students become skillful in cutting through a paragraph to find a main idea, they next examine each detail, sifting through them to select those that are most important for remembering. Important details are often buried in elaboration! A single section of a fact-packed chapter may have hundreds of details. Not all of them are important! Knowing a technique for selecting only those details that are essential to the main idea is invaluable.

After the "main-idea sequence" is developed, paragraphs that contain signal words are introduced. Students quickly move from reading the very obvious full signals: *"First ....Second....Third...."* to more subtle half signals: *"For one thing* he*....Another* quality was*....Furthermore,* he had*....*But, *above all,* he*...."*

Now follows application of this skill to textbooks. Alerted to the extensive use of signals in texts, students readily admit that before this practice they were overlooking many of the subtle signals that now guide them quickly to main points.

Students are now returned to paragraphs that have few or very subtle signals. Having been trained to use signals as guides to organization, they find themselves fairly facile at imposing upon a paragraph signals of their own, as they look for "another, and another, and another" point.

In the next step students apply what has been learned to longer selections. Attention is called to "series" paragraphs, where ideas are introduced in one paragraph and further developed in succeeding paragraphs. Then they progress to a full-length article; finally they apply all skills learned to their textbook chapters.

2. *A second organizational technique much needed in study-type reading is finding thought patterns.* As important as main idea is, it is only a general paragraph structure within which there is often a more specific pattern. The need to teach thought patterns in content reading is stressed by Smith. Here is an example of her approach.

Your chapter on "The Rise of Industry" discusses a chain of causes and effects. First, it tells of several causes that produced the rise of industry. Then industry itself became a cause and produced several effects. Finally, wealth, one of the *effects* of industry, became a cause and produced effects of its own.

In doing your assignment, try this procedure:
1. Preview the chapter to get the over-all picture of the causes and effects described.
2. Read the selection concentrating solely on causes and the effects produced. Associate each cause with the effect that belongs with it.
3. Just get major causes and effects. Don't bother with details.
4. When you finish reading the selection, fill in causes or effects in the skeleton outline I have provided.[2]

The use of thought patterns will aid comprehension. If students read the above assignment unaware of the pattern, for example, they will likely be lost in details. However, if they approach the assignment as suggested, identify the cause and effect pattern immediately and then read, concentrating on the causes and effects that each produced, they should comprehend the ideas clearly.

3. *A third way to help students organize the content is to teach them to formulate a question for each section in the book.* This has been called the "Go in with a question, come out with an answer" technique and is perhaps the most important step in the popular SQ3R or PQRST methods of study.[3]

Students can be trained to turn boldface headings, topic sentences, the headings of lists, and boldface terms into questions; then, to read for the answers. In a history book, for example, the boldface heading **"Centers of Early Civilization"** becomes "What were the centers of early civilization?" In an earth science book the boldface term **seismograph** becomes "Just what is a seismograph?"

Any student who becomes proficient in just the three organizational techniques described above will be better able to handle and understand his textbook assignments.

---

2 Nila Banton Smith. *Be a Better Reader,* Book IV, pp. 112-15. Englewood Cliffs, N.J.: Prentice-Hall, 1959.

3 For a description of the SQ3R method see Francis P. Robinson, *Effective Study,* chaps. ii and iii. Rev. ed. New York: Harper & Bros. 1961. For a description of the PQRST method see Thomas F. Stanton, *How To Study.* Montgomery, Ala.: 2208 Woodley Rd., 1954.

ABILITY TO USE SUPPLEMENTARY MATERIALS

A skill basic to success in most content subjects is the ability to use a variety of supplementary materials that complement textbooks.

Most textbooks are fact-jammed! An analysis of a fifth-grade text used widely in Indiana revealed that basic facts came "crowding in" at the rate of two facts per fifteen words. The danger in keeping students at the fact level of their textbooks is the stressing of information and memorization rather than thinking. Many teachers, realizing this, have abandoned the single textbook approach and have turned assignments into problem-solving.

The retarded reader, thrown into activities that take him to many sources, will need special help. He will need assistance in finding supplementary materials plus help in the use of reference skills. He will need much aid in evaluating the material he finds, and then will need help in collating and organizing it.

DEVELOPING FAVORABLE ATTITUDES

Favorable attitudes toward reading can best be developed by the teacher who first interests students in the topic and then provides activities with real opportunities to use reading for a purpose. Many retarded readers, however, will find it difficult to set purposes on their own; therefore help must be provided. You can set purpose for students with a statement: "The author of the article you will read for tomorrow contends that many a youngster nowadays finds that his high school has assumed the aspects of a carnival. Read the article carefully to decide whether or not you agree with the author's idea." You can set purpose with a question: "What difference has it made to us that the Greeks rather than the Persians won in the Persian Wars?" You can set purpose co-operatively with students as they begin an assignment: Ask "What would you like to know about this subject?" Learn what is most important to them; then organize a study outline around *their* questions.

Also essential to establishing favorable reading attitudes is providing material that is within the capacity of the student. The reading teacher will foster good attitudes by securing the co-operation of the classroom teacher in an adjusted program of learning whenever needed; for it is only through such an adjustment that the student can build skills successfully and thus reach a point where he can move along at the same pace as his regular group.

DOUGLAS F. BATES

Behavior Modification:
A Pigeon, A Grandma, and You

*Both developmental and remedial instruction try to bring
about a change in children's reading techniques — they try to
modify their reading behavior. Perhaps we should be pragmatists
rather than theorists; if a method works, we should use it, not
reject it because it isn't compatible with our theory of learning.
And because the task of treating children with reading difficulties is so monumental, we should be willing to try any
technique that seems rational and sound or has been shown to be
efficacious. One goal of this book is to acquaint teachers with
some unique, little known, and avant-garde ideas — and to
encourage them to apply those ideas in their teaching. Hence
this original article.*

*In what ways would diagnosis be different from traditionally
accepted notions if you adopted behavior modification
techniques? Formulate a measure appropriate to reading instruction for each of the four possible types of records. What
types of consequences do you think would be most appropriate
for the type of reading instruction and children you are involved
with? Have you ever used techniques similar to this? Do you
think there are any cautions which need to be exercised in using
this technique? What values other than improved reading
achievement might this technique produce?*

Once upon a time, in an obscure laboratory hidden deep in the
bowels of a dark, unobtrusive building filled with rats, pigeons,
cages, and mysterious equipment, there lived a scientist who
spent years watching little birds and animals, making them toil

An original article written for this book by Douglas F. Bates, doctoral
candidate, University of Kansas, Lawrence. Supported in part by PHS training
grant NB05362 to the Bureau of Child Research, University of Kansas.

long hours pushing bars and pecking disks to get enough food to stay alive. Eventually, he was able to make these little captives work harder for less than anyone had ever been able to do before. He became very famous and lived happily ever after.

The man was B. F. Skinner, and the techniques which he developed came to be known as "operant conditioning." Skinner was intensely interested in the potential human applications of his findings, but it was many years after he began his initial work with small animals that one of his students, Ogden R. Lindsley (now at the University of Kansas), undertook the first human operant conditioning experiments. As applied to human beings, "operant conditioning" became known as "behavior modification."

Behavior modification has expanded greatly from its early beginnings and today includes much that is far removed from Dr. Skinner and the animal labs. Despite this, the beginning was there. Many people are embarrassed at this, feeling defensive about using techniques with people that were first tested with animals. This is rather foolish. If we were to throw out all of the techniques which we commonly use today that were first tested with animals, medicine would be back in the stone age, the astronauts would be sitting on the ground staring at the moon, and the whole educational complex would collapse (because after all, the first school was probably of fish). Should we search back in our own family trees we would likely all find a few birds roosting securely in the branches and a few rats gnawing on the roots; behavior modification is no exception.

Now you may well ask at this point, "What is behavior modification?" Since behavior modification is many things, ranging from faddish foolishness to meticulous research, the question is an extremely difficult one to answer. Nevertheless, I shall try. Dr. Skinner found, in the course of his studies, that he was able to influence the behavior of his laboratory animals by controlling what happened after they behaved. That is, if he wanted a pigeon to peck a disk on the side of its cage, he fed the pigeon for pecking and didn't feed it for not pecking. Since the pigeons were hungry, they soon learned to peck the disk. Now we do not ordinarily feed people when they behave as we would like and refrain from feeding them when they do not behave as we would like, unless those people are children and we give them dessert for being good and send them to bed without any supper for being bad. Thus we cannot use food deprivation as Dr. Skinner did when we work with people. But there is a great difference between using a general technique and using all of its parts. Dr. Skinner's general finding that behavior is heavily influenced by what happens after it occurs is one that we may very effectively use in our work with people even if we do not use food and hunger in connection with it.

Behavior modification is very similar to other approaches in education so far as the goals are concerned; whether one is a "behaviorist" or a "traditionalist," an advocate of Summerhills or military academies, the primary interest is still the child. Major differences can be found, however, in the initial orientation towards a behavioral problem (using the term "behavior" in a very broad sense to include everything from eating to learning — in short, to include everything that people do) and in the procedures followed to deal with the problem.

Traditional approaches towards behavior in education have been heavily involved with testing, labelling and searching for reasons. All of this is done to improve the "understanding" of the behavior problem. Too often, however, the result is the reverse: the extended, expensive testing and evaluation procedures simply result in more sophisticated labels which don't help the teachers (who must apply the findings) understand anything. We have not made a very significant contribution towards the solution of a reading disability, for instance, if after administering a battery of tests we are then able to authoritatively replace the labels which a teacher has placed upon some unfortunate child's brow — "not too bright, poor reader" — with "WISC I.Q. 87, apparent dyslexia." Our contribution has been towards obfuscation (look it up — I had to), not clarification.

Before demanding more sophisticated labels and perceptive reasons, we should first ask ourselves what good they will be once we get them. A skunk by any other name would smell as foul; a label by and of itself can solve nothing. The same is true of reasons. The basic reasons for or causes of poor reading, for example, usually lie within the child's environment. Suppose we are able to determine this for a given child — suppose, as is not at all uncommon, that the reason little Billy doesn't do well in reading is that he happens to be one of many children belonging to a family suffering from the absentee parent syndrome (parents usually absent due to work or other reasons; when home, too busy with other things to spend much time with the children). By the time such a child enters school he will have suffered under these reasons and causes for a good many years, and as a teacher or reading specialist you will be powerless to do much about any of them. You may shed a few tears of compassion for Billy and his unfortunate past, but in the end you will still be faced with Billy and his reading problem no matter how well you may "understand" why he has it or how cleverly you can label it.

Behavior modification does not concern itself with reasons or causes lying outside the control of the therapist. There are two major reasons for this. In the first place, you can't do anything about reasons and causes lying outside your control anyway, so when you spend time chasing them down you are not really helping the child — you are simply satisfying your curiosity. In the second place, as was stated earlier in this article, one of Skinner's early findings was that behavior is heavily influenced by its consequences. This means that, regardless of the reasons for or causes of a given behavior which may be lying in the dim obscurity of the past, the primary reasons for the behavior's continuance into the present may be found in the present consequences.

In general, the behavior modification approach to a problem is individualized and extremely personal. The basic requirements, other than the people involved, are a pinpoint, a record and a consequence.

THE PINPOINT:

A pinpoint is a precise designation of the behavior to be modified. Too often behavior is described in largely meaningless terms which inflate problems to such ridiculous proportions through sheer verbiage that the child himself is obscured. Pinpoints deflate these descriptive balloons and leave something that can be understood and manipulated without seven years of college and an unabridged dictionary. Pinpoints are not: (a) generalized or subjective descriptions of problem behavior (i.e. "Jimmy can't read worth a hoot"); (b) suggestive hints about causation (his daddy's a loafer, his mother drinks, the only decent piece of furniture they have is a color TV, and I think he's mentally retarded); (c) psycho-medical descriptions (minimal brain damage, dyslexia, bradylexia, paralexia, alegia); (d) grade level designations (oral reading level 2.3, paragraph meaning 1.8, sentence meaning 1.3). *Pinpoints are: specific designations of the behavior (word omissions, transpositions, words read correctly in oral reading) which make it possible to identify the behavior readily when it occurs.*

THE RECORD:

Behavior modifiers use records (generally in the form of charts or graphs) to indicate the success of the procedures which they are using. The types of data which they record on the charts or graphs vary widely. Behavior modifiers may measure quantity, quality (accuracy), duration, speed (frequency or rate) or some combination of these. Each type of data has advantages and disadvantages, and the teacher must decide what is most important in a given situation before deciding which type of data to record.

Quantity records show the number of times something occurs — number of questions correctly answered, number of pages read, etc. Such records are commonly used for reporting attendance and other things where totals are of prime importance, but they are of little value for recording behaviors for which accuracy, speed, and/or time spent on a given task are important variables.

Records of accuracy or quality may take the form of value estimates such as letter grades on papers or report cards, or they may take a more objective form such as a percent figure. Behavior modifiers generally try to avoid subjective value estimates, but often use percent measures. Such a measure is of value if quality or accuracy is most important; it is not as valuable in cases where the amount of work done, the time spent working, and/or working speed are also important. Percent figures must also be computed, making record keeping more burdensome.

Duration records measure the time spent on a given task. Often these records are combined with percent, and a behavior modifier may report that a child spent 25% of his time reading, 50% doing other work and 25% annoying the teacher. A duration record is worthwhile if the time spent on a task is most important. It may be misleading if output is also important — some children (and adults) can spend hours working without accomplishing anything that is particularly worthwhile.

Speed records indicate how fast something is done. Since such a record combines both the number of things done (quantity) and the time spent working (duration) it is a very sensitive measure. Speed, also known as rate or frequency, is computed by dividing the number of things done by the time spent, and is reported as number of things per unit of time (as in words per minute). As was the case for percent, such computation imposes an extra burden. This may be considerably relieved, however, by using time samples which make division easy. For example, we could decide to measure a child's reading speed by giving him a whole story and asking him to read it through. This might leave us with 1,357 words read in 26 minutes and 49 seconds, a rather messy division problem. Or we might simply ask the child to read for five minutes, then count the number of words read, double this figure and move the decimal point one place to the left (253 words in five minutes = 506 words in ten minutes = 50.6 words in one minute).

Frequency records (another name for speed or rate records), while sensitive to both number and time, do not indicate the total number or total time, nor do they reveal accuracy of output unless separate records are maintained for correct and incorrect responses.

Since each of the records mentioned is strong in some respects and weak in others, behavior modifiers commonly utilize two or more measures at the same time, either of the same (as in measuring both frequency correct and frequency incorrect) or of different (as percent time) types. Dr. Ogden R. Lindsley, mentioned earlier in this article, has developed a rather unique composite system called Precision Teaching which combines features of quantity, quality, duration and speed on a single standard chart form which has been so designed that teachers are able to measure a fifth dimension of behavior — acceleration, or proportional change in frequency over time. Using this behavioral dimension, teachers are able not only to describe behavior as it was, but also to predict in many cases the course it will follow in the future.

One very important question that needs to be answered during all of this talk about records is who's going to keep them.

Of course, a certain amount of record keeping is a normal part of any teacher's day. As additional helps, some behavior modifiers have developed simple forms and procedures to lighten the load; others recommend using observers or aides, while others (including Lindsley in his Precision Teaching approach) train children to keep their own records, thus relieving the teacher of almost the entire record-keeping burden. The choice remains the teacher's; she must analyze her own situation and adapt procedures to fit it.

THE CONSEQUENCE, AND "GRANDMA'S LAW":

Consequences are things that happen because something else happened. They can be enjoyable (a kiss for being good), distressing (a spanking for being naughty), or neutral. Consequences influence everything that we do: we keep working at a particular job because we enjoy the work, because we feel we are making a contribution, and because we get paid; we drive slowly through radar-controlled speed zones because we believe in honoring and upholding the law and because speeding tickets are expensive; we read articles on behavior modification because we have an insatiable thirst for knowledge and because the professor has promised to include a couple of questions about it in the next test. If any of these consequences were to be manipulated, our behavior would very likely change — how long would you keep working at a job if they stopped sending you a check?

A behavior modifier tries to find consequences that will strongly influence the pinpointed behavior in the desired manner. The behavioral record provides information concerning the effect of a given consequence, in essence helping the behavior modifier to "manage" the behavior in question. Commonly used consequences in school are praise, attention, recognition, grades, "privileges" (such as going out to recess, being able to choose a free-choice activity for a short period, etc.), and the usual punishments. Some teachers have used more tangible consequences, such as stars on foreheads, little candy or cookie "treats," pennies, tokens that could later be traded for various things (including "privileges") and even trading stamps. Although such consequences are often effective, they are not generally necessary.

Because some behavior modifiers have used tangible consequences such as M&M candies, money, or tokens in some of their work, particularly that involving severely disturbed or retarded children, some misinformed souls have described behavior modification as systematic bribery. This is nonsense. Bribery is something that is done to corrupt people, or encourage things illegal or immoral. A teacher is no more guilty of bribery when she uses tangible consequences when they are necessary than she is guilty of accepting a bribe when she cashes her paycheck.

How should a teacher then go about using behavior modification in school? She should choose the pinpoint, record, and consequence that best fit her program and the needs of the child, and get to work. The pinpoint should be reasonable and within the capabilities of the child. The record should be such that the necessary information can be gleaned from it quickly and easily; data should be recorded daily when possible, so that the record can more accurately reflect the child's progress. The consequence should be effective, and as natural (that is, as close to the normal consequence) as possible — in other words, don't implement a complicated system using points and stars if a pat on the head and a smile work just as well. Not all consequences are equally effective, and many lose their effect after a period of time has passed. The daily behavioral record provides the information necessary to determine which consequences should be used and when. Above all, the teacher should be consistent; there is nothing that can destroy a program for behavior modification faster than haphazard, inconsistent teacher behavior.

Last of all, a teacher should remember "Grandma's Law," named after Dr. Lindsley's grandmother who first taught it to him: "If at first you don't succeed, try, try again." Good luck, and may all your consequences be enjoyable!

HELEN K. SMITH

Junior High Remedial Reading

Junior high school may simultaneously be both the "no-man's land" of education and education's stepchild. Few articles have been written specifically about teaching in the junior high school, and either elementary or secondary certification can usually be used to teach in junior high. Smith zeroes in on some specific needs and techniques appropriate to this level.

Do Smith's ideas on ways to make instruction meaningful seem feasible and meaningful to you? Are some of these suggestions equally applicable to both elementary and high school instruction? What kinds of things are necessary if curricular adjustments are to occur and be helpful to the students? What kinds of things does Smith not mention? Do Johnson's suggestions in the next article give you any insights as to how to develop and broaden reading interests?

Appropriate remedial instruction for students with reading difficulties may be the most important single aspect of the junior high school curriculum. The evidence is abundant that many junior high school students need remediation in reading; yet many are neglected because no provisions have been made to help them overcome their reading difficulties. Successful reading remediation is essential for the satisfactory performance of these students in the content area subjects, both in junior and senior high schools, and may prevent some youth from becoming dropouts a few years hence.

Retarded readers are the ones who, for various reasons, are

Reprinted from *Reading Difficulties: Diagnosis, Correction, and Remediation,* William K. Durr, ed. (Newark, Delaware: International Reading Association, 1970), pp. 260-268, by permission of Helen K. Smith and the International Reading Association.

reading below their potential, if their potential can be satisfactorily estimated. They have the mental ability to be good or able readers but have not yet learned to read in harmony with their ability. Such a definition includes any student who is not reading in harmony with his mental ability, whether he is a bright student who is capable of reading beyond his grade placement but is reading at grade level, or an average or bright student who is reading considerably below his grade placement. The concern in this paper is with the latter group, those who are capable of reading materials at their grade level or beyond but who cannot keep up with their peers because of their reading disability.

Four suggestions will be given concerning how to help retarded readers at the junior high school level. One assumption has been made throughout the paper: that teachers and/or administrators have identified the students whose major difficulty is deficient reading ability from those who are slow learners or discipline problems and from those who are so disturbed that they cannot profit from reading remediation.

LEARNING ABOUT RETARDED READERS

In order to help junior high school retarded readers, teachers should learn as much about these young people and their reading problems as possible. Among the keynotes to successful reading experiences are the motivation of the pupils to learn and to read, their interest in reading, and sufficient background experiences to make reading meaningful. Teachers should use every opportunity to learn what these students are really interested in, how they really feel about reading and school, and what their real desires or life goals are. Cumulative records, interviews with parents and students, day-by-day observation, interest inventories, and informal conversations with students are some of the sources teachers can use to know their pupils as real people. This understanding of and knowing the student is a continuous process. Spending a few moments occasionally with a student may well reap its rewards in a short period of time. These few moments may give the teacher much insight about what, how, when, and why the students read, their progress, their difficulties, their interests, their ideas, and their dreams. In addition, rapport between the teacher and student is usually strengthened when the student realizes that the teacher's interest in him is genuine.

Teachers need to learn as much as they can about the student's reading difficulty. They need to investigate, if at all possible, when the problem was first noted, what has been done to alleviate the difficulty, and what the past progress was if special teaching had been provided. Interviews with parents or information from cumulative records may provide teachers with insights not only about the reading problem but also about any factors which may be inhibiting the student's progress in reading.

Diagnosis of the reading problem is essential for the planning and conducting of successful reading instruction for retarded readers. This does not imply that a complete, intensive diagnostic examination should be made of every retarded reader assigned to the teacher. Time is saved and frustrating experiences for both students and teachers can be avoided if instruction is directed from the beginning to the skills each student needs. The extent to which diagnosis is carried out is dependent upon the numbers and kinds of each student's reading deficiencies. Diagnosis should systematically continue until the major areas of the reading difficulty are identified and a reading improvement program can be planned for each student. When teachers are familiar with many kinds of standardized tests, informal testing procedures, and conference and observational techniques, they will know which diagnostic avenues yield the kinds of information desired.

Because there will probably be a wide range of abilities and achievement among a group of junior high school retarded readers, teachers should be prepared to identify and to provide remediation in any area of reading: word recognition, vocabulary, comprehension — both literal and nonliteral — study skills, and/or rate of reading. Since students may be weak in one, two, or all of these areas of reading, the teacher must know which skills logically precede others, as difficulty in one area may reflect a problem in a more basic area. For example, comprehension may be influenced by poor word recognition skills, or rate of reading may be slow because of poor comprehension or a small stock of word meanings. Within each area of reading there is a myriad of skills which need to be assessed for possible gaps.

Diagnosis, of course, does not end with the initial assessment of the reading, but continues as long as the teacher is helping the student. As progress in reading is made, new and different reading needs may become apparent. As a result of new insight about the reading of students, teachers can change their instructional plans to suit the needs of their pupils.

PROVIDING MEANINGFUL INSTRUCTION

Teachers can help junior high school retarded readers by providing them with meaningful instruction in reading. Instruction should be often, preferably four or five times a week. It should be based upon the findings of the diagnosis and should be as individualized as possible by being geared to the needs of each student. Instruction should emphasize the skills which the student does not possess but which are important for further growth in reading. Teachers should capitalize on the strengths of the student, as revealed in the diagnosis, and strengthen areas of weakness. Both students and teachers should be aware of long range goals. When students help in the formulation of their own goals, instruction is usually more meaningful for them. To insure immediate success, which these students need very badly, the first goals should be easily attainable but should gradually become more difficult so that students are challenged and progress in reading is attained.

All students who are deficient in reading need much meaningful practice if they are to make progress. This aspect of reading remediation is often omitted because teachers think if students can state a generalization and apply it to a few selected words, they will automatically apply these principles to anything which they read. It is only after much meaningful practice that most retarded readers can apply their newly learned skills effectively. This practice should accompany skill development and not be left to chance or a later time. Meaningful practice should be an integral part of the instructional period so that the skills can be strengthened as they are being learned.

Meaningful practice can be attained through the student's reading of easy books for fun or information and the use of a variety of practice materials which require the understanding of running context. The student's own textbooks are sometimes suggested as a source of materials for meaningful practice. The principal limitation of the latter suggestion is that students who require special instruction in reading do not always have the necessary skills to read their textbooks. The whole purpose of remedial reading instruction may be defeated if students are given materials which are inappropriate.

If instruction in a reading class or group can be organized around a topic of interest, students have a meaningful setting in which to practice the skills they are learning. For example, they may wish to study occupations in which they are interested. By reading materials on levels which they can handle about a vocation of their choice, all can contribute information in group discussions and each can learn from the others. Written work can also be based upon the topic of the unit. Selected successful people within some of the occupations could talk to the classes and perhaps make suggestions about the importance of reading to their field of endeavor. How much more meaningful a unit approach would be than an overabundance of drill on isolated words!

Meaningful practice can take place in situations other than in the classroom. Some junior high students may gain practice by reading easy books to younger brothers or sisters or to younger pupils in the lower grades, provided they have had the opportunity to practice the reading. In these cases, the vocabulary load of these books should be in harmony with the reading level of the junior high student. The books may not be appropriate for the interest levels of junior high students but may be acceptable since they are reading the stories to children who will enjoy them. Reading materials for content area subjects, if selected commensurate with the reading achievement of students, are another source of meaningful practice.

Both instructional and leisure reading materials should be interesting to the learner and harmonious with the goals of instruction. Because of the wide diversity in the needs and achievements of junior high school retarded readers, no one book is appropriate for all students. Materials used for instructional purposes should provide for the sequential development of the skills needed by each student. When selecting instructional materials for retarded readers, teachers should be aware of the fact that students may be unable to accomplish work on the reading level indicated by their test scores, which may represent their frustration levels. They can stretch to these levels on tests but should not be expected to maintain them at all times. It is wise, especially when reading instruction is initiated, to select instructional materials one or two years below the test scores and leisure reading materials on even lower levels.

Evaluation should be a part of the instructional program and should be continuous so that remediation can move in the direction which will be most profitable for the students. Both students and teachers need to be aware of what has been accomplished and what is left to be done. Records kept jointly by students and teachers help to motivate students. For some students it is very important that daily progress be noted and honest praise from the teacher be given; if these things are done, students do not become so discouraged as they might otherwise. Although standardized tests are often used as a means of assessing reading growth, especially at peak periods during instruction, teachers should not overlook informal ways of evaluation at other times. When asked when she evaluated the reading progress of her students, one able teacher said, "I evaluate them and my teaching every day I teach them."

MAKING CURRICULAR ADJUSTMENTS

Curricular adjustments should be made for most retarded readers. Remedial reading teachers have long been concerned about the plight of their pupils when they are in other classes and are expected to fulfill the same reading requirements as their peers who have had more fortunate reading experiences. Such a situation can only inhibit growth in reading because retarded readers, who cannot possibly read the materials, may, understandably, give up in their frustration.

Content area subjects provide an opportunity for students to practice in a natural setting the reading skills which they are acquiring. Today, because there is an abundance of materials written for poor readers, it is possible for teachers to select materials which their pupils can read. Tradebooks, newspapers, magazines, textbooks in some subject areas, workbooks, and pamphlets on different reading levels are currently available. When a unit approach is used in content area subjects, retarded readers can contribute to the discussion if they have been provided with materials which they can read. The foregoing makes more work for teachers, especially the first time they make necessary adjustments in materials. However, if they are willing to help and to stimulate retarded readers with appropriate materials, the experience will be more fruitful to all than the reading of a single textbook.

If no adjustments are made in instructional materials or course requirements, other alternatives must be substituted. With each year that passes by, retarded readers become further and further behind their peers in the development of important concepts because they have not been able to read their textbooks. One alternative strongly recommended is to have assignments read to them by someone with whom the student feels comfortable: a parent, a brother or sister, a volunteer tutor, or a classmate. If the foregoing is impossible, tape recordings should be made of textbooks or similar sources, either totally, partially, or in adapted form for use by retarded readers. These tapes could be placed in listening laboratories and become a part of the learning materials of the school. By listening to either the oral reading of the assignment by another person or to tape recordings, students would have opportunities to gain insight into the topics being studied in their classes and to keep abreast with the concepts and ideas being discussed. Films, filmstrips, and pictorial presentations may also be used in a similar manner.

Other curricular adjustments may be necessary for the severely disabled readers. They may need to be assigned to fewer courses or have less reading assigned to them than other students.

Every teacher must accept the responsibility for helping retarded readers. Such a statement does not imply that all should attempt to teach the reading skills per se, which they need; in order that the student does not become more confused than he is, one teacher should be responsible for his skill development. Communication among those who work with retarded readers should be as often as feasible, for it is through a combined effort that the poor reader will be most greatly benefited.

DEVELOPING AND BROADENING READING INTERESTS

Teachers should use every available means to stimulate students to develop and broaden their interests in reading. By the time retarded readers enter junior high school their dislike for reading has snowballed to such an extent that teachers must be cautious, especially at first, in their approach to leisure reading. Yet, because of the importance of leisure reading in the strengthening of skills which students are learning, it is essential to reach these students. The development of reading interests has long been in the realm of the English department, but all teachers should share the responsibility. Sometimes a science or social studies teacher can use the student's interest in the subject to make suggestions for leisure reading. Implied in the last statement is that these teachers are informed about the reading status of their pupils and know books which retarded readers can read. Some inservice work may be a necessity in junior high schools.

One of the obvious reasons that disabled readers do not enjoy reading is that they have not had access to books which they could read. In many instances, they have been forced to try to read materials which were too difficult for them. Sometimes the problem of lack of interest is solved by helping the student find an exciting book which is easy enough for him to read. When this occurs, students have been known to say that they enjoyed a book for the first time. It will be easier to help them with a second book for they are on their way.

A second reason retarded readers do not enjoy reading is that in many schools they must prepare book reports. Since they are also usually poor in writing and spelling, they have no appetite for the preparation of these reports. Book reports have never been known to stimulate free reading and do not accomplish the goals for which they have been intended. It is surprising that an educational practice with such a small amount of promise as the book report has been continued for so many years. For these particular students it is much better for the teacher to say, "Has anyone read a good book lately?" and to permit the discussion to move from there. Since these students need the stimulation of group discussions, they can share books they have read informally through buzz sessions, group discussions, or informal conversation. Classtime should be provided for free reading so that students realize this kind of reading is important. When students need as much instruction as retarded readers do, free reading is often neglected for skill development. However, teachers must not lose sight of the fact that one of the major reasons for improvement in reading is the enjoyment which it should bring.

As teachers work with junior high retarded readers, two important factors must be remembered. First, retarded readers really want to be able to read satisfactorily. Some may conceal this desire by wearing a front and letting others believe that the matter is not important. However, they really wish to prove to themselves and to others that they are not dumb and that they can read as well as their peers. Second, almost all can learn to read adequately if they receive proper instruction adjusted to their needs and interests. These students need help so that they can make worthwhile contributions to society. It is urgent that schools find effective ways to help retarded readers.

LAURA S. JOHNSON

If It's Fun, It Can't Be Reading!

Who, if given an alternative, would choose to be a secondary-school remedial reading teacher in an inner-city school? Does any teacher have greater responsibilities, challenges, and tasks? I doubt it. Lucidly, specifically, and inspiringly, Johnson tells how she tackles her problems. Hopefully there are numerous ideas you can use or adapt.

Do you believe that materials such as newspapers can make as much difference in attitude and interest as Johnson implies? Would all school administrators enthusiastically support such an approach? Is Johnson's approach compatible with Cohen's "Taxonomy" described in an earlier article in this section? How does it agree with Emeruwa's article in Part Four and with Smith's, earlier in this section? What relationship does it have to Edward's advocacy of the language-experience approach earlier in this section?

Let us pretend for awhile today that this is the first Thursday after the first Tuesday in September. The ivy on the ledge outside our open classroom window grasps the sill and, finding support, surges with the color and vibrance of its nature as it seeks to move on into the room. We think of Dylan Thomas and the force that through the green fuse drives the flower. We feel, as we look at the ivy, that students too, given support, have a power for moving the way they were meant to go.

Yes, Ivy's got a good thing going. Maybe there's something in it for us.

Reprinted from *English Journal,* 59 (September 1970), pp. 837-845. Copyright © 1970 by the National Council of Teachers of English. Reprinted by permission of the publisher and Laura S. Johnson.

Editor's Note: This paper was read at the NCTE Convention in Washington, D.C., November 1969.

And now let our eye move inside the classroom, to the students sitting in front of us in even rows, five abreast. The reds, the oranges, and the greens of their dashikis shout the way they'd like to be. Bright, full of life, ready to be a part of the scene. But their faces tell another story. These faces exude gloom; they register dislike; some even show hatred; all bear tight lines of tension, as if bracing to confront the worst again. Within this group there is no joy. Something has struck out. Perhaps I should begin by reading them *that* poem; if I did, they'd have company in their misery of a lost ball game.

But they are depressed enough as it is. Why add to it? A November day does not glower more darkly nor sigh with greater vehemence than do most students in a Remedial Reading I class on the first day of school. For most of them, this is the eighth, ninth, or even tenth year they have been in a class labeled "poor reader." No wonder they are tired of the whole thing and have already called it quits. Their attitude says that though their counselor may have scheduled them into this course, they will be darned if they do anything while they are here.

My eye sweeps over them as I hunt for someone, or something, to open the way and let me in.

Zekiel, Abram, Hank, Bill, and Sue — on the back row. No help there.

Each of them occupies a seat at the head of a row, and each has just crashed into the wall directly behind himself. Now in mock surprise and with abject consternation they all bounce back into line but with such force that they rebound to the wall.

This, I know, will go on until Bill's chair shoots off at a tangent and bumps Sue's chair. Then she will flop down onto the floor, pick herself up with a shriek, and head toward Bill with a karate chop. Anything to get him to look at her, or her to look at him — or me to look at all of them — anything goes in these first few moments when we meet and establish our lines of communication and territoriality.

But we could forestall all of this imminent disaster. We could go out and come in again. Let's do. But before we come back in, let's reset the stage and add something very significant in the way of props.

Let's place near the door an irresistible object. Say, a stack of fresh, daily newspapers. Just off the truck. We can still smell the printer's ink. It even rubs off on our hands. But that's good. It tells us that what we have here is alive — not old, not sterile, not yesterday.

With this fresh sight in front of them, the students enter the room and pause momentarily in disbelief. Then following the instinctive urge to know what's going on, each picks up a newspaper. The next need, then, is to find a place to sit down so that they can read. Right off, a group of boys grab some seats, rearrange them into a circle, and turn at once to the baseball scores.

I do not need to utter one word to them about reading for a purpose, nor do I need to tell them the importance of skimming, nor how to do it. They take care of oral reading spontaneously and without embarrassment. What they have got going for them already knows what to do — when it counts. Like the ivy, all the kids need is a sill to hang onto. For them, crucial battles are being fought out on Wrigley Field and in Shay Stadium. Once the scores are located and the standings figured out, their talk turns to the Cubs, the Mets, and the Baltimore Orioles. Their voices rise in the heat of argument. They refer to the text in the newspaper again and again for proof of their point of view.

In another part of the room a couple of girls sit off by themselves intent on Dear Abby. The distance between their understanding of her advice on personal problems and *Mr. and Mrs. Bojo Jones* (over on the bookrack) is not great. Perhaps by the time the girls are juniors, they may even be able to comprehend *The Scarlet Letter*.

A few boys are deeply and solitarily absorbed in the opening pages of the newspaper. What *are* Nixon and Laird going to do about Vietnam? People say the war is going to last a long time, and these boys know the distance between fifteen and eighteen is only three short years. Not much time as the kid grows.

As I see my students satisfied and at ease by finding gratification for their desire to know, I am aware that they have brought their own readiness into the classroom. All I need do is recognize it, channel it, and sustain it. They sense something is coming their way, something that says "Yes" to them, rather than "No." Something's going on in reading class that they haven't run into before. Why, Man, here in this one, you can read!

The following day, beside the stack of newspapers, the students find a pile of records.

"Hey, look! The Miracles!" Irene exclaims.

"You got to be kiddin'," says Bobbie.

"No, honest," she answers. "And to prove it, here's a record player."

"You mean we gonna jam today?" Billy breaks in.

"If you like," I say. "Today we are going to have a chance to listen and read."

The news is greeted with a clamor as I hand out dittoed sheets with the words of "Here I Go Again." Some students read the song in silence, others orally, and some begin to sing it. Somewhere in here, among the litany, the record player gets turned on and the impact of Smokey Robinson gathers them all into a union which ends with a sigh as the music dies away. A silence falls then, as if the audaciousness of it all is just too much of a good thing. It is suddenly broken by Sammy, tall, dark, and serious.

"How come?" he asks. "I thought we's sposed to be in a Readin' class. And jammin' ain't readin'."

"Man, you crazy," says Bo. "You readin', ain't cha?"

"Yeah," says Sammy slowly. "But this is fun. And if it's fun, it can't be readin'."

Well, can't it?

For most of them the daily newspaper soon becomes an absolute must. Likewise, the songs and the things they say and do when put on tape. These also become an important part of what they read.

The newspaper puts them into the habit of reading every day, a thing many of them have never done before. They gain a sense of continuity about events, too, as they read, for most major news stories extend over two or three days. This gives the students a chance to relate what's happening now to something which happened in the past as they read about it in history, or as something artistically conceived in literature, music, and art.

In this class, of course, there are a few students who cannot even read a newspaper. Their reading level is nil or else so low that even the sixth-grade vocabulary of the paper is beyond them. But I have something for them, too, so that they won't feel embarrassed or look left out because they are not reading like the other students.

For them I have magazines. The student who can't read can always look at pictures and make it seem as if he is reading. And this is what he will do until such time as I can test him individually and know better how to help him. Our range of magazines is wide, with heavy emphasis on cars and sports for the boys, clothes and looks for the girls. Several copies of *Hot Rod* and *Sports Illustrated* have never been too many; and cartoon books about cars are really great. The girls go for *Teen, Seventeen, Jet,* and *Ebony,* and they could care less about things mechanical or enervating.

Along with the magazines and the newspapers, two spindles of paperback books are a great attraction for the better readers in the group. Once the newspaper urge for the day is satisfied, these better readers descend upon the paperback books like bees upon clover. Sports, humor, cars, and the supernatural offer the greatest attraction in this kind of reading. Ethnic fiction is popular, too, much more so than is nonfiction among this fifteen- and sixteen-year-old group. Most of them are not yet ready to take on remaking the world. Perhaps this will come later, and tempered then by the degree to which they have succeeded earlier in feeling respected as individuals.

Ready access to all of this reading material is very important, and we are generous in its availability to the students. Newspapers can be cut up or taken home when they are a day old. Magazines need to be noncurrent before they can be taken apart. I try to keep the books moving in and out, and yet still keep a good supply on hand, for the books are a very important part of the reading program. Many of the students come from homes that have no books. So I believe it is especially important for the students to be surrounded by them at school. And yet this presents a problem. For if, in this openness the books go out and do not come back, a part of our reading program disappears. For it to be effective, it must have something for everybody. We need to have all of its parts. The biggest culprit, so far as loss of books is concerned, turns out to be the nonreader.

But we can forestall this kind of thing if we offer the student something else first, something he'd rather have anyway. An analysis of why he takes and destroys a book he can't read supplies the remedy.

Let's say the boy takes *Stock Car Racer,* even though he

can't read it. But it has an exciting picture of a car and a boy on the front cover. Gee! He'd like to own that car, and be that boy, and win that race! But he can't, really. He knows a dozen reasons why none of these things will ever happen. And yet, wouldn't it be great fun if he could just read the story and pretend for a while that it could happen?

So he takes the book for which he feels a real need — he wants to be, for a little while, the boy in the picture on the cover of that book. Possessing it, he feels good for another reason too. He sees the other fellows taking out books to read. He wants to do what they are doing. He doesn't want to look stupid, which is what will happen if he walks out without a book. So he picks *Stock Car Racer* off the rack.

The illusion is good while it lasts. He's like the rest of the kids, and he's winning the race! But as soon as he gets outside of the room, away from the other books and kids and the teacher, the dream vanishes. That's when he pitches the book into the nearest wastebasket. Now if it only had some pictures, it might stand a chance of being looked at and perhaps of even making a trip back into the Reading Center. But without pictures, it will never return unless a perceptive janitor rescues it from the trash can and brings it back.

So what can the teacher do to cut down on this kind of loss and still have a paperback library? One of the things he can do is have enough magazines with pictures in them so that the poor reader will take them instead of the books. For unless he is totally illiterate, he can make some sense out of what he reads by looking at the pictures and by figuring out some of the words through context. After all, that is the way he learned to read Dick and Jane about ten years ago. He is simply carrying over a little longer into high school what he was exposed to in the first grade. So what if he misses a few things along the way, like the middles and the endings of words? That's nothing new for him. He's been making his way on pictures and by guessing for a long, long time.

But not just any picture.

Though his desire for pictures in magazines must be met, the magazines must look just as adult and respectable as the paperback books. A boy once put it very accurately to me when he said, "I like *True* magazine because it says right here on the cover it's a man's magazine." A statement like this emphasizes.

the young man's need to be treated as if he were an adult. And most of them can make a legitimate claim for this treatment. They look the part; they have jobs of a sort; a lot of them have transportation such as cars or bikes, and some even have a girl. So appeal to them should be made through adult-slanted materials. By reading materials which recognize their growing maturity, they achieve an improved self-image, and when this occurs through a reading class, they begin to feel more kindly toward reading. They discover that there is something in it for them.

When I sense that they are leaning this way, I have my first evidence that their attitude is changing in favor of the positive, that I have begun to score with them. For from the start, I have considered my first task with them to be one of changing their attitude about reading from negative to positive. Most of them have come to me with a strong antipathy for it, and until I disperse this, I cannot do much of lasting benefit for them. There is, of course, a great deal more I need to do, and will hope to get done; but changing their attitude so that they are willing to bring their power to bear on eliminating their reading problem must come first. I believe that until I can change their attitude toward reading, I cannot effect a permanent change in them. And this is what I am most concerned about.

I am primarily interested in what I can do that will have transfer value. I ask myself, "What will they do with reading after they leave my class?" And I answer, "If they are not moved to read on their own after they get out of my class, I have not done much to help them." I know that if they are to keep any gains they make in decoding in this class — if they are to improve at all in the skill of reading, they will have to be motivated to practice it. Unless they do this, daily and consistently and over a lifetime, the drills I can give them to raise their vocabulary achievement a few test points in June will not be worth a thing as transfer in the following September's test. They may not even register in that fall test because what they drilled on earlier did not become an integral part of their language pattern. And it did not become a part of that pattern because it was not rooted in an interest of theirs. So unused, unrelated, over a period of three months, the drills disappeared and the student had no carryover.

But worse than a poor showing testwise is the time the

student could have been reading, finding out things he didn't know. For of course he didn't read because it had no pleasure for him. He had never found fun in it. So why do something so unpleasant if he did not have to?

For high school students I try to plan a reading program which emphasizes the pleasure and self-satisfaction in reading. I try to make it fulfilling rather than depleting.

The free ranging we begin through newspapers, magazines, and paperback books on the first day of class is continued on all the other days whenever a student finishes his assigned work and has some free time. But to assure every student's having some chance for free reading every day, each class period begins with ten minutes of reading; most students read the newspaper during this period. Once this habit becomes established, it is almost impossible to break. But who wants to? Who can justify not reading in Reading? I dare to predict a mutiny if we tried to begin a reading class now without a newspaper. I have students from other classes stop by my room and beg for newspapers; I have heard them speak with regret of not being able to read in their classes. Somehow, it seems as though we ought to be able to do something about this.

At the beginning of the year, too, each student fills out an informal inventory on which he indicates his attitude toward reading and his preferences in it. This inventory does several things for both of us. It gives him an opportunity to state privately just what he really feels and thinks about reading. It tells him, too, that I am on his side because I have asked his opinion about what he wants to work with in this class.

And I discover, from what and how he writes, a great deal about his language patterns. This is important because I view reading as just one part of the total language process. I need to see reading in relation to a whole if I am to work with the part successfully. I must view reading in its relationship to the (1) subconscious or perceptive nature of the individual, (2) to the manner in which he speaks, (3) listens, (4) reads, and (5) writes. When I know his *total* pattern, I know more about him as a reader.

When I read what he writes, I know something of how words look to him when he reads. I know, too, something of how they sound to him when he listens. I discover that he is totally unaware of tense and of plurals; I see that phonetic spelling is the rule rather than the exception; I find odd combinations of consonants in his writing; I see him omitting vowels, structure words, and marks of punctuation; I find him reversing letters. I learn, in short, that for him, reading is an excursion into a foreign language, most of which he does not get because he does not recognize its printed form. What he has been able to learn rests mostly on what he has been able to pick up from listening and looking at pictures.

If he is to *read* I must take him back to that place in the primary or intermediate grades where his missing techniques still await him; I must return with him to the place where, for a host of reasons, he either missed or rejected what he needed the first time around. But he must come willingly with me if he is to acquire it this time, for reading is not a skill easy to acquire. Now that he is fourteen, fifteen, or sixteen years old, he is psychologically not at all the person he was when he first encountered the code-breaking process.

Though he may need the same things at sixteen which he needed at age six, I cannot teach them in the same way. At age six he was still curious and eager to learn. Then he entered school, wanting to learn to read. He still thought he could find out what he wanted to know by reading. Also, as a child, he had a built-in love for repetition. This was the time when he liked to hear the same story over and over again. This was the time when he could still take the repetitive drills necessary for learning the shapes of letters, the sounds of consonants, and vowels, digraphs, blends, and the like. This was the time when his teacher could discover any ineptness in him and correct it.

But it was, unfortunately, also the time when she did not do this. Perhaps her class was so large that she couldn't get around to helping the children who were slower at catching on to the system for decoding. Or perhaps her teaching situation was so deprived that she could not do what she knew she ought to do. Perhaps the child himself brought handicaps to learning — perceptual, environmental, or otherwise. Whatever the reason for his lack of success in reading in the first grade, he kept falling further and further behind as he went on through the elementary school. With each passing year he took more verbal and emotional abuse from parents, teachers, and peers because of his failure. A lowered self-image, frustration, lack of motivation, and hostility thus become built into his personality so strongly that by the time he arrives in the ninth-grade reading class, I have more than just a decoding problem to solve for him. I need to be something of a counselor and a therapist as well.

From the very first day he enters that ninth-grade reading class he needs to meet some success and some pleasure. The best way for this to happen is to give him something to read or look at or listen to that interests him. Once he has become confident that he can count on finding these things in the reading classroom every day, he relaxes and becomes more willing to try decoding again. I make it more palatable to him, too, and more relevant by using newspaper and magazine materials as the basis for our drill materials. In fact, prefixes and suffixes may be more at home in an article on Operation Breadbasket than in the traditional reading workbook. Vocabulary words such as *hostile, deliberate,* and *incriminate* somehow make more sense and stick in the memory longer if taken out of a newspaper account of the Conspiracy Trial than if listed, out of context, in a word book.

Using the current and daily newspaper like this, of course, requires my getting to school early before my first class so that I can go through the paper carefully enough to spot the one or two articles in it which I am sure will have most appeal to my students. Then I must quickly adapt these articles to the use I intend to make of them that day.

If, for example, I am working on comprehension and want students to recognize the logical order of ideas, I can copy onto ditto stencils the beginning three or four paragraphs of an article, but I will not place them in sequence. I will put them in a scrambled order and ask the students to number them in 1,2,3,4 order. After they have done this, we will discuss the word clues and the idea clues which are present to help a reader know what comes first, then second, then third, and finally fourth. Again, paragraphs such as a local march on the City Hall for better housing are better materials for an exercise like this than some in a workbook about events totally unrelated to the students.

To help them see how much there is in the newspaper and in reading as an activity for them, each student is asked to make a scrapbook of clippings related to an interest of his. Over a three-week period, each student learns to select a topic — and for the really unmotivated ones this in itself becomes a major project. Once a topic is selected, the next step is to read, looking only for articles related to that one idea. Here the student practices reading for a purpose skimming, categorizing, vocabulary, comprehension. He delves deeper and learns to ask questions about his reading, and he also provides answers for them. He may write a theme about his interest, or read a magazine article or a book relating to it. When he has finished his project, his scrapbook provides a graphic representation in print of something interesting to him.

Records offer him a strong inducement to read too. When a student brings us a pop record to play to the class, he also brings along the words which go with it. If it has no words, he provides them for the way it makes him feel when he listens to it. I type the words onto ditto master sheets and produce copies for each student so that as he listens, he can also follow the words in print. Many students, learning to read this way, discover that in print many a word has sounds and letters which they do not know it has, judging from the way they say it and write it. For students whose native dialect is not standard English, this tape-listening-reading situation is very helpful. Of course, any materials that appeal to the students can be used this way: poems, stories, essays, plays, jokes — almost anything they want to bring and record can be transcribed into print to be read while they listen. For many students, this eye-ear connection has never been made before. For some, it is the road out of their reading problem.

Every Friday we have a reading review. It never takes the same form twice. Sometimes it is oral; sometimes it is written. One aspect of it has slowly but steadily grown in importance. To impress upon these so-called nonreaders their dependence upon reading, and also to demonstrate to them that they are not nonreaders, I ask them to list everything they can think of that they have read during the week. When we began this listing, most of the students said they never read anything. But questioning on my part soon showed them that they read more than they thought. Now their lists contain not only newspapers, magazines, books and history lessons, but also their journals for English, science lab reports, basketball schedules, marching band formations, menus, sales checks, price tags, street signs, prayer books, hymnals, candy wrappers, traffic tickets, and

even a court summons. From their written reviews, I type
excerpts and ditto them to use again as reading when the
material has been put on tape. The first time we did this, one
student was so impressed by what she had done that she ex-
claimed, "Do you know? This is the first time I've ever been in
print."

A comment so pointed and honest as this makes me realize
anew the importance of recognition for the student who almost
never has a chance to shine or excel in school. As a teacher of
regular classes, I was always aware of those three or four very
poor students who were scraping along at the bottom of the
roster of thirty-five; but what does anybody ever have time to
do for them? The papers and the reports and the meetings and
the demands on the usual English teacher are so heavy that the
poor kid who just can't keep up rarely gets the daily individual
help he needs if he is ever to have a chance at all.

So though the taped-typed contribution of someone in a
remedial reading class would look meager when viewed on the
continuum of a regular English class, in the larger space which
this remedial student has in his much smaller reading class,
what he does begins to assume importance. And this feeling of
importance, of being somebody, is what he must have if he is
ever to pull himself out of the slough of failure in which he has
been stuck for so many years.

Occasionally a few students will become so involved in a
news event that they will want to carry on with it even after it
leaves the front page. Two boys in one of my classes got into a
terrific argument one day about Paul McCartney. Was he alive
or was he dead? They squared off for a debate, but each asked
for a week to get prepared. When their day came, each was
ready with support he'd gleaned from a week of going through
magazines, collecting pictures, and playing excerpts from
several Beatles albums. We taped the debate, included snatches
of the songs; all of us listened carefully to the supposedly buried
clues which proved, or disproved, that Paul is dead — or is still
alive. Fortunately, for the debater who contended that Paul
McCartney is still alive, *Life* magazine came out that week with
a strong supporting article just at the right time. The class voted
at the end of the debate, but the count was a tie. However, even
though the decision was not clear, the popularity of Beatles'
albums is still undisputed.

For me, however, the real issue was not Paul; mine was reading. Did they read or didn't they? Did they read on their own time? Was it spontaneous? Was it voluntary? Was it something they didn't have to do, but they did it anyway — because they wanted to?

I felt I won that one.

As the weeks go by and the students come to feel more and more that reading is something they must have in order to satisfy some deep inner need, I find myself becoming more and more involved with getting them what they want to read. Mitch, for example, has had me scouring every one of the five bookstores I patronize for books on cars. When I couldn't find any more, I channeled him into science fiction. This kick should hold him for a while; but when I see it waning, I hope to have some indication from him of the next direction to take. From the start, Mitch has been the best reader in all of my classes, being about only one grade below level when he came. Perhaps he should not even have qualified for remedial reading because he was so good, when compared with the rest of the kids. But quickly I sensed his morale building qualities for me and the other students, furnishing as he did a shining example of what it was like to be a good reader. So I let him stay. Now he comes into class each day, breezes in five minutes through the assignment the other kids will spend twenty minutes on, and then spends the rest of his time off by himself in a corner reading. But, of course — this *is* a class in reading!

Sammy, who earlier in the year doubted the validity of a reading class that was fun, had a problem with words, which he finally got up nerve enough to talk about with me. He came up one day after class and asked, "Could you get me somethin' I always wanted to read?"

"Sure," I said. "What is it?"

"It's this thing about ice. I hear people talkin' about it." So the next day I handed him *Soul on Ice*. A week later he brought it back and sadly deposited it on my desk.

"What's wrong?" I asked. "Don't you like what Eldridge Cleaver has to say?"

"It's not that," he said. "It's just I can't read it. But that's the way it always is. Them great books always has them big hard words in them."

Knowing how disappointed he felt, and remembering that

his news scrapbook was entitled "Black People Who Did Something Important," I gave him another paperback which I was sure he could read — a simplified version of Gordon Parks' *A Choice of Weapons.* He got it on a Thursday afternoon; the following Monday he brought it back and said happily, "Gee, that was great. What else have you got?" *Harlem Summer* was nearby, so he took that out. Again he read it in less than a week. Next came an easy book on Frederick Douglass. This was followed by *Roosevelt Grady* and *South Town.*

Now, he is eager to read, and so convinced of the benefit to him of reading extensively and on a level easy enough to give him no trouble with words, that he is following my suggestion of going to the young people's section of the public library to hunt for books for a fictitious sixth-grade brother. And I am willing to predict that Sammy's brother will hurry through sixth grade and graduate into junior high in record time, for Sammy has a great thing going. He's got himself. And he's going to move along and make up for lost time. And when the day comes that finds him reading *Soul on Ice,* it will happen, I think, because for him reading did become fun.

ALBERT J. HARRIS

What About Special Theories
of Teaching Remedial Reading?

Excruciatingly slow progress and little or no improvement despite intensive or long-term instruction have caused many educators to question some of the commonly accepted assumptions and remedial methods and to search for other approaches in hopes of achieving better results. And there is no doubt but that methods deviating drastically from traditional ones will spew forth in an increasing torrent in the near future as new insights into human behavior are discovered and older ones are resurrected. Educators desiring to be professional must not only know of these approaches but also form sound, cogent opinions about them. One of the most outstanding and respected figures in remedial reading instruction, Albert J. Harris, does precisely that in the following discussion.

In what way does Harris believe these methods are similar? Which of these four are you familiar with? For which of them would reading of original sources benefit you? For whom are these methods generally aimed? Are there any ideas in Part Two of this book that could have stimulated educators to reject traditional approaches and adopt these special methods? How would you summarize Harris's opinions on these methods — cautious, enthusiastic, cynical, skeptical, or reserved? Has this discussion whetted your appetite for more information on these and other rather exotic methods?

Majority opinion among remedial specialists has for many years favored the policy of beginning remedial reading by using perceptual and memory abilities which are normal or least impaired and, while the child is learning by a method with

---

From *Current Issues in Reading*, Nila B. Smith, ed. (Newark, Delaware: International Reading Association, 1969), pp. 392-407. Reprinted with permission of Albert J. Harris and the International Reading Association.

which he can achieve some success, working to strengthen those perceptual and associative abilities that are particularly weak. Major emphasis has been on capitalizing on strengths with minor emphasis on building up areas of weakness.

The contrast between the general remedial viewpoint and a newer point of view has been clearly stated by Silver and Hagin *(39)*:

> Our initial concept had been that compensation was a basic principle; i.e., after assessing perceptual assets and deficits, we should train in the areas of greater perceptual strength, via the most intact modalities. Results of the follow-up studies, however, suggest that this technique does not appear to enhance perception or to effect lasting improvement in reading. Efforts now are directed to the stimulation of the defective perceptual areas. This is almost a complete reversal of our earlier approach. Our purpose now is really to enhance cerebral maturation, to bring neurological functioning to the point where it is physiologically capable of learning to read.

This paper will attempt to explore several new approaches to remedial reading which share the viewpoint expressed by Silver and Hagin, to review the research currently available concerning them, and to arrive at tentative conclusions concerning their readiness for widespread adoption.

The writer had originally hoped to be able to include, under "special methods," those that attempt to simplify the reading task by using special alphabets, applications of programed instruction and reinforcement psychology, and various forms of psychotherapy. However, limitations of time and space have made it necessary to limit the scope of coverage.

Most of the approaches to be discussed agree with the statement of Krippner *(25)*: "Often a program of perceptual training, dominance establishment, and/or motor coordination improvement is needed before reading improvement will be helpful." The four major approaches to be discussed place emphasis on 1) developing neurological organization 2) establishing a firm motor and perceptual base, 3) developing specific perceptual skills, and 4) using drugs to improve the learner's accessibility to instruction.

In attempting to appraise any new approach one must realize that the first efforts to study the value of an innovation are usually case reports or small-scale and poorly controlled pilot studies which may indicate whether the procedure is worth more careful evaluation — but which cannot do much more. An everpresent danger is the placebo effect described by McDonald *(29)* — the power of positive suggestion which tends to enhance the effects of any innovation when used by its creator or by a devoted disciple. A second danger is the Hawthorne effect, the built-in advantage that almost any new experimental procedure has over the routine and comparatively unglamorous procedure assigned to a control group. A third problem is that of broad generalization from results obtained with small groups of doubtfully representative subjects over a short period of time. A fourth problem in evaluating the evidence is the reasearcher's temptation to use a statistical method which tends to maximize the possibility of finding a statistically significant difference, whether it is the most appropriate way to treat the data. In reviewing the evidence the writer has tried to keep these possible sources of error constantly in mind.

One must keep in mind, also, that as yet there is no good statistical evidence on the frequency of neurologically based reading disability or the percent of retarded readers whose problems fall into this category. Recently Morris *(30)*, in a large-scale study, reported that ". . . the poorest readers were not in any reasonable interpretation of the term a neurological problem, and that the study as a whole lends little support to the idea that 'specific developmental dyslexia' is an identifiable syndrome distinct from 'reading backwardness.' In other words, if 'word blindness' exists as a condition which cannot be treated by good teaching within the state educational system it must be a rare condition indeed."

Nevertheless, there are many specialists in learning disabilities who believe in a special condition caused by heredity, severe environmental deprivation, or brain damage which makes it extremely difficult for some children with otherwise normal intelligence to learn to read. Among the characteristics stressed as frequently found in this group are poor visual and auditory perception, poor ability to make visual-auditory associations, and directional confusion; distractibility, motor restlessness, clumsiness, and short attention span are reported in many cases *(20)*. Most of the special remedial methods have been advocated especially for this subgroup of disabled readers.

THE DELACATO APPROACH:
NEUROLOGICAL INTEGRATION

Delacato has explained his theoretical basis and remedial procedures in three books *(8, 9, 10)*. Obviously only a very sketchy summary can be given here. Very briefly, he believes that in some children a failure to achieve neurological integration below the cortical level of the brain is basic and must be corrected by such activities as sleeping in a particular position and learning to crawl and creep properly. When subcortical integration is present or has been developed, the major problem is lack of clear and consistent dominance of one cerebral hemisphere over the other. A variety of treatment procedures have the common purpose of strengthening the consistent use of the dominant hand and compelling the child to rely on the eye on the same side as the dominant hand. Among the procedures used are eliminating music, occluding one eye to force reliance on the other, creeping, crawling, and so on. Once neurological integration has been achieved, the child is said to learn to read by normal developmental teaching methods.

In his books Delacato has presented brief versions of fifteen studies, for several of which he did the statistical work on data supplied by others. A careful analytical review of these studies has recently been made by Glass and Robbins *(18)*, who analyzed each of the studies in detail, considering research design and statistical treatment. Their conclusions are summarized in the following quotation:

> Twelve experiments are analyzed in light of the controls which were lacking in their execution and the shortcomings of the reported statistical analysis. Serious doubts about the validity of any of the twelve experiments are raised. An analysis of correlation studies reported by Delacato reveals a conclusion quite contrary to the implications drawn by him from the data. Without exception, the empirical studies cited by Delacato as a 'scientific appraisal' of his theory of neurological organization are shown to be of dubious value.

The writer had read the fifteen studies before seeing the Glass and Robbins critique and reread them afterward. He finds himself in close agreement with their criticisms.

Recent research has cast doubt on the idea that crossed dominance — having the preferred eye on the opposite side from the preferred hand — had any relation to success in reading, although Delacato considers this condition sufficient evidence of neurological immaturity. In the writer's own research *(21)*, crossed dominance was not significantly more frequent in severe reading disabilities than in an unselected school population, while mixed-handedness and directional confusion were found in a substantially higher proportion of reading disabilities. A study by Stephen, Cunningham, and Stigler *(43)* recently found no relationship between crossed dominance and reading readiness in kindergarten children.

Independent studies bearing on the Delacato approach have not produced supporting evidence. Yarborough *(46)* studied the value of the Leavell Language-Development Service, a procedure for strengthening the use of the eye on the same side as the preferred hand. Using a stereoscopic technique similar to one used by Delacato, she found no evidence of significant benefit in reading. Robbins *(35, 36)* tried out Delacato procedures with second graders. Not only did he find no benefit in reading but, after the training to establish consistent sidedness, there were two more children with crossed dominance than before the training.

Anderson *(1)* tried cross-pattern creeping and walking exercises with kindergarten children and found no significant improvement in readiness in the experimental as compared with a control group. He did a similar study with intermediate grade students and again found no significant differences for the total population, for lower I.Q. children, or for those with lower initial reading ability.

It may turn out eventually that the Delacato approach is useful for a small percentage of children with severe reading disabilities. However, the research efforts to date have failed to provide evidence of its value. In view of the widespread publicity given to these procedures and the considerable number of children who at present are spending a substantial part of their school time creeping and crawling, definitive impartial research on the Delacato system is urgently needed.

A rather extreme version of a point of view resembling that of Delacato is expounded by a private organization in Chicago called The Reading Research Foundation *(33)*. In a brochure explaining its program the following statements are made:

> Development of the capacity to sustain concentration is influenced by continuous changes in the stimulus cues for the appropriate response-pattern and for signaling success and error of response. Furthermore, the intensity of the signals (loud hollers, for example) are used as one way of developing the stability of concentration. Cross-lateral patterns of movements are used extensively in order to promote neurological organization in each of the cerebral hemispheres as well as an integration in their functioning.

The writer has received from this organization two mimeographed papers reporting small-scale tryouts of their procedures with first grade children. Although differences between the final reading scores of total experimental and control groups were not significant in both studies, the authors argue for significance in one case by restricting the comparison to low groups of twelve children each and in the other by disregarding a nonsignificant analysis of variance and stressing a comparison of gain scores, which is, in the writer's opinion, a dubious statistical procedure *(27, 28)*.

A very recent feature article in the *Chicago Daily News* describes this program and reports comments by two visitors. The following is a direct quotation from the article: "Dr. E. R. Simmons, director of the Texas Reading Institute, San Antonio, visited the school and saw teachers shake, pinch, and pull the hair of students. He described his attitude as disbelief giving way to anger and distress. . . . James Weddell, director of Purdue University's Achievement Center for Children said some of his staff were 'appalled' by the approach, fearing it may 'tear some kids asunder emotionally.'" It is not necessary for me to add to these comments.

KEPHART: MOTOR AND PERCEPTUAL TRAINING

Kephart *(23)* has advocated programs for slow or disabled learners in which much emphasis is placed on developing readiness. In a recent paper coauthored with Dunning occurs the following: "Readiness for learning. . . consists of a hierarchical build-up of generalizations which allows the child to deal more effectively with his environment. Learning difficulties may be viewed in terms of difficulties in this developmental sequence. When such difficulties occur, then there are gaps in the sequence which will affect all future learning either by limiting or distorting it" *(11)*. In the Kephart approach emphasis is placed on helping children change from stereotyped, rigid movement patterns to variable, adaptive, and purposeful mόvement patterns. Specific graded sequences of exercises are suggested to develop balance and locomotion and to improve laterality, directionality, ocular pursuit, and temporal rhythm and succession. Essentially the same basic program seems to be recommended for mentally retarded, brain-injured, and reading-disability children.

There is as yet little published research on the effectiveness of the Kephart approach in improving reading. Rutherford *(38)* studied the effect of Kephart-type activities on the Metropolitan Readiness Test scores of kindergarten children. He found a significant gain for the boys in the experimental group but not for the girls. Whether this program would induce better reading later on is not known. Roach *(34)* used perceptual-motor training of the Kephart type with groups of reading-disability children averaging twelve years old and found no significant differences in oral reading. LaPray and Ross *(26)*, selecting first graders who were low in both reading and visual perception, compared a group given training in large-muscle activities and visual training with one given extra time with simple reading materials; the former group improved more on perceptual tests and the latter on reading tests. The writer has not yet found any controlled research that shows the Kephart approach to be useful in the treatment of reading disabilities.

Points of view quite similar to those of Kephart have been expressed by Barsch *(3)*, Getman *(17)*, and Batemen *(4)*. The writer has not been able to find controlled research relevant to their theoretical positions.

Since establishment of directionality is one of the objectives of Kephart, it may be appropriate at this point to mention a new method of preventing and correcting reversal tendencies. Daniels *(7)* has described a simple procedure which he says requires only one 20-minute session and is effective two years later. He uses paired cutout forms which are mirror images, such as locomotives facing right and left. The child is shown a pair and then practices fitting each part into the correct formboard depression; this procedure is then practiced with many similar pairs. Daniels states that one lesson at about the age of four prevented reversals at the age of six. Certainly this procedure deserves to be tested by others; if it should be found to work, one of the big problems in reading could be eliminated for most children.

SPECIFIC PERCEPTUAL TRAINING

Emphasis on developing specific perceptual skills received major impetus with the publication of the Illinois Test of Psycholinguistic Abilities *(24)* and the Marianne Frostig Developmental Tests of Visual Perception *(16)*. With analytical tests available, training programs were developed to improve the particular functional weaknesses disclosed by the tests. Although this approach seems reasonable and in accord with common sense, both the diagnostic validity of the tests and the value of spending time on perceptual training instead of remedial reading are at present questionable.

Olson *(31, 32)*, studied the predictive value of the Frostig test and found that it had some predictive value when correlated with reading scores in grades two and three, but neither the total score nor the individual part scores were substantial predictors of specific difficulties in reading. Rosen *(37)* compared twelve experimental classes which received a half hour of Frostig training per day with thirteen classes receiving reading instruction only. The differences on reading tests consistently favored the control group but were not significant when adjustments were made to equate the groups for readiness.

According to Weener, Barritt, and Semmel *(45)*, the Illinois Test of Psycholinguistic Abilities falls short of the statistical requirements for a satisfactory diagnostic test. They found that the reliabilities of I.T.P.A. subtests are too low, both split-half and test-retest, for adequate prediction and diagnosis from individual profiles.

Thus both of these tests, which have been widely adopted in reading clinics and by school psychologists, are imperfect instruments. A remedial program based on their high and low subtest scores may or may not fit the child's needs. It is to be hoped that revised versions or new perceptual tests will provide more accurate diagnostic analyses of perceptual and linguistic skills, information which will in turn permit research to determine whether remedial programs based on such tests will be valuable.

It should be noted that Frostig's descriptions *(15)* of her own remedial approach are broader and more flexible than study of her perceptual training materials might lead one to expect. She states that she includes physiotherapy, physical education, eye exercises, and help with fine motor coordination when indicated in an individual diagnosis *(14)* and employs varied teaching procedures for reading, including picture cues, phonics, and kinesthetic procedures when indicated *(13)*.

Concentrated training in auditory perception as a preparation for remedial reading is advocated by Daniels *(7)*, who reported that a group of retarded readers given one term of auditory training followed by two terms of phonics-oriented remedial reading improved more than a matched group given three terms of remedial reading. Since the control groups final average-age score was only 6.3, the quality of its remedial instruction would not seem to have been very high.

Silver, Hagin, and Hersh *(40)* have issued a progress report on what seems to be a quite important study. One group of disabled readers was given training in auditory and visual perception for half a year, followed by remedial reading during the second half year; the other group had remedial reading for the first half and perceptual training during the second half. However, the remedial teaching consisted of using a basal reader and following the teacher's manual — hardly an optimal remedial procedure. The authors concluded: "The results so far suggest that where perceptual defects are first trained out, reading instruction at intermodal and verbal levels will have a better chance of success. This is particularly true of the more severe language disabilities, those with defects in multiple modalities, and those in whom 'soft' neurological signs may be found." The final report of the study is not yet available.

A quite sophisticated study of the value of training in auditory perception was conducted by Feldmann and Deutsch *(12)* with third grade Negro and Puerto Rican children in New York City; all of the children were initially reading below

middle second grade. The experimental children were instructed in small groups of two to four, three times a week for
five months. In the first study there were three experimental
groups: remedial reading only, auditory training only, and
separate periods of reading and auditory training. None of the
experimental groups did significantly better than the others or
better than the control group that received only regular
classroom reading instruction. On the assumption that the
instruction program needed improvement, a second study was
conducted with new but similar children. Changes were made in
the auditory training program, and a new variable integrating
auditory training with remedial reading was added. Again the
results showed the control group doing as well as the experimental groups and no significant differences among the
experimental groups.

The results of the Feldmann and Deutsch study demonstrate that one cannot assume that training in auditory perception will necessarily benefit retarded readers; transfer of
what is learned during perceptual training to the act of reading
is not automatic and sometimes does not take place.

DRUG TREATMENT FOR READING DISABILITY

The most ambitious effort to provide a theoretical and experimental basis for a drug treatment approach as an adjunct to
remedial teaching is that of Smith and Carrigan *(41)*. Starting
with the hypothesis that reading disability is based on a
physiological difficulty in the transmission of nerve impulses in
the brain, they developed theoretical models for five syn-
dromes, based on various patterns of excess or deficiency in two
chemicals, cholinesterase and acetylcholine. They then
analyzed the results of a test battery given to 40 cases of reading
disability and reported that most of the cases fell into groups
that corresponded to the models. Some of the children were
given drugs chosen on the basis of the kind of change assumed
to be needed in the child's brain chemistry. Statistically better
response to remedial reading was reported for those taking
medication as compared to other children not receiving
medication. In 1961 the writer *(19)*, prepared an evaluation of
this study which may be briefly summarized as follows: the
theoretical base is highly original, most interesting, and still

possibly correct; the experimental evidence is unconvincing because of technical errors in design and execution. It is a pity that nobody has attempted to replicate the Smith-Carrigan study.

Staiger *(42)* studied the effects of a drug called Deanol on perception and reading improvement. He found a gain in perceptual speed for those taking the medication, but not in reading.

Baldwin and Kenny *(2)* tried twenty medications, singly and in combination, with 100 children having behavior disorders involving hyperactivity, impulsiveness, etc. The most effective treatment in reducing symptoms was a combination of Benadryl and Dilantin which produced some improvement in two-thirds of the cases to whom it was given, while only one child got worse. For children who are very hard to teach because of behavior disorders, the use of drugs to make them amenable to instruction seems quite plausible.

However, one should not confuse expectations with results. Valusek *(44)* did a carefully controlled study on the use of drugs with retarded readers in a state mental hospital using Thorazine, Cytomel, and Dexedrine, tranquilizers that are quite popular in psychiatric practice. He found no significant differences between the medication and placebo groups in oral or silent reading or on psychological tests.

An interesting report of successful drug treatment for a specific subgroup of disabled readers comes from Calvert and Cromes *(5)*. In the eye-movement photographs of children who were not responding to remedial tutoring they found evidence of fine tremors or spasms occurring at intervals of about 18 seconds. Treatment of a few of these children with Primidone both stopped the tremors permanently and was followed by improved learning. The writer has not found any other study reporting either similar tremors or the use of Primidone, so this study certainly seems worth replicating.

These are the only studies the writer has found on the use of drugs with children having reading disabilities, studies which are certainly not definitive. It would seem logical that when children with reading disability are hyperactive or sluggish or depressed, appropriate drug therapy should be a useful adjunct to remedial teaching. New discoveries with animals open up possibilities of improving human mental functioning chemically, but as yet this area is something for the future. Certainly any use of medication should be prescribed and supervised by a physician, and we need much more research on the use of drugs with poor readers.

SUMMARY AND CONCLUSIONS

This paper has considered four main approaches to the treatment of reading disability by procedures other than teaching reading skills. All are interesting, but none has yet been firmly substantiated.

Most radically innovative is the Delacato's stress on neurological organization and laterality. Both Delacato's basic theories and the practical value of his procedures for treating reading disabilities are very much open to question. Publicity has far outstripped proof. Hopefully, careful objective studies will be done to discover if the method really helps any children with reading problems and, if so, how to identify the cases to which the method may be applicable. Adoption of cross-pattern creeping and attempts to alter patterns of lateral dominance are not justified for either schools or reading clinics on the basis of present evidence.

The Kephart approach, stressing the improvement of motor control and flexibility, the development of hand and eye coordination, and directionality, has not yet found verification as an improvement in remedial reading programs. However, it would seem to have some intrinsic value apart from reading. Better control of one's body can be a desirable goal in itself. Perhaps this kind of training will find a home in the physical education program rather than be judged in terms of whether it makes a direct contribution to academic learning.

Since there is ample evidence that visual and auditory perception are both significantly correlated with success in beginning reading, the main question would seem to be how to give perceptual training rather than whether to give it. Can it be most effective when it proceeds or parallels reading instruction or when it is an integral part of reading instruction and emphasizes alphabetic shapes and the sounds of words and word parts? Here the evidence is somewhat conflicting. In the absence of proof to the contrary, the writer's preference is to combine perceptual training as closely as possible with reading instruction.

The fourth and final special approach considered here, the use of drug medication, is one in which future possibilities far outstrip the present inconclusive findings. If the particular drugs tried so far have not produced remedial reading miracles, perhaps some drug not yet discovered will do so. We must keep a close watch on the possible contributions of pharmacology to remedial education, and we should encourage continuing research in this area.

This paper began by pointing out the contrast between the classical emphasis on making use of the child's best avenues for learning and some newer approaches which concentrate on building up deficiency areas. As yet, the newer approaches have not provided convincing proof of their effectiveness. Those who have been obtaining satisfactory results with established methods of remedial teaching would do well to wait for more conclusive evidence before adopting any of the newer procedures that have been discussed here.

REFERENCES

1. Anderson, Russell W. *Effects of Neuro-Psychological Techniques on Reading Achievement.* Greeley: Colorado State College, 1965.
2. Baldwin, Ruth R. and Thomas J. Kenny. *"Medical Treatment of Behavior Disorders,"* in Jerome Hellmuth (Ed.), *Learning Disorders,* 2. Seattle: Special Child Publications, 1966, 313-325.
3. Barsch, Ray H. "Six Factors in Learning," in Jerome Hellmuth (Ed.), *Learning Disorders.* Seattle: Special Child Publications, 1965, 323-343.
4. Bateman, Barbara. "An Educator's View of a Diagnostic Approach to Learning Disorders," in Jerome Hellmuth (Ed.), *Learning Disorders,* 1. Seattle: Special Child Publications, 1965, 219-237.
5. Calvert, James J. and George F. Cromes. "Oculomotor Spasms in Handicapped Readers," *Reading Teacher,* 20 (December 1966), 231-236.
6. Cronbach, Lee J. *Educational Psychology,* (2nd ed.), New York: Harcourt, Brace and World, 1963.
7. Daniels, J. C. "Children with Reading Difficulties," *Slow Learning Child,* 13 (March 1967), 138-143.
8. Delacato, Carl H. *The Diagnosis and Treatment of Speech and Reading Problems.* Springfield, Illinois: Charles C. Thomas, 1963.
9. Delacato, Carl H. *Neurological Organization and Reading.* Springfield, Illinois: Charles C. Thomas, 1966.

10. Delacato, Carl H. *Treatment and Prevention of Reading Problems.* Springfield, Illinois: Charles C. Thomas, 1959.

11. Dunning, Jack D. and Newell C. Kephart. "Motor Generalization in Space and Time," in Jerome Hellmuth (Ed.), *Learning Disorders,* 1. Seattle: Special Child Publications, 1965, 77-121.

12. Feldmann, Shirley C. and Cynthia P. Deutsch. *A Study of the Effectiveness of Training for Retarded Readers in the Auditory Perceptual Skills Underlying Reading.* U. S. Office of Education Title VII Project No. 1127. New York: Institute of Developmental Studies, Department of Psychiatry, New York Medical College, 1965.

13. Frostig, Marianne. "Corrective Reading in the Classroom," *Reading Teacher,* 18 (April 1965), 573-580.

14. Frostig, Marianne and David Horne. "An Approach to the Treatment of Children with Learning Disorders," in Jerome Hellmuth (Ed.), *Learning Disorders,* 1. Seattle: Special Child Publications, 1965, 293-305.

15. Frostig, Marianne and David Horne. *The Frostig Program for the Development of Visual Perception.* Chicago: Follett, 1964.

16. Frostig, Marianne, D. W. Lefevre, and J. R. B. Whittlesey, *The Marianne Frostig Developmental Test of Perception.* Palo Alto, California: Consulting Psychologists Press, 1964.

17. Getman, G. N. "The Visuomotor Complex in the Acquisition of Learning Skills," in Jerome Hellmuth (Ed.), *Learning Disorders,* 1. Seattle: Special Child Publications, 1965, 49-76.

18. Glass, Gene V. and Melvyn P. Robbins. "A Critique of Experiments on the Role of Neurological Organization in Reading Performance," *Reading Research Quarterly,* 3 (Fall 1967), 5-52.

19. Harris, Albert J. "A Critical Reaction to: The Nature of Reading Disability," *Journal of Developmental Reading,* 3 (1960), 238-249.

20. Harris, Albert J. "Diagnosis and Remedial Instruction in Reading," in *Innovation and Change in Reading,* Sixty-seventh Yearbook, Part II, of the National Society for the Study of Education. Chicago: University of Chicago Press, 1968, 159-194.

21. Harris, Albert J. "Lateral Dominance, Directional Confusion, and Reading Disability," *Journal of Psychology,* 44 (1957), 283-294.

22. Hasman, Karen. "What's All the Shouting About?" *Chicago Daily News,* April 2, 1968, 25.

23. Kephart, Newell C. *The Slow Learner in the Classroom.* Columbus, Ohio: Charles C. Merrill, 1960.

24. Kirk, Samuel A. and James J. McCarthy. "The Illinois Test of Psycholinguistic Abilities: An Approach to Differential Diagnosis,"

American Journal of Mental Deficiency, 66 (November 1961), 399-412.

25. Krippner, Stanley. "Etiological Factors in Reading Disability of the Academically Talented in Comparison to Pupils of Average and Slow-Learning Ability," *Journal of Educational Research,* 61 (February 1968), 275-279.

26. LaPray, Margaret and Ramon Ross. "Auditory and Visual Perceptual Training," in J. Allen Figurel (Ed.), *Vistas in Reading,* Proceedings of the International Reading Association, Vol. II, Part 1, 1966 (Copyright 1967), 530-532.

27. McCormick, Clarence C., et al. *Improvement in Reading Achievement through Perceptual-Motor Training.* Chicago: Reading Research Foundation, July 1967 (mimeographed).

28. McCormick, Clarence C., Janice N. Schnobrich, and S. Willard Footlick. *The Effect of Perceptual-Motor Training on Reading Achievement.* Chicago: Reading Research Foundation, Inc., July 1967 (mimeographed).

29. McDonald, Arthur S. "The Placebo Response in Reading Research," *New Developments in Programs and Procedures for College-Adult Reading.* Twelfth Yearbook of the National Reading Conference, 12 (1963), 220-229.

30. Morris, Joyce M. *Standards and Progress in Reading.* London: National Foundation for Educational Research in England and Wales, 1966.

31. Olson, Arthur V. "Relation of Achievement Test Scores and Specific Reading Abilities to the Frostig Developmental Tests of Visual Perception," *Perceptual and Motor Skills,* 22 (1966), 179-184.

32. Olson, Arthur V. "School Achievement, Reading Ability, and Specific Visual Perception Skills in the Third Grade," *Reading Teacher,* 19 (April 1966), 490-492.

33. *Perceptual-Motor Training:* A Program of Exercises Designed to Effect Remediation for Disorders Involving Underachievement, Learning Disabilities, Perceptual Handicaps, Minimal Brain Damage, Mental Retardation. Chicago: Reading Research Foundation, 3849 West Devon, 1967.

34. Roach, Eugene G. "Evaluation of an Experimental Program of Perceptual Motor Training with Slow Readers," in J. Allen Figurel (Ed.), *Vistas in Reading,* Proceedings of the International Reading Association, Vol. 11, Part 1, 1966 (Copyright 1967), 446-450.

35. Robbins, Melvyn P. "Creeping, Laterality, and Reading," *Academic Therapy Quarterly,* 1 (1966), 200-206.

36. Robbins, Melvyn P. "The Delacato Interpretation of Neurological Organization," *Reading Research Quarterly,* 1 (Spring 1966), 57-78.

37. Rosen, Carl L. "An Experimental Study of Visual Perceptual Training and Reading Achievement in First Grade," *Perceptual and Motor Skills,* 22 (1966), 979-986.

38. Rutherford, William L. "Perceptual-Motor Training and Readiness," in J. Allen Figurel (Ed.), *Reading and Inquiry,* Proceedings of the International Reading Association, Vol. 10, 1965, 194-196.

39. Silver, Archie A. and Rosa A. Hagin. *Specific Reading Disability: An Approach to Diagnosis and Treatment.* New York: Department of Neurology and Psychiatry, New York University Bellevue Medical Center, 1966 (mimeographed).

40. Silver, Archie A.; Rosa A. Hagin; and Marilyn F. Hersh. *Specific Reading Disability: Teaching Through Stimulation of Deficit Perceptual Areas.* New York: Department of Neurology and Psychiatry, New York University Bellevue Medical Center, 1965 (mimeographed).

41. Smith, Donald E. P. and Patricia M. Carrigan. *The Nature of Reading Disability.* New York: Harcourt, Brace and World, 1959.

42. Staiger, Ralph C. "Medicine for Reading Improvement," *Journal of Developmental Reading,* 5 (Autumn 1961), 48-51.

43. Stephens, W. E., E. Cunningham, and B. J. Stigler. "Reading Readiness and Eye Hand Preference Patterns in First Grade Children," Exceptional Children, 30 (March 1967), 481-488.

44. Valusek, John E. *The Effect of Drugs on Retarded Readers in a State Mental Hospital,* doctoral dissertation, University of Michigan, 1963.

45. Weener, Paul, Loren S. Barritt, and Melvyn I. Semmel. "A Critical Evaluation of the Illinois Test of Psycholinguistic Abilities," *Exceptional Children,* 30 (February 1967), 377-380.

46. Yarborough, Betty H. "A Study of the Effectiveness of the Leavell Language-Development Service in Improving the Silent Reading Ability and Other Language Skills of Persons with Mixed Dominance," doctoral dissertation, University of Virginia, 1964.

BARBARA LINDEMAN
MARTIN KLING

Bibliotherapy:
Definitions, Uses, and Studies

Many children with reading problems also have "emotional" problems. Sometimes it is possible to kill two birds with one stone by combining reading instruction and therapy. The use of books in which the characters face and solve problems similar to ones of the child has reportedly helped many children simultaneously improve their reading and develop more stable personal-social adjustment patterns. This article reviews and summarizes the literature on this technique, which may be just as "special" as the methods described by Harris in the preceding article.

Has reading ever helped you solve a personal problem? What knowledges and skills are required by the teacher who wishes to investigate the use of bibliotherapy? What kinds of adjustment problems do you think would best lend themselves to this approach? Are you familiar with any material that could be used this way? Are any selections in basal readers appropriate? Are materials especially written for this purpose? Would this approach add a new dimension to Cohen's "Taxonomy" earlier in this section? What cautions would you want to observe in using this technique with any child?

Webster (1961) defined bibliotherapy as "the use of selected reading materials as therapeutic adjuvants in medicine and psychiatry; also guidance in the solution of personal problems through directed reading." This definition concisely suggests two approaches to bibliotherapy: one a scientific technique, the other an informal one. Russell & Shrodes (1950), representing the latter view, called bibliotherapy:

Reprinted from *Journal of School Psychology,* 7 (2, 1968-69), pp. 36-41, by permission of Journal of School Psychology, Inc. and Barbara Lindeman and Martin Kling.

a process of dynamic interaction between the reader and
literature — interaction which may be utilized for personality
assessment, adjustment, and growth. This definition suggests
that bibliotherapy is not a strange, esoteric activity but one that
lies within the province of every teacher of literature working
with every child in a group. It does not assume that the teacher
must be a skilled therapist, nor the child a seriously maladjusted
individual needing clinical treatment. Rather it conveys the idea
that all teachers must be aware of the effect of reading on
children, and must realize that, through literature, most children
can be helped to solve the developmental problems of adjustment which they face (p. 335).

Darling (Witty, 1964) considered bibliotherapy described in this
way a misnomer, since little difference is indicated between
bibliotherapy and teaching in the classroom or reader guidance
in the library. "Certainly it is mental hygiene, but it lacks the
basic requirement of therapy which seems to require that an
illness be present to treat (p. 453)."

A composite definition, based on the results of a
questionnaire sent to a selected group by a Committee on
Bibliotherapy, June, 1961, puts the "therapy" back into
bibliotherapy, and reflects the medical-psychiatric viewpoint.
Tews (1962) defined bibliotherapy as:

a program of selected activity involving reading materials,
planned, constructed, and controlled as treatment under the
guidance of the physician for emotional and other problems. It
must be administered by a skilled, professionally trained
librarian within the prescribed purpose and goals. The important
and dynamic factors are the relationships which are established,
the patient's reactions and responses, and the reporting back to
the physician for interpretation and evaluation (p. 99).

There is agreement, then, that in bibliotherapy some interaction, often beneficial, takes place between the reader and
what is read.

Differences in definition depend upon whether one is
talking about bibliotherapy for the mentally ill, as treatment for
the maladjusted, or as a natural part of the classroom
curriculum used in meeting the developmental needs of
children. Differences also depend upon who does the defining;
the physician, the counsellor, or the teacher.

BIBLIOTHERAPY FOR THE MENTALLY ILL

The earliest literature on bibliotherapy concerned its use for the mentally ill and how it could be made an exacting science. One of the first to use the term "bibliotherapy" was Crothers (Beatty, 1962): "Bibliotherapy is such a new science that no wonder there are so many erroneous opinions as to the actual effect which any particular book will have" (p. 106). Junier (1962) indicated continued concern with the lack of agreement among researchers on how to make bibliotherapy a science. He raised questions as to consensus on the meaning of the term, how much of what is done in hospital libraries is actually bibliotherapy, and who is educationally equipped to provide it. This trend was reflected in a historical review of the research by Beatty (1962), who described the prevailing interest and belief in the therapeutic value of the hospital library, the more scientific concerns of qualifications of the bibliotherapist, and the importance of keeping case studies and records

Alston (1962), unlike some of his predecessors, thought that the development of a highly standardized, precise form of bibliotherapy was unlikely. In explaining the relationship between psychotherapy and bibliotherapy, possible values for the mental patient are: (*a*) information and instruction; *(b)* courage to enter therapy by reading about it; (*c*) the opportunity to discuss a situation in a book, rather than the situation as it applies to himself; (*d*) greater insight into problems; (*e*) the acquisition of language and ideas with which to communicate his problems; (*f*) the opportunity for him to focus attention outside of himself; (*g*) skills in socialization; and (*h*) relaxation and diversion.

While Alston recognized the degree to which many people are influenced by books, he reminded us that not everyone reads, and not everyone is so deeply affected. Furthermore, the patient's illness may prevent him from distinguishing between what does and does not apply to him. Bibliotherapy, then, must be used with appropriate discussion; misunderstanding or trying to apply wrong principles may create resistance to therapy.

READING AND ADJUSTMENT

Advocates of bibliotherapy as a guidance technique with the maladjusted are concerned with its use as an informal aid in the solution of personal problems. Shrodes (1955) saw an integral relationship between the dynamics of personality and the nature of vicarious experience, which includes identification (both projection and introjection), catharsis, and insight. This interaction can provide the reader with increased self-awareness, an opportunity to see his problems objectively, and a feeling of belonging.

Others concerned with the adjustment potential of reading see bibliotherapy as a real or imagined affiliation with characters which may increase feelings of belonging, augment self-esteem, and provide insights into one's motivations and needs (Russell, 1952); an opportunity to solve personal problems through acquaintance with others who are timid, lonely, or handicapped (Jenkins, 1967); a counteraction to the meagerness of one's own environment and interpersonal situations (Jackson, 1962); a situation in which the writer creates and resolves a conflict in the reader which helps the reader resolve his own conflict (Jackson, 1962); and an incorporation of reading materials by means of identification, projection, and insight, the organization of which depends on the literature itself and on what the reader brings to it (Jackson, 1965).

BIBLIOTHERAPY IN THE CLASSROOM

Witty (1947) emphasized the parallelism between fictional situations and actual adolescent conflicts. Many adolescents need release from tensions and worries; others need help acquiring emotional stability. When bibliotherapy is used in the classroom, guidance is important in helping the child apply to his problems the principles which he discovered in reading (Keneally, 1949).

Meeting the personality needs of students has become a new purpose for many teachers who believe there has been too much emphasis on mechanics and not enough on content (Bristol, 1947). These teachers see as part of their role the guidance of students through recreational reading, in which a youngster may identify with a problem or situation similar to his own. To do this successfully, the teacher must, of course, be familiar with both the child's problem and children's books (Koch & Lindahl, 1952).

The teacher can learn about a child's personal life through interest inventories, the anecdotal method, and his writing. The developmental reading program can then be designed to meet the student's emotional as well as academic needs (Witty, 1952). The school librarian, perhaps within the framework of the Library Club, can also capitalize on his knowledge of the student's reading interests and the available books in order to help normal youngsters develop emotionally under directed reading (Emeruwa, 1958).

MEETING CHILDREN'S NEEDS THROUGH BOOKS

Bailey (1956) suggested five types of insecurities which reading can help the child overcome: (*a*) relations with peers, (*b*) family dynamics, (*c*) repeated failures, (*d*) economic factors, and (*e*) physical factors.

A committee for the determination of high school book selection found that reading should help a pupil to gain a better understanding of himself, his personal environment and his social environment, and to acquire deeper satisfactions, enjoyment and escape (Henry, 1948). Lind (1936) added that reading should have an organizing influence on the personality and should help solve practical problems. Bibliotherapy can also be used preventively (Moore, 1946, & Wenzel, 1948).

A number of books have appeared in recent years which can be used to meet these and other needs. A change in the context of books from the period of 1920-1940 to 1940-1960 was noted by Homze (1966), who found increasing emphasis on the problems and adjustments of individual child characters. The problems of people and their world are also being represented more realistically (Wenzel, 1948).

Elementary Grades. A bibliography best suited for the elementary level, but sometimes useful for junior high and high school students, includes books on responsibility to family and others, emotional conflicts, physical handicaps, intergroup relations, and achieving through hardship (Smith & Dechant, 1961).

Another list on this level suggests stories which may help children face situations of motherless, fatherless or parentless homes, homes with stepparents, and children living with relatives and in other people's homes (Eno, 1949).

Middle Grades. A bibliography for these grades includes books on problems of adjusting to school, economic insecurity, feelings of not belonging, feelings of superiority, meeting trouble and facing responsibility, personal fears, physical handicaps, and racial insecurity (Koch & Lindahl, 1952).

The selected problems of the eight to twelve-year old child were divided into three categories by Homze (1964); adjustment to families, to groups of children, and to personal problems. *Ginger Pye* is described (Tyler, 1965) as being particularly appealing to this age group.

Adolescence. Brooks (1950) has compiled a list related to the following developmental tasks of adolescents: (*a*) accepting physique and the masculine and feminine role; (*b*) new relations with age mates, male and female; (*c*) emotional independence of parents and other adults; (*d*) assurance of economic independence; (*e*) selecting and preparing for an occupation; (*f*) desiring and achieving socially responsible behavior; (*g*) preparing for marriage and family.

Additional Bibliographies. Brooks (1947) listed books at each level from kindergarten through junior college concerned with everwidening areas of human relationships from the family to the community. Another bibliography by Brooks (1950) catalogs separate individual needs at the primary, intermediate and high school and college levels. Lenrow (1940) also developed a comprehensive list of books which aid pupils in understanding themselves and their environments.

Other useful bibliographies are by Strang et al..(1944), Rue (1943, 1950), and Kircher (1945). An annotated bibliography of 138 references was recently edited by Ross (1968) and issued by the International Reading Association.

BIBLIOTHERAPY FOR EXCEPTIONAL STUDENTS

Gifted. Bibliotherapy is particularly useful for the gifted child because he enjoys vicarious experiences more than the average child (Barbe, 1961), and, because he often feels rejected in a group of the less gifted, he needs help in social relations (Strang, 1951). Since the gifted child generally likes books, bibliotherapy is an especially appropriate means of helping him adjust.

Retarded Reader. Bibliotherapy is equally applicable to the retarded reader. Kantrowitz (1967) believes that a meaningful reading that answered a particular individual's need would produce gains in learning, a different attitude towards books, and perhaps a better self-concept. Carefully selected materials, centered around interests, can provide the retarded reader with identification and motivation.

Handicapped. Books for the handicapped appeared in previously mentioned bibliographies, but Cohoe (1960) compiled a special list designed to improve the attitude of the handicapped and to help him accept the attitudes of others. The problems included are: under-size, over-size, speech defects, unattractive facial features, deafness, blindness, and crippling condition.

EXPERIMENTS AND CASE STUDIES

There have been very few experimental or case studies to support the uses of bibliotherapy, perhaps because books are used formally and informally, in and outside the classroom, so that their therapeutic usefulness is taken for granted. Also, the effects of bibliotherapy are difficult to measure, especially over a long period of time.

A few experimental efforts and several case studies do exist. An experiment in the use of literature for guidance purposes in the classroom was reported by Elkins (1949). Information on the children was obtained from sociometric tests, individual interviews, compositions by the children on "wishes" and "worries," diaries kept for two days, and sociodrama. Two main areas of problems emerged: those related to family and those related to peer relationships. Books were chosen in both areas, and the reading was followed by class and panel discussions. The teacher was able to judge, from written work and discussion, differences in reactions. She found greater understanding in approaching a problem, deeper understanding of others' feelings, greater readiness to accept differences in others, and the ability to bring greater resources to the consideration of a problem.

Webster (1961) was able to reduce fear of the dark and of dogs in first grade children by reading stories showing the positive attributes of what was feared, and by the undirected discussion which followed. Each of two groups, 35 afraid of the dark, and five afraid of dogs, read one story for each of five weeks. Interviews, repeated three months after completion of the final story, indicated that fear was reduced in 29 of those who feared the dark, and in all five who feared dogs. Webster attributed the change to the possibility of relearning and the reinforcement of pleasant experiences in group discussion. Whether or not the change in attitude in these experiments was accompanied by a change in behavior is not known.

Lind (1936) obtained information from 44 adults, using interviews and life histories, on the effects of childhood reading. The effects were categorized as escape, diversion, definition of role, and interests. The obvious weakness of this study is that its conclusions are based entirely on recall.

Smith (1948) conducted a similar study with children, asking them to name books, stories and poems which changed their lives. Two-thirds reported changes in attitude as a result of reading, and 10% reported changes in behavior. With one exception, no two children named the same book; this indicates the personal nature of reading and the problem of using bibliotherapy effectively.

Moore (1944) described a special type of bibliotherapy developed by the Delaware State Society of Mental Hygiene: an attempt was made to teach seventh and eighth grade pupils wholesome reactions to emotional crises in order to prevent mental breakdowns in later life. Filmstrips were used to stimulate discussion; then, stories were told, dramatized by students, and discussed. Some of the topics were: the importance of friends, facing up to personal problems, overcoming handicaps, and the relationships with siblings, parents and relatives. It is not known whether or not this experience was actually beneficial.

Case studies appearing earlier in this paper, as well as others reported by Moore (1944) and Witty (1964), also described children who were helped to adjust successfully to school, personal and family problems.

SUMMARY AND CONCLUSIONS

Bibliotherapy has been defined as an interaction between the reader and certain literature which helps him make personal adjustment. Bibliotherapy has been used in mental hospitals, with maladjusted individuals, and in the classroom, for the gifted and retarded reader and for the average student. Various needs which can be met through reading and relevant bibliographies have been suggested. A few experiments and case studies have been offered as evidence of the effectiveness of bibliotherapy, and the quantitative and qualitative limitations of these experiments have been discussed.

While the use of bibliotherapy for the mentally ill seems to be most in question or subject to controversy, the evidence indicates that bibliotherapy can benefit the maladjusted individual who is, or can be, motivated to read. In the school, bibliotherapy, used by the resourceful teacher, can be a useful part of a developmental program designed to prepare young people for present and future life situations.

REFERENCES

Alston, E. F. Bibliotherapy and psychotherapy. *Library Trends,* 1965, *2,* 159-176.

Bailey, M. A candle of understanding. *Education,* 1956, *76,* 515-521.

Barbe, W. B., & Williams, T. E. Developing creative thinking in gifted children through the reading program. *The Reading Teacher,* 1961, *15,* 198-201.

Beatty, W. K. A historical review of bibliotherapy. *Library Trends,* 1962, 106-117.

"Bibliotherapy." *Webster's Third New International Dictionary.* Springfield, Mass.: G. C. Merriam Co., 1961.

Bristol, R. Techniques in promoting well being through reading in the primary grades. In W. S. Gray (Ed.), *Supplementary Educational Monographs,* No. 64. Chicago: University of Chicago Press, 1947.

Brooks, A. R. Books that contribute to personal well being. In W. S. Gray (Ed.), Promoting personal and social well being through reading. *Supplementary Educational Monographs,* No. 64. Chicago: University of Chicago Press, 1947.

Brooks A. R. Integrating books and reading with adolescent tasks. *The School Review,* 1950, *58,* 211-219.

Cohoe, E. Bibliotherapy for handicapped children. *National Education Association Journal,* 1960, *49,* 34-36.

Elkins. D. Students face their problems. *The English Journal,* 1949, *38,* 498-503.

Emeruwa, L. Bibliotherapy via the library club. *School Activities,* 1958, *29,* 145-146.

Eno, I. V. Round table, books for children from broken homes. *The English Journal,* 1949, *38,* 457-458.

Henry, N. B. (Ed.) Reading in the high school and college. *The 47th yearbook, part II, National Society for the Study of Education.* Chicago: University of Chicago Press, 1948.

Homze, A. Children face themselves through books: A bibliography. *Elementary English,* 1964, *41,* 788-792.

Homze, A. Interpersonal relations in children's literature, 1920-1960. *Elementary English,* 1966, 43, 26-28.

Jackson, E. P. Bibliography and reading guidance: A tentative approach to theory. *Library Trends,* 1962, *2,* 118-126.

Jenkins, W. A. Reading for enjoyment and personal development. *Educational Leadership,* 1967, *24,* 404-406.

Junier, A. Bibliotherapy: Projects and studies with the mentally ill patient. *Library Trends,* 1962, *2,* 136-146.

Kantrowitz, V. Bibliotherapy with retarded readers. *Journal of Reading,* 1967, *11,* 205-212.

Keneally, K. G. *Therapeutic value of books: Youth, communication and libraries.* Chicago: American Library Assoc., 1949.

Kircher, C. *Character formation through books: A bibliography.* Washington, D.C.: Catholic University of America Press, 1945.

Koch, K., & Lindahl, H. Bibliotherapy in the middle grades. *Elementary English,* 1952, *29,* 390-396.

Lenrow, E. *Reader's guide to prose fiction.* New York: Appleton Century Crofts, 1940.

Lind, K. N. The social psychology of children's reading. *American Journal of Sociology,* 1936, *41,* 454-469.

Moore, T.V. *The nature and treatment of mental disorders.* New York: Grune & Stratton, 1944.

Ross, R. (Ed.) *Bibliotherapy, IRA annotated bibliography No. 16.* Newark, Delaware: International Reading Association, 1968.

Rue, E. *Subject index to the primary grades.* Chicago: American Library Assoc., 1943.

Rue, E. *Subject index to the intermediate grades.* Chicago: American Library Assoc., 1950.

Russell, D. H. & Shrodes, C. Contributions of research in bibliotherapy to the language arts program, I. *The School Review,* 1950, *58,* 335-342, 411-420.

Russell, D. H. Reading and the healthy personality. *Elementary English*, 1952, *29*, 195-200.

Shrodes, C. Bibliotherapy. *The Reading Teacher*, 1955, *9*, 24-29.

Smith, H. P., & Dechant, E. *Psychology in teaching reading*. Englewood Cliffs, N. J.: Prentice-Hall, Inc., 1961.

Smith, N. B. Personal and social values of reading. *Elementary English*, 1948, *25*, 490-500.

Strang, R., et al., *Gateways to readable books*. New York: H. W. Wilson Co., 1944.

Strang, R. Mental hygiene of the gifted child. In P. A. Witty (Ed.), *The gifted child*. Boston: D. C. Heath and Co., 1951.

Tews, R. M. Bibliotherapy. *Library Trends*, 1962, *11*, 97-105.

Tyler, L. Books and children. *Elementary School Journal*, 1965, *65*, 253-257.

Webster, J. Using books to reduce fears of first grade children. *The Reading Teacher*, 1961, *14*, 159-162.

Wenzel, E. Children's literature and personality development. *Elementary English*, 1948, *25*, 12-31.

Witty, P. A. Reading and personal well being. In W. S. Gray (Ed.), Promoting personal and social well being through reading, *Supplementary Educational Monographs*, 1947, No. 64.

Witty, P. A. Reading to meet emotional needs. *Elementary English*, 1952, *29*, 75-84.

Witty, P. A. Meeting developmental needs through reading. *Education*, 1964, *84*, 451-458.

6

The Extras That Count

With more public schools establishing special reading services, particularly those including diagnostic and tutorial
services, reading specialists must provide guidelines for the
most effective ways to organize and administer them. For
example, many people still do not understand the role of the
special teacher in relation to the classroom teacher.
Throughout this volume, it has been suggested that in most
cases of severe reading disability much more than reading
handicaps are involved, making obvious the need for
multidisciplinary therapy — yet many reading teachers attempt
to "go it alone." Certainly the utilization of two readily
available resources — parents and children — has been
neglected. And finally, existing special reading programs must
be evaluated to see what effect they have had.

In this section we cannot pretend to provide all the answers. We hope to increase the reader's awareness of
possibilities not comprehensively treated in professional textbooks and to whet his interest in exploring other promising
avenues.

It is folly to focus totally on corrective and remedial programs if some reading problems are the result of existing reading instruction. To what extent is current instruction contributing to the number of reading problems we have? And to
what degree could different procedures, emphases, and
materials decrease this number? The first two articles in this
section investigate the problem of early prevention and intervention — possibly the most important of all the "extras"
discussed in this section.

The third article in this section provides some guidelines
for establishing a remedial reading program, as well as some
pitfalls to avoid. The following articles provide information

about, and insight into, the components of a comprehensive reading services program: the role of the special reading teacher in the school, auxiliary services in the reading program, parent-teacher relationships, use of students as tutors, and evaluation of the success of a clinical program.

MILDRED C. ROBECK

An Ounce of Prevention

If remedial reading teachers are our "pound of cure" then obviously the regular classroom teachers in kindergarten and grade one are our "ounce of prevention." It makes little sense to hire numerous well-trained remedial teachers while slighting or ignoring the pre-reading learnings of the children who may eventually wind up in remedial instruction. "Don't lock the barn door after the horse is stolen." This article and the following one focus on crucial aspects of this significant problem.

Do the readiness programs you know about consider and provide for the adequate development of each of the five abilities discussed by Robeck? What would the implementation of these suggestions in your school demand in the way of commercial material? of teacher training? of evaluative instruments? What abilities other than the five discussed by Robeck does your knowledge and experience lead you to believe are equally critical? What information in Part Two of this book suggests or implies critical but overlooked aspects of pre-reading programs?

Most of the sickness, frustration, and regret in our world could have been prevented. The prevention of reading disabilities is difficult but the treatments are even more difficult and the cures are often impossible. The educational casualties that accrue from poor reading account for most of the dropouts, the delinquents, and the unemployed. Much more difficult to estimate — but very real to the victim and his parents — is the erosion of self-esteem that accompanies school failure. Our technological society is a world of readers, where the person

---

An original article written for this book by Mildred C. Robeck.

who is functionally illiterate cannot hope for full participation. This fact of modern living — the need to read — becomes apparent very early to most children who measure their own accomplishments in reading, as in other skills, against the accomplishments of their peers. Prevention of reading failure becomes increasingly urgent in highly developed societies because the options for poor readers become increasingly limited.

Young children are particularly vulnerable to negative conditioning during the early stages of learning to read. In part, this is because they have accumulated few successes to balance the difficulties they encounter. Lower animals — flatworms, pigeons, monkeys — learn rather quickly to turn toward and take in those things which satisfy their needs or are pleasurable, and to avoid those situations which are not. School children, even the least bright, learn very quickly to seek activities which bring them satisfaction and to avoid situations which cause them to feel inadequate. Most reading clinic children underestimate their own learning potential and reveal negative conceptualizations about themselves as learners while still in second or third grade *(7)*. Social and psychological evidence has been accumulating which supports both the need for prevention and the notion that prevention of reading disability — as distinct from some temporary difficulty — is both possible and essential.

The concept of prevention is based on several assumptions which are basic to issues and recommendations in this paper. First, the prevention of reading disability, if it occurs, will take place early in the school life of children, probably in the primary and pre-primary classrooms. Second, all children except those severely retarded intellectually can learn to read. Third, the success of each child will need to be assured from the beginning of activities he identifies as reading. Fourth, the knowledge of how children learn to read and the technical skill for teaching them is presently available. The formula for prevention, in simplistic and overstated terms, is success plus more success, as this is seen by the child himself. A sustained motivation for reading is learned from the beginning by pleasurable associations which the child himself must feel in the reading situations. The teacher may give the child favorable feedback at many points but cannot indefinitely substitute external criteria for internal satisfaction, if the child is to read on his own. The evidence for the kind of affective learning that is taking place during reading can be observed on a day-to-day basis by the teacher who works with the child. Prevention of reading disability requires an early and continuous awareness of the interaction between cognitive and affective learning generally.

In order to learn to read at a pace and with the facility that is inherently reinforcing, the child must have learned particular functions that are basic to the act of reading. This paper will focus on five critical abilities a child must bring to the reading situation if his success from the beginning is probable. Each of these skills can be observed prior to reading or taught to criterion levels: (1) Visual perception of letters and words, (2) Auditory perception of phonemes within words, (3) Language development of conventional syntax and vocabulary, (4) Sensory-motor integration, and (5) Potential for school learning.

VISUAL PERCEPTION

Perception is the individual's immediate interpretation or organization of information from the senses. The logical criterion performances for testing the child's visual readiness for learning to read are those tasks which correspond closely to the reading process itself. Prior to formal instruction in reading, the child should have learned to distinguish between letters that are similar in appearance, should be able to recognize groups of letters as words and know that spaces separate one word from another, and should also have conceptualized the idea that word symbols stand for units of speech and that the arrangement of letters in a particular word is invariate.

When designing the *Kindergarten Evaluation of Learning Potential (KELP) (10)*, an item was needed which teachers could use to observe and to teach these criterion behaviors in visual perception. The "safety sign" item proved useful, both as a curricular activity and as an evaluation tool. At the association level of learning, the children use the signs (STOP, GO, SLOW, SCHOOL, etc.) to play games. The teacher notes who among them is responding to the signs meaningfully. These children are taught to match a small black sign of the correct shape with the large full-color sign and then to build the words on the black shapes with letter cut-outs. By keeping the model on the left, most children learn very quickly to match the order and the direction of the letters and to read back the words to the teacher. The children who can discriminate the letters and build as many as six of the signs usually make the conceptualization that groups of letters make a word and that the letters must be consistently ordered.

Children who have difficulty building the safety signs may need practice in easier visual discrimination tasks such as bead stringing, block design, or some of the figure-matching activities in the readiness books.

AUDITORY PERCEPTION

Another perceptual ability critical in beginning reading is auditory discrimination of phonemes, the sound units, within words. Research has shown positive correlations between auditory discrimination of word parts and reading achievement. Low scores on the *Wepman Auditory Discrimination Test* were highly significant in predicting reading failure *(9)*. It is important for teachers to be able to observe when a child learns to discriminate a particular phoneme and in what position in the word he can make the discrimination — initial, medial, or final. A child cannot learn the grapheme corresponding to an auditory symbol if he is unable to discriminate that symbol auditorily. The child who lacks only the difficult discriminations such as the short /e/ or /i/ may do quite well in learning to decode if the teacher begins with consonant sounds that are easily discriminated, probably in the initial position.

When *KELP* was being developed, an item was needed at that level which taught and tested the ability to hear beginning sounds, distinct and apart from their printed equivalent. A box with three compartments was used, along with eighteen or more toys whose names began with sounds easy to discriminate, *B, M,* and *T.* At the association level of learning, the child learns the name of the toys: bear, ballerina, banana, binoculars, boat, and butterfly. At level two, the child is expected to discover, when naming one of the three groups of toys, that they all begin the same way. Having made the conceptualization that words can be grouped by their beginning sound, the child can demonstrate his ability to discriminate auditorily by sorting the toys according to compartments identified with pictures of a bed, a monkey, and a turtle.

Another auditory skill that is important is sound blending — the ability to identify a word after hearing its separate phonemes. Marion Monroe sampled this and other auditory abilities in the *Reading Aptitude Tests (5)*, a prediction and analysis test published in 1935 which has been reissued and is still useful.

SENSORY INTEGRATION

The third critical ability for beginning reading is the integration of the sensory systems to the extent that the child is able to learn (1) left-to-right sequencing of letter symbols, (2) hand-eye coordination in printing, (3) modality shifts from receiving through one sensory system and responding in another, and (4) sequencing of sound symbols in words. These skills require neural mediation between two or more sensory systems. An evaluation of reading readiness should include observations of the child's sensory motor integration in activities such as these and competence should be developed before expecting the child to succeed in reading, or the instruction should be adapted to his unique characteristics. Much of the learning during the sensory motor period (ages 0 - 2) and in the pre-operational period (ages 2 - 4), as Piaget defined them, is the integration of the different sensory systems *(6)*. Although speech and reading require highly integrated neural structures for processing language symbols, most children are neurologically ready for reading before they enter first grade.

Left-to-Right Sequencing

Reading from left to right is a characteristic of our culture which the child needs to learn. The child can demonstrate this ability by learning to write his name. Practice, short of reading or writing, is possible through games such as stringing bead cards from left to right, listening to stories while sitting beside the reader, or interpreting series of pictures.

Hand-Eye Coordination

Most children learn control of their hands while watching their own reaching and grasping movements. Children whose hand-eye coordination is retarded need many skill-building activities prior to pencil-and-paper tasks. Some children can cope with blackboard writing before their finger control is adequate for reading-related work at their desks.

Modality Shifts

Many studies have been made of the relative importance of visual, auditory, and tactile-kinesthetic modalities in learning communication skills. A question which is related, but more complex, is the process of receiving information through one modality, such as visual symbols of print, and responding with spoken words, as in oral reading. Katz and Deutsch *(7)* compared the rate of visual, auditory, and cross-modality shifts in good and poor readers among Negro boys of Harlem. They found no difference between the groups in visual perception, a difference favoring the good readers on auditory perception tests, and significant differences between good and poor readers in their ability to shift the input-output mediation from one sensory modality to the other. The poor readers took longer to make these kinds of responses, even when the stimuli for the responses were non-reading materials.

Sequential Ordering of Phonemes

The ability to recall sounds in their proper temporal sequence is related to auditory memory span and to the acquisition of language *(11)*. Most children come to first grade with adequate sensory integration for learning to read and write, but children who hear normally but have poor articulation or jumble the order of words when repeating a sentence may need to be referred for a diagnostic test. The *Illinois Test of Psycholinguistic Abilities* has nine subtests which analyze the input-mediation-output processes including auditory-vocal sequencing *(4)*.

LANGUAGE DEVELOPMENT

The fourth critical area of readiness is language development. The knowledge of standard syntax, or sentence structure, is at least as important as vocabulary, or meaning units, in beginning reading. The number of words that slum children know — Chicano and black children — is approximately as extensive as the vocabulary of middle-class children in the 1930's and 40's.

The size of vocabulary did not keep middle-class children from learning to read then nor was their reading instruction delayed. The more likely handicap is irregularity in sentence order between the slum child's language and that used in books. This problem raises the question of whether minority group children should be taught to read their own dialects. The hazard in doing this seems to be the delay in learning to speak and read standard English at a time when the child is developmentally very efficient in learning language. The number of words that a child is required to know in beginning reading is not extensive; however, a successful beginning in reading seems to depend on his having internalized the basic patterns of speech that are used in the reading material.

LEARNING POTENTIAL

The fifth concern in evaluating readiness for reading is rate of learning. The notion of a chronological or mental age of six-and-a-half is no longer considered an appropriate criterion for beginning to read. Children with IQ's in the 50's can learn to read if they are not started too soon and if their program is built on success. On the other hand, children with IQ's of 120 to 145 can be severely retarded in reading *(7)*.

Young children show individual and cultural differences in their relative functioning in verbal versus non-verbal ability and in their understanding of versus their expressing of ideas. A recent study compared American Indian and Caucasian children in their ability to perform non-verbal cognitive tasks and to learn simple English vocabulary (names of colors, days of the week, and number words) as compared with their functioning in English. The results in mean scores at the end of the kindergarten year are shown in Table 1. Indian children were

Table 1
Analysis of Functioning in English

	Non-Verbal Performance	Understanding Directions	Expressing Ideas	Language Potential
Indian (N = 17)	3.88	4.41*	2.76	4.24
White (N = 58)	3.53	3.67	3.05	3.67

*CR = 3.51

from the Umatilla reservation where English is commonly used to communicate among the several tribes which live there. These children showed significantly greater strength in listening to than in expressing ideas and they showed significantly better responses than white children did to tasks which required a careful listening to directions. To check against a possible bias in the kindergarten teacher's observations, the *KELP Summary Test,* a pencil-and-paper instrument designed for program evaluation, was administered to the children in groups of ten at the end of the kindergarten year. No significant differences were found between Indian and white children on association learning, conceptualization, and creative self-direction (Table 2.). These Indian children are typical of Indian children all over the country in showing low achievement and early dropout. Quite likely affective factors rather than general intelligence are important in the poor achievement records of several sub-culture groups.

Table 2
Comparison of Means on KELP Observations

	Level 1	*Level 2*	*Level 3*	*Total*
Indian (N = 17)	10.41	6.35	5.00	21.76
White (N = 58)	10.05	5.98	4.37	20.37

None of these differences is significant.

CONCLUDING COMMENTS

Perhaps the greatest obstacle to a significant and rapid reduction in the proportion of reading failures the schools produce is the success shown by about three-fourths of the students, whatever approach used in teaching them to read. The national norms for reading achievement are revised upward with each passing decade, giving proof of gradual improvement in reading programs. The visible success of the children who learn to read effectively tends to reinforce teachers and clinicians in the continued use of materials and techniques. Unfortunately this same visible success of the many intensifies the confusion and self-denigration of those who fail. Much progress could result if the clinic curtain (the epistemological barrier between developmental and remedial teachers of reading) were lowered so that the analytical and individualized techniques of the clinic would be practiced in the typical classroom and the broader base of the developmental programs would be made to function in the typical reading clinic.

1. deHirsch, Katrina, Jeanette J. Jansky, and William S. Langford, *Predicting Reading Failure*. Harper and Row, New York, 1966.

2. Frostig, Marianne, "Visual Modality — Research and Practice," *Perception and Reading*, Helen K. Smith, ed. International Reading Association, Newark, Delaware, 1968, pp. 25-33.

3. Katz, Phyllis, and Martin Deutsch, *Visual and Auditory Efficiency and Its Relationship to Reading in Children*. Institute for Developmental Studies, Department of Psychiatry, New York Medical College, New York, 1963.

4. Kirk, Samuel A., and Winifred Kirk, *Further Studies on the ITPA*. University of Illinois Press, Urbana, Ill., 1971.

5. Monroe, Marian, *Reading Aptitude Tests*. Houghton Mifflin Co., 1963.

6. Robeck, Mildred C., "Affective Learning in the Language Development of Young Children," *Journal of Research and Development in Education*, 3 (Fall 1969), pp. 32-42.

7. Robeck, Mildred C., "Intellectual Strengths and Weaknesses Shown by Reading Clinic Subjects on the WISC," *Journal of Developmental Reading*, 7 (Winter 1964), pp. 120-129.

8. Robeck, Mildred C., and John A. R. Wilson, "Application of a Learning-Motivation Model to the Development and Appraisal of Learning Ability in Young Children." Invitational paper presented to the 17th Congress of the International Society of Applied Psychology, Liege, Belgium, 1971.

9. Wepman, Joseph M., *Auditory Discrimination Test*. Language Research Associates, Chicago, 1958.

10. Wilson, John A. R., and Mildred C. Robeck, *Kindergarten Evaluation of Learning Potential: A Curricular Approach to Evaluation*. McGraw-Hill Book Co., Webster Division, St. Louis, 1967.

11. Witkin, Belle Ruth, "Auditory Perception — Implications for Language Development," *Journal of Research and Development in Education*, 3 (Fall 1969), pp. 53-71.

LEO M. SCHELL

A Second Ounce of Prevention

There is virtually no hope that remedial instruction alone will help us attain the goal of the Right to Read effort. We cannot expect any more special reading teachers than we now have, nor can we anticipate materials or methods that will radically improve the results of remedial instruction. Drastic reductions in the number and proportion of reading difficulties can probably be achieved in only two ways: (1) pre-school parental cooperation and (2) improved primary-grade reading instruction. This discussion focuses on the latter; Wynn's essay, also in this section, deals with the former.

In what ways does this discussion repeat the main theme of Zaeske's study in Part Three? Do you agree that improved primary-grade instruction can decrease the number and proportion of children with reading problems? To what degree can such instruction accomplish this? What educational practices, other than those discussed, do you believe contribute to the creation of children with reading difficulties? Has reading this article caused you to question some traditional practices you are cognizant of?

One of the intriguing — and horrifying — facts that specialists in remedial reading generally believe is that "the vast majority of disability cases are brought about through faulty learning or lack of educational adjustment of one sort or another" (3:138). John Sherk, director of the reading clinic at the University of Missouri at Kansas City, states, "The school system's reading program may be *creating* reading problems while the clinic is trying to cure them" (18:357). Truly a chilling and sobering thought!

An original article written for this book by Leo M. Schell.

Treating the problems of reading disability after the fact is a cruel, useless, nonviable, impractical solution. The time to treat reading problems is as close to the inception of the difficulty as possible. What can interested, dedicated educators do to intervene, to prevent creating reading problems? No definitive answers are possible but an examination of a few outstanding characteristics of children with reading difficulties can suggest some minimal imperatives.

READING READINESS

Smith and Carrigan (1:6) state that

> Clinicians are like a small group standing beside a river full of drowning people. The victims are being swept seaward by the current of time. The clinicians can pull out a few, but the rest are lost. Few of the group are willing to go upstream to find out how the victims got into the river in the first place.[1]

It seems obvious that the farther upstream we go, the closer we get to the source of the river, the better chance we have of deterring the flood of drowning people. Bond and Tinker (3:140) note:

> Reading disability is frequently caused by starting a child in a standard reading program before he has acquired the readiness which will assure success in classroom reading activities....he is unable to achieve enough of the learnings day by day to handle satisfactorily what is coming next. He gets farther and farther behind as time goes on. He may even come to hate reading and all persons and activities connected with reading activities.

Detailed longitudinal knowledge of numerous disabled readers has indicated that even though during "ground school" there were numerous indications that they would have difficulty soloing, many were still shoved into a plane only to fly erratically — or even crash. Kindergarten teachers predicted it, readiness tests indicated it, and first-grade teachers suspected it. Still the child was expected to solo — with the predicted and inevitable results.

A comprehensive, detailed description of appropriate

---

[1] D. E. P. Smith and Patricia Carrigan, *The Nature of Reading Disability*, Harcourt, Brace and Co., Inc., 1959. Reprinted by permission.

readiness experiences is beyond the scope of this discussion; nevertheless, two crucial, often slighted or neglected items will be discussed.

Auditory and Visual Screening

The roles of hearing and sight are so evident that no justification needs to be made here for such examinations except to say that they should be *administered by the school system to every child* (6:174). However, two cautions are in order. One, the Snellen chart is totally inappropriate for visual screening. An optical instrument diagnosing nearsightedness is imperative. And two, it is essential that referrals be con-summated. A depressing percentage of cumulative records note that parents were informed of suspected deficiencies, but there is no record or evidence that a professional examination was made.

Implementation of Readiness Assessment Data

Readiness should be assessed by a combination of standardized tests and teacher observation. Then this information must be translated into instructional practices. "Study and Implement" should be our motto rather than "File and Forget"! With some children these data suggest an extended readiness period.

As long ago as 1936, in a pioneer investigation into factors determining success and failure in beginning reading, Gates and Bond asserted, "The study emphasizes the importance of recognizing and adjusting to individual limitations and needs before and after the beginning of reading" (9:683). They felt strongly that formal, systematic beginning reading instruction might be profitably postponed for some children, provided this time is filled with appropriate and worthwhile learning activities that will develop a higher level of readiness. As a part of the well-known USOE-funded first-grade reading studies, Spache (20) experimented with this general idea of intensifying and extending the readiness period. He concluded that not only was the achievement of experimental and control groups quite similar despite the delay in the introduction of formal reading to the majority of experimental pupils, but the experimental readiness program was of significant value to educationally disadvantaged pupils. That is, "The effectiveness of the program appeared to increase as the ability of the pupils decreased" (20:584). When it is considered that formal reading was delayed as long as four to six months for some of these pupils, it seems we should more closely examine some of our readiness practices and our expectations for beginning first-grade children.

However, the content and orientation of this readiness program is of utmost importance, particularly for children typically identified as potential failures. As a result of her study of children who read upon entering first grade, Durkin tentatively suggested that "children of relatively lower intelligence especially benefit from an early start.... slower children [might] need contact with learning to read that is spread out over time.... they [might] need an earlier start with it" (7:150). The curricular and instructional implications of this hypothesis seem so self-evident that they hardly need explication.

Thus, it seems that not only may readiness skills need to be emphasized over a longer period of time as stressed by Spache but also children may need to be immersed in a reading environment from their first day in school. There seems no better way to accomplish this than to use components of the language-experience approach *(11,12,23)*. Focusing on the concept of what reading is and what it can do while simultaneously strengthening skill deficiencies seems to be one minimal imperative in preventing reading failure. These two approaches used jointly merit much greater acceptance and use.

LOWER SOCIOECONOMIC BOYS

Up to 90 percent of the youngsters referred for remedial help are boys. And any city-wide survey of reading achievement invariably reveals that the lowest achievers, even in comparison with their reading potential, are from the lower socioeconomic levels. This type of information should indicate where we need to focus our attention! And some insights as to possible causes of this situation may help us better understand the problem and formulate instructional procedures.

Boys seem to have three strikes against them before they start!

In their summary of the USOE-funded first-grade reading studies, Bond and Dykstra (2:121) found that girls tended to have a greater degree of readiness for reading at the beginning of first grade. Even though they point out that this finding applies only to averages of groups and not to individual children, it is obvious that a far greater proportion of boys than girls wind up at the bottom of the readiness scale. Strike one?

Also there is much persuasive evidence that elementary teachers, in general, discriminate in varied subtle ways against boys *(1, 8, 10, 14)*. It is hypothesized that this discrimination — conscious or unconscious — contributes to lowered reading achievement by boys. Strike two?

And traditional first-grade basal readers seem to have a definite feminine orientation and bias that does not strongly appeal to or interest boys *(4, 15)*. Strike three?

Instructional Implications

Several classroom implications can — and should — be drawn from these facts. One, in light of Bond and Dykstra's finding, the point of view on readiness taken earlier in this paper takes on even more crucial significance. But they also specified some other areas where, in general, girls were more advanced than boys. Two of these were visual discrimination and auditory discrimination. This information should be used in planning the skill aspect of the readiness program.

Two, primary-grade teachers need to examine carefully their expectations of, and behavior toward, boys. Bond and Dykstra state: "It is necessary for teachers to make differential expectations concerning the mean achievement of boys and girls. On the average, boys cannot be expected to achieve at the same level as girls" (2:122).

Stanchfield (21:205-209) carries this beyond simple reading achievement. She describes eight areas of basic differences in learning patterns of boys and girls and implies that teachers need to make adaptations to them. The areas are:

1. Personality style
2. Activity levels
3. Verbal facility
4. Auditory discrimination
5. Listening skills
6. Attention span
7. Goals and motivations
8. Interests

Since primary-grade teachers are almost totally women, it is reasonable to assume that behavior standards are set in terms of female values — and middle-class female values at that. One simple fact points out the need for different behavior standards for boys and girls: Boys exhale more carbon dioxide than do girls; boys burn more energy than do girls and have more residue to exhaust. This, coupled with social conditioning and expectations, should be recognized in developing standards more in accord with the realities of masculine development. Educators must make an exhaustive search for ways to provide for this phase of individual differences, and teachers must introspectively reflect on their own standards and pupil-teacher interaction.

A third implication relates directly to Stanchfield's last item, interests of boys. More material in the primary grades needs to reflect known masculine interests. Children who are captivated by such TV shows as "Lost in Space" and "Gunsmoke" have nothing more adventurous and exciting than two children and their dog playing train in cardboard boxes or riding a pony on Grandpa's farm. Many remedial programs thrive on high-interest, low-vocabulary books, and research has shown that this material can be successfully used for beginning reading instruction *(21)*.

Research clearly indicates that when given their choice, primary-grade children do not choose to read the types of stories found in typical basal readers *(15, 25)*. We need to experiment with various high-interest, low-vocabulary type materials[2] either as the core of the reading program or as frequently used supplementary books (that is, co-basals). Stanchfield's new series *(22)* definitely deserves serious consideration in this regard.

And teachers should ponder the possibilities and potential of the language-experience approach in helping satisfy and provide for the interests of these boys. Even a cursory survey should reveal almost unlimited possibilities as children, not books, become the focus of the reading program.

---

[2] An excellent source of titles and publishers is Spache's *Good Reading for Poor Readers*. Garrard Press, Champaign, Illinois, 1970. His annotated bibliography is also valuable, *Sources of Good Books for Poor Readers*, International Reading Association, Newark, Delaware, 1969. Most texts on remedial reading instruction also list such materials.

SKILLS LEARNING

Sherk has written that "Eighty-five percent of the clinic cases referred to us . . . are cured of their reading problems by simple reteaching of basic skills. . . . This suggests that, if the pupil had been approached properly concerning reading from the beginning, he would not have become a disabled reader " (18:357). An examination of any professional text on remedial reading gives substance to this statement, as dominant emphasis in these books is skills instruction! Over a time, inadequate mastery of individual skills snowballs into a cumulative deficit so huge that even long-term remediation seldom succeeds in restoring the child to his potential level. An ounce of prevention is imperative.

Teacher Knowledge of Subskills

Only when teachers know the specific sub-skills of reading will they be able to diagnose accurately and instruct meaningfully. Vilscek states, "Reading behaviors must be precisely classified and sufficiently specified so that they might be observed and evaluated" (24:174). Camp *(5)* and numerous other specialists concur wholeheartedly. [Some suggestions for implementing this idea are given in the article "Meeting Individual Differences in Reading Skills" in Part Four of this anthology. — *Editor*]

Attention to Potential Deficiencies

Children with reading problems almost universally have two outstanding deficiencies: a small and unreliable stock of sight words and the inability to merge sounding techniques with the use of context clues. The first of these problems is treated in all reading methods textbooks and is amplified in the article "How to Prevent and Correct Word Identification Problems," in Part Five.

Wyatt *(26)* lists four differences between "normal progress readers" and "retarded readers," two of which emphasize the need to combine sounding with context clues.

1. The good reader more often relies on use of context and a broad oral vocabulary than does the poor reader.
2. The good reader produces several approximations of a word and constantly matches his approximations with words he knows which would make sense in the context he is dealing with.

Who has not heard a child read:

> The Indian had a new *father* in his headdress, or We can't find *there* it went.

Such errors shout, "I confuse similar appearing words and I don't demand that my reading jibe with my oral language!" It is easy to say, "J.D., read that sentence again," or "No, that word isn't *there*, it's..." Unfortunately such techniques have not been shown to be effective.

Kindergarten teachers must begin to sensitize pupils to the structure and predictability of oral language. (This is not the place to delineate a complete program on the use of context; McKee's text *(13)* is recommended.) Then, this foundation must be extended and applied to the reading situation. No better way seems possible than by the child seeing his oral language become written symbols. Teachers should use experience charts and stories judiciously with first-grade youngsters and remedial readers, all the while incidentally pointing out and refining the sense of context. And when skill sheets are checked, it is not sufficient merely to determine right and wrong and enter a score in the grade book. A discussion of the whys and wherefores of rights and wrongs is a much better preventive medicine!

CONCLUSION

A better understanding of some of the educational practices that frequently contribute to the creation of problem readers hopefully will result in revised and different practices. May we unite in the rallying cry, "Let's abolish the remedial reading teacher!"

REFERENCES

1. Austin, David, et al, *Reading Rights for Boys.* New York: Appleton-Century-Crofts, 1971.
2. Bond, Guy L., and Robert Dykstra, "The Cooperative Research Program in First-Grade Reading Instruction," *Reading Research Quarterly,* 2 (Summer, 1967), 5-142.
3. Bond, Guy L., and Miles A. Tinker, *Reading Difficulties: Their Diagnosis and Correction.* New York: Appleton-Century-Crofts, 1967.

4. Byers, Loretta, "Pupils' Interests and the Content of Primary Reading Texts," *Reading Teacher,* 17 (January, 1964), 227-233.

5. Camp, Gloria S., "Take the Child Where?" *Reading Teacher,* 24 (December, 1970), 239-243.

6. Cotter, Kathryn C., "First Grade Failure: Diagnosis, Treatment, Prevention," *Childhood Education,* 44 (November, 1967), 172-176.

7. Durkin, Dolores, "An Earlier Start in Reading?" *Elementary School Journal,* 63 (December, 1962), 147-151.

8. Felsenthal, Heley, "Sex Differences in Teacher-Pupil Interaction in First Grade Reading Instruction," ERIC: ED 039 106.

9. Gates, Arthur I. and Guy L. Bond, "Reading Readiness: A Study of Factors Determining Success and Failure in Beginning Reading," *Teachers College Record,* 37 (May, 1936), 679-685.

10. Grambs, Jean D., and Walter B. Waetjen, "Being Equally Different: A New Right for Boys and Girls," *National Elementary Principal,* 46 (November, 1966), 59-67.

11. Hall, Mary Anne, *Teaching Reading as a Language Experience.* Columbus, Ohio: Charles E. Merrill, 1970.

12. Lee, Dorris M., and R. V. Allen, *Learning to Read Through Experience, 2nd ed.* New York: Appleton-Century-Crofts, 1963.

13. McKee, Paul, *Reading: A Program of Instruction for the Elementary School.* Boston: Houghton Mifflin, 1966.

14. Manning John C., *An Evaluation of Level-designed Visual-Auditory and Related Writing Methods of Reading Instruction in Grade One.* Cooperative Research Project No. 2650, USOE, 1966.

15. Meisel, Stephen, and Gerald G. Glass, "Voluntary Reading Interests and the Interest Content of Basal Readers," *Reading Teacher,* 23 (April, 1970), 655-659.

16. Palardy, J. Michael, "What Teachers Believe — What Children Achieve," *Elementary School Journal,* 69 (April, 1969), 370-374.

17. Putnam, Lillian, "Prevention of Reading Difficulties," *Vistas in Reading,* J. Allen Figurel, ed. Newark, Delaware: International Reading Association, 1967, 240-243.

18. Sherk, John K., "School Clinics," *Reading and Realism,* J. Allen Figurel, ed. Newark, Delaware: International Reading Association, 1969.

19. Smith, D. E. P., and Patricia M. Carrigan, *The Nature of Reading Disability.* New York: Harcourt, Brace & Co., 1959.

20. Spache, George D., et al., "A Longitudinal First Grade Reading Readiness Program," *Reading Teacher,* 19 (May, 1966), 580-584.

21. Stanchfield, Jo M., "Differences in Learning Patterns of Boys and

Girls," *Reading Difficulties: Diagnosis, Correction, and Remediation,* Wm. K. Durr, ed. Newark, Delaware: International Reading Association, 1970, 202-213.

22. Stanchfield, Jo M., *Our Beautiful Land — America.* Chicago: Century Consultants, 1967.

23. Stauffer, Russell, *The Language-Experience Approach to the Teaching of Reading.* New York: Harper & Row, 1970.

24. Vilscek, Elaine C., "Increasing Instructional Efficiency, A Preventive Measure," *Psychological and Physiological Aspects of Reading,* Donald L. Cleland, ed. Pittsburgh: School of Education, University of Pittsburgh, 1968, 171-179.

25. Wiberg, John L., "A Comparison Between the Content of First Grade Primers and the Free Choice Library Selections Made by First Grade Students," *Elementary English,* 47 (October, 1970), 792-798.

26. Wyatt, Nita M., "Pinpointing Specific Skill Needs," *Forging Ahead in Reading,* J. Allen Figurel, ed. Newark, Delaware: International Reading Association, 1968, 174-178.

ROBERT BYRNE

Do It Right the First Time!

Out of his personal experience with numerous reading programs, the author of this essay proposes specific do's and don'ts to school systems in the process of developing special reading services. The continuing establishment of new programs involving remedial teachers in public schools makes this article not only timely but "must" reading for both experienced and inexperienced teachers and administrators.

What cautions does the writer suggest? Are there other suggestions you would offer to a school system regarding selection of students? pupil-teacher ratio? methods and materials?

"Do it right the first time...don't spend your career trying to patch up mistakes..."

This is the word of advice from many a reading consultant who has been through the process of giving birth to a new remedial reading program. — Once things get started on the wrong foot, they're often close-to-impossible to rectify.

If your school system is in the process of establishing a new remedial reading program, it might pay you to invest a few moments in the following article...

So you're about to set up a new remedial reading program?

Good luck. It's probably one of the most difficult tasks you'll ever tackle.

It's not the design that makes it difficult. Nor the methods of instruction you'll want to use. It's just that everybody in almost every school system has a number of rather concrete ideas about how a remedial reading program should work.

Reprinted from *Reading Newsreport,* 2 (February 1968), pp. 25-31, by permission of Multimedia Education, Inc., and Robert Byrne.

And just about everybody is ready to give free (often erroneous) advice.

THE SUGGESTIONS

Among the most common examples of poor advice which may come your way:

Work with the older children, not the younger ones. ("The older ones need help first.")

It's better to work with more children once a week than less children every day. ("There are so many children who need help — we can't refuse to give it to some when we are giving it to others.")

The remedial reading teacher doesn't need a special room. ("There are plenty of rooms available during the day which she can use... the teacher's room... the library... the nurse's office... the closet in the hall...")

The classroom teacher should decide what times children should leave her room for remedial reading. ("After all, she has a regular, planned program — the remedial teacher doesn't.")

SOME POINTERS

According to Dr. Robert Byrne of Eastern Kentucky University, steering clear of ill-founded advice is one of the most difficult tasks a reading supervisor faces in setting up a new reading program. And, "although compromise may look like the answer in the beginning," says Byrne, "it isn't... Experience has shown that it's far better to establish a remedial reading program in the right way at the outset than to try to 'correct it later.'"

"Correcting it later," as many an unhappy supervisor has discovered, "is a close-to-impossible task."

Here's a list of pointers which Dr. Byrne has drafted for school systems which are about to embark on the establishment of new remedial reading programs:

SELECTION OF STUDENTS

Various surveys indicate that the number of children with severe reading problems may range from 5 percent to 50 percent of the total school population. Many of these children with reading problems may be helped within their regular classrooms by skillful teachers using a variety of methods and materials. Other students have problems that are not only difficult to diagnose and correct but also require considerable time and more specialized techniques before progress is made.

A special committee made up of administrators, classroom teachers, the reading coordinator, and remedial teachers should meet to establish criteria for the selection of the students to be serviced by the remedial reading program.

Unless a procedure is developed and a set of criteria adopted and followed, administrative personnel and remedial teachers may find themselves under constant pressure by parents, teachers, principals, and board members who make special requests to include particular children who may not have been selected otherwise.

The following selection procedures and criteria may prove to be helpful:

Identify the retarded readers in the first and second grades and begin remedial instruction as early as possible. Although the poorer readers will probably not need major curriculum adjustments until they have difficulty with the more extensive reading begun in most fourth grades, remediation should begin before the problem becomes further complicated by other factors. Social and emotional maladjustment, parent concern, and a negative peer group evaluation become much more apparent after the third grade. Research has clearly indicated that the longer a reading problem exists, the more difficult it is to correct.

The regular classroom teacher should refer those children who are below grade level in reading according to the standardized test results and/or the teacher's evaluation of daily performance. Although there are good arguments for giving remedial instruction to the children with high intelligence but only average reading achievement, it is recommended that the selection be made from those children who are the most retarded in achievement. These lower reading level students are the ones who will have the greatest difficulty in succeeding in other subjects that require reading. These are the children who are in greater danger of becoming socially and emotionally maladjusted because of their low reading levels. A much larger number of these children will become the high school dropouts, delinquents, and the unemployed. When selecting children who are the farthest behind in reading, it is recommended that a percentage or ratio factor be used rather than so-many-years below grade level. (A second grade child reading on a first grade level is much more a potential problem than is a sixth grade child who is reading on a fifth grade level, although both children may be considered as being a year retarded in reading.) Children could be selected who are 25 percent below average, or perhaps children who are 3 months retarded in the first grade, 4 months in second, 5 months in third grade, etc.

By using both formal and informal means of evaluation, select those children who meet the above retardation in reading achievement criteria and who have the greatest intellectual potential.

Some teachers have found the use of a formula to estimate how much a child's reading level is below his intellectual or expected level to be helpful. One of the methods for estimating this amount of reading disability is to subtract a child's actual reading achievement from his expected reading grade level. This expected level can be computed by multiplying his I.Q. score, as if it were a percentage, by the number of years that he has attended school and then adding 1.0 to the product. A child who is in the middle of the third grade, for example, would, if not retained any year, have been in school for 2.5 years. If he had an I.Q. of 120, his expected level would be 4.0, (1.20 X 2.5 + 1.0). Such a child would have a reading disability of 1 year if he were only reading on a 3.0 reading level (4.0 expected level– 3.0 reading achievement grade level = 1.0 amount of reading disability). Similarly a child with an 80 I.Q. at the end of the fourth grade who has a reading achievement score of 4.1 would not be classified as a disabled reader, although according to his grade level of 4.9 he is .8 behind the average fourth grade group.

Do not exclude children with social, emotional, and physical abnormalities if they meet the other criteria for selection. Although the remedial program should not become a dumping ground for behavior problems, many children who are difficult to instruct in the regular classroom can achieve in the small-group, informal program. A child who is a behavioral or psychological problem in small group or individual instruction should probably be referred to the psychologist or guidance counselor for further study.

PUPIL-TEACHER RATIO

How many students should a remedial teacher have at one time? How often and for what length of time should the classes meet? Who schedules the sessions and organizes the groups? What duties other than teaching will the teacher be requested to perform? Who will do the selecting and diagnosing of new cases?

The problem of pupil-teacher ratio and time schedules must, of course, be considered as part of the total reading program. Assuming that the remedial teacher will perform all the duties implied by the questions listed in the preceding paragraph, it must be assumed that the teacher will meet with the children in smaller groups than would often times be possible in their regular classrooms. To ask a remedial teacher to instruct more children in less time than would be expected of a regular teacher would be inviting a program to fail. With these ideas in mind, it is recommended that:

The children should be scheduled for remedial instruction every day. These remedial cases need reinforcement every day if they are to progress. If the child has remedial reading on an irregular schedule, the classroom teacher must continue the same program as the one prescribed by the remedial teacher. A child with a learning problem should usually be presented fewer skills each day but have more reinforcement of the same skills by a greater variety of approaches.

The periods should usually average approximately forty minutes in length. Some older children may have a longer attention span and thus may profit more from longer periods. Younger children or children with shorter attention spans may achieve better from two short periods each day. A program may be organized into two instructional periods, one for individual or small group skills development and the other for interest and practice activities in larger groups.

The remedial teacher should usually organize his enrollment with an average of five children per group. However the teacher must be allowed enough flexibility to group according to children's specific needs and abilities. Initial grouping usually is done according to reading achievement rather than the child's grade in school. It is generally considered that the lower a group's reading level, the smaller should be the group size.

The teacher may instruct a maximum of sixty children a year, but should probably not enroll more than thirty children during any one part of a year. (Six periods a day times five children per period.)

The first few weeks at the beginning of each year and the last few days at the end of the year should be reserved exclusively for the selection and diagnosis of remedial cases and other non-teaching duties.

The remedial teacher should have responsibility for preparation of materials and for selecting and grouping children for instruction. Teachers, administrators, and other school personnel may request that a child be admitted to the remedial program, but the final responsibility *must* rest with the remedial teacher.

The remedial reading program should have priority over all other school subjects or extracurricular activities. If a remedial teacher is required to group the children according to the regular teacher's preference of time, the remedial program will be handicapped from the beginning.

METHODS AND MATERIALS

Are the methods and materials any different for remedial reading than those used in the developmental reading program? Who will purchase and store materials? Where should remedial instruction take place?

Most reading authorities seem to agree that remedial methods and materials are not really different from those used in developmental reading. A good classroom program should include as great a variety of methods and materials as a remedial program. There are, however, some elements that need to be stressed in the remedial program.

The remedial teacher should probably employ a greater variety of methods and materials than is ordinarily found in a developmental program.

The instruction should be more individualized and specific enough to correct particular weaknesses. Evaluate, teach, evaluate, re-teach should be the pattern for remedial instruction.

The remedial teacher should have an independent budget and should not be expected to beg, borrow, or steal from other teachers nor to use outdated materials or sample copies. Since children with learning problems usually need more repetition or reinforcement, a larger variety of materials will be needed for each skill being developed.

There must be a special room set aside for the unrestricted use of the remedial program. Remedial teachers find it more than a little difficult to teach while the dentist is examining teeth, teachers are mixing their coffee, lunch is being prepared, or the custodian is firing the boiler in a "temporary" remedial reading room. Many rural schools have found the mobile unit to be an excellent facility for special instruction.

A center should be established in each school to avoid the necessity for the remedial teacher to cart materials from place to place.

Remedial teachers have become quite efficient in their ability to pack most materials in the trunks of their cars. They have even learned to rationalize that another box of workbooks is more important than the spare tire.

However, such inconvenience is an unnecessary handicap for the remedial teacher. It should be avoided whenever possible.

PITFALLS TO AVOID

Included below are some of the common pitfalls that should be avoided in establishing a new remedial reading program. Although this list may simply be a negative statement of some of the recommendations already suggested, it may prevent some systems from making the same mistakes that others have made in the past.

Remember that the remedial or special reading program is only one part of the total language experience that the school should provide. Integration and coordination of these experiences is important.

Since the remedial program is only a small part of the total reading program, a comprehensive survey of the entire reading program should be conducted before any remedial services are initiated. One of the other types of programs mentioned earlier may be more appropriate for a particular system.

Avoid the numbers game of trying to provide a little instruction for a large number of children. Evaluate the program in terms of the number of children helped rather than the number of children in the program. If the children can be instructed in larger groups than is usually recommended for remedial reading, they probably would profit as well in the regular programs as they would in a special program. The coordinator may wish to supply additional materials for the regular teacher's use with these children.

The coordinator and remedial teachers should have the final word in the selection of children, methods, and materials. This authority should be limited only to the extent that it involves other curricular or personnel decisions. Grouping decisions should be made by the remedial teacher. *Do not allow the regular classroom teacher to control the class period in which the children will leave the room for remedial instruction.* When children are grouped by reading levels and needs instead of school grade levels, each could possibly have remedial reading at a different time, even though several may be from the same regular classroom.

Remember that the remedial teacher must not be scheduled every period for instruction, but must have time for diagnosing, preparing materials, coordination, and other professional but non-teaching responsibilities.

Do not order materials without evaluating the specific purposes for which they will be used. Itemize the needs and order a variety of materials for each category. Materials requested by teachers are usually more widely used than those ordered from a central office.

Allow ample time and money for inservice education programs and group involvement both before the program begins and as it develops.

And remember. . .

Reading is indeed the key to education, but a poorly organized program may be the unopened lock.

J. ESTILL ALEXANDER

Teacher Roles in the
Special Reading Program

This article delineates a position relative to roles of the special reading teacher and the classroom teachers, suggesting procedures for their working together more effectively.

Do you agree or disagree with the position presented in this paper? Why or why not? Why, in your opinion, is the concept of "joint effort" still at the lip-service level?

One result of federal funds available for education during the 60's was the creation of special reading programs for disabled readers. A good remedial program is a *joint effort* of the central school administration, the building staff (principals, teachers, counselors, school nurses, and teacher aides), other professionals (psychologists, physicians, social workers, and optometrists), parents, and community agencies. Unless there is an effective working relationship among these groups, the program will be weak and rather ineffective.

This paper presents a position relative to the roles of the special reading teacher and the classroom teacher and suggests procedures for their working together. The special teacher is defined as an individual who works with youngsters taken out of the classroom for special instruction in reading and/or assists teachers in the classroom, not as a supervisor and evaluator (1:99), but as a consultant and/or helping teacher. Although the International Reading Association *(4)* has identified responsibilities and desirable qualifications for such special teachers, there seems to be a lack of understanding of the role

---

Based on a paper presented to the Reading Section of the East Tennessee Education Association, 1970, by J. Estill Alexander.

of the special teacher in relation to the classroom teacher, extending from the classroom teacher to the school administration.

ROLE OF THE CLASSROOM TEACHER

Both the classroom teacher and the special teacher have roles in the reading program for the disabled reader (7:223-226). The classroom teacher, in addition to primary responsibilities for the developmental program, shares responsibilities with the special teacher in the remedial program for formal and informal diagnosis, classroom remediation, and evaluation of performance. Additional responsibilities include follow-up and reinforcement instruction for those pupils taught by the special teacher.

A vital public relations function may be performed for the special program by the classroom teacher since he usually knows the parents well and generally has developed a rapport with parents such that they may be accepting of his explanation of the child's difficulty and the remediation plan to be effected through the combined efforts of both teachers.

ROLE OF THE SPECIAL TEACHER

The role of the special teacher is two-fold. First, he should be more than a person who works with a small group of students in a special room; he should be the *reading leader* in his building *(2. 6)*. Second, and of lesser importance in the view of the writer, he is a teacher of children with reading disabilities.

Role as a Reading Leader

In order for the special teacher to be an effective reading leader, it is assumed that he is a good teacher of reading who excels in knowledge of the reading process, has competence in the diagnosis and correction of reading difficulties, and has those personal qualities which enable him to work effectively with others. Many special teachers, as yet, do not possess these competencies; they must assume the responsibility for improvement as quickly as possible. School systems should encourage and reward their efforts to do so. Too, state certification agencies must move in establishing a minimal level of preparation, such as that suggested by the International

Reading Association *(4)*, as certification requirements. To do less is to shortchange the children of today.

Establishing Inclusion-Exclusion Criteria. A major responsibility of the special teacher, as a reading leader, is the establishment of a special reading program which meets the individual needs of the students in his building. A first task in the development of a special program is the selection of inclusion-exclusion criteria for identifying pupils for additional help in the classroom or the reading room. These criteria must be understood and accepted by all school personnel to prevent the special program from becoming a dumping ground for discipline problems or mentally retarded students whose intellectual capacities do not permit them to profit from special instruction.

Wheelock (6:230) suggests that first priority for special help in the reading room should be given to those pupils who are moderately deficient in selected reading skills. These pupils may be remediated and phased out of the special program in a relatively short time, returning to function at ability level in the regular program. Then attention may be given to more severe cases where progress will be of a long-term nature.

If pupils are removed from the classroom, the activity that is missed should be determined on an individual basis. According to Wheelock (6:227), this instruction should not occur during skills classes, such as reading and mathematics, since the fundamental knowledge gained in these classes is essential for effective growth in other curricular areas. Too, the time should not come from an area that the pupil especially enjoys (such as art, music, physical education, or break time) since the reading room should be viewed as a place to learn and not as a place of punishment.

Opinions differ on the amount of time to be spent weekly in the special program and on the frequency of special class meetings. Suggestions range from daily half-hour classes to hour-long classes meeting twice weekly (5:26). The nature of the disabilities should be the determining factor here.

The same priorities are appropriate for selecting pupils for special reading instruction in the regular classroom. This instruction may be given by the special teacher, the classroom teacher, or both.

Securing Interdisciplinary Effort. Adequate diagnosis of and remediation strategies for many reading problems require a specialization of knowledge often not possessed by special teachers of reading. Other professionals, who have competencies in fields related to the teaching of reading, may assist in the diagnostic and remediation processes. These specialists include psychologists, counselors, physicians, school nurses, and social workers. It is the responsibility of the reading teacher to secure the services of these specialists, when needed, and to coordinate their efforts so that a balanced view of the problem may be obtained. Effective channels of communication between reading teacher and specialists must be developed and maintained.

Community agencies, such as civic clubs, may also assist with the reading program. The development of rapport with community agencies is imperative since these agencies often supply the financial resources needed to effect adequate diagnosis and remediation.

Consulting with Teachers. The special teacher also provides reading leadership through consulting with teachers in his building, assisting them in the developmental and corrective programs with testing, grouping, materials, teaching strategies, motivation and reinforcement techniques, and evaluation of progress. This role function may be accomplished through planning sessions with classroom teachers, classroom demonstrations, and presentations and discussions at faculty meetings. Appropriate topics for faculty meetings include: (a) the development of goals and objectives of the reading program; (b) analysis of recent literature in the field; (c) diagnostic and evaluation techniques; and (d) identification of teaching strategies for special reading problems (such as reversals, substitutions, how to read critically, and others).

Diagnosing Reading Difficulties. As noted earlier, both the classroom teacher and the special teacher perform diagnostic functions. Smith (5:16), in the paradigm which follows, refers to four levels of diagnosis appropriate in a good reading program.

Attention is called to the fact that the first two levels are the responsibility of the classroom teacher. However, the special teacher may assist classroom teachers with selection

Levels of Diagnosis of Reading Disability

Level of Diagnosis	*Look for*	*By*	*How*
I. Description of performance	Skill strengths and weaknesses	Classroom teacher	Observation Teacher tests Standardized group tests
II. Behavior affecting reading performance	Attitudes toward reading	Classroom teacher	Observation Attitude and personality tests
III. Specific analysis of reading process	Strength and weaknesses in specific skills, perception, etc.	Remedial reading teacher	Standardized tests of specific skills Informal testing and observation
IV. Determination of mental ability	Intelligence Memory Association Reasoning	Clinician	Standardized tests of intelligence

and/or construction of tests, testing techniques, and interpretation of results. His own role in the specific analysis of the reading process (level III) will be crucial in selecting those pupils who need specially formulated treatments for remediation.

Role as a Teacher of Reading

The second major role of the special teacher is that of working directly with those pupils who need individually prescribed treatments. It is assumed that the special teacher will demonstrate expertise in those areas discussed in connection with his role as consultant (diagnosis, motivation, materials, methods, reinforcement, and evaluation). He must also be able to communicate effectively what he is doing in the special program to the classroom teacher so that effective follow-up (mentioned earlier) may be provided. A basic goal of special instruction should be the return of the student to the regular school program as a functioning member as quickly as possible.

Special Secondary School Roles

Although the ideas presented thus far are pointed in general toward the elementary school level, many of the same roles and functions are applicable at the secondary level. There are differences, however. In his role as a secondary reading leader, the special teacher has the responsibility for establishing and maintaining a developmental program within the content areas. At this level, his in-service role and his role as a consultant will receive high priority. He must convince secondary teachers that reading skills can and should be taught in content area classes, and he must be able to help content teachers improve these reading skills once they have been recognized as important.

Special secondary programs, outside the regular classroom, should be dual in nature — a remedial program for those students with significant skill deficiencies and a developmental program for those good students who wish to become more proficient in reading. The special teacher must assume responsibilities in each area.

COORDINATION BETWEEN TEACHERS

Coordination in two basic areas, planning and teaming, is the cornerstone of an effective working relationship between the special teacher and the classroom teacher.

Planning

Coordinated planning has been implicit in each aspect of the reading program discussed in this paper. Basic to effective planning is a full sharing of knowledge between the classroom teacher and the special teacher so that the special teacher may be armed with all available input to help him plan remediation and so that the classroom teacher may know how to build on the work of the special teacher or to formulate effective remediation strategies himself. In order that planning may occur, it is essential that the administrator build planning time into the school schedule (5:32).

Teaming

Teaming, in which both teachers work in the same room concurrently, is a fruitful instructional pattern for a special reading program. The special teacher could work with individuals or small groups in the classroom with great professional benefit to the classroom teacher who would see good techniques in operation. Such an arrangement would also aid in removing some of the stigma attached to the "special room" concept.

Palmatier's suggestion (3:222-225) for "satellite" teachers seems worthy of serious consideration as an instructional pattern. In his suggested program, resource teachers in reading, under the direction of a reading supervisor, would be assigned to given buildings. These teachers would work in the classroom with the regular teacher, assisting with diagnosis and serving as a consultant to the teacher. Only those pupils with severe difficulties would be removed from the classroom to a special clinic staffed by highly trained personnel centrally located in the school system. This represents a revised functioning of the reading clinic as it is usually known and would represent a forward step.

COMMENTS

To be an effective special teacher of reading is no small order. He may need to be satisfied with small beginnings, building on his own state of readiness and on the readiness of those classroom teachers with whom he works.

REFERENCES

1. Campbell Barbara. "Resource Teacher Program," *Forty States Innovate To Improve School Reading Programs,* Berlie J. Fallon and Dorothy J. Filgo (eds.). Bloomington, Indiana: Phi Delta Kappa, Incorporated, 1970, pp. 99-104.
2. Otto, Wayne, and Richard J. Smith. *Administering the School Reading Program.* Boston: Houghton Mifflin Company, 1970, Chapter 7.
3. Palmatier, Robert A. "Clinical Remediation and Diagnosis in the Elementary School: A Research View of Status and Needs," *Reading Difficulties: Diagnosis, Correction, and Remediation,* William K. Durr (ed.). Newark, Delaware: International Reading Association, 1970, 215-225.
4. "Roles, Responsibilities, and Qualifications of Reading Specialists." Professional Standards and Ethics Committee, International Reading Association; Newark, Delaware, 1968.
5. Smith, Carl B. *Treating Reading Disabilities: The Specialist's Role.* Newark, Delaware: International Reading Association, 1969, Chapters II, III, and IV.
6. Wheelock, Warren H. "Corrective and Remedial Reading and the Role of the Special Reading Teacher," *Reading Difficulties:*

Diagnosis, Correction, and Remediation, William K. Durr (ed.). Newark, Delaware: International Reading Association, 1970, 226-231.

7. Wilson, Robert. *Diagnostic and Remedial Reading for Classroom and Clinic.* Columbus, Ohio: Charles E. Merrill Publishing Company, 1967, Chapter II.

HELEN M. ROBINSON

The Role of Auxiliary Services in the Reading Program

The view throughout this anthology has been that a true remedial program must be interdisciplinary. The first step in such a program — prevention — also demands such an approach. This article outlines fundamental services that can help in both the correction and prevention of reading problems.

In such a program, what is the role of the special reading teacher? What is the role of the classroom teacher? Who is responsible for initiating such services? Are there possible organizational and communicative problems involved in supplying such services?

Special services in the reading program may be classified into two broad categories. The first includes the work of reading specialists of different types with varying responsibilities; and the second is composed of the services of specialists in related professions. The purpose of this paper is to explore the latter category, in view of the fact that the former has been considered by the writer in a previous article (2). However, the reading specialists (consultant, remedial teacher, etc.) are often the key persons in coordinating the different services with the reading program.

In this paper the services of allied specialists will be called auxiliary services. In most schools these services are limited and, as a result, are available only to selected children. Therefore, auxiliary service must be supplied by parents or other agencies.

From *The Reading Teacher*, 14 (March 1961), pp. 226-231. Reprinted with permission of Helen M. Robinson and the International Reading Association.

PURPOSES OF AUXILIARY SERVICES

Auxiliary services are designed to enhance all learning, and particularly learning to read. At the present time the services of specialists in these areas are more often used to help pupils who are retarded in reading. It is not unusual for a retarded reader to be referred to a school psychologist, speech correctionist, school nurse, or to a psychiatrist. The services are here performed for individual pupils. The service is usually diagnostic, but correction of the difficulty is essential if the pupil is to be helped to make progress with the guidance of a remedial teacher.

Another function of auxiliary services is evolving at varying rates in different schools. This function is prevention of learning difficulties. Prevention of reading deficiency is ideal if it is possible. To the extent that research, case study, and personal insight permit specialists to identify factors that inhibit reading progress, effective preventive procedures can be developed, evaluated, and applied. Today experimentation by reading specialists and auxiliary specialists is taking many new and unconventional forms. However, evaluation is too often subjective, and before adequate research has been completed the experimental procedure is adopted as a partial panacea.

In view of the fact that auxiliary personnel tend to have training and competence in fields allied to the teaching of reading, it follows that they often find it difficult to evaluate reading progress unless they are part of a team. Ideally, a team of auxiliary specialists will work with the reading specialist in serving retarded readers or in planning programs for preventing reading failure. This type of cooperative plan is more likely to insure better service to children and youth than an individual approach, particularly in experimental stages.

In most schools, however, individual pupils with difficulties are referred for auxiliary services. It is urgent that either written or oral reports accompany each referral, and that the auxiliary personnel reciprocate with adequate reports. Both the diagnosis and the plan for therapy should be described in terms that the reading specialist can understand. Very often a conference is needed to plan the instructional program in reading so that it will not interfere with therapy by auxiliary personnel.

TYPES OF AUXILIARY SERVICES

The special services may be classified several ways. In this paper, however, they will be considered in relation to the physical, psychological, and social aspects of their special contributions, although some serve in more than one of the three categories.

Physical Services. The school nurse is usually responsible for all aspects of health, several of which appear to be related to reading progress. She often uses special devices for screening pupils who may need referral to experts for diagnostic and corrective purposes. In some schools a physician is also available, at least part time, to advise concerning screening procedures and to make decisions about questionable referrals. In such a school preventive plans are more likely to be available.

Visual screening is often done by the school nurse, perhaps assisted by laymen under her supervision. Too few schools have the services of vision specialists for this purpose. An exception is represented by the Orinda study in California (1), where it was shown that at approximately the same cost per pupil professional visual examiners markedly increased the accuracy of referrals for visual care.

One of the problems faced by school personnel is the lack of uniform views held by ophthalmologists and optometrists. Consequently, it is highly desirable to include representatives of both groups serving on an advisory committee to establish procedures for visual screening in schools, especially of pupils who are retarded in reading. Sweeting reports excellent results in New Haven, Connecticut (3), where co-operative efforts of the two professional groups resulted in improved service. The visual screening procedure developed there resulted in the referral of about 20 per cent of the pupils, in contrast to an approximately 10 per cent referral based on the Snellen test alone. Several studies show that retarded readers tend to pass the Snellen test even though they really need visual care. Therefore, improved visual screening which is endorsed by both groups of professional refractionists is particularly helpful.

When pupils fail visual screening tests, the final diagnostic examination and corrective procedures remain at the discretion of the parents. In order to coordinate the efforts of different refractionists who examine children and prescribe visual care for them, it is very useful to develop a standard "report form," which is sent out by, and returned to, the person designated by the school to make such referrals. Returned forms should then be made available to teachers and reading specialists.

Screening for loss of hearing is usually done by the school nurse with the use of an audiometer. Referral to a specialist known as an otolaryngologist is made when persistent hearing losses are found. A report from this specialist is also needed by the classroom teacher and reading specialist. If the hearing loss is only temporary, or if it can be corrected fairly easily, the teacher may need to review some aspects of the work missed by the pupil. On the other hand, in cases where no correction is made, the teacher needs to make adjustments in the instructional program to provide maximal opportunity for success.

Although the relationship of endocrine disturbances to all aspects of learning, and especially to reading success, is controversial, this factor should not be overlooked. In individual cases hypothyroidism has been found to contribute to learning difficulty. Pupils who give evidence of endocrine imbalance should be referred to an endocrinologist. However, considerable care should be taken in making wholesale referrals in this as in other areas.

Of recent interest is the possibility that minimal brain damage may affect the learning of a considerable number of children. Research in this area is limited, and many neurologists can identify the difficulties only if there are obvious physical concomitants. Furthermore, experimentation in corrective procedures, as well as in remedial instruction, is only in the embryonic stage. In all probability, however, this is an area in which new devices for selecting pupils for referral will be forthcoming.

The auxiliary services related primarily to physical factors are highly significant to the reading program in individual cases. At present, however, the effect of preventive procedures is still controversial. Both research and experimental programs of prevention are needed in this general area.

Psychological Services. The school psychologist is often used largely as a psychometrist whose main function is to estimate capacity to learn. This is a significant service to the teacher and reading specialist, especially for pupils who are already retarded in reading or for those who come from underprivileged homes, different cultures, or who have little command of the English language.

However, the well-trained psychologist should be of much greater assistance to the reading teacher than providing adequate measures of intellectual ability. He should be able to assess the extent of emotional inhibition in learning to read. If the emotional difficulty appears to be the result of reading failure, the reading teacher can often be successful in alleviating both problems, under the guidance provided by the psychologist. If the emotional problem seems to be more basic, the psychologist may be able to carry forward the necessary therapy. However, severely disturbed children are usually in need of psychiatric care. The psychologist would make the referral and usually serve in a liaison position, offering assistance to the classroom teacher or the reading teacher.

In addition to offering therapy to pupils with emotional disturbances, the psychologist and psychiatrist can aid in preventing personal problems. Their assistance in helping teachers provide a climate that promotes maximal learning helps to prevent an undetermined amount of retardation in reading.

The speech therapist should have an excellent psychological background, although he must be familiar with the physical problems basic to incorrect speech. However, according to many reports, the proportion of speech defects due to physical abnormalities is relatively small, and for this reason the speech specialist has been included in the category of psychological services.

Speech therapy helps children recognize and produce the language which they will learn to read. Since oral language is basic to learning printed symbols, speech correction offers strong support for the reading program.

Many investigators concerned with the relationship between speech problems and reading difficulty have sought another factor which underlies both. One such factor has been emotional problems. Another which is currently under investigation at several centers is auditory discrimination.

Wepman *(5)* has concluded that auditory discrimination matures at different ages, in some cases as late as eight years. Furthermore, he has found that pupils with inadequate auditory discrimination usually exhibit unique speech problems which are not amenable to treatment until the auditory discrimination is adequately developed. On the other hand, he hypothesizes that retarded readers without speech problems may be taught to discriminate among similar sounds in words. Investigations of this type are extremely important as they may illuminate the difficulties experienced by certain pupils in learning phonics at early ages. Furthermore, such insight might point to the use of other sensory avenues for beginning reading among selected pupils.

Speech therapy is an essential auxiliary service in correcting reading difficulties. It also offers promise for preventing reading failure among selected pupils.

All of the psychological services have proved to be useful in diagnosis and in remedial instruction. However, a great deal of research and experimentation is needed to develop an adequate plan to prevent reading failure in all aspects of psychological services.

Social Services. The visiting teacher or school social service worker is usually most concerned with families of children who present school problems. In serving retarded readers especially, the visiting teacher can appraise the socio-economic status of the home and determine the kinds of expectations and motivations provided. Some parents are over-ambitious while others have little academic expectation for their children.

Another type of service which must be performed is to follow up on referrals for physical and psychological difficulties. For example, a pupil whose parents have been notified of the need for a professional visual examination may fail to take the recommended steps. The visiting teacher may learn that the parents cannot afford such professional care and call to their attention a service that is free or relatively inexpensive.

In instances where referral for psychiatric or child guidance services has been made, the visiting teacher may need considerable time to help parents accept and secure this help. Occasionally, medical service is not compatible with parental beliefs, and the remedial or classroom teacher must be alerted to this fact so that compensations in teaching can be made.

The visiting teacher should also be informed of the reading difficulty exhibited by each child so that it can be explained to parents. Some parents, however, do not feel satisfied without direct conferences with the classroom or remedial teacher. Whenever such conferences are scheduled, the visiting teacher should be included.

So far, few planned programs of prevention of reading difficulty have been attempted in this area. Undoubtedly the paucity of trained personnel and the great demand on the time of the few who are available account for this fact.

ORGANIZATION OF AUXILIARY SERVICES

Throughout this paper reference has been made to referral of pupils to specialists who supply auxiliary services. The referral is based on the assumption that the remedial reading teacher or reading consultant is already dealing with the pupil who appears to exhibit certain problems. However, in some school systems, the reverse is true. For example, the school psychologist may be the first to examine a pupil. If the psychological appraisal reveals evidence of reading difficulty, then referral to a special reading center is made. If this plan is followed, the school psychologist must be fully aware of the characteristics of the retarded reader, and referral to the reading specialist must be easily done.

In order to facilitate communication, some schools organize special services under one administrator. In other instances the special services are brought together in a child guidance center. In either plan the administrator must have sufficiently broad experience and training to enable him to give proper emphasis to each type of special service. Otherwise, one type of service may be over-emphasized, while another is given little opportunity to develop properly.

Few schools have sufficiently large budgets to provide auxiliary personnel for research or to experiment with preventive programs. Hence, it seems likely that within the foreseeable future schools will continue to seek more effective devices for identifying individuals who need special care, will assist the parents in providing it, and will then correct the resultant reading difficulty.

CONCLUDING STATEMENT

Special services to the reading program include several within the school and many others supplied by parents. Varied services are needed because, as Vernon *(4)* points out, our present methods of clinical diagnosis have failed to isolate any factors which appear only among retarded readers. The reading specialist in the school must be responsible for requesting different types of special services as they are needed. He must also be sure that he is informed of the steps taken, the difficulties corrected, and he must maintain proper communication with each of the auxiliary services. The coordinated efforts are far more effective than permitting each specialist to proceed without full knowledge of the efforts of others. The existing special services should be organized administratively to make most effective use of each in order to correct existing retardation in reading and to learn how to prevent many such failures in the future.

REFERENCES

1. Peters, Henry B., *et al.* "The Orinda Vision Study," *American Journal of Optometry,* 36 (Sept., 1959), pp. 455-69.
2. Robinson, Helen M. "The Role of Special Services in the Reading Program," in *New Frontiers in Reading,* J. Allen Figurel, Ed. Vol. 5, pp. 160-64. New York: Scholastic Magazines.
3. Sweeting, Orville J. "An Improved Vision Screening Program for the New Haven Schools — A Case Study," *Journal of the American Optometric Association,* 30 (May, 1959), pp. 715-22.
4. Vernon, M. D. *Backwardness in Reading*, p. 186. Cambridge: University Press, 1958.
5. Wepman, Joseph M. "Auditory Discrimination, Speech and Reading," *Elementary School Journal,* 60 (Mar., 1960), pp. 325-33.

SAMMYE J. WYNN

The Ancillary Role of Parents
in the Prevention and Correction
of Reading Difficulties

Believing that most parents desire the very best for their children, Wynn proposes what can be done to improve teacher-parent coordination, particularly when the aim is to prevent or alleviate a reading difficulty.

What suggestions are made for making parent-teacher cooperation more effective? How does this article relate to the Chandler study in Part Two? Coleman's study in the same part? Davey's article in Part Five? If feasible, develop some detailed and specific materials for topics 1, 2, 7, 8, 9, and 10 proposed for a parent education program. What additional topics would you consider appropriate?

Traditionally educators have looked within the school for ways of preventing reading failures and solving the pervasive problem of reading difficulty, while overlooking their most natural and concerned ally, parents. The strategic position held by parents enables them to play a major role, not only in the correction of reading difficulties, but their prevention as well. Why has this readily available source of help been overlooked or minimized? Could it be the feeling that only professionals can make a contribution to the education of children? Could it be the opinion that educators are the sole purveyors of education? With acceptance and proper guidance, this great unharnessed parent force can be used to tremendous advantage in developing effective readers in our schools. As stated by Schell and Burns:

> Teachers usually indicate grave concern for the pupil experiencing a reading problem but this concern does not always

---

An original paper written for this book by Sammye J. Wynn.

encompass the pupil's parents. Yet don't the parents' feelings and attitudes extend to the child "for better or for worse"? *(3)*

INFLUENCE OF THE HOME

Reading instruction is initiated long before the child has his first encounter with the school. Since it is a matter of public information that parents are the first and most long-term teachers of their children, why then cannot educators with intellectually-oriented insights use this information as an aid in preventing and correcting reading difficulties? Parents are shapers and developers of the beginning reader: talking with the child, sincerely listening to him, introducing him to his world and broadening his horizon, pointing out signs and labels, calling attention to likenesses and differences, helping him to perceive relationships, and reading to him are all activities which lay the foundation for success in reading.

The above mentioned activities abound in some homes, contributing immeasurably to the development of readiness for reading and learning in general. It is no fortuitous occurrence that children from such homes generally experience success in reading; they have been groomed for this successful encounter since infancy. The informal learning activities provided these children might be referred to as the "home prep school." It is as though a "hidden curriculum" is operative in the homes. This suggests that a concerted effort should be made to help other parents develop this "hidden curriculum" in their homes as one means of preventing reading difficulties.

Schools can no longer afford to ignore the important role which parents can play in the education of their children. Educators must look beyond the confines of the school for answers to an effective reading program. Children cannot be insulated from the influence of the home, as it is the learning arena for them during their first and most impressionable years; therefore, a portion of the school's total reading effort must be directed toward parent involvement. Bloom, Davis, and Hess support this philosophy in the following statement:

> The home environment has been studied as a means of understanding the factors which influence development of children. Studies repeatedly show that the home is the single

most important influence on the intellectual development of children, particularly in the pre-school years. The ways in which parents spend time with their children at meals, in play, and at other times during the day have been found to be central factors in developing skills which prepare children for school. The objects in the home, the amount of parental interest in learning and the amount of practice and encouragement the child is given in conversation and general learning have been found to be significant influences on language and cognitive development, development of interest in learning, attention span, and motivation to the child. *(1)*

DEVELOPING A COALITION
BETWEEN PARENTS AND TEACHERS

A coalition between parents and teachers must be developed, with the school taking the initiative. In many instances, however, the school must engage in extensive "fence mending" before this coalition can become a reality. In the past, parents have not been perceived as allies in education; their help has not been sought. Generally they have not even been welcomed in the schools. This has especially been true in regard to poor parents and those of minority groups. The school has knowingly or unknowingly discriminated against these parents.

It is imperative that this picture be changed. How can this change be effected? A first crucial step could be an attitudinal change on the part of educators: perception of parents as a source of help, rather than as peripheral people to be tolerated. The school must accept the assistance currently available in many homes and actively seek to find avenues through which less-prepared parents may be helped to develop in their homes an environment which provides readiness for reading and promotes continued successful learning.

Presupposing the development of effective home-school relations and eradication of the notion that only professionals can contribute to the education of children, parents can be helped to assume their supporting roles in the prevention and correction of reading problems. Generally, parents want to help. They want to make a contribution to their children's reading success, but many lack the background needed and are sensitively aware of this deficiency. Those parents can be provided the needed background information and a vote of confidence in their abilities to function in this arena. They must not only be given general background information, but specific how-to-do instructions related to their supporting roles in their children's reading success.

Appropriate background content for the parent could center around such topics as the following:

1. What We Know About How Children Learn
2. The Importance of the Self-Concept in Learning
3. Listening to and Talking with Children
4. Exploiting the Community for Learning Situations
5. Reading to Children — How It Helps
6. Making Maximum Use of the Public Library
7. The Use of Learning Games (commercial and parent-constructed)
8. Using Mass Media for Learning
9. Supervision of Home Study (special place, special time, special atmosphere)
10. Parents as Pace Setters in Reading

Information about such topics could be disseminated through home visitations, parent-teacher conferences, study groups, television presentations, or organized parent programs.

SOME DETAILS ABOUT
PARENT EDUCATION PROGRAM

Whatever the mode of presentation, the main thrust of any program should be helping parents create in their home an environment where learning abounds and everyday living is related to development of reading readiness and reading skills. Parents must be helped to understand how specific activities contribute to reading success. A further elaboration is made upon several of the topics proposed above.

Listening to and Talking with Children

Generally parents do not recognize that sincerely listening to and talking with their children, and encouraging further conversation, is laying the foundation for success in reading. Parents must be helped to understand that talking with their youngsters provides a backlog of information that is basic to reading progress. This activity also aids in developing the concept that printed symbols represent "things" that exist in life. Children learn many words through conversations with their parents — names for objects and words for expressing ideas. As parents listen to children, they are conveying the idea that the child has something worthwhile to say which encourages him to speak more often and more freely.

It is not suggested that parents make special preparation or provide specific structured content as they talk with the child; rather that they share some of the things parents already know and perhaps take for granted that the child understands. For example:

time: minutes make hours; hours make days; days make weeks; weeks make months; months make years.

seasons: the four seasons; what the seasons are like in terms of temperature, activities, etc.

special holidays: origin; how observed

animals: where they live; classifications; how they help humans

food: sources

transportation: different modes

weather: wind, clouds, storms, rain cycle, snow, changes.

Parents need to recognize that as they talk with and listen to their children they are contributing to reading readiness and success through developing an enlarged listening and speaking vocabulary, oral language facility, and an extended backlog of information needed for concepts.

Exploiting the Community for Learning Situations

As the community is exploited for learning situations, an enriched experiential background is developed, thus enabling the child to read materials of wide diversity with understanding. A community void of learning situations is nonexistent. An awareness of the numerous opportunities for acquiring background information from the community should be developed: a trip to the supermarket, dime store, drugstore, bank, service station, airport, and a nature walk are a few examples. Envision this parent-guided tour of the supermarket as the various departments are introduced and discussed.

"This is the meat department. Here we have all kinds of meat and sea foods. We get our meat from selected animals such as the cow, hog, chicken, lamb, and duck. Animals such as the fish, oyster, and shrimp give us seafood. They live in water which is sometimes called the sea. This is beef. The cow is the animal that gives us beef. When the meat is cut, the different parts are given names such as steak (which you see here), hamburger, roast, and liver. The cow not only gives us beef, but milk as well which is used to make butter, cheese, ice cream, and other dairy products."

"We call this the produce department. Fresh vegetables and fruits are found here. Vegetables and fruits come from plants which grow in the ground. These green beans grow on a bush or vine. We call these greens 'leafy vegetables' because we eat the leaves. With potatoes it is a different story: only the roots of the potato are eaten."

Fruits could be discussed in a similar manner. On subsequent trips to the supermarket, other departments could be explored, providing information about the sources and classifications of foods. The role of the farmer and grocer as community helpers and the equipment used in a supermarket provide further opportunities for "talk-starters."

Using the community as a backdrop, parents can be guided into planning countless activities which can provide background of experiences and stimulate learning. As parents draw on information received in the proposed parent education program, hopefully they will develop further facility in communicating concepts and serve, more and more, as sources of information for their children. In addition, as parents and children share these experiences, much conversation between them will be stimulated, thus further promoting facility in oral language which is crucially important to reading success. It is understood that parents in the lowest income stratum are often preoccupied with the problem of survival — all their energies may be expended on immediate necessary goals; nevertheless, every effort should be made to inform parents of the wealth of available learning situations in the community.

Reading to Children — How it Helps

In addition to a shared enjoyable experience, many valuable by-products accrue when parents read to children. Facility in the use of oral language is developed which is a prime prerequisite to success in reading. As the child asks questions, describes pictures, repeats favorite parts, develops an awareness of rhyming words, and retells the story, he is getting an excellent foundation in essential reading skills. The child's listening and speaking vocabularies are increased as he learns the usage and meanings of words through pictures, context, and parent definitions. Children are able to experience vicariously, storing valuable background information to be drawn on later for interpretative purposes. (When it is considered that children interpret all that is read in light of their experiences, it becomes increasingly important that an extended experiential background be developed. The background information acquired also aids in concept formation and clarification.) As a result of being read to, children are able to see the connecting link between speech and printed symbols: they begin to understand at an early age the relationship of oral language to print. This basic understanding enables the children to move with greater ease into the world of books. As parents read to child, proficiency is developed in the use of context clues as the children start to anticipate appropriate words which fit and 'make sense' with preceding context. This skill will be useful as the child begins to read on his own. Reading to children not only lays the foundation for success in reading, but it aids in developing a permanent interest in reading as well. These are some of the myriad ways in which reading to children contributes to reading success.

Making Maximum Use of the Public Library

Such information as the following might be presented to parents as a series of vignettes:

Introduce your child to the public library at an early age.

Help him develop the concept that the library is a supermarket of knowledge, information, and fun-type reading.

See that your child has his own library card. Take him to the library often to check out books in line with his interests and level of development.

Acquaint your child with the various departments and services of the library: children's department, reference, audio-visual, story hour, and reading clubs.

Explain the organization of the library as an aid in locating materials. Fiction is shelved alphabetically according to last name of author. Non-fiction is arranged according to Dewey Decimal System.

Biographies are arranged according to the last name of the person the book is about.

Catalog cards are filed alphabetically in drawers by author, subject, and title.

Give more than lip-service to the notion that reading is important. Use the library with enthusiasm as a source of pleasure and information. Let your children observe you enjoying books.

PARENT ROLE IN ALLEVIATING READING DIFFICULTIES

To this point, the major focus has been upon some ways parents can help in preventing reading problems. Operating on the valid assumption that parents want the best education possible for their children and are willing to become actively involved given the needed background information, we must actively seek their support in working with children experiencing difficulty in reading. It is erroneous to assume that parents are unable or unwilling to contribute to the correction of reading problems. In this regard, Lieben states:

> If the child is badly delayed in reading, then the statement "Leave him alone" is ineffective advice for both the teacher and the parent. The teacher needs to teach; the parent who is filled with anxiety, whether rightly or otherwise, needs to help the child through difficulties. The problem is how each can supplement the other's efforts. To solve the problem requires that the mother be involved in the treatment plans for the child and that she and the teacher identify the possible things she may do to help. *(2)*

Slossen *(4)* further buttresses this belief by suggesting specific ways in which parents may cooperate at home in helping their children overcome reading difficulties. Slossen suggests a daily "reading game" of short duration using material at a predetermined, comfortable level of reading. Readiness for the reading game is established by the parent who informs the child that each day for about ten minutes they will play a reading game which will help him improve his reading.

In essence, the "reading game" consists of having the child read a few lines orally as the parent records the words repeatedly missed. These words are referred to as "stickler" words. In the oral reading, the missed words are printed on index cards and efforts are made to help the child remember these words through silent re-reading of orally read materials, using the word in a sentence, using the index card as a flash card, or using phonic and structural clues.

Slossen recommends that each day's reading session begin with a review of "stickler" words to determine how many had been remembered. All known "stickler" words are given a plus sign: the objective of the game is to get five plus signs on all "stickler" words. These cards are then filed alphabetically as learned words and periodically reviewed. Hopefully, the child will acquire a large collection of learned words and fewer "stickler" words as the daily reading progresses. This reading game is reported to be highly effective as children are motivated to read successfully. Success naturally gives the child confidence that he can improve his reading. In the game situation, parents often read interesting stories to the child, advancing the idea that reading is a delightful pleasure time pursuit.

A PILOT PARENT PROGRAM

That parents can contribute to the prevention and correction of reading difficulties was demonstrated by a pilot parent program conducted by the author over an eight-year period. Though designed for parents in the low-socio-economic group, this program has implications for all parents. The program was conducted in a depressed area of Knoxville, Tennessee, for parents of first graders. The median income of participating families was about $2,000 per year with many welfare recipients involved. Limited experiences were provided for the children; excursions outside of the community were very rare. Although a public library was within walking distance, few families used it. Reading material in the homes was extremely limited and there were few toys of any kind.

The program was initiated because of the appalling number of reading failures noted in the school-grades one through six. The rationale was that parents could do much to supplement and reinforce the school's reading efforts in view of the long period of time the children spent with parents, as opposed to the short period spent with the teacher. To lay the groundwork for initiating the program the first year, home visits were made the first three weeks of school, followed by organization of a First Grade Parents' Study Group. A program of parent education and involvement was designed; the program was explained in detail to parents who were told that the school needed their help in order to improve the reading achievement of their children. As each component of the program was explained, the parents were shown how it was related to reading readiness or development of reading skills.

The parents' group had evening meetings, using the format of a social hour. Information was presented in an informal manner. Each year a mother was chairman and "sparkplug" of the group; it was she who sent out notices regarding meetings and kept other parents interested and involved. During the course of the school year topics discussed included how parents can help their children make better progress in school: (a) vignettes from the area of child growth and development; (b) the importance of the self-concept; (c) booklists, television logs, and lists of inexpensive learning materials; (d) organization and use of the public library; and (e) supervised home study. At one meeting each year, the librarian from the public library would bring a collection of books including offerings for the entire family; she encouraged the parents to use all services of the library.

Although money was a source of difficulty, parents seemed able to rearrange somewhat their financial priorities. They pooled their resources to provide buses for children for trips to places of interest such as the bakery, dairy farm, bottling company, TVA dam and zoo. Many of the mothers accompanied the children on trips and seemed to derive as much pleasure and stimulation from these experiences as did the children. These shared experiences provided many opportunities for conversation between parents and children.

Through the years, the name of the parent organization changed, but the objective remained the same. As time progressed, a positive change in child-rearing practices was noted: parents spent time reading to their children; parents and children used the library; inexpensive picture dictionaries, paper back books, recordings and learning games were bought with a portion of the family's meager income. The children showed strong improvement both in reading skills and interest in reading. Not only did this changed home environment affect the lives of the children enrolled in the first-grade class, but the pre-schoolers and school-aged children in these families benefitted as well. There were fewer reading problems as the pre-schoolers reached first grade and the school-aged children generally showed improvement in their reading achievement and interest.

This pilot program supports the efficacy of involving parents in an ancillary manner as a means of preventing and correcting reading difficulties. This does not imply that parents are to take over the function of the teacher; rather that they are to function in a supporting role.

REFERENCES

1. Bloom, B. S., Davis, A. and Hess, R., *Compensatory Education for Cultural Deprivation*, New York: Holt, Rinehart and Winston, 1965, p. 69.
2. Lieben, Beatrice, "Attitudes, Platitudes, and Conferences in Teacher-Parent Relations Involving the Child with a Reading Problem," *Elementary School Journal*, 58 (February 1958), pp. 279-286.
3. Schell, Leo, and Burns, Paul C., *Remedial Reading: Anthology of Sources*, Boston: Allyn and Bacon, Inc., 1968, p. 404.
4. Slosson, Richard L., *A Game to Improve Your Child's Reading*, East Aurora, New York: Slosson Educational Publications, 1963.

HERBERT ROSNER

Facets of a Cross-Grade Tutorial Reading Program

In this article, Rosner provides a clear and practical "recipe" for the use of student tutors. He gives attention to preplanning, attitudinal emphasis, orientation, materials, organizational structure and supervision, and record keeping, and he cites some testing results of the program.

What are some possible pitfalls in such a proposed program? Would such a program be feasible in your situation? Why or why not?

The idea of students helping students is not a new one. It can be traced back to the "monitorial system" devised by Joseph Lancaster and Andrew Bell in England in 1841. As a matter of fact, Comenius advocated tutoring as far back as 1632. Many cross-grade tutorial programs have surfaced during the past decade with varying degress of success. Educational journals are reporting an ever increasing amount of research on this subject. This portends an upsurge of interest in this direction and presages a definite trend.

The purpose of this program is to fulfill a specific need. The primary grade teacher is supplied with an approach towards reaching a greater number of children at an early age. An important avenue for the primary teacher to reach this goal is the use of other students. There are ways in which a child can reach another child where adults cannot.

Teachers of the upper grades report that a new interest in learning has been kindled in the tutors. This newly generated

This is an abridged account of a paper presented at the 1970 convention of the International Reading Association. Reprinted by permission of Herbert Rosner.

enthusiasm in learning on the part of the tutors permeates the entire upper grade classroom and gives the teacher additional leverage in the added aspirational goals. The much sought ingredient of "motivation" occurs repeatedly as children seek knowledge which they can transmit and put to immediate use. There is a need to know "now," and there is an immediate sense of satisfaction in putting this knowledge to use.

Reading teachers welcome the injection of a "new spirit" into the remedial situation. The reading room is now much sought after. Children seek out their teacher in the hope of becoming a tutor. Such contact in itself is very valuable; moreover, the character-building values developed through a desire to serve are immeasurable. Reading teachers find relief from the routine of pure remedial work and look forward to the realization of ever higher enrichment goals as high-achievers are drawn into the program to serve as tutors.

ATTITUDINAL EMPHASIS AND APPROACH

A successful tutorial program must begin with the fullest cooperation and help of administrators, teachers, tutors, and tutees. With the first signs of success there develops a greater sensitivity on the part of all concerned. This leads to a smoother functioning of the program.

Teachers and members of the faculty must be apprised of the total strategy and plan. They will be interested in knowing that the program does not burden them with extra work. On the contrary, the tutors will reinforce their teachings and will add new dimensions to the classroom learning situation.

Administrators are delighted to see the learning that takes place. They are also pleased by the negligible extra costs, and are heartened by the extensive community support.

Arrangements are made through the school administration for the use of the school auditorium, library, or lunch bench area for the tutoring hour. It is important that the pairs be well-separated one from another, as close quarters may bring interference and diminish the program's effectiveness.

Teachers sometimes need to reschedule classroom subject matter, but they invariably feel the gains involved in the tutorial program warrant such modifications in scheduling.

The tutees are recommended in consultation with the

administration and the classroom teacher. They are then tested by the reading teacher. The children with deeper-rooted reading or emotional problems are screened out, since they are in need of the more direct specialized and expert care of the professional. Tutors are selected in the same manner. They, too, are screened and tested. Potential tutors should have desirable personality traits, such as pleasant and positive demeanor.

The selection process referred to above cannot be defined with any hard and fast rule. Only the general principle has been enunciated; namely the need to be aware of deep seated aberrations which require the special attention of a highly skilled counselor. It should be noted, however, that sometimes students who are seemingly emotional deviates have been selected at the discretion of the reading specialist with highly beneficial results, both as tutors and tutees.

After tutors and tutees have been selected, orientation sessions for tutors begin. These sessions are conducted by the reading teacher. Emphasis is placed upon gaining a pleasant, relaxed, cordial relationship. This attitude pervades in all areas of tutor-tutee activities and helps to produce and nurture favorable reading and learning experiences.

Each tutor is introduced to a much broader outlook via the "SPACE AGE" tutoring principles which become part of his understanding. "SPACE AGE" is a mnemonic device which covers the following principles, comprising the main themes of the orientation sessions:

> **S**uccess experiences for all involved.
> **P**atience and understanding with youngsters.
> **A**ccept your tutee as he is and help him.
> **C**ompliment him for learning and cooperation.
> **E**nter daily results of your accomplishments.
> **A**sk your reading teacher when you need help.
> **G**ive your child the best of yourself.
> **E**njoy school by helping others.

During their early orientation sessions, tutors select a chairman, co-chairman, and secretary. Only the chairman calls for the tutees, in order to minimize classroom disruptions. The co-chairman is the official timekeeper during the tutoring period. The secretary takes minutes during the orientation sessions. This organization is taken quite seriously by the children and helps growth in leadership, democracy and responsibility.

> Tutors are furnished a kit which contains:
> A basal textbook
> A library book
> Various tools for learning:
>> A pocket tachistoscope
>> A word-wheel
>> Alphabet card
>> A lap chalkboard, chalk, and cloth
>> A pad, pencils with erasers

Tutors learn the organizational structure of the program and how to use the materials in the kit. They are now ready for their tutees.

ORGANIZATIONAL STRUCTURE

The tutoring period consists of 40 minutes three days a week. The remaining days of the week are set aside for tutor's orientation and enrichment activities. The program is conducted in cycles of ten weeks, or twenty tutorial hours. At the end of each tutorial cycle, a week is set aside for testing, analysis, and evaluation. Decisions as to who should be reinvited to join the new cycle are based upon gains made.

The 40-minute period is divided into four sections. This division allows for a variety of approaches with multisensory activities. These diverse activities assure maximum attention-getting and holding power. Time allotments are flexible, however, and tutors are not required to adhere to them rigidly. They may vary their individualized reading program to suit the tutee's mood, interests, and to take advantage of the "teachable moment."

The basic time allocations are:

1. *Oral Reading and Comprehension — A Basal-Visual Approach.* The tutee reads to his tutor from a basal text series, and tutor asks comprehension questions. The reading teacher tests the tutees periodically and sets the pace. The pace must not be too fast or too difficult. A tendency for tutors to compare

and compete with each other must be discouraged. At no point should the child be exposed to the frustration level of learning.

Once a tutor wrote: "I happened to be looking around in the auditorium while my student was reading. He said to me: 'Hey, are you listening?' Now, I really have to listen to every word he says, or he catches me."

2. *Phonics — Auditory Approach.* The tutee is given practice in auditory discrimination, such as recognizing consonants, blends, and digraphs in various positions. Such practice takes place with the help of paired pictures and word rhymes. A number of workbooks are suitable for this type of activity. Phonics cards are also used for reinforcement value.

3. *Vocabulary Practice — Kinesthetic-Manipulative Approach.* The tutor may use any of the learning tools in his kit to practice high-frequency vocabulary words, both in isolation and in context.

The lap chalkboard, for example, is an indispensible tool. It allows for an infinite variety of stimulating learning activities. Tutors take delight in "inventing" new uses for the chalkboard in a tutoring situation. Many tutors eagerly anticipate the orientation sessions where they may share their creative ideas. The interested peer group will listen, and credit the valuable suggestions, thereby boosting the ego of the innovator, while the secretary officially records these ideas in the minutes.

4. *Story-Time — A Literary Approach.* A limited but choice selection of books covering a wide range of high interest potential is available in the reading room. The tutor guides his tutee in the selection of one such book. The tutee now has a book of "his" choice read to "him" alone. This personal attention helps to extend further the tutee's appreciation for books. The story-time approach serves to lengthen the attention span and provides for a valuable exercise of good listening habits.

Now tutor's own diction, expression, and appreciation for punctuation show improvement. His reading is meaningful and purposeful. A genuine need for clear, effective articulation and communication exists. Many a tutee's desire for additional information has sent the tutor scurrying through available reference books.

In all the above interactions, a unique social relationship develops which has its own educational dimensions. It will be readily recognized that such friendships once developed are in themselves rather important secondary gains of the tutorial program.

THE MULTI-MEDIA DIMENSION

Tutors at orientation sessions are trained in the use of various multi-media techniques and in the care of all those used. Learning centers are set up in the reading room and tutors make use of them on a rotational basis.

The following items have been used successfully by the tutor-tutee pairs.

Viewing Centers:
  Filmstrip projector
  Overhead projector
  Large chalkboard

Listening Centers:
  Record player
  Tape recorder
  Filmstrip projector in conjunction with the record player
  Other electronic hardware

Kinesthetic-Manipulative Centers:
  The typewriter (progressing from the alphabet and leading up to the Language Experience Approach)
  Puzzles for perceptual conceptualizations (forms, letters, words, and sentence puzzles)
  Large three-dimensional letters (forming words, and tracing)
  Realia kits (three-dimensional objects used as conversational stimulants, role-playing simulations, representations of consonants, blends, and digraphs in initial, medial, and final positions)

Tutors gain practice in the use and care of these valuable learning tools during orientation sessions. They are eager to transmit their newly acquired skills to their tutees. Tutors are rated by the reading teacher for attitude, responsibility, and dependability. A very simple rating scale is used, such as a "plus" sign for "excellence," and an "equals" sign for "satisfactory."

THE READING TEACHER'S ROLE

The reading teacher is an integral part of the program throughout. He is totally aware of all that is going on. He makes notes for items he wishes to discuss or clarify at each orientation session. He inspires, guides, and encourages creativity. He sets high but attainable standards with short- and long-term goals. Children's scholastic aspirational levels are raised continually, but always kept within reach. The reading teacher is a fully accepted member of the tutorial team as he "sits in" and tunes to with each pair, with an occasional encouraging or helpful comment, and enjoys the full flavor of the "happenings."

A master check list containing each child's reading level, skill attainments, learning pace, attitude, books, and materials covered, dates, etc., is necessary. This master check list is kept current by referring to the tutor's log record, consultations with tutors and tutees, discussion during orientation sessions, and results of an ongoing testing program.

COMMUNITY INVOLVEMENT

The community is pleasantly involved by invitations to come and see the program in action. Visitors repeatedly express enjoyment as they see the children working together in such harmony. The children are so absorbed in their activity that they do not realize the presence of the guests. At least they do not give any outward indication. They just carry on!

Parents participate in the making of felt badges with a 'T' for tutor. Tutors wear these with justifiable pride. It is quite an honor to be selected as a tutor.

TESTING RESULTS

Following are test results of one tutoring cycle, representative of many others during a six-year period in which this program has been operative.

Thirteen fifth and sixth graders, all remedial students themselves, were matched as tutors with a like number of second and third graders as tutees for a ten-week tutorial cycle. All the children were pre and post tested with the *Gates McGinitie Vocabulary and Comprehension Tests*. In addition, the second and third graders were administered the *Stanford Reading Test,* while fifth and sixth graders took the *Comprehensive Tests of Basic Skills, Reading Section.*

At the start of the program, the children, both tutors and tutees, averaged two years or more below their reading grade level.

At the end of the 10 week cycle, the second and third graders averaged 4 months reading growth in the *Stanford Reading Test* and 5 months reading growth in the *Gates-McGinitie Tests.* Maximum gain by any one student was 1 year 5 months on the *Gates-McGinitie.*

The fifth and sixth graders who tutored in the mornings and received remediation in the afternoons had an average of 1 year 5 months gain on the *CTBS* and 1 year gain on the *Gates-McGinitie.* Maximum gain by any one student was 2 years 2 months on the *Gates-McGinitie.*

Similar results have been charted each year of the six years that this program has been in effect.

CONCLUSIONS

This tutorial program incorporates characteristics which are conducive to maximizing the learning appeal including: preplanning with school personnel; attitudinal emphasis; orientation enrichment sessions with tutors; varied multisensory approaches coupled with multi-media learning centers; record keeping by tutors; ongoing supervision, analysis, direction, and evaluation by the reading teacher in charge; and community participation.

The results produced in a relatively short period of time were significant. Equally important to the academic gain is the development of personal image through success-oriented, school-centered involvement.

STELLA M. COHN

Procedures for Evaluating a
Reading Clinic Program

*Those who provide reading services to pupils should always
be interested in following up the program to see what effect the
services have had. This report of the Special Reading Services in
New York City suggests some evaluation procedures that may be
used.*

*After studying the procedures suggested by Cohn, decide on
what grounds she believes the testing program, the learning
ratio, and the reading accuracy ratings to be important criteria.
Are there other important aspects that are not measured by
these suggested procedures? Of what value are evaluations by
classroom teacher, parent, and the pupil? Does the article
suggest that remedial instruction can be a qualified success?*

Before it is possible to discuss in detail procedures for
evaluating a reading clinic program, it is important that an
understanding of the aims, scope, and special design of the
particular clinic be spelled out. Where the authority lies, of
course, also determines what kind of evaluation will be possible.
A college or university clinic may have less opportunity to set
up a comprehensive program of evaluation of the services it
provides to school children than would a clinic which is part of
a public school system and can obtain the approval of the
superintendent of schools for the procedures used. On the other
hand, a university-sponsored clinic may benefit from the
careful design of research planning by highly trained personnel.

From *Vistas in Reading,* J. Allen Figurel, ed., (Newark, Delaware: International Reading Association,1967), pp. 566-570. Reprinted with permission
of Stella M. Cohn and the International Reading Association.

To begin with, let us assume that the reading clinics with which we are concerned provide service to a population of school children within clearly delimited geographic areas. The administrator of such a school district will undoubtedly expect to receive at the close of the school term (or at other specially requested periods) a report from the director of a reading clinic in general child-accounting terms. For example, the total number of children given service will be reported; and perhaps this figure will be set against the number of children referred for service, and the number discharged, with reasons given. Some administrators will want to evaluate how the various schools are taking advantage of such a special service and may want the above data broken down by schools. Usually the overall administrator under whom the reading clinic is organized will want to have a copy of a complete report of the sort which could be patterned on the plans suggested here.

INITIAL STAGES IN EVALUATION — THE DIAGNOSIS

If the reading clinic has specially qualified teachers of reading and also clinical personnel able to give diagnostic and treatment services, then the usual procedure calls for a careful reading diagnosis by the reading teacher plus a casework evaluation by a social worker and individual examination by a psychologist. On the basis of the findings of these three workers, enough data can usually be assembled to provide a tentative diagnosis of the problem and plan for treatment. The child will have had several reading tests to measure his reading achievement and to analyze special difficulties in reading such as are revealed by various oral tests of phonetic skills. Objective scores obtained on reading tests will have been recorded in terms of age or grade scores, percentile points, etc., which will serve as a basis for measuring later improvement. The reading teacher will also have learned from the regular school staff what behavior and/or personality problems the child manifests so that these reports, together with her own first observations of behavior, may be entered in the anecdotal record and later used as a basis for evaluation of changes in behavior.

Depending on the extent to which the parents are concerned with the child's difficulty and can contribute their own observations and expression of attitudes, the parent-child relationships will be clarified by the clinicians and can be assessed for their bearing upon the child's learning and behavior difficulties. In some cases a very full study, perhaps including a careful medical history and present examination by pediatrician, neurologist, eye or ear specialist, as well as a psychiatrist, may be in order. Special cases may include those which need individual medical attention, correction of sensory defects, or assistance with a related problem such as a speech defect. Notation concerning all of these conditions must be entered in the case records so that their handling may not be overlooked nor their later evaluation omitted in regard to the response to such treatment.

Another more informal method which includes evaluation in a consultation procedure is followed in the New York City clinics. On the one specified day of the week when reading teachers are scheduled to come to the school in which the clinic center of a district is housed, conferences are scheduled by the coordinator of the clinic. During these conferences the reading teachers meet with the clinic staff (psychologist and social worker, with the psychiatrist joining also in special cases) to have case conferences on individual children.

These may be "intake" conferences, at which the purpose is to share information and interpretation made from the initial studies before the children are accepted into the program. Plans as to the type of handling the child seems to need are agreed upon by the staff members and are recorded in a special report, copies of which are placed in both the reading teacher's anecdotal record and in the confidential case record maintained by clinicians. Later conferences on these cases are usually held at the request of the reading teacher, especially if the child does not respond as had been anticipated to the reading instruction.

Other types of conferences are also helpful — for example, at the request and with the participation of a child's class teacher or other school personnel. All of these group processes, which almost certainly lead to closer cooperation of the various people concerned with an individual child, involve evaluation directly or indirectly.

INTERIM OR YEAR-END EVALUATION —
THE TESTING PROGRAM

To return to the more general evaluation of the reading progress made by children attending a clinic, it is desirable to have a regular program for retesting the children with alternate, equivalent forms of the same reading tests or with succeeding tests included in the same series previously given. Hopefully, scores on such tests are graded on the same scale or by age or grade standards which have known and equivalent units. In our New York reading clinics we have used both the N. Y. Tests of Growth in Reading, devised by our N. Y. Board of Education's Bureau of Educational Research, and also other commercially available tests of reading such as the Metropolitan Reading Tests and the various tests devised by Arthur Gates and published by the Bureau of Publications of Columbia University.

The obvious way to evaluate the reading achievement of a child or a group of children is to compare the scores obtained on reading tests at the close of a school term, or after a certain significant length of time during which clinical help was given, with the scores obtained at the beginning of such a period of clinical instruction and guidance. Reading gains are obtained by simple subtraction of the original from the subsequent or terminal grade scores. As an example, the May 1965 results for the New York City reading clinic for 1,350 children measured by the N. Y. Tests of Growth in Reading showed a median reading gain of 1.3 grade scores, whereas median length of service was 1.0 years.

YEAR-END EVALUATION — THE RATIO OF LEARNING
PRIOR TO AND AFTER
ADMISSION TO THE CLINIC

In order to evaluate these findings in somewhat greater detail, a plan was devised whereby the average reading growth per month of schooling was determined for each child, first, prior to admission to the reading clinic and, later, whenever a testing program was desired. The first step is to compare for each child the reading grade score with the "grade equivalent" of the child. If the child has been held back once or more than once, the time for such repetitions of grades should be added to his "grade equivalent" to determine the expected achievement. Thus, if a child is in the third month of grade three, which he is repeating at the time, his expected reading achievement in grade score should be grade 4.3 (3.3 + 1.0). If his obtained reading grade score is 2.8 (the equivalent of eight months through grade 2), it is the latter scores which are to be compared. For example, when the child actually achieves 2.8 he has theoretically learned 1.8 years in reading (2.8 − 1.0)*whereas he should have acquired 3.3 grades in the course of his 4.3 years of instruction (4.3 − 1.0). The ratio between 1.8 and 3.3, or .55, represents the average reading growth per month of instruction which has occurred prior to reading clinic assistance to this child.

Similarly, such ratios may be obtained for all the children in the clinic's caseloads; and these percentages will roughly represent their learning efficiency at the time of acceptance into the clinics. At the time an evaluation is made, each child's total reading test score may be converted to a grade score. If the efficiency with which he has responded to the reading program is to be compared with his original ratio, the difference between the two scores must be divided by the months of reading-clinic attendance. For example, if the child who began with a reading grade score of 2.8 reached a grade score of 4.5 after 1.4 years of instruction, his average ratio of growth during the period of clinic attendance is obtained by dividing the gain (4.5 − 2.8) or 1.7 years or 17 months by 14 to obtain 121%or an average of 1.21 months of grade score per month of instruction. This figure represents a considerable gain over the .55 months — a gain which was characteristic of the child on admission to the clinic service. If such figures are available for all the children, they may be dealt with by various statistical procedures to show the changes in learning efficiency. The data may be totaled and/or separated into subgroups by grade groups, by teaching caseloads, or by groups provided with varying lengths of service; and the scores distributed so that central tendencies can be ascertained. For example, in one of our reading clinics, the statistics for the 1964-65 school year showed at the close of the school term an average reading growth per month of 120 percent. The same children, upon

---

* Standardized Tests of Achievement in Reading usually begin with 1.0.

entering our clinic program had had an average reading growth of only 43 percent per month. These are easily understood, meaningful figures which can be given to school personnel and even to the public in general, who may want to know if a clinic program actually results in children's improved learning.

YEAR-END EVALUATION —
A COMPARISON OF
"READING ACCURACY RATINGS"

Another way of evaluating the reading growth of children after a period of special instruction is to note the reduction in errors made on silent reading tests. The N. Y. Tests of Growth in Reading provide "reading accuracy ratings" which are based on the number of correct items divided by the number of attempted items. Initial versus final reading results may be evaluated by comparing these "accuracy ratings" in terms of the percentages obtained at each level. Thus in our New York City reading clinics, for a total of 1206 children* given service during the school year 1964-65, seventy percent obtained "medium" or higher accuracy ratings, whereas of these same children, on admission to the clinic program, only 26 percent had reached "medium" or higher accuracy. (The test norms for the standardization population were 60 percent with medium or better than medium accuracy.)

YEAR-END EVALUATION —
THE PRINCIPAL, THE CLASS TEACHER

Regarding the guidance aspects of the program, evaluation will depend on the nature of the work carried out and its apparent outcomes. The opinions of the referring schools may be solicited by letter to the principal with answers to questions, such as: "To what extent has there been evidence of improvement of the children? Do the class teachers express evidence of having received help through consultations with the clinic staff or through demonstration lessons by the reading specialist? Have they observed changes in the behavior of the

---

*Excluded from the grand total of the official caseload were 144 pupils whose achievement was not high enough on admission to the clinics for them to be tested with the reading tests which provide accuracy ratings. Many were non-readers.

children concerned? etc. It is well to also allow for negative criticism by asking directly if there are suggestions for improvement of the service.

It is important to have the opinion of the class teacher regarding the child's personal-social adjustment both prior to and following attendance in the reading clinic. The form shown here may be used either for a written communication or as a basis for consulting a class teacher:

> Has there been evidence of positive change in the child's attitude toward reading and other school subjects?
>
> Has there been growth in the child's relationships with his classmates? Is he better integrated with the group? Is the group accepting him?
>
> Is the child showing evidence of increased participation in the classroom activities?
>
> What problems does he present?

YEAR-END EVALUATION — THE PARENT

The parents may also provide data for evaluation. The social workers or other clinicians dealing with the parents, individually or in groups, may ask them to estimate the progress made by their children, to give criticism of the service they have received. (Do they want to continue with treatment? Does the child show any increase in self-confidence, in wishing to go to school? Does he seem happier at home? Does he show increased ability to get along with siblings, playmates?) While answers to these questions may be influenced somewhat by a parent's wishes, the general tenor of a parent's evaluation is likely to be fairly dependable, especially if his comments are compared with his report about his child's problems at the time of the intake interview.

YEAR-END EVALUATION — THE PUPIL

The children themselves may also be asked to evaluate their own reading progress; and, if this is done by checking written answers to questions phrased and read to them by their reading teachers, the replies may be evaluated by teachers other than their own in order that they may be interpreted as objectively as possible. (See form below.)

CHILD'S ESTIMATE OF
HIS PROGRESS IN READING

Directions: Pupil is to check any statement which he considers to be true of him.

_____

                I think that during the present school year

_____   I have learned more about reading than in any previous school year.

_____   I have gained as much in reading power as I did last year.

_____   I have enjoyed reading more than ever before.

_____   I still have trouble with new words.

_____   My school marks are not as high as they used to be.

_____   My marks have improved
                 _____   a good deal.
                 _____   somewhat

_____   I want to continue in the reading program.

           Signed _____
                               (Pupil)

               Grade_____

Reading Teacher's Evaluation: Taking the above into account, the class teacher's report, and also the test results, check one of the following as representative of this child:—

_____   No improvement

_____   Fair improvement

_____   Very good progress

_____   Excellent progress

           Signed _____
                               (Reading Teacher)

           Checked by _____

This report has been patterned on the procedures and the resulting experience of Special Reading Services in the City of New York. Other clinics which may have more uniform patterns of instructional or other procedures will accordingly vary their evaluative procedures. Also, as research advances our knowledge as to the most effective methodology, it is expected that evaluation procedures will be guided by relevant research findings.

Index